I0643627

Recommended Reference Books for Small and Medium-sized Libraries and Media Centers

American Reference Books Annual
Advisory Board

Susanne Bjørner
  Bjørner & Associates

Joe Janes
  Associate Dean for Academics
  Information School, University of Washington

Judith Matthews
  Head of Biomedical and Physical Sciences Library
  Michigan State University

Steven Sowards
  Assistant Director for Collections
  Michigan State University Libraries

Arthur P. Young
  Director
  Northern Illinois Libraries

RECOMMENDED REFERENCE BOOKS

for Small and Medium-sized Libraries and Media Centers

Volume 32

2012 Edition

Shannon Graff Hysell, Associate Editor

LIBRARY
ARAPAHOE COMMUNITY COLLEGE
5900 S. SANTA FE DRIVE
P.O. BOX 9002
LITTLETON, CO 80160-9002

LIBRARIES UNLIMITED

AN IMPRINT OF ABC-CLIO, LLC
Santa Barbara, California • Denver, Colorado • Oxford, England

Copyright © 2012 ABC-CLIO, LLC
All Rights Reserved
Printed in the United States of America

No part of this publication may be reproduced, stored in a retrieval
system, or transmitted, in any form or by any means, electronic,
mechanical, photocopying, recording, or otherwise, without the
prior written permission of the publisher.

LIBRARIES UNLIMITED
An Imprint of ABC-CLIO, LLC
130 Cremona Drive
P.O. Box 1911
Santa Barbara, California 93116-1911
www.abc-clio.com

Library of Congress Cataloging-in-Publication Data

Main entry under title:

Recommended reference books for small and medium-
  sized libraries and media centers.

  "Selected from the 2012 edition of American
reference books annual."
  Includes index.
  I. Reference books--Bibliography. 2. Reference
services (Library)--Handbooks, manuals, etc.
3. Instructional materials centers--Handbooks,
manuals, etc. I. Hysell, Shannon Graff
II. American reference books annual.
Z1035.1.R435   011'.02   81-12394
ISBN 978-1-61069-180-2
ISSN 0277-5948

Contents

Introduction xi

Contributors xiii

Journals Cited xix

Part I
GENERAL REFERENCE WORKS

1—General Reference Works

Acronyms and Abbreviations 3
Almanacs 3
Bibliography 5
  Bibliographic Guides 5
Biography 6
  International 6
Dictionaries and Encyclopedias 6
Directories 8
Government Information 9
Handbooks and Yearbooks 10
Museums 11
Periodicals and Serials 11
Quotations 12

Part II
SOCIAL SCIENCES

2—Social Sciences in General

General Works 15
  Dictionaries and Encyclopedias 15
  Handbooks and Yearbooks 16

3—Area Studies

United States 19
  General Works 19
  Alaska 19
Africa 20
  Angola 20
  Ethiopia 20
  South Africa 21

Asia .21
  Afghanistan 21
  India .22
Australia and Oceania 23
Europe 24
  Hungary 24
  Ireland 24
Middle East 25
  General Works 25
Polar Regions 25

4—Economics and Business

General Works 27
  Bibliography 27
  Catalogs and Collections 27
  Dictionaries and Encyclopedias 30
  Directories 31
  Handbooks and Yearbooks 31
Business Services and Investment Guides . .32
  Catalogs and Collections 32
  Handbooks and Yearbooks 32
Consumer Guides 33
Finance and Banking 34
  Catalogs and Collections 34
  Handbooks and Yearbooks 34
Industry and Manufacturing 35
  Catalogs and Collections 35
  Dictionaries and Encyclopedias 35
Insurance 36
  Directories 36
International Business 37
  General Works 37
    Catalogs and Collections 37
    Handbooks and Yearbooks 37
  Asia .38
Labor .39
  General Works 39
    Dictionaries and Encyclopedias 39
    Handbooks and Yearbooks 40
  Career Guides 41
Management 42
  Handbooks and Yearbooks 42

NOV 01 2012

Marketing and Trade 43
   Catalogs and Collections 43
Office Practices 43

5—Education

General Works. 45
   Almanacs 45
   Dictionaries and Encyclopedias 45
   Handbooks and Yearbooks 46
Elementary and Secondary Education. . . .47
   Biography. 47
   Catalogs and Collections 47
   Handbooks and Yearbooks 48
Higher Education 49
   General Works 49
     Dictionaries and Encyclopedias 49
     Directories 50
   Financial Aid 51
     Directories 51
     Handbooks and Yearbooks 52
Nonprint Materials 52
Special Education 53

6—Ethnic Studies and Anthropology

Anthropology 55
Ethnic Studies 55
   General Works 55
     Dictionaries and Encyclopedias 55
   African Americans 56
     Almanacs 56
     Biography. 57
     Dictionaries and Encyclopedias 57
   Australian Aborigines. 58
   Indians of North America. 59
     Bibliography 59
     Dictionaries and Encyclopedias 59
     Handbooks and Yearbooks 61
   Jews. 62
   Latin Americans 62

7—Genealogy and Heraldry

Genealogy 65
   Directories 65
Personal Names 66

8—Geography and Travel Guides

Geography 67
   General Works. 67
     Atlases. 67
     Dictionaries and Encyclopedias. 68
Travel Guides. 68
   General Works. 68

9—History

American History 71
   Atlases 71
   Catalogs and Collections 71
   Dictionaries and Encyclopedias 72
   Handbooks and Yearbooks 74
Asian History 75
   Singapore 75
European History 75
   General Works 75
Latin America and the Caribbean 76
Middle Eastern History 77
World History 78
   Atlases 78
   Dictionaries and Encyclopedias 78
   Handbooks and Yearbooks 80

10—Law

General Works. 81
   Dictionaries and Encyclopedias 81
   Handbooks and Yearbooks 82
Criminology and Criminal Justice 83
   Chronology 83
   Dictionaries and Encyclopedias 84
   Handbooks and Yearbooks 86
Environmental Law 88
Human Rights 89
   Dictionaries and Encyclopedias 89
   Handbooks and Yearbooks 89
Immigration Law 90

11—Library and Information Science and Publishing and Bookselling

Library and Information Science 91
   Reference Works 91
     Bibliography 91
     Handbooks and Yearbooks 94

Publishing and Bookselling 96
   Directories 96

12—Military Studies

General Works. 99
   Almanacs 99
   Chronology 99
   Dictionaries and Encyclopedias 100
   Handbooks and Yearbooks 102
Navy .103
Weapons 104

13—Political Science

General Works. 105
   Dictionaries and Encyclopedias 105
   Handbooks and Yearbooks 105
Politics and Government 108
   United States 108
      Biography. 108
      Chronology 108
      Dictionaries and Encyclopedias . . .109
      Directories 110
      Handbooks and Yearbooks 111
   China 113
   Europe 113
Ideologies. 114
International Relations 115
Public Policy and Administration 116
   Dictionaries and Encyclopedias 116
   Handbooks and Yearbooks 118

14—Psychology

Psychology 119
   Bibliography 119
   Dictionaries and Encyclopedias 119
   Handbooks and Yearbooks 120

15—Recreation and Sports

General Works. 123
   Atlases 123
   Dictionaries and Encyclopedias 123
   Handbooks and Yearbooks 124

Baseball 125
Basketball 126
Bodybuilding and Weight Training 126
Cycling 126
Football. 127
Golf 127
Ice Skating 128
Soccer. 128
Tennis. 129

16—Sociology

Death .131
Disabled 131
Family, Marriage, and Divorce. 132
Gay and Lesbian Studies 132
Philanthropy 133
   Catalogs and Collections 133
   Directories 133
   Handbooks and Yearbooks 134
Poverty. 134
Sex Studies 135
Substance Abuse. 135
   Dictionaries and Encyclopedias 135
   Handbooks and Yearbooks 136

17—Statistics, Demography, and Urban Studies

Demography 139
   Catalogs and Collections 139
   Dictionaries and Encyclopedias 139
   Handbooks and Yearbooks 140
Statistics 142
   General Works 142
   United States 142
      Catalogs and Collections 142
      Handbooks and Yearbooks 142
Urban Studies 143
   Handbooks and Yearbooks 143

18—Women's Studies

Dictionaries and Encyclopedias 147
Handbooks and Yearbooks 148

Part III
HUMANITIES

19—Humanities in General

General Works 153

20—Communication and Mass Media

General Works 155
Authorship 156
   General Works 156
   Style Guides 157
Journalism 158
Newspapers 158
Radio, Television, Audio, and Video 159

21—Decorative Arts

Collecting 161
   Coins 161
   Firearms 162
Crafts 163
Fashion and Costume 164
   Dictionaries and Encyclopedias 164
   Directories 165

22—Fine Arts

General Works 167
   Dictionaries and Encyclopedias 167
   Handbooks and Yearbooks 169
Architecture 169

23—Language and Linguistics

General Works 171
English-Language Dictionaries 172
   General Usage 172
   Rhyming 173
   Terms and Phrases 173
   Thesauri 174
Non-English-Language Dictionaries 174
   French 174
   German 175
   Spanish 176

24—Literature

General Works 177
   Bibliography 177
   Bio-bibliography 177
   Dictionaries and Encyclopedias 178
Children's and Young Adult Literature . . 179
   Bibliography 179
   Dictionaries and Encyclopedias 183
   Handbooks and Yearbooks 184
Fiction 184
   General Works 184
   Crime and Mystery 186
      Bibliography 186
      Biography 187
   Science Fiction, Fantasy, and Horror . . 187
National Literature 188
   American Literature 188
      General Works 188
      Individual Authors 189
   British Literature 190
      Individual Authors 190
   Canadian Literature 192
   Spanish Literature 192
Nonfiction 193
Poetry 194

25—Music

General Works 195
   Bibliography 195
   Dictionaries and Encyclopedias 195
   Handbooks and Yearbooks 196
Instruments 197
   Piano 197
   Violin 197
Musical Forms 198
   Classical 198
   Orchestral 199
   Popular 199
      General Works 199
      Hip-Hop 200

26—Mythology, Folklore, and Popular Culture

Folklore 201
Mythology 203
Popular Culture 203

Dictionaries and Encyclopedias 203
Handbooks and Yearbooks 204

27—Performing Arts

General Works. 207
Film, Television, and Video 208
   Biography. 208
   Catalogs. 208
   Dictionaries and Encyclopedias 209
   Handbooks and Yearbooks 212
Theater 213
   Chronology 213
   Dictionaries and Encyclopedias 215

28—Philosophy and Religion

Philosophy 217
Religion. 217
   General Works 217
   Bible Studies 219
      Handbooks and Yearbooks 219
   Buddhism 220
   Christianity 220
   Hinduism 222
   Islam 222
   Judaism 223

Part IV
SCIENCE AND TECHNOLOGY

29—Science and Technology in General

Catalogs and Collections 227
Handbooks and Yearbooks 228
Indexes 229

30—Agricultural Sciences

General Works. 231
Food Sciences and Technology 232
   Catalogs and Collections 232
   Chronology 232
   Dictionaries and Encyclopedias 232
   Handbooks and Yearbooks 235
Horticulture 236
   Dictionaries and Encyclopedias 236
   Handbooks and Yearbooks 237

31—Biological Sciences

Biology 241
   Dictionaries and Encyclopedias 241
   Handbooks and Yearbooks 243
Anatomy 243
Botany 244
   General Works 244
      Dictionaries and Encyclopedias . . . 244
      Handbooks and Yearbooks 245
   Flowering Plants 245
   Fungi 245
   Trees and Shrubs 246
Natural History 247
   Dictionaries and Encyclopedias 247
   Handbooks and Yearbooks 247
Zoology 248
   General Works 248
      Dictionaries and Encyclopedias . . . 248
      Handbooks and Yearbooks 249
   Birds 249
      Atlases 249
      Handbooks and Yearbooks 250
   Fishes 251
   Marine Animals. 251
   Reptiles and Amphibians 252

32—Engineering

General Works. 255
Biomedical Engineering 255
Civil Engineering 256
Electrical Engineering. 256

33—Health Sciences

General Works. 259
   Bibliography 259
   Dictionaries and Encyclopedias 259
   Directories 261
   Handbooks and Yearbooks 262
Medicine 264
   General Works 264
      Catalogs and Collections 264
      Dictionaries and Encyclopedias . . . 264
      Handbooks and Yearbooks 266
   Alternative Medicine 268
   Specific Diseases and Conditions. 269
      AIDS 269

Arthritis 269
Autism 269
Cancer 270
Diabetes 270
Heart Disease 271
Sexually Transmitted Diseases 271
Sleep Disorders 272
Nursing 272
Pharmacy and Pharmaceutical Sciences . . . 272
Handbooks and Yearbooks 272

34—Technology

General Works 275
Directories 275
Handbooks and Yearbooks 275
Games 276
Internet 276
Dictionaries and Encyclopedias 276
Directories 277
Handbooks and Yearbooks 278
Telecommunications 278
Directories 278

35—Physical Sciences and Mathematics

Physical Sciences 279
Earth and Planetary Sciences 279
Astronomy 279
Climatology and Meteorology 280
Ecology 282
Oceanography 282
Paleontology 283
Volcanology 283
Mathematics 284

36—Resource Sciences

Energy 285
Directories 285
Handbooks and Yearbooks 285
Environmental Science 286
Dictionaries and Encyclopedias 286
Handbooks and Yearbooks 288

37—Transportation

General Works 289

Author/Title Index 291

Subject Index 303

Introduction

Recommended Reference Books for Small and Medium-sized Libraries and Media Centers (RRB), now in its thirty-second volume, is designed to assist smaller libraries in the systematic selection of suitable reference materials for their collections. It aids in the evaluation process by choosing substantial titles in all subject areas. The increase in the publication of reference sources and availability of reference databases in the United States and Canada, in combination with the decrease in library budgets, makes this guide an invaluable tool.

Following the pattern established in 1981 with the first volume, RRB consists of book reviews chosen from the current edition of *American Reference Books Annual*. This nationally acclaimed work provides reviews of reference books, CD-ROMs, and Internet sites published in the United States and Canada within a single year, along with English-language titles from other countries. ARBA has reviewed over 66,500 titles since its inception in 1970. Because it provides comprehensive coverage of reference sources, not just selected or recommended titles, many are of interest only to large academic and public libraries. Thus, RRB has been developed as an abridged version of ARBA, with selected reviews of resources suitable for smaller libraries.

Titles reviewed in RRB include dictionaries, encyclopedias, indexes, directories, bibliographies, guides, atlases, gazetteers, and other types of ready-reference tools. General encyclopedias that are updated annually, yearbooks, almanacs, indexing and abstracting services, directories, and other annuals are included on a selective basis. These works are systematically reviewed so that all important annuals are critically examined every few years. Excluded from RRB are regional guides in the areas of biological sciences and travel guides. All titles in this volume are coded with letters that provide worthwhile guidance for selection. These indicate that a given work is a recommended purchase for smaller college libraries (C), public libraries (P), or school media centers (S).

The current volume of RRB contains 522 unabridged reviews selected from the 1,388 entries in ARBA 2012. These have been written by nearly 200 subject specialists throughout the United States and Canada. Although all titles in RRB are recommended acquisitions, critical comments have not been deleted, because even recommended works may be weak in one respect or another. In many cases reviews evaluate and compare a work in relation to other titles of a similar nature. All reviews provide complete ordering and bibliographic information. The subject index organization is based upon the *Library of Congress Subject Heading*. Reference to reviews published in periodicals (see page xix for journals cited) during the year of coverage are appended to the reviews.

The present volume contains 37 chapters. There are four major subdivisions: "General Reference Works," "Social Sciences," "Humanities," and "Science and Technology." "General Reference Works," arranged alphabetically, is subdivided by form: bibliography, biography, handbooks and yearbooks, and so on. The remaining three parts are subdivided into alphabetically arranged chapters. Most chapters are subdivided in a way that reflects the arrangement strategy of the entire volume: a section on general works and then a topical breakdown. The latter is further subdivided, based on the amount of material available on a given topic.

RRB has been favorably reviewed in such journals as *Booklist, Journal of Academic Librarianship*, and *Library Talk*. The editors continue to strive to make RRB the most valuable acquisition tool a small library can have.

In the coming year ARBA and RRB will be teaming up with another highly esteemed reviewing source, *Library Media Connection* (LMC), to recognize the Best of Reference in the areas of children's and young adult library resources. Both publications are known for featuring high-quality, critical reviews that enable librarians to select the best reference sources for their young researchers' needs. We will be seeking out the "best of the best" in the areas of children's reference, young adult reference, electronic reference for K-12, and best professional guide for school and youth librarians. The editors and reviewers of ARBA and RRB look forward to celebrating the best in children's and youth reference in the coming year.

In closing, the editors at Libraries Unlimited would like to express their gratitude to the contributors whose reviews appear in this volume. We would also like to thank the members of the Advisory Board, whose ideas and input have been invaluable to the quality of ARBA, ARBAonline, and RRB.

Contributors

Stephen H. Aby, Education Bibliographer, Bierce Library, Univ. of Akron, Ohio.

Anthony J. Adam, Director, Institutional Assessment, Blinn College, Brenham, Tex.

Michael Adams, Reference Librarian, City Univ. of New York Graduate Center.

Jim Agee, Library Assoc. Director, Nazarbayev Univ., Astana, Kazakhstan.

Adrienne Antink, Medical Group Management Association, Lakewood, Colo.

Salvador Avila, Branch Librarian, Las Vegas Public Library, Nev.

Susan C. Awe, Asst. Director, Univ. of New Mexico, Albuquerque.

Christopher Baker, Professor of English, Armstrong Atlantic State Univ., Savannah, Ga.

Thomas E. Baker, Assoc. Professor, Department of Criminal Justice, Univ. of Scranton, Pa.

Catherine Barr, Editor, Children's and Young Adult Literature Reference Series, Libraries Unlimited.

Mark T. Bay, Electronic Resources, Serials, and Government Documents Librarian, Hagan Memorial Library, Cumberland College, Williamsburg, Ky.

Leslie M. Behm, Reference Librarian, Michigan State Univ. Libraries, East Lansing.

Kim M. Belknap, Librarian, Penn London Elementary School, West Grove, Pa.

Suzanne S. Bell, Economics/Data Librarian, Rush Rhees Library Reference Dept., Univ. of Rochester.

Michael Francis Bemis, Asst. Librarian, Washington County Library, Woodbury, Minn.

Laura J. Bender, Librarian, Univ. of Arizona, Tucson.

Elaine Lasda Bergman, Bibliographer for Reference and Gerontology, Dewey Graduate Library, University at Albany, N.Y.

Helen Margaret Bernard, Reference and Interlibrary Loan Librarian, Writing Center Director, Southwestern Baptist Theological Seminary, Fort Worth, Tex.

Allison L. Bernstein, Educational Materials Reviewer, Cortlandt Manor, N.Y.

Barbara M. Bibel, Reference Librarian, Science/Business/Sociology Dept., Main Library, Oakland Public Library, Calif.

Sally Bickley, Coordinator of Reference Services, Texas A&M Univ.—Corpus Christi.

Daniel K. Blewett, Reference Librarian, College of DuPage Library, College of DuPage, Glen Ellyn, Ill.

James E. Bobick, Former Head of the Science and Technology Dept. at the Carnegie Library of Pittsburgh, Pa.

Polly D. Boruff-Jones, Director of Library and Information Services, Drury Univ., Springfield, Mo.

Christine Brandt, Science Teacher, Wissahickon High School, Ambler, Pa.

Nelda Brangwin, Cherry Valley Elementary School, Duvall, Wash.

Alicia Brillon, Reference Librarian, Univ. of Colorado, Boulder—Law Library.

Georgia Briscoe, Assoc. Director and Head of Technical Services, Law Library, Univ. of Colorado, Boulder.

Simon J. Bronner, Distinguished Professor of Folklore and American Studies, Capitol College, Pennsylvania State Univ., Middletown.

Frederic F. Burchsted, Reference Librarian, Widener Library, Harvard Univ., Cambridge, Mass.

Joanna M. Burkhardt, Head Librarian, College of Continuing Education Library, Univ. of Rhode Island, Providence.

Greg Byerly, Assoc. Professor, School of Library and Information Science, Kent State Univ., Kent, Ohio.

Diane M. Calabrese, Freelance Writer and Contributor, Silver Springs, Md.

Danielle Marie Carlock, Reference and Instruction Librarian, Arizona State Univ. at the Polytechnic campus, Mesa.

Bert Chapman, Government Publications Coordinator, Purdue Univ., West Lafayette, Ind.

Boyd Childress, Reference Librarian, Ralph B. Draughon Library, Auburn Univ., Ala.

Dene L. Clark, (retired) Reference Librarian, Auraria Library, Denver, Colo.

Barbara Conroy, Career Connections, Santa Fe, N.Mex.

Rosanne M. Cordell, Head of Reference Services, Franklin D. Schurz Library, Indiana Univ., South Bend.

Kay O. Cornelius, (formerly) Teacher and Magnet School Lead Teacher, Huntsville City Schools, Ala.

Gregory A. Crawford, Head of Public Services, Penn State Harrisburg, Middletown, Pa.

Alice Crosetto, Coordinator, Collection Development and Acquisitions Librarian, Univ. of Toledo, Ohio.

Cynthia Crosser, Social Sciences and Humanities Reference, Fogler Library, Univ. of Maine, Orono.

Gregory Curtis, Executive Director Information Services, Univ. of Maine, Presque Isle.

Wendy Diamond, Business and Economics Librarian and Head of Reference at California State Univ.—Chico.

R. K. Dickson, Asst. Professor of Fine Arts, Wilson College, Chambersburg, Pa.

Scott R. DiMarco, Director of Library Services and Information Resources, Mansfield Univ., Mansfield, Pa.

Margaret F. Dominy, Information Services Librarian, Drexel Univ., Philadelphia.

Lucy Duhon, Serials Librarian, Univ. of Toledo, Ohio.

Joe P. Dunn, Charles A. Dana Professor of History and Politics, Converse College, Spartanburg, S.C.

Bradford Lee Eden, Assoc. University Librarian for Technical Services and Scholarly Communication, Univ. of California, Santa Barbara.

Patricia A. Eskoz, (retired) Catalog Librarian, Auraria Library, and Asst. Professor Emeritus, Univ. of Colorado, Denver.

Kay Evey, NBCT Teacher-Librarian, Tukwila Elementary School, Wash.

Benet Steven Exton, St. Gregorys Univ. Library, Shawnee, Okla.

Elaine Ezell, Library Media Specialist, Bowling Green Jr. High School, Ohio.

Judith J. Field, Senior Lecturer, Program for Library and Information Science, Wayne State Univ., Detroit.

Josh Eugene Finnell, Reference Librarian, William Howard Doane Library, Denison Univ., Granville, Ohio.

Virginia S. Fischer, Reference/Documents Librarian, Univ. of Maine, Presque Isle.

Charlotte Ford, Asst. Professor, School of Library and Information Science, San Jose State Univ., Calif.

Eric Forte, Member Services Consultant with OCLC.

Kenneth M. Frankel, Assoc. University Librarian, Florida Atlantic Univ., Boca Raton.

David O. Friedrichs, Professor, Univ. of Scranton, Pa.

Brian T. Gallagher, Access Services Librarian, Univ. of Rhode Island, Kingston.

Denise A. Garofalo, Systems and Catalog Services Librarian, Curtin Memorial Library, Mount Saint Mary College, Newburgh, N.Y.

Renee Byers Gentry, Media Coordinator, North Wilkes High School, Hays, N.C.

John T. Gillespie, College Professor and Writer, New York.

Caroline L. Gilson, Coordinator, Prevo Science Library, DePauw Univ., Greencastle, Ind.

Sue Ellen Griffiths, Public Services Librarian 1, Pasco County Library System, Hudson, Fla.

Laurel Grotzinger, Professor, Univ. Libraries, Western Michigan Univ., Kalamazoo.

Linda W. Hacker, Reference Librarian, SUNY Brockport, Brockport, N.Y.

Patrick Hall, Director of the Library, Univ. of Pittsburgh, Pa.

Ralph Hartsock, Senior Music Catalog Librarian, Univ. of North Texas, Denton.

Karen D. Harvey, Assoc. Dean for Academic Affairs, Univ. College, Univ. of Denver, Colo.

Muhammed Hassanali, Independent Consultant, Shaker Heights, Ohio.

Maris L. Hayashi, Asst. University Librarian, Florida Atlantic Univ., Boca Raton, Fla.

Lucy Heckman, Reference Librarian (Business-Economics), St. John's Univ. Library, Jamaica, N.Y.

Mark Y. Herring, Dean of Library Services, Winthrop Univ., Dacus Library, Rock Hill, S.C.

Joseph P. Hester, SRO-Learning, Claremont, N.C.

Ladyjane Hickey, Reference Librarian, Austin College, Tex.

Susan Tower Hollis, Assoc. Dean and Center Director, Central New York Center of the State Univ. of New York.

Mihoko Hosoi, Public Services Librarian, Cornell Univ., Ithaca, N.Y.

Ma Lei Hsieh, Librarian, Rider Univ., N.J.

Jonathan F. Husband, Program Chair of the Library/Reader Services Librarian, Henry Whittemore Library, Framingham State College, Mass.

Shannon Graff Hysell, Staff, Libraries Unlimited.

Melissa M. Johnson, Reference Services, NOVA Southeastern Univ., Alvin Sherman Library, Ft. Lauderdale, Fla.

Tom Johnson, Technology Integration Specialist, The Hockaday School, Dallas, Tex.

Sandi Jordet, District Library Media Coordinator, Brush Public Schools, Colo.

Edmund D. Keiser Jr., Professor of Biology, Univ. of Mississippi, University.

Abe Korah, Reference Librarian, Sam Houston State Univ., Huntsville, Tex.

Lori D. Kranz, Freelance Editor, Chambersburg, Pa.

Betsy J. Kraus, Librarian, Lovelace Respiratory Research Institute, National Environmental Respiratory Center, Albuquerque, N.Mex.

Karla Krueger, Asst. Professor in School Library Studies at the Univ. of Northern Iowa, Cedar Falls.

George Thomas Kurian, President, Encyclopedia Society, Baldwin Place, N.Y.

Robert V. Labaree, Reference/Public Services Librarian, Von KleinSmid Library, Univ. of Southern California, Los Angeles.

Sharon Ladenson, Gender Studies and Communications Librarian, Michigan State Univ. Libraries, East Lansing.

Linda L. Lam-Easton, Assoc. Professor, Dept. of Religious Studies, California State Univ., Northridge.

Lizbeth Langston, Reference Librarian, Univ. of California, Riverside.

Peter Larsen, Physical Sciences and Engineering Librarian, Univ. of Rhode Island Libraries, Kingston.

Martha Lawler, Assoc. Librarian, Louisiana State Univ., Shreveport.

Chris LeBeau, Research and Instruction Librarian for Business and Public Administration for the Henry Bloch School of Management, Univ. of Missouri—Kansas City.

Charles Leck, Professor of Biological Sciences, Rutgers Univ., New Brunswick, N.J.

Tze-chung Li, Professor and Dean Emeritus, Dominican Univ.

Charlotte Lindgren, Professor Emerita of English, Emerson College, Boston, Mass.

Megan W. Lowe, Reference/Instruction Librarian, University Library, Univ. of Louisiana at Monroe.

Tyler Manolovitz, Digital Resources Coordinator, Sam Houston State Univ.—Newton Gresham Library, Huntsville, Tex.

Sara Marcus, Asst. Professor of Education, Touro University International, N.Y. and MALS Student at Empire State College.

Ron Marinucci, Adjunct Professor of History, Mott and Oakland Community Colleges, Mich.

Michelle Martinez, Librarian, Newton Gresham Library, Sam Houston State Univ., Huntsville, Tex.

Melinda F. Matthews, Interlibrary Loan/Reference Librarian, Univ. of Louisiana at Monroe.

Kevin McDonough, Reference and Electronic Resources Librarian, Northern Michigan Univ.—Olson Library, Marquette.

Peter Zachary McKay, Business Librarian, Assoc. Chair for the Social Sciences, Univ. of Florida Libraries, Gainesville.

Lillian R. Mesner, Arbor City Indexing, Nebraska City, Nebr.

G. Douglas Meyers, Chair, Dept. of English, Univ. of Texas, El Paso.

Seiko Mieczkowski, Cocoa Beach, Fla.

Bill Miller, Director of Libraries, Florida Atlantic Univ.

Richard A. Miller, Professor of Economics, Wesleyan Univ., Middletown, Conn.

Terry Ann Mood, Professor Emeritus, Univ. of Colorado, Denver.

Paul M. Murphy III, Director of Marketing, PMX Medical, Denver, Colo.

Ann Bryan Nelson, Volunteer Media Specialist and Guest Teacher, Thompson Ranch Elementary School, Dysart Unified School District, Surprise, Ariz.

Charles Neuringer, Professor of Psychology and Theatre and Film, Univ. of Kansas, Lawrence.

Herbert W. Ockerman, Professor, Ohio State Univ., Columbus.

Lawrence Olszewski, Director, OCLC Library and Information Center, Dublin, Ohio.

Ray Olszewski, Independent Consultant, Palo Alto, Calif.

John Howard Oxley, Faculty, American Intercontinental Univ., Atlanta, Ga.

Mike Parchinski, Brookfield, Conn.

J. Carlyle Parker, Librarian and Univ. Archivist Emeritus, Library, California State Univ., Turlock.

Amy B. Parsons, Reference and Catalog Librarian, Courtright Memorial Library, Otterbein College, Westerville, Ohio.

Gary L. Parsons, Reference Librarian, Florida Atlantic Univ., Boca Raton.

Nick Petrosino, School librarian, Harmon Middle School, Pickerington, Ohio.

Jack Ray, Asst. Director, Loyola/Notre Dame Library, Baltimore, Md.

Allen Reichert, Electronic Access Librarian, Courtright Memorial Library, Otterbein College, Westerville, Ohio.

Barbara Ripp Safford, Assoc. Professor at the School Library Media Studies, Univ. of Northern Iowa, Cedar Falls.

Nadine Salmons, (retired) Technical Services Librarian, Fort Carson's Grant Library, Colo.

William O. Scheeren, Lecturer in Education at St. Vincent College, Latrobe, Pa.

Diane Schmidt, Biology Librarian, Univ. of Illinois, Urbana.

Ralph Lee Scott, Assoc. Professor, East Carolina Univ. Library, Greenville, N.C.

Colleen Seale, Humanities and Social Sciences Services, George A. Smathers Libraries, Univ. of Florida, Gainesville.

Ravindra Nath Sharma, Dean of Library, Monmouth University Library, West Long Branch, N.J.

Stephen J. Shaw, Library Director, Antioch University Midwest, Yellow Springs, Ohio.

Scott Alan Sheidlower, Asst. Professor, York College/City Univ. of New York, Jamaica.

Brian J. Sherman, Head of Access Services and Systems, Noel Memorial Library, Louisiana State Univ.—Shreveport.

Susan Shultz, Reference and Instruction Librarian, DePaul Univ., Chicago, Ill.

Jack Simpson, Curator of Local and Family History at the Newberry Library in Chicago, Ill.

Mary Ellen Snodgrass, Freelance Writer, Charlotte, N.C.

Lisa Kay Speer, Special Collections Librarian, Southeast Missouri State Univ., Cape Girardeau.

Ellen Spring, Library Media Specialist, Rockland District Middle School, Maine.

Kay M. Stebbins, Coordinator Librarian, Louisiana State Univ., Shreveport.

John P. Stierman, Reference Librarian, Western Illinois Univ., Macomb.

John W. Storey, Professor of History, Lamar Univ., Beaumont, Tex.

William C. Struning, Professor, Seton Hall Univ., South Orange, N.J.

Philip G. Swan, Head Librarian, Hunter College, School of Social Work Library, New York.

Rosalind Tedford, Asst. Head for Research and Instruction, Z. Smith Reynolds Library, Wake Forest Univ., Winston-Salem, N.C.

Polly J. Thistlethwaite, Associate Librarian for Public Services, CUNY Graduate Center, New York.

Susan E. Thomas, Head of Collection Development/Assoc. Librarian, Indiana Univ. South Bend.

Linda D. Tietjen, Senior Instructor, Arts and Architecture Bibliographer, Auraria Library, Denver, Colo.

Diane J. Turner, Science/Engineering Liaison, Auraria Library, Univ. of Colorado, Denver.

Robert L. Turner Jr., Librarian and Assoc. Professor, Radford Univ., Va.

Linda M. Turney, Cataloging Coordinator, Sam Houston State Univ., Huntsville, Tex.

Leanne M. VandeCreek, Social Sciences Reference Librarian, Northern Illinois Univ., DeKalb.

Anthony F. Verdesca Jr., Reference Librarian, Palm Beach Atlanta Univ., West Palm Beach, Fla.

Stephanie Vie, Asst. Professor of Composition and Rhetoric, Fort Lewis College, Durango, Colo.

J. E. Weaver, Dept. of Economics, Drake Univ., Des Moines, Iowa.

Karen T. Wei, Head, Asian Library, Univ. of Illinois, Urbana.

Lucille Whalen, Dean of Graduate Programs, Immaculate Heart College Center, Los Angeles, Calif.

Robert L. Wick, Professor Emeritus, Auraria Library, Univ. of Colorado, Denver.

Maren Williams, Reference Librarian, Univ. of Louisiana at Monroe.

Mark A. Wilson, Professor of Geology, College of Wooster, Ohio.

Julienne L. Wood, Head, Research Services, Noel Memorial Library, Louisiana State Univ. in Shreveport.

Anita Zutis, Adjunct Librarian, Queensborough Community College, Bayside, N.Y.

Journals Cited

FORM OF CITATION	JOURNAL TITLE
AG	*Against the Grain*
BL	*Booklist*
C&RL News	*College & Research Libraries News*
Choice	*Choice*
JAL	*Journal of Academic Librarianship*
LJ	*Library Journal*
LMC	*Library Media Connection*
RUSQ	*Reference & User Services Quarterly*
SLJ	*School Library Journal*
TL	*Teacher Librarian*
VOYA	*Voice of Youth Advocates*

Part I
GENERAL
REFERENCE
WORKS

1   General Reference Works

Acronyms and Abbreviations

C, P

1.   **A Guide to Federal Terms and Acronyms.** Don Philpott, ed. Blue Ridge Summit, Pa., Government Institutes, 2011. 2v. $175.00/set. ISBN 13: 978-1-60590-712-3.

As the publisher of this ready-reference source points out, mastering the acronyms, abbreviations, and terms of the U.S. federal government is nearly the equivalent to mastering a second language. As one looks through this tome they are sure to agree with this assessment. Having this book on hand, therefore, would make it much easier for those writing government reports or working within the federal government. The book is comprehensive in scope, covering terms, acronyms, and abbreviations used in each major federal government agency. The format is user friendly, allowing users to look up terms by department or subject matter. This volume is a must-have for anyone writing documents for the federal government on a regular basis and will be a necessary volume in most academic and public libraries as well.—**ARBA Staff Reviewer**

Almanacs

P, S

2.   **Factmonster.com. http://www.factmonster.com/.** [Website]. Upper Saddle River, N.J., Pearson Education. Free. Date reviewed: 2011.

Factmonster.com is a freely available almanac for children online. It draws on the contents of the print *Time for Kids Almanac* and offers information in various categories: World, United States, People, Science, Math and Money, Word Wise, and Sports. The Cool Stuff link includes information on art, architecture, business, entertainment, fashion, holidays, music, and worldwide dating and marriage customs. *Factmonster.com* also offers a Game and Quizzes area and a Homework Center. The Word Wise section includes information on children's literature, language facts, and a handy grammar and spelling resource. This reference also has a Reference Desk area. One can search all the information on the site through a simple keyword search box on the homepage. For general information for children this is a good online source to consult.—**Adrienne Antink**

P, S

3.   **National Geographic Kids Almanac 2012.** Washington, D.C., National Geographic Society, 2011. 351p. illus. maps. index. $13.99pa. ISBN 13: 978-1-4263-0783-6.

This annual provides facts and quirky stories about animals, the environment, science, world cultures, nature, history, government, and geography. It also provides listings of upcoming events in 2012 of interest to children, plus a section of games and puzzles. Information is presented in easy-to-read sections. Interspersed throughout the publication are Web resources to further engage the reader, reinforce learning, and provide additional information. A notable feature is the QR (quick response) smart phone codes that link to videos, games, and more. If the child does not have a smart phone, the same material is available online. Each section ends with a Homework Help page. As an example of how the topics are tied together with digital resources, the Awesome Adventure section has a QR code to explore the world, stories about dinosaur tracks, crystal caves, what to do in the event of a lion attack and Homework Help on how to write an essay on your adventure. The Super Science section provides a QR to conduct a science experiment, a sky calendar for 2012, a NASA Website to go to learn about the future of space travel, Homework Help advice on developing a research project, and tips for participating in a science fair. This book is sure to appeal to 8-12 year olds. After all, who can resist a publication that offers step-by-step instructions on how to get out of quicksand?—**Adrienne Antink**

C, P, S
4.   **Time Almanac 2011.** Alexandria, Va., Time-Life Books, 2011. 864p. illus. maps. index. $34.95pa. ISBN 13: 978-1-60320-164-3.

C, P, S
5.   **Information Please Almanac Online. http://www.infoplease.com.** [Website]. Free. Date reviewed: 2011.
       The *Information Please Almanac* has been published annually since 1947 by a series of publishers with variant titles. Its most recent title is the *Time Almanac*. "Information Please" was the name of a famous radio quiz program. The this almanac is very similar to The World Almanac both in content and in style. The print in the Time almanac is more readable than that of *The World Almanac and Book of Facts* (see ARBA 2012, entry 12), and the *Time Almanac* indexes more personal and place names. Each almanac has some information the other almanac does not. The *Time Almanac*, for instance, has a Time 100 list of influential individuals for the year but does not have a glossary for scientific concepts that appear frequently in the news.
       The *Information Please Almanac* online (http://www.infoplease.com) includes information from the *Time Almanac* and the *ESPN Sports Almanac*. The almanac information is integrated with the *Random House Unabridged Dictionary* and the *Columbia Encyclopedia* (6th edition) into a single reference source with a wealth of facts. The search page offers several ways to find information, including a keyword box, an index of topics, and a directory of information divided into the following categories: World and News, United States, History and Government, Biography, Sports, Arts and Entertainment, Business, Calendars and Holidays, Health and Science, Homework Center, and Fact Monster. One can click the Daily Almanac link near the top of the search page to access such features as "This Day in History," "Today's Word Quiz," "Today's Weather Fact," and "Today's Birthdays." The site is continuously updated, offering more recent information than can be found in the paper edition.—**Adrienne Antink**

C, P, S
6.   **The World Almanac Online. http://www.worldalmanac.com/.** [Website]. New York, Facts on File/Infobase. Price negotiated by site. Date reviewed: 2011.

P, S
7.   **The World Almanac for Kids Online. http://www.worldalmanacforkids.com/.** [Website]. New York, Facts on File/Infobase. Price negotiated by site. Date reviewed: 2011.
       Almanacs are handy collections of fascinating facts about a wide variety of people, places, and things. *The World Almanac and Book of Facts* is an excellent example of this type of reference source and for the first time Facts on File has made it available in an easy-to-navigate online resource. The publisher offers it in two formats: *The World Almanac Online* (for users from high school age and up) and *The World Almanac for Kids Online* (for kindergarten through middle school ages).

The World Almanac Online can be searched by keyword or browsed by category (e.g., Year in Review, Crime, Military Affairs, Health and Vital Statistics, Consumer Information, Science and Technology). It includes many additional features apart from the print edition such as daily articles on "This Day in History," "This Day in Sports," and "Quote of the Day." In addition users can export data into Excel; see full-color maps, flags, and graphs; and get citation help in the forms of MLA and *Chicago Manual of Style*.

The World Almanac for Kids Online provides extensive resources for students that goes well beyond what the print edition provides. These include: resources for homework, reports, and projects; image and video galleries; interactive games and quizzes; Homework Help tools; and Search Assistant technology that will help kids figure out the best way to research a topic. The site can be searched by keyword or browsed by topic (e.g., Animals, Career Ideas, Space and the Solar System, U.S. Presidents). There is also a Reader's Corner where children can discover books in particular genres, by specific authors, or best-sellers. The homepage is filled with news of the day, such as famous person's birthdays, "Today in History," and "Today in Sports."—**Shannon Graff Hysell**

Bibliography

Bibliographic Guides

C

8. **MLA International Bibliography. http://www.mla.org/bibliography.** [Website]. New York, Modern Language Association of America. Price negotiated by site. Date reviewed: 2011.

The *MLA International Bibliography* is produced by the Modern Language Association of America, and is one of the longest running indexes still in existence. The Association itself was founded in 1883, and began publishing a printed index in 1921. (Materials in the online database, however, date back to 1884; another example of an electronic product that has expanded beyond its print counterpart.) In a situation similar to that at the National Library of Medicine, the staff of the Modern Language Association Department of Bibliographic Information Services works with outside bibliographers from around the world to produce the *Bibliography*. It is a huge cooperative effort.

The *MLA International Bibliography* is vast in many ways: the scope of topics include sources, document types, number of records, and publication dates. Topical coverage is described broadly as "all forms of human communication"—literature, folklore (including music and art), the study of linguistics and languages, literary theory and criticism, the dramatic arts, and the history of printing and publishing. Coverage of the "history, theory, and practice of teaching language, literature, and rhetoric and composition," from 1998 onward, was added to the scope of the *Bibliography* in 2000. More than 100,000 subject-indexed records, representing the entire runs of the journals in JSTOR's Language and Literature collection, have been added to the *Bibliography*, which extends coverage of journals such as *Modern Language Notes* and *PMLA* back as far as the 1880s (ProQuest, 2008). As indicated in the title, sources from all over the world are reviewed for entry into the database. (The "Language of Publication" thesaurus list is probably the longest and most esoteric you will ever encounter.) Document types covered include types you would expect, such as books, book chapters, and journal articles, but also indexed are reference works, published working papers, conference papers and proceedings, citations for dissertations listed in *Dissertations Abstracts International*, electronic publications, and works related to teaching (e.g., handbooks, textbooks, anthologies).

The "numbers" for the *Bibliography* are equally impressive: there are over 2 million records in the database, and new additions total about 66,000 records per year. Subject terms used to describe records come from the *MLA Thesaurus*, which includes over "49,000 topical terms and 327,000 names." A database about literature is, obviously, very concerned with names: names of writers and names of characters.

The *Bibliography* is OpenURL compliant: it supports full-text linking technologies. It is also possible to run the *MLA International Bibliography* in concert with, or as a module in, a full-text database called *Literature Online.*—**Suzanne S. Bell**

Biography

International

C, P, S

9.   **Almanac of Famous People.** 10th ed. Farmington Hills, Mich., Gale/Cengage Learning, 2011. 2v. index. $267.00/set. ISBN 13: 978-1-4144-4548-9.

For those who need to know who was born or died in their hometown or want to know what happened in the year they were born, the *Almanac of Famous People* is the resource to consult. It is also a handy source for those needing the names of well-known actors, army officers, astrologers, shipping executives, or librarians. Although, it funny, there seem to be more famous actors and army officers than there are famous librarians.

Bearing entries for more than 42,000 famous and infamous newsmakers, celebrities, and otherwise noteworthy people, this popular standard almanac now includes death dates for the deceased and often place of death, along with birthdates and birthplaces, pseudonyms, nicknames, nationalities, occupations or fame-making activity, and even a one-line description of the "famous." Perhaps the most useful elements of these brief entries are the "source codes" to original references—over 1,500 of them by this reviewer's count. The *Almanac of Famous People* is culled from an impressive array of important biographical sources. In turn, the *Almanac* functions as a useful birth date, death date, occupation, and geographic index to the original sources. Great for middle school, high school, junior college, and four-year college libraries, the *Almanac* will satisfy the whims of many casual researchers and trivia buffs.—**Polly J. Thistlethwaite**

P, S

10.   **The Britannica Guide to the World's Most Influential People.** Chicago, Britannica Educational Publishing, 2010. 8v. illus. index. $53.00/vol.

This series from Britannica provide biographical information for 100 influential people in a variety of fields: inventors, musicians, artists, philosophers, scientists, women, world leaders, and writers. Each article in each book describes the background of the subject including childhood and education, their work, and any honors they may have received. Pictures of a person's work, where appropriate, are included as well as black-and-white pictures of some of the people. Each book includes an introduction, followed by readable articles of varying length. The format is similar to that of an encyclopedia, and each title includes a bibliography, glossary, and index. Any one of the titles would be a good addition to the library collection as need dictates.—**Sandi Jordet**

Dictionaries and Encyclopedias

C, P, S

11.   **Britannica Online. http://www.britannica.com/.** [Website]. Chicago, Encyclopaedia Britannica. Price negotiated by site. Date reviewed: 2011.

Britannica Online maintains the high standards that are the hallmark of the print version, *Encyclopaedia Britannica*, and augments what is available in the print edition. *Britannica Online* is available in a variety of packages, including the school edition, the academic edition, and the public library edition, which offers two interfaces, one for children and one for adults. Depending on the edition, articles come from *Encyclopaedia Britannica, Britannica Concise Encyclopaedia, Compton's by Britannica*, and other Britannica titles, as well as the *Book of the Year*. Textual information is supplemented by a wealth of images, multimedia, tables, and figures. Searches can be conducted across multiple titles or limited to any combination thereof. Browsing is available by time period, index, and subject (in an easy-to-use arrangement similar to the *Propaedia*, which topically organizes the multivolume *Encyclopaedia Britannica*). Special features include interactive timelines, statistical profiles of countries worldwide, the *Merriam-Webster's Collegiate Dictionary*, a biography of the day, a "The Day in History" link, headline news from *The New York Times* and BBC News, and a list of recently updated articles.—**Shannon Graff Hysell**

S

12.   **Marshall Cavendish Digital. http://www.marshallcavendishdigital.com/.** [Website]. Tarrytown, N.Y., Marshall Cavendish. Price negotiated by site. Date reviewed: 2011.

Marshall Cavendish Digital is a "virtual online encyclopedia" of topics in the natural and social sciences and literature. Searching can be done by category, which includes animals/plants, biography, geography, health, literature sciences, social studies, and world cultures, or by title. Marshall Cavendish titles include Heath Encyclopedia, The Aquatic World, The Civil War, Supreme Court Milestones, Elements, The Muslim World, The Old West, The Ancient and Medieval World, and dozens more. Clicking on a title directs users to outlines, dozens of relevant articles, glossaries, maps, portraits of people, places, and more. Primary source documents are included. Information covers all eras; key facts and quick reference materials are presented. The variety of subjects covers all time periods and parts of the globe as well as controversial issues. The site is easily accessed and navigated. Black-and-white and color illustrations (drawings, photographs, and maps) are found throughout the site. Some of the reading will be difficult for high school students, but the outlines and glossaries will help with their research. This site is recommended for high school libraries.—**Ron Marinucci**

P, S

13.   **World Book Encyclopedia 2012.** Chicago, World Book, 2012. 22v. illus. maps. index. $975.00/ set. ISBN 13: 978-0-7166-0112-8.

P, S

14.   **World Book Advanced. http://www.worldbookonline.com/.** [Website]. Chicago, World Book. Price negotiated by site. Date reviewed: 2011.

In publication since 1917, this well-known and well-respected encyclopedia now comprises 22 volumes, including a special research guide and index volume. With each new edition a significant amount of material is revised and many new entries are added. This edition includes data from the 2010 United States census, resulting in more than 1,000 updated population figures and updates in some 380 articles. It also includes updates for each state's representatives of Congress and electoral votes, and population data on all of the United States major ethnic groups. Many of the updates are to be expected because of the vast amount of new information that has emerged about these topics within the past year, such as the entries on carbon footprint, DNA fingerprinting, Facebook, hoarding, IEDs (improvised explosive devices), and text messaging. Contributing to this update, more than 27,500 illustrations, photographs, and maps are presented here, including reproductions of fine art and well-drawn illustrations of the human anatomy.

Another key element of *The World Book Encyclopedia* is the plethora of research aids provided. Some examples include: "Facts in Brief" tables, which highlight important facts on counties; "Tables of Terms," which define highly technical entries; "Table of Important Dates," which provide a chronology of historical dates; lists of "Additional Resources" (arranged by difficulty); and a listing of "Related Articles."

World Book has a roster of 4,000 experts who work as contributors, authenticators, reviewers, and consultants. Content of the encyclopedia is determined by what the publisher refers to as the Classroom Research Project. This project allows for the publisher to poll students in kindergarten through high school classrooms and find out what they are researching, how they are researching, and if *The World Book Encyclopedia* is useful in their research. This encyclopedia is based on the schools' curriculum needs and national and state standards. For this reason, this *Encyclopedia* is most useful in K-12 school media centers and children's reference departments of public libraries.

The World Book Encyclopedia is available on an Internet version (by subscription) so libraries will have a choice of the most useful format for their library. The online edition offers hundreds of thousands of encyclopedia articles and primary source documents. It also includes thousands of complete e-books to help students with research. The e-books can be accessed in English as well as Spanish, French, German, Italian, Dutch, Latin, Flemish, and Portuguese. Research tools include an atlas, dictionary, and local and country research guides. Users can create and save their personal research along with their notes and citations. The Timeline Builder allows students to create their own illustrated timeline with content pulled from the *Encyclopedia*. Although the print version is bulky, it does provide stunning illustrations and will teach young users valuable research skills.—**Shannon Graff Hysell**

Directories

C, P

15. **Associations Yellow Book: Who's Who at the Leading U.S. Trade and Professional Associations. Winter 2011 ed.** New York, Leadership Directories, 2011. 1425p. illus. index. $400.00pa. (annual subscription); $380.00pa. (automatic renewal). ISSN 1054-4070.

This detail-filled, informative directory includes a user's guide, A-Z listing of associations, an industry index, a geographical index, a budget index, a political action committee index, a foundation index, a name index, an acronym index, and an organization index. Each entry on an association provides acronyms, addresses, telephone numbers, e-mail addresses, thorough paragraphs explaining the associations, members, goals, how many workers, finances, date originated, and annual conferences. The entries feature a picture of the president of the group and the president's credentials. The listing provides the other employees, secretaries, and contact data. The catalog shows the affiliated government department and contact information. Foundation research is mentioned. Divisions of the corporations throughout the United States and other countries are given. The listing reveals any items published. Committee and board members are highlighted.

The eight indexes with page numbers go the extra mile. The industry index uncovers associations by type of subject. The geographical index categorizes associations by state. The budget index records organizations by millions in finances. The political action committee index reports groups by politics and causes. The foundation index features foundations supporting the organizations. The name index supplies all people included in the association directory. The acronym index notes association acronyms. The organization index points out all organizations in the book. Clearly, *Associations Yellow Book* is one of the best complete catalogs of associations for any type of library.—**Melinda F. Matthews**

C, P

16. **National Trade and Professional Associations Directory 2011.** Bethesda, Md., Columbia Books, 2011. 1425p. index. $299.00pa. ISSN 0734-0734.

C, P

17. **AssociationExecs.com. http://www.associationexecs.com/.** [Website]. Bethesda, Md., Columbia Books. $699.00 (basic); $4,000.00 (premium). Date reviewed: 2011.

Trade and professional associations are an excellent and sometimes overlooked source of information. This work provides a method of finding organizations that patrons can turn to with their information queries. The more than 7,800 organizations are presented in an organizational list by title. Each entry provides contact information, membership, number of staff, budget, key personnel, organization publications, and historical notes.

The annually updated book also provides a number of methods to cross-reference entries. Associations are indexed by subject; city and state headquarters; budget; executive; association acronym; and by city in which the next annual meeting will take place. New in this edition is information on certifications provided by each association and city and state organizational meeting trends for the past three years.

The information provided within this volume can also be found in the publisher's online database, *AssociationExecs.com*. The database contains the contents from this title as well as one of the publisher's other directories, *State and Regional Associations* (22d ed.; see ARBA 2012, entry 48). The online database provides access to 45,000 association executives and over 16,000 national and state associations. Users can search by subject/industry, budget, annual meeting place, membership size, state, type of organization, job function, or zip code. The Website is updated on a daily basis, eliminating the problem that print directories have of the information being outdated quickly.

The *National Trade and Professional Associations of the United States* provides basic information and serves as a jumping off point for further investigation. When compared to *Associations Unlimited* (Gale/Cengage Learning), the amount of data in each entry is limited. For robust information needs, *Associations Unlimited* will be the superior resource. However, in most situations, the simplicity of search and cross-reference provided by this book should efficiently serve patrons' needs. This resource is recommended for academic, public, and corporate libraries.—**Abe Korah**

Government Information

C, P

18.   **The Book of the States 2011. Volume 43.** Lexington, Ky., Council of State Governments, 2011. 490p. illus. maps. index. $99.00pa. 978-0-87292-773-5.

The Book of the States, published biennially, offers a wealth of factual information about individual states in one place that is unmatched online. *The Book of the States* is the standard ready-reference source to check for recent information on state officials, state legislatures, and the state judiciary, as well as on state elections and finances. Whether seeking information on the qualifications of secretaries of state, the methods for the removal of judges and filling of vacancies, or allowable state investments, this source is the place to start. Tables about state excise tax rates, motor vehicle laws, and time-series data on state minimum wages are examples of what can be found here. State mottoes, flowers, songs, birds, and so forth are also given.—**Shannon Graff Hysell**

C, P

19.   **USA.gov. http://www.usa.gov/.** [Website]. Free. Date reviewed: 2011.

The U.S. General Services Administration is responsible for a third federal resource that functions as the primary portal to federal government information online, as a government services directory, and as a reference tool and also points to basic directory information. USA.gov was begun as Firstgov.gov by entrepreneur Eric Brewer in 2000 and, after some uncertainty, became the official single portal to federal government information (the E-Government Act of 2002 further pushed development of government Internet sites and services and effectively served to provide funding for, and legitimize, USA.gov). It became know as USA.gov in 2007. USA.gov offers subject-based access to government information, as well as a series of in-depth, user-friendly portals aimed at seniors, student, exporters, workers, small businesspeople, and people with disabilities, to name a few. It also provides access to state, local, and tribal government Websites. It is organized centrally by broad topics, such as Consumer Guides, Jobs and Education, Science and Technology, and Travel and Recreation, to name a few. Convenient interactions with government are facilitated. "Shop Government Auctions," "Passport Application," "Flu Clinic Locator—Get Your Flu Shot," and "Loans—GovLoans.gov" are examples illustrative of its service-delivery focus. USA.gov features specialty portals for citizens, business and nonprofits, government employees, seniors, military and veterans, and visitors to the United States. USA.gov also includes a Spanish-language version.—**Julienne L. Wood**

Handbooks and Yearbooks

C, P, S

20.   **Britannica Book of the Year 2011.** Chicago, Encyclopaedia Britannica, 2011. 880p. illus. index. $75.00. ISBN 13: 978-1-61434-452-8.

Yearbooks can cover general or specific areas of knowledge and one popular general yearbook for libraries is the *Britannica Book of the Year*. It updates articles in the *Encyclopaedia Britannica* and is a chronicle of the events of a given year. It bridges the gap between editions of the *Encyclopaedia Britannica*. The majority of each yearbook is a review of happenings of the previous year. In addition, about one-third of each volume provides a largely statistical description of the nations of the world, called "Britannica World Data." Sections cover images of the year and people of significance in the previous year, as well as obituaries for prominent people who died during the previous year. Special reports appear throughout the "Year in Review" and provide several-page discussions of topics of current interest. A cumulative, decennial index is an important feature of the *Britannica Book of the Year* because it allows the user to locate information when the exact year is not known. Unlike many almanac indexes, yearbook indexes also contain personal names. In the decennial index, the date of the yearbook is indicated by boldface type followed by a page number; for example, 89:14 refers to page 14 of the 1989 yearbook. The *Britannica Book of the Year* is included in *Britannica Online* (see entry 11). Articles from the yearbook are identified in the search results list after performing a search. The online edition offers the advantage of single-stop searching but is not necessarily more current than the print version.—**Shannon Graff Hysell**

S

21.   **Crabtree Connection Series.** New York, Crabtree, 2011. 18v. illus. index. $21.27/vol.; $6.95pa./vol.

This is a series that is very broad in scope, covering everything from science and geography to history and recreation. The idea behind the series is to get students to connect everyday things in their lives to the topics that they study in school. The books cover such topics as bugs and pets, the ocean, ecosystems and the environment, sports and nutrition, and medicine and invention. The books are filled with enlarged color photographs and fun facts; the history behind each subject is addressed as well. Each volume concludes with a glossary, a list for further reading (books and Websites), and an index—all of which are very brief in nature. These books are designed with elementary age and middle school age students in mind and would be fun books for children in this age group to use to explore new topics.—**Sara Marcus**

C, S

22.   **Top Stories 2010: Behind the Headlines.** Farmington Hills, Mich., Gale/Cengage Learning, 2011. 350. illus. index. $105.00. ISBN 13: 978-1-4144-8889-9.

This new, yearbook-style resource provides an in-depth look into 10 worldwide issues that caught the attention of people all over the world and dominated the global press. The book looks at such things as conflict, collaboration, global development, and world security, and touches on how these key concepts affect all nations and all people. This 1st edition covers the following headline stories: The Afghan War;

The Chilean Miners' Rescue; The Global Economic Crisis; The Gulf Oil Crisis; Haiti's Earthquake and Its Aftermath; Iran's Nuclear Program; Islam in the West; Mexico's Drug War; Migrants, Immigrants, and Refugees; and Security in the Digital Age. The entries are written in a dramatic style that will encourage classroom discussion, and each story provides historical, cultural, and economic context so that it can be fully understood. The work has full-color photographs that will further capture the imagination of young adults. Priced at $105, this new series is one that will be of interest to high school and undergraduate libraries, as well as large public libraries.—**Shannon Graff Hysell**

Museums

C
23.   Danilov, Victor J. **America's College Museums Handbook & Directory.** 2d ed. Millerton, N.Y., Grey House Publishing, 2011. 687p. illus. $185.00. ISBN 13: 978-1-59237-674-2; 978-1-59237-675-9 (e-book).

America's College Museums is a directory of over 1,700 museums at over 800 academic institutions in the United States. The text is divided into two main sections. The first section opens with a look at the history of academic museums in the United States starting with the College of William and Mary in 1732. This chapter is followed by a second that considers the main types of academic museums: art museums, science museums, and history museums. Subsequent chapters examine the governance, organization and staffing of museums; the mission of museums; their collections and research role; their exhibits and programs; their facilities and attendance; and the reasons for both their closures and openings over the years. The first section closes with an index of the section's chapters and 19 pages of black-and-white photographs. The second section is a directory arranged by categories of major subject concentration, ranging from agricultural museums to zoology museums. Within a subject concentration the museums are alphabetically arranged by the name of their institution. A brief history of each museum is provided followed by a brief summary of the collection and, often times, a listing of the annual attendance. The contact information of each museum is provided along with the name and contact information of the museum director. The text closes with indexes, which pair universities to their museums and vice versa, along with a geographic index and an index of key personnel. This is followed by an appendix of founding dates and a bibliography.—**Philip G. Swan**

Periodicals and Serials

C, P
24.   **Ulrich's Periodicals Directory 2011.** New Providence, N.J., R. R. Bowker, 2011. multivolume. index. $1260.00/set. ISBN 13: 978-1-60030-134-6.

Ulrich's Periodicals Directory is an annual guide to more than 201,000 currently available periodicals and, since 1993, newspapers. The arrangement is by broad subject area, with separate indexes providing access to title, ISSN, and publications of international organizations. Providers of online periodicals and serials on CD-ROM are listed alphabetically in separate sections. Entries include the information needed to order the title: publisher, address, price, and ISSN. In addition, frequency, beginning date, circulation figures, advertising rates, refereed status, and telephone and fax numbers are usually included. *Ulrich's* has several other features that greatly increase its usefulness in the reference collection. Each entry lists the indexes and online databases that cover the contents of the periodical. This feature allows the librarian or other user to locate the complete citation for an article in a periodical by identifying the index or database where the citation can be found. Another valuable feature is the list of cessations, which lists periodicals that have ceased publication during the previous three years. Since

1988, *Ulrich's* has incorporated *Irregular Serials and Annuals* in its coverage and title, thus providing publication and ordering information for most directories, almanacs, and yearbooks.

Web-based access to *Ulrich's* is now provided by Serials Solutions as *Ulrichsweb*. Quick search options include ISSN, keyword, subject, exact title, and keyword from title. Entries can be browsed by general subject or by a variety of indexes, including country of publication, language, Dewey Decimal number, and LC classification number. The advanced search option allows more complex combinations of fields. The database is updated weekly.—**ARBA Staff Reviewer**

Quotations

C, P, S

25. **Bartlett's Familiar Quotations.** 17th ed. New York, Oxford University Press, 2010. 1155p. index. $50.00. ISBN 13: 978-0-19-923717-3.

The core quotations source is *Bartlett's Familiar Quotations*, now in its 17th edition, published since 1855. With 25,000 quotations from more than 2,000 authors, Bartlett's covers a wide variety of subjects, time periods, and people, from the Bible and Shakespeare to such contemporary authors as Maya Angelou and Frank McCourt. It is arranged chronologically and includes an author index and a keyword index to provide and enhance access. Its moderate price puts it within the reach of many libraries' budgets, and for the content and history contained in *Bartlett's*, it should be part of every library's collection.—**ARBA Staff Reviewer**

Part II
SOCIAL SCIENCES

2 Social Sciences in General

General Works

Dictionaries and Encyclopedias

C, S

26. **Encyclopedia of Contemporary Social Issues.** Michael Shally-Jensen, ed. Santa Barbara, Calif., ABC-CLIO, 2011. 4v. illus. index. $372.00/set. ISBN 13: 978-0-31339-204-7; 978-0-31339-205-4 (e-book).

Drawing upon a series of books published previously by Greenwood Press entitled Battleground, this set, entitled *Encyclopedia of Contemporary Social Issues*, updates, revises, and even replaces some articles benefiting from the scholarship of previous writers. In four volumes, the editor and over 170 contributors have created a research tool that will be a valuable resource for years to come. The intention of this series is to provide a "bridge" between in-depth scholarship and those new to the subjects it covers. The 200 entries in these volumes create a useable research tool complete with subtopics, referencing and cross-referencing, and a useable appendix. Although social issue books seem caught in time and become outdated rather quickly, by building on past research and selecting topics that have dominated the social landscape for many decades, and by setting these issues in a historical context, these volumes will have lasting quality. For convenience, each of these four volumes concentrates on a different set of issues: Business and the Economy; Criminal Justice; Family and Society; and Environment, Science, and Technology. Impressive are the depth of coverage and the clarity of writing which makes these volumes an excellent foundational tool for high school students, college undergraduates, and a starting place for graduate research. The articles present controversial arguments from a variety of perspectives representing an expanded version of the sociological tradition that focuses on social problems and the many ways by which these problems can be and have been researched and analyzed.—**Joseph P. Hester**

C, P

27. **Encyclopedia of Power.** Keith Dowding, ed. Thousand Oaks, Calif., Sage, 2011. 784p. index. $175.00; e-book available. ISBN 13: 978-1-4129-2748-2.

This large, 784-page encyclopedia contains 381 entries written by a group of 157 internationally based authors. Within the entries cover topics related to the concept of power as it relates to a variety of social sciences, many of which are obvious such as political science and organizational studies, and some that are less obvious, including social-psychology and urban planning. The editor provides a Reader's Guide that categorizes each term into one of several categories, which include Biography, Social Psychology, Social Theory, Political Science, Decisions and Game Theory, and Urban Studies. Each term is clearly defined with examples and links to other areas presented. The entries all include a list for further reading, *see also* terms, related topics, and each is signed by its author. The majority of the terms fall under the categories of political science (96) and concepts related to power (99), with fewer falling under the categories of interpersonal relationships (14), interpersonal matters (10), and institutional issues (24). The terminology used is mainly appropriate for undergraduates and older. The broad cross-section of ethical, cultural, sociological, and economic topics makes this a worthwhile resource for most public and academic libraries.—**Shannon Graff Hysell**

S

28.   **Issues: Understanding Controversy and Society. http://www.abc-clio.com/Previews/index. aspx.** [Website]. Santa Barbara, Calif., ABC-CLIO. Price negotiated by site. Date reviewed: 2011.

Issues: Understanding Controversy and Society has several features that distinguish it from its closest competitors, *The CQ Researcher Online* (CQ Press/Sage) and *Opposing Viewpoints in Context* (Gale/Cengage). First of all, it is now available in a middle and high school version, or in an academic version for undergraduate libraries. This database currently contains information on 150 of today's most significant social issues, accessing 7,000 articles and 4,500 primary sources. Following the pattern of ABC-CLIO's other outstanding online products, the basic narratives are supplemented with links to thousands of related biographies, organizations, statistics, events, maps, video and audio clips, still images, timelines, court cases, quotations, and primary source documents.

Controversial issues included in this database are divided into six categories: society, criminal justice, environment, gender/ethnicity, government/law/politics, and science/technology. Multiple specific issues are listed under each category. These issues range from traditional subjects, such as gun control, air pollution, and capital punishment to more contemporary issues, such as hate crimes, outsourcing, weapons of mass destruction, and obesity. The basic format for investigating the issues is the same throughout the database.

Each issue is introduced with an overview article, signed by the author, beginning with an attention-grabbing example. The issue is then placed in historical and social context and is written in a way that encourages student inquiry and critical thinking. Tools allow quick access to people and organizations, timeliness (impressively up to date), and statistics, as well as what is going on right now and likely to happen in the future. On the right side of the screen are the links to supplemental materials (e.g., events, images, objects, places). Internal links and images designed for individual exploration are also included. Articles can be formatted for printing and e-mailing. Pictures can be copied or saved for student presentations, and statistics can be downloaded to spreadsheets. The statistics, however, are presented in tables that need interpretation. Navigating the database met expectations with multiple routes, folder tabs, breadcrumbs, back buttons, and back to top buttons all present, yet unobtrusive.

Although this new database does not have the scope of the thousands of issues in the online version of *CQ Researcher*, or the broad base of outside articles provided in *Opposing Viewpoints in Context*, it does offer a Web-based multimedia approach to studying issues that today's students will appreciate. The flexibility of its organization gives library media specialists and teachers a wide variety of ways to help students find information. The excellent layout and navigation also make it simple for students to use independently.—**Barbara Ripp Safford**

Handbooks and Yearbooks

S

29.   **At Issue Series.** Farmington Hills, Mich., Greenhaven Press/Gale/Cengage Learning, 2011. index. $31.80/vol.; $22.50pa./vol.

Greenhaven's At Issue Series has been in publication since 2001 and in that time more than 450 titles have been published (both in hardcover and in paperback). The series is grouped into smaller subtopics, including health, civil liberties, and crime. The goal of the series is to provide a wide range of opinions on specific social issues. The titles vary greatly in the breadth or narrowness of each topic discussed; for example, users will find a title on the very broad topic of food safety as well as a title on the much more narrowly focused subject of the benefits of organic food. To provide opinions for each side to the argument the book uses eyewitness accounts, governmental views, scientific analysis, and newspaper and magazine accounts. A bibliography and a list of organizations at the back of each book points readers to other sources for further information.

These books are an excellent source for middle and high school readers to enhance their critical thinking skills. They could easily be used as jumping off points for research projects and debate topics. At $31.80 for the hardcover copies and $22.50 for the paperback versions this set as a whole is expensive. School librarians will most likely need to be selective if they choose to purchase books within this series.—**Shannon Graff Hysell**

S

30.   **Basher Basics Series.** Boston, Kingfisher/Houghton Mifflin, 2011. 3v. illus. index. $7.99/vol.

Created by Simon Basher, these handy little guides present the basics of essential curricular subjects in a fun and interesting manner. Titles include: *Punctuation: The Write Stuff!*, *Chemistry: Getting a Big Reaction!*, and *Math: A Book You Can Count On!* With characters who correspond to the specific content area, color coordinated chapters provide one page of explanation and full-page illustration. The colorful characters, fun facts, do's and don'ts, and casual writing will appeal to struggling students or visual learners, although some of the terms and descriptions may be difficult for some. These guides would make a nice supplement to the teaching and learning process. Users can look at the creator's Website for more instructive ideas (http://www.basherbooks.com). Each book includes a glossary, table of contents, and index.—**Nick Petrosino**

C, P

31.   **Statesman's Yearbook 2011.** 147th ed. New York, Palgrave Macmillan, 2011. 2000p. maps. index. $250.00. ISBN 13: 978-0-23020-603-8.

A long-time favorite of ready-reference librarian is the *Statesman's Yearbook*, issued annually since 1863. The first part of this book gives excellent coverage of international organizations, starting with the United Nations and including numerous other organizations. Part 2 is a listing of countries of the world. For each country the publications includes a map, along with information on the country's history, population and social statistics, politics and government, industry, communications, social institutions, religion, and culture. Brief biographies of current leaders are also provided, may of which are fascinating.

An online version of the *Yearbook* is available to subscribers at http://www.statesmansyearbook. com/. The online product is updated on a regular basis and provides extensive further reading lists and more than 1,500 Web links for further research. Special features include the monthly Editor's Spotlight (focusing on anniversaries in modern history), a chronology of events that led up to the current economic credit problem, and an essay discussing online competition of news media.—**Charlotte Ford**

3 Area Studies

United States

General Works

C

32.   Lavin, Stephen J., Fred M. Shelley, and J. Clark Archer. **Atlas of the Great Plains.** Lincoln, Nebr., University of Nebraska Press, 2011. 335p. illus. maps. $39.95. ISBN 13: 978-0-8032-1536-8.

While there are several reference books about the American West, there are very few that focus so completely on this particular region aside from the publisher's previously published and well reviewed *Encyclopedia of the Great Plains* (2004). This historical atlas chronicles the history of the Great Plains, including its social and political developments. It does so through the use of more than 300 original full-color maps, all of which are accompanied by explanatory text. Users will get a full presentation of the geography of the regional as well as a better understanding of the settlement patterns of both Native Americans and white settlers, agriculture, voting history, crime rates, and even health and medical services. It includes maps of both the United States and Canada, showing exactly the breadth of this vast region. The maps are beautiful to look at and will help readers gain a better appreciation of geography, people, and wildlife that inhabit this region. All of the authors have published extensively. Lavin is a professor of geography at the University of Nebraska—Lincoln and co-author to several other titles, including *Historical Atlas of U.S. Presidential Elections, 1788–2004* (see ARBA 2007, entry 585). Every library in the plains region will of course need this title in its reference collection; outside of that huge region, it would be most useful in academic and larger public libraries.—**Mark T. Bay**

Alaska

C, P

33.   Naske, Claus M., and Herman E. Slotnick. **Alaska: A History.** Norman, Okla., University of Oklahoma Press, 2011. 504p. illus. index. $39.95. ISBN 13: 978-0-8061-4040-7.

The 3d edition of this now classic history of Alaska has undertaken a large update in the 24 years since the 2d edition. The 15 chapters of the 2d edition have been expanded into 26 chapters and subdivided into five parts, covering just over 400 substantive pages. Part 1 is about the land and native peoples. It takes up just 15 pages. Part 2 on Russian Alaska covers 65 pages. Part 3 on territorial Alaska includes the gold rush and the Cold War in 120 pages. Parts 4 and 5, "Alaska as a State" and "Modern Alaska" cover 185 pages. As such, this history is strongest on the economic and political history of the last 50 years.

Issues that are covered in detail with many illustrative tables, maps, and appendixes, include the oil resources, native land claims, military presence, and political power struggles of well-known Alaskans like Ted Stevens and Sarah Palin. Scholars will appreciate the many footnotes and the "Bibliographical

Essay on the Sources of Alaska's History." For the generalist user in the public library, a new 12-page introduction in the front of the book, fascinating subjects in text boxes, and over 100 black-and-white photographs make the history come to life.

As the largest state and the only one with arctic and subarctic climate and with an abundance of natural resources, this survey of Alaskan history is fascinating and will be of interest to many. This book can be used as a reference tool, for perusing, or as a textbook.—**Georgia Briscoe**

Africa

Angola

C

34.   James, W. Martin. **Historical Dictionary of Angola.** 2d ed. Lanham, Md., Scarecrow, 2011. 347p. (Historical Dictionaries of Africa). $95.00. ISBN 13: 978-0-8108-7193-9; 978-0-8108-7458-9 (e-book).

Angola was a Portuguese colony from 1482-1961. Portugal exploited Angola's people and its resources by sending the wealth of Angola to Portugal, and leaving no economic infrastructure, hospitals, education, or political systems in place for the Angolans. Finally, in 1961 Angolan revolutionary groups ousted the Portuguese. Conflicts ensured among some of the rival tribes that drove the country into a civil war for 27 years. Finally, in 2002 the Angolans were able to form a unified government for themselves. Today, Angola is a country rich in abundant resources such as fertile soil, minerals, oil reserves, and a hearty people who want Angola to continue to be a free nation. Currently it is on its way to becoming a regional African power with global influence.

This is a 2d edition and it continues the coverage of the personalities, organizations, geography, institutions, and historical events of Angola (see ARBA 2005, entry 84, for a review of the 1st edition). There are black-and-white maps in this dictionary, a chronology, and updated lengthy bibliographies of historical documents, books, journal articles, and Websites. The appendixes cover Heads of State and their officers, and the country's provinces and their cities.

This new edition of the *Historical Dictionary of Angola* is highly recommended for academic and large public collections. It is also recommended for corporate business and government country study collections, especially if your company or group is doing business in Angola and other neighboring African countries.—**Kay M. Stebbins**

Ethiopia

C, S

35.   Milkias, Paulos. **Ethiopia.** Santa Barbara, Calif., ABC-CLIO, 2011. 544p. illus. maps. index. (Africa in Focus). $85.00. ISBN 13: 978-1-59884-257-9; 978-1-59884-258-6 (e-book).

Most Americans know little about this African country, but we need to. It has the second largest population on the continent, is the headquarters of the African Union, and is of strategic importance to the United States because of its location next to Somalia, a haven for terrorist groups and the operating base of the pirates menacing shipping off the coast of North Eastern Africa. And, Ethiopians are one of the fastest growing immigrant groups in the United States.

In this book, Milkias introduces readers to Ethiopia—its people, its history, its geography, its culture, its economy, its political development, and the current issues impacting it. Designed for the general reader, this book tells us Ethiopia is the birthplace of Lucy, the ancestor of all human beings, who lived 3.2 million years ago. Coffee was first domesticated in Ethiopia. Ethiopia's indigenous writing system dates back more than 2,600 years and there are historic annals dating back to that same time.

During the period of European colonialism in Africa, only Ethiopia remained independent. Features include the Ethiopian alphabet and common phrases as well as appendixes with statistical information, a list of Ethiopian holidays, country-related organizations with Web addresses, and an annotated bibliography.—**Adrienne Antink**

South Africa

C

36.   **Encyclopedia of South Africa.** Krista Johnson and Sean Jacobs, eds. Boulder, Colo., Lynne Rienner Publishers, 2011. 373p. index. $95.00. ISBN 13: 978-1-58826-749-8.

This single-volume encyclopedia of more than 300 pages provides many entries that are relevant and appropriate to South Africa. Both breadth and depth are apparent as it truly is "encyclopedic" in scope. Entries range from the more general topics such as "immigration" and "music" to the obvious "Robben Island" or more esoteric "Fanagalo" language. There are many well-known and lesser-known biographical entries, and relevant geographical sites such as "Mozambique" and "Lesotho" that explain the essential information of this vast and diverse nation. The book is well laid out and bound, it has excellent entries that vary in length according to the significance of the topic, but are of uniformly high quality for researchers. Many entries have a bibliography, while both *see* and *see also* headings guide the reader to specific and additional information. Occasional black-and-white photographs give visual relief, although their overall content and relevance are of less value than the individual entries. Whether the alphabetically arranged entry topics are biographical, political, sport, historical, or any of the many other categories, they are very well presented. Both logical arrangement and thoughtful contributors' content make this volume easy to use and an important resource. Six well-designed appendixes show: chronology, heads of state, government structures, geography, political parties, and key legislation. Timelines, tables, and illustrations keep the appendixes informative, neatly available, and clear for the reader. A list of more than 100 acronyms is a useful back-of-the-book tool. Also, about 23 pages of very thorough index add significant value for any researcher.

This volume deserves to be included as an addition to any collections of African, Black History, or many other historical, demographic, political, geographic, or cultural areas. This is a valuable print volume for community college, university, some special, and many large public libraries. More than 50 scholars form the team of diverse international contributors with oversight by an International Advisory Board. The diligent effort of Johnson and Jacobs is evident in this excellent volume that is highly recommended.—**Jim Agee**

Asia

Afghanistan

C, P

37.   Adamec, Ludwig W. **Historical Dictionary of Afghanistan.** 4th ed. Lanham, Md., Scarecrow, 2012. 569p. (Historical Dictionaries of Asia, Oceania, and the Middle East). $95.00. ISBN 13: 978-0-8108-7815-0; 978-0-8108-7957-7 (e-book).

The first substantive section of this dictionary is a chronology of events which goes up to March 2011. Next is a concise introduction (eight pages) on the geography, people, religion, and history of Afghanistan. While there is mention of Afghan ties to Ariana (1500 B.C.E.), the historical analysis focuses on the early nineteenth century onwards, with special consideration for events leading up to the Soviet occupation and its aftermath. The same focus is true for the dictionary of terms. This is in line with the work's stated scope to concentrate "on the political history of contemporary Afghanistan." Following the dictionary are appendixes, which outline major terms of the Durand Agreement, Taliban Codex, Rules for Political Parties, Durrani genealogy, and a thematically arranged bibliography.

While the 4th edition provides coverage of recent events, some of the appendixes in the 3d edition are not in the current one (3d ed.; see ARBA 2004, entry 114). These include Soviet report on Intervention of Afghanistan, Military Technical Agreement, and Commission for Loya Jirga. As the bibliography is thematically arranged, references to some entries require greater effort to look up. This work is not immune from errors of omission that general works like this one are prone to suffer. Its best work is the thorough descriptions of significant personalities, organizations, geographical places, and historical events. These entries make it is more of an encyclopedia than a dictionary, making it an excellent starting point for scholars and general readers interested in contemporary political Afghanistan.—**Muhammed Hassanali**

India

C, P, S
38. **India Today: An Encyclopedia of Life in the Republic.** Arnold P. Kaminsky and Roger D. Long, eds. Santa Barbara, Calif., ABC-CLIO, 2011. 2v. illus. maps. index. $189.00/set. ISBN 13: 978-0-313-37521-7; 978-0-313-37463-0 (e-book).

India is the birth place of four major religions of the world—Hinduism, Buddhism, Jainism, and Sikhism. Over one billion people live in this secular country and it is the most successful parliamentary democracy in the world. India became an independent and free country in 1947 and has made good progress in many aspects of life since independence from the British. The book under review is a two-volume encyclopedia that deals with the progress since 1947. It includes 250 articles written by 80 scholars arranged alphabetically A to Z. They are all signed articles from 300 words to 5,000 words and include many cross-references as well as lists of further reading. Both volumes have many black-and-white photographs, illustrations, and maps. Volume 2 has an extensive bibliography for further research. The entries cover many good topics including politics, religion, cities, states, biographies of many politicians and other prominent leaders, and social and economic aspects of modern India since 1947. The encyclopedia also has a selected chronology of events in the country since independence and a topic finder. According to the editors India is one of the most remarkable, diverse, and fascinating countries in the world and they have proved it by including very selective entries to educate readers. They have provided a very good research tool for scholars. This encyclopedia is recommended very highly for all types of library collections that serve students, researchers, and scholars.—**Ravindra Nath Sharma**

C
39. Hoover, William D. **Historical Dictionary of Postwar Japan.** Lanham, Md., Scarecrow, 2011. 423p. (Historical Dictionaries of Asia, Oceania, and the Middle East). $95.00. ISBN 13: 978-0-8108-5460-4; 978-0-8108-7539-5 (e-book).

This volume, written by William D. Hoover, a retired professor at the University of Toledo, belongs to the series of Historical Dictionaries of Asia, Oceania, and the Middle East, edited by Jon Woronoff. The book consists of five parts: a chronology, an introduction, the main text, appendixes, and bibliography. The chronology covers essentially post-World War II Japan to the present: events that occurred from August 15, 1945, when the Emperor broadcast Japan's surrender, to July 11th, 2010 when the Democratic Party of Japan became the majority party in the election for the House of Councilors.

In the introduction, the author discusses history, population, economy, foreign policy, and other topics. Although the treatment of each topic is brief, it is enough to provide a picture of Japanese development. The volume's main part, the A-Z dictionary, has about 350 pages. Its topics include people of various professions, such as athletes, businessmen, educators, journalists, movie stars, politicians, royal families, singers, and more.

This section also covers architecture, the automobile industry, banks, cities, companies, diplomacy, religion, and trade unions. The explanations of social groups like *burakumin* and *yakuza*, companies like Nintendo and Sony, and traditional sports like sumo, will hold the reader 's interest and provide lively breaks from other, more standard topics. The manifold entries are alphabetically listed and some are as short as five or six lines, while some cover more than one page. Appendix A lists names of the prime ministers from August 17, 1945 to June 2010, while Japan 's Defense Expenditures, percentage increases in GDP, and other useful statistics and facts are shown from appendices B to N. The bibliography aids further study.

The beginning of the book contains two useful, reader-friendly features: three pages of abbreviations and acronyms and a map of present-day Japan with names of main cities and the seas surrounding the country. Throughout the book, most entries of Japanese people's names appear with the surnames and first names in that order, first in roman letters, with the Japanese characters following. The names of companies and institutions also appear with roman letters first, and Japanese characters following. Some entry names are written in English only, including those for the constitution, foreign policy, labor organizations, literature, and women. The book gives ample information about post-World War II Japan and it is recommended for college and university libraries as well as large public libraries.—**Seiko Mieczkowski**

Australia and Oceania

P, S

40.   **World and Its Peoples: Sub-Saharan Africa, Australasia, and the Pacific.** Tarrytown, N.Y., Marshall Cavendish, 2011. 11v. illus. maps. index. $499.95/set. ISBN 13: 978-0-7614-7912-3.

In this day and age of online reference resources, e-books, and Google, sometimes it is easy to forget that there is more to an information resource than the information it provides. Occasionally, it is good to be reminded that a book, or set of books, is often an artifact in and of itself, and can provide the user with an aesthetic experience that is missing from electronic resources. The *World and Its Peoples: Sub-Saharan Africa, Australasia, and the Pacific* is one such reference resource. Not only is it valuable for the information that it presents, but it presents this information in a well-organized and attractive package. The set is comprised of 11 volumes, divided geographically, with the last volume an index and collection of charts and tables. Each volume starts off with an examination of the geography, climate, history, and movement of peoples of the covered area as a whole. Then, each country in the covered area is examined in depth. There is a short narrative summary of the country, its culture, and its history, followed by tables of demographic and geographic information. Then, the history, culture, economy, and government are explored in greater detail. Each section is illustrated with color photographs and useful maps.

The authority of the large group of editors and consultants associated with *World and Its Peoples: Sub-Saharan Africa, Australasia, and the Pacific* is hard to question. The information is accurate and the writing is free from obvious bias. The writing is excellent and is accessible to users with a middle school and higher reading level. While the cost of the set is prohibitive to smaller libraries, this resource would be an excellent addition to the reference collection of any library that ever fields questions about geography and history of the areas covered.—**Mark T. Bay**

Europe

Hungary

C, S

41.　Buranbaeva, Oksana, and Vanja Mladineo. **Culture and Customs of Hungary.** Santa Barbara, Calif., Greenwood Press/ABC-CLIO, 2011. 212p. index. (Culture and Customs of Europe). $50.00. ISBN 13: 978-0-313-38369-4; 978-0-313-38370-0 (e-book).

Culture and Customs of Hungary is a lively, readable guide to the diverse cultures and traditions of Hungarian society. The authors place contemporary issues and trends in a historical context. The text focuses primarily on the twentieth century, with frequent attention paid to the countries geographical position and the role it has played in European history and politics. Topics covered include (among others) religion, language, gender, customs, media, literature, cinema, music, and architecture. The text has a chronological list of events, from prehistory to the present; a country map; a short glossary; a selected bibliography for the entire book; and an index. Each chapter includes a list of notes.

The authors not only describe national traditions, but also do an effective job of identifying and exploring regional cultures. Although the book is mainly about contemporary culture, the authors explore some history in this volume especially as it relates to Hungary's contributions to literature, music, architecture, philosophy, natural science, and political thought. There are a handful of black-and-white photographs found within the text. This work is recommended for academic, school, and public libraries.—**Sharon Ladenson**

Ireland

C, P

42.　**Atlas of the Irish Rural Landscape.** 2d ed. F. H. A. Aalen, Kevin Whelan, and Matthew Stout, eds. Toronto, University of Toronto Press, 2011. 422p. illus. maps. index. $75.00. ISBN 13: 978-1-4426-4291-1.

When the 1st edition of this atlas appeared in 1997 it was lauded as a treasure trove of information on Ireland and multi-disciplinary in scope, providing geographical, environmental, historical, and architectural information on Ireland in one volume. This 2d edition has been expanded by 30 percent and the format has been revamped to be more user-friendly and functional. Of the nearly 1,000 photographs, maps, and diagrams, nearly 50 percent are new to this edition. Five new regional case studies have been added: Tory Island (Donegal), the Wicklow Uplands, Inistioge (Kilkenny), Aughris (Sligo), and Point Lance in Newfoundland. Also included in this edition are a list of 50 books on the Irish landscape, a guide to the Irish landscape online, and an expanded index. User will find an abundance of information on everything Ireland here, including archaeology, farming, transportation (railways, roads, canals), mining, and castles and churches. Essays are provided on history of the early Irish landscape, the modern landscape, and the future of rural Ireland. The text ties in very well with the photographs, maps, and diagrams making this an all-around and pleasurable book to both consult in research or browse.—**Shannon Graff Hysell**

Middle East

General Works

C, S

43.   **The Middle East: A Guide to Politics, Economics, Society, and Culture.** Barry Rubin, ed. Armonk, N.Y., M. E. Sharpe, 2012. 2v. index. $299.00/set. ISBN 13: 978-0-7656-8094-5.

Divided into seven topical parts, this two-volume resource discusses the Middle East's complex history, political problems, and many of the misconceptions that people hold on this region. The seven parts are: Politics of Governing in the Middle East; Middle East Economics; Middle East Media; Religion in the Middle East; Middle East Cultures; People of the Middle East; and Women in the Middle East. Interspersed within each section are stories of the Middle East's modern history and the way it has shaped the lives of its people and the worldviews of others in the region. The set could be used by high school and undergraduate students studying everything from the politics of the Middle East, to the various cultures living there, to the lives and status of women in the region. Each essay ends with a list of references and a concluding index pulls the entire set together. This work would serve well as a general reference on this region for high school and undergraduate libraries.—**Shannon Graff Hysell**

Polar Regions

C, P

44.   Stewart, John. **Antarctica: An Encyclopedia.** 2d ed. Jefferson, N.C., McFarland, 2011. 2v. index. $495.00/set. ISBN 13: 978-0-7864-3590-6; 978-0-7864-8917-6 (e-book).

This is the 2d edition of *Antarctica: An Encyclopedia.* It is the first update of this encyclopedia since 1990. The 30,000 entries are alphabetically arranged in two volumes. The only missing part in the 2d edition is the chronology. The two volumes cover the geography, the geology, and the expeditions and explorations of the continent. Short biographical entries of the explorers are available, with extensive entries for Captain James Cook's expedition and the Richard E. Byrd expedition. The entries are very detailed with geological and geographical information as well as entries on pertinent scientific terms, birds, animals, insects, and flora. Additional information from English and Spanish gazetteers has been translated to be beneficial to the reader. There are extensive cross-references for the various names of the same locations' place-names by various countries.

These two volumes cover every aspect of the scientific and technological information about this fascinating continent. I would recommend this encyclopedia for academic and public libraries. [R: LJ, Jan 12, p. 140]—**Kay M. Stebbins**

4 Economics and Business

General Works

Bibliography

C, P

45.   **ALA Guide to Economics & Business Reference.** Chicago, American Library Association, 2011. 505p. index. $65.00pa.; $58.50pa. (ALA members). ISBN 13: 978-0-8389-1024-5.

Part of the ALA Guide to Reference series, this source focuses on "print and electronic sources that are key to economics and business reference" (Editors Guide). Subjects covered include: Basic Industry Information; Company Information; Economic Conditions and World Trade; Functional Areas of Business (among these areas are Accounting and Taxation; Finance and Investments; Electronic Commerce; Management, Marketing, Advertising, and Public Relations; and Operations Management); General Works (including Biography, Directories, Periodicals, Quotations); Occupations and Careers; Regional Economic Sources; and Specialized Industry Information (including Agribusiness, Computers, Food and Beverage, Retail Trade, Transportation, and Utilities). Each chapter contains subsections with annotated lists of sources. For example the Chapter Basic Industry Information contains subsections on Financial Ratios, Indexes, Abstract Journals, Overviews, and Statistics. Each entry contains the title, author (when applicable), place of publication, and publisher with call numbers in Dewey Decimal System and Library of Congress call numbers. ISSN numbers are provided for serial publications and Web addresses for Websites. The annotations are generally one paragraph and provide descriptions of each item, including content, special features, and formats available. There is an index by entry number (with main entry number in bold and entry number in light type to refer to mention of items in other annotations) to the entries included.

This guide is suitable for public and academic libraries, business researchers, students and faculty of business schools, librarians developing both public and academic library collections, and library and information science students. It is highly recommended.—**Lucy Heckman**

Catalogs and Collections

C, P

46.   **AllBusiness. http://www.allbusiness.com/.** [Website]. Short Hills, N.J., Dun and Bradstreet. Free (some content for sale). Date reviewed: 2011.

AllBusiness covers the finer aspects of starting and operating a new business, and it does so in a very consolidated way. The Dun & Bradstreet site offers tools for the new business owner, short multimedia clips covering tips, and more than 5 million journal articles written by in-house staff and by the Gale Cengage Learning staff. While the main body of content is free, there is much for sale on the site offered through memberships. One must wind a path through the advertising of related products such as forms.

An entire section is devoted to franchises. The franchise directory lists several hundred franchise opportunities. Franchise entries give brief information, including required investment amounts, business descriptions, an all-star ranking, and the number of employees needed to operate a franchise. Entries also include a three-year growth rate based on the numbers of units, the franchise and royalty fee, the net worth and capital requirements, and franchise-sponsored financing. *AllBusiness* runs an all-star ranking of 300 listed franchises. All of this is accompanied by feature articles with tips for buying, growing, and franchising a business. The franchise directory is a particularly good addition to this well-organized site, packed with valuable content for the new business owner.—**Chris LeBeau**

C, P

47. **BEOnline: Business and Economics Online. http://www.loc.gov/rr/buisness/beonline/.** [Website]. Free. Date reviewed: 2011.

Compiled by the Library of Congress Business Reference Services for researchers, under Subject Guides, you will find a lengthy list of business topics like associations, business plans (forms), companies by industry, data sets, e-commerce, franchises, economic indicators, legal resources, and more. If you click on Associations, you are in an Associations Database which includes contacts, descriptions, addresses, and events data for the organizations listed. More than 10,000 business organizations in the United States are listed. Find here a link to the Herb Growing and Marketing Network or the Association of Bridal Consultants. Under the Title Listing, you will find Airlines of the Web, America's Business Funding Directory, American Chambers of Commerce Abroad, American City Business Journals, and much more.—**Susan C. Awe**

C

48. **Business Source Premier. http://www.ebscohost.com/academic/business-source-premier.** [Website]. Ipswich, Mass., EBSCO. Price negotiated by site. Date reviewed: 2011.

Business Source Premier fills the need for access to general business journals, magazines, and trade journals. Its 3,300 titles cover the fields of marketing, management, MIS, production, operations, accounting, finance, and economics. A little more than 50 percent of the titles are academic, one-quarter are trade titles, and the remainder are business magazines. The database has expanded its content to encompass nearly 100 books, including the Blue Ibex "Doing Business in …" series, case studies mostly from Datamonitor, country reports from sources including Business Monitor International, ICON Group International, Country Watch, Economist Intelligence Unit, and the Superintendent of Documents, domestic and international industry reports from Datamonitor, and company profiles containing SWOT analyses. Market research reports are dated and very limited. *Business Source Premier* carries some unique titles, particularly *Harvard Business Review*.—**Chris LeBeau**

C

49. **Gale Business Insights: Global. http://www.gale.cengage.com/businessinsights/academic. htm.** [Website]. Farmington Hills, Mich., Gale/Cengage Learning. Price negotiated by site. Date reviewed: 2011.

Gale Business Insights: Global is a new online international business reference database that discusses such topics as global companies, rankings and statistics, company histories, market share data, and industry research reports. It is full of full-text articles from academic journals, business periodicals, newswires, and media outlets and provides hundreds of economic indicators that allow users to analyze various economies, companies, and industries across the globe. Case studies have been included from the publisher's *CaseBase* (see entry 70) as well as from other publishing partners. In all, text and resources from nearly 2,500 resources have been pulled into this searchable database. There is video provided on management and leadership tips, as well as live charts for economic and business indicators that will allow researchers to generate their own analyses and custom charts for reports and presentations. It will be most useful for students and researchers needing information on international business and trade. It will aid in business research and help them interpret their findings. It would be a useful research tool in academic libraries but libraries are encouraged to register for the publisher's free trial to see if the material and the functions of the database are right for your clientele and reference needs.—**Shannon Graff Hysell**

C, P

50. **ProQuest Entrepreneurship. http://www.proquest.com.** [Website]. Ipswich, Mass., ProQuest. Price negotiated by site. Date reviewed: 2011.

The audience for *ProQuest Entrepreneurship* spans the needs of the practitioner to the educator and student. This well-designed database features menus with major business concepts the average entrepreneur or small-business owner would seek. The topical approach lists sources for start-ups, management, legal issues, marketing and sales, operations, product development, and profit and financial management. Topic links connect searchers to 115 journals, 50 trade publications, working papers, conference papers—in all, a little over 400 sources are included.

The practitioner or business planner has access to forms, tips from successful business owners, and start-up toolkits and guides. The basic search screen walks searchers through topics such as product development and design, innovations, business planning issues, marketing, advertising, pricing, sales, cash flow, purchasing, and technology use. Expectedly, there is a topic heading for start-ups. Start-up information covers idea creation, feasibility, and industry and competitor analysis. It also includes forms of ownership and franchising. Users can find business models, as well as location and planning resources. A special section is devoted to family-owned business, women-owned and minority-owned business, Web-based business, and native and aboriginal business.

But there is even more content. The database also includes approximately 60 books and journals. Also included are very short video clips on topics such as business valuation, exit strategies, and promotion. These come complete with a text copy of the video. A future enhancement will be the addition of 400 business plans from the University of Texas—Austin's Business Plan Competition.—**Chris LeBeau**

C, P

51. **Small Business Resource Center. http://www.gale.congage.com/smallbusiness/.** [Website]. Farmington Hills, Mich., Gale/Cengage Learning. Price negotiated by site. Date reviewed: 2011.

This database is an all-inclusive mix of sources for the small business owner or entrepreneur. The *Small Business Resource Center* covers all major areas of starting and operating a business, including accounting, finance, human resources, management, marketing, tax, and more. It covers nearly 190 journal and magazine titles suited to small business and some key newsletters. It also contains some of the famous Gale reference publications, such as *Business Plans Handbook*, *Encyclopedia of Major Marketing Campaigns*, and *Encyclopedia of Small Business*. Users will find more than 10 years worth of business plans from *Business Plans Handbook*, plans for everything from bed-and-breakfast accommodations to microbrewers.

The *Small Business Sourcebook*, although included, is quite disassembled to make its contents searchable. Alone it offers a wealth of resources for the entrepreneur. By entering a type of business and limiting to this source, users will find business start-up information, the best associations and trade organizations, reference and statistical sources, the best trade journals for a line of business, trade shows and conventions, consultants, computerized databases, videos, and libraries to refer to.

The database is searchable a number of different ways but it also is designed to suggest quick paths to needed information. In addition to business plans, there is a lengthy list of Business Topics including everything from handling brand image to tax planning. The Types of Businesses section lists several dozen commonly researched lines of business. Once one is selected, the searcher finds information organized into sections for business plans, articles, an overview of the business type, and reference directories. Another special section is labeled "How To ...," featuring helpful guides: How to Start a

Small Business, How to Write a Business Plan, How to Buy a Business, How to Finance Your Business, How to Grow Your Business, and How to Locate and Expand Your Business.

The database includes some well-chosen books including titles like: *How to Incorporate: A Handbook for Entrepreneurs and Professionals*, *How to Start Your Own S corporation*, *Specialty Shop Retailing: How to Run Your Own Store*, *SBA Loans: A Step-by-Step Guide*, *The Unofficial Guide to Marketing Your Small Business*, and *Attracting Investors: A Marketing Approach to Finding Funds for Your Business.*—**Chris LeBeau**

Dictionaries and Encyclopedias

C, P

52.   **Encyclopedia of Small Business.** 4th ed. Farmington Hills, Mich., Gale/Cengage Learning, 2010. 2v. index. $663.00/set. ISBN 13: 978-1-4144-2028-8.

The *Encyclopedia of Small Business* features over 600 entries, including 39 new entries since the publication of the 3d edition in 2007. According to the publisher some 566 of the entries have been revised to reflect the dramatic changes in industry and the economic times.

The *Encyclopedia* features entries covering the many aspects of owning and operating a small business, from computer crimes to accounting to benchmarking to overtime. Each term is defined plus applications of the term to small business is described. Each entry is comprised of two to three pages on average, plus each has a bibliography for further reading. In addition to terms, entries are provided for organizations related to small business among which are the Better Business Bureau, Equal Employment Opportunity Commission, National Venture Capital Association, and the Small Business Administration. This new edition has timely and updated entries on such topics as financing, business market creation, market analysis, tax planning, and human resources issues. It also addresses the realities of the economic times we live in—a time in which many small business owners are those who have been recently laid off or forced into retirement. This source has an index of subjects with the pages of specific entries for the subject highlighted in bold typeface. Cross-references are provided via *see also* headings at the bottom of the text of each article.

According to the publisher, this encyclopedia is intended as a resource for the small business owner, for the would-be entrepreneur, and for students of business generally. It should serve as an excellent starting point for students and practitioners and also as a source of quick reference information. It is recommended to academic libraries supporting a business program and to larger public libraries.—**Lucy Heckman**

C, S

53.   Folsom, W. Davis. **Encyclopedia of American Business.** rev. ed. New York, Facts on File, 2011. 2v. index. (Facts on File Library of American History). $125.00/set. ISBN 13: 978-0-8160-8112-7; 978-1-4381-3592-2 (e-book).

The newly revised edition of *Encyclopedia of American Business*, under the general editorship of W. Davis Folsom, provides a comprehensive and user-friendly guide to the concepts and terms that characterize current business practices in the United States. The 2-volume set contains over 800 alphabetically arranged entries, prepared by more than 120 contributors, largely drawn from business faculties of American universities. The entries can be understood by nonprofessionals as well as by students, while yet retaining adequate rigor and embodying sufficient information to serve as references or refreshers for professionals. Many of the entries are followed by suggestions for further readings. Cross-references are used where appropriate, to provide useful relationships with other entries. A list of entries and an index facilitate searches for specific terms. The book also contains a list of contributors and a bibliography.—**William C. Struning**

Directories

C, P

54. **Plunkett's Almanac of Middle Market Companies 2012.** Jack W. Plunkett, ed. Houston, Tex., Plunkett Research, 2011. 450p. index. $299.99pa. (includes online edition). ISBN 13: 978-1-60879-647-2; 978-1-60879-909-1 (e-book).

Plunkett's Almanac of Middle Market Companies 2012 is designed to be a business development tool for business professionals, marketers, those in sales, and consultants needing to learn more about middle market American companies. A second use for this volume would be for job placement companies, recruiting and human resources professionals, and job-seekers. The bulk of this book profiles 500 leading middle market companies based in the United States with annual revenues of $100 million to $1 billion. It includes a variety of industries, including information technology, health care, telecommunications, energy, and more. For each company complete directory information is included: company name, ranks, business activities, type of business, brands/divisions, contacts, financials, salaries and benefits, competitive advantage, growth plans, and locations. The directory also has a glossary, a list of business contacts and a list of industry associations and government agencies. Multiple indexes are provides for ease of use. This would be a worthwhile investment for academic libraries with business collections and public research libraries.—**Lucy Heckman**

Handbooks and Yearbooks

C, P

55. **Business Statistics of the United States, 2011: Patterns of Economic Change.** 16th ed. Lanham, Md., Bernan Associates, 2011. 642p. index. $154.00. ISBN 13: 978-1-59888-486-9. ISSN 1086-8488.

The 16th edition of *Business Statistics of the United States: Patterns of Economic Change* continues to be a valuable, comprehensive source of U.S. economic data gathered from several federal government agencies. The economic and industry statistics comprising this work are largely drawn from the Bureau of Labor Statistics, the Bureau of Economic Analysis, the Board of Governors of the Federal Reserve, and the Census Bureau. These statistics are presented in approximately 3,500 economic time series, with coverage dating back to the 1950s and 1960s for the majority of these; however, 150 of these series date back to 1929.

In addition to the richness of the data, a considerable strength of this work is the explanatory information appearing throughout the volume. The preface describes the history, organization, and design of the work. The "Notes and Definitions" sections supplement each chapter by providing details about sources, explanations of concepts and terms, and information about data revisions and availability. New to this edition is additional information on industrial production (going back to 1919), annual data from the Bureau of Labor Statistics on hours worked per person going as far back as 1948, and additional data on inflation rates among major industrialized countries.

Business Statistics of the United States will be an important resource for students, scholars, practitioners, and consumers to understand the historical implications of the current recession we are in. This reasonably priced reference work is recommended for public and academic libraries.—**Susan Shultz**

C, P

56. **21st Century Economics: A Reference Handbook.** Rhona C. Free, ed. Thousand Oaks, Calif., Sage, 2010. 2v. index. $325.00/set. ISBN 13: 978-1-4129-6142-4.

This handbook from Sage is testament to the fact that interest in economics is at an all-time high among business owners, academics, and the general public. In light of the current economy's struggle with high unemployment, rising inflation, and failures of businesses and banks, people are looking for answers to how traditional economic theories fit into modern-day economics. This resource, available in both print and electronic format, was contributed to by 100 economists and is arranged into 92 chapters. A large majority of the chapters are on economic theories and models in the areas of micro and macro economics. There are several key chapters also discussing cutting-edge topics that provide new approaches to traditional economic theories that help explain the economic climate of today and what may be to come in the future. The chapters are laid out in a way that students and researchers can learn more about interconnected topics or can conduct new research projects. For the most part the editor has tried to keep the chapters as jargon-free as possible, though students will probably need some background in economics and statistics to understand the majority of the text. Entries are arranged under seven major topics: Economic Analyses of Issues and Markets; Emerging Areas in Economics; International Economics; Macroeconomics; Microeconomics; Public Economics; and Scope and Methodology of Economics. For each entry there are a list of related topics and a list of further readings. All entries are signed and a list of contributors is provided with their credentials mentioned. The electronic version of this work also links to other Sage titles that may be of interest. This is a well-researched and easy-to-use resource that will be of interest to academic libraries with economics studies at the undergraduate and graduate levels.—**Shannon Graff Hysell**

Business Services and Investment Guides

Catalogs and Collections

P

57.   **Venture Deal. http://www.venturedeal.com/.** [Website]. Menlo Park, Calif., Venture Deal. $25.00/month. Date reviewed: 2011.

This is a low-priced way for investors and entrepreneurs to follow the funding and trends in the venture capital markets. *Venture Deal* maintains a database of deals of start-up companies, venture capital firms, and company financings, dating back to 2003. Information is updated on a daily basis. Funding range, venture capital, private equity, angel groups, corporate lenders, hedge fund, and public market investors all can be identified with this resource. Areas for funding include everything from agriculture to banking to technology. Searches can be tailored to the major regions of the country. One of the most common search modes is "transaction type." In this search mode, searches may be run for technology companies, venture investors, transactions, and executives. In venture capital jargon a "series" is a funding round of which there are a number of levels. *Venture Deal* offers search criteria for Series A-F funding rounds, IPOs, and an "undisclosed" category.

A venture investor detailed record includes the focus area of the deal, and brief information about the investors. Records also include the activity level of the investor company, which is the number of deals currently in progress. Records include a transaction history displaying the recipients of funding and the amounts. This is valuable information for the funding seeker and for a competitor as well.—**Chris LeBeau**

Handbooks and Yearbooks

P

58.   **TheStreet Ratings' Ultimate Guided Tour of Stock Investing, Spring 2011.** Millerton, N.Y., Grey House Publishing, 2011. 288p. $249.00pa. (single issue); $499.00 (four quarterly editions). ISBN 13: 978-1-59237-807-4.

It's a jungle out there so *TheStreet Ratings' Ultimate Guided Tour of Stock Investing* is organized to provide a road map to get you on the right path to building an investment portfolio while avoiding "the quicksand, the rocks and the wild animals." The *Guide* is divided into three trails: The Basics, Your Goals, and Stock Selection. Throughout the volume a "Wise Guide" helps you along the trail with advice. The signposts entitled "Survival Tips," "Be on the Lookout," and "Deserves Another Look," are also scattered through the text to provide additional information.

Part 1, "Know the Jungle," consists of 4 chapters that cover stock investment basics. The 6 chapters in part 2, "Know the Map," are designed to help you map out your goals for investing. Part 3, "Know the Trail," is comprised of 10 chapters that cover stock selection. A stock comparison worksheet included in this section is particularly helpful. The brief chapters in these three parts are designed to provide enough information without overwhelming the novice investor in the process. A glossary of investment terminology is also provided.

If you do not need to follow the beginner's trail, you can skip straight to the back, to a section that provides ratings on more than 5,000 stocks. The alphabetic listing provides the company name, ticker symbol, an industry abbreviation, the stock exchange, the market index if listed, an overall investment rating, a performance rating, and a risk rating. The ratings have the backing of Jim Cramer, founder of the TheStreet.com, a leading authority on financial news and analysis, and its acquisition, Weiss Ratings, a well-known, independent financial rating agency. Data are provided by Compustat, Standard & Poor's, a division of McGraw-Hill Companies, Inc.

This is a quarterly publication and the spring issue examined for this review used data analyzed on March 31, 2011 for the stock ratings. Since current information is an important aspect of stock investing, there is also a companion guide online at the TheStreet.com Website. The book's chief value is in providing an excellent source of basic information in an easy to use format for first-time investors. The printed stock information would be dated for most active investors who could refer to the website (which is not without a number of online competitors such as Yahoo Finance, Motley Fool, CNBC and SeekingAlpha among others). Although pricey, the annual subscription is a better value for this title than a single issue.—**Colleen Seale**

Consumer Guides

C

59.   **Encyclopedia of Consumer Culture.** Dale Southerton, ed. Thousand Oaks, Calif., Sage, 2011. 3v. index. $595.00; $750.00 (e-book). ISBN 13: 978-0-8728-9601-7; 978-1-4129-9424-8 (e-book).

Editor Dale Southerton set an impressive task with this encyclopedia, explaining how consumerism has become a function of everyday lives, and plays a role in defining our identity and how we perceive the world. The goal of the work is to provide authoritative entries and broad coverage on consumer related topics making the information accessible to a general audience. This three-volume set contains more than 340 signed entries. Contributors come mainly from academia with a few exceptions of experts in the field. While the entries are displayed in alphabetic order there is a Reader's Guide at the beginning of each volume that provides greater context for the individual entries. There are 9 topic areas and they range from Geographies and Histories of Consumer Culture to Politics and Consumers, and Social Divisions and Social Groups. Even though the same entry may be displayed in multiple topic areas this section is very useful in collocating related items. Entries range from a couple of pages to several pages. All entries contain a *see also* section and a brief bibliography of further readings. While a visible effort was made to make every entry accessible to a general audience, some topics lend themselves to complicated explanations. Overall, the text is jargon-free and understandable. The third volume concludes with a nice index that includes *see also* entries. This is a must have for all academic and large public libraries.—**Melissa M. Johnson**

Finance and Banking

Catalogs and Collections

C, P

60.   **Federal Reserve Statistics & Historical Data. http://www.federalreserve.gov/econresdata/ releases/statisticsdata.htm.** [Website]. Free. Date reviewed: 2011.

This preeminent producer of popular economic indicators is the Federal Reserve, whose mission is largely to manage the nation's money supply. It and its highly visible chairman have become more prominent in recent decades as their role in managing the economy has become perceived as more influential than may have been the case earlier. Key indicators from the Federal Reserve measure consumer credit and money stocks. Arguably its best-known activity is its control of the interest rate (popularly known as the prime rate or the federal funds rate), which may change after a meeting of the Fed's Open Market Committee. Announcements of changes to the prime rate are very closely watched by business, economic, financial, and even general interests. FRASER—the Federal Reserve Archival System for Economic Research (http://fraser.stlouisfed.org/)—contains data from the Federal Reserve, as well as other U.S. economic data.—**Eric Forte**

Handbooks and Yearbooks

C, P

61.   **The AMA Handbook of Financial Risk Management.** By John J. Hampton. New York, AMACOM/American Management Association, 2011. 303p. index. $75.00. ISBN 13: 978-0-8144-1744-7.

In the preface, the author states "Managerial financial risks is all about understanding how to reduce a complex business environment to workable concepts and models. Everything starts with risk" and adds that *The AMA Handbook of Financial and Risk Management* "provides the tools for dealing with what are arguably the most important areas of financial decision making." Hampton has created this handbook as a reference guide for those looking for specific knowledge of an aspect of financial risk management and states that provided are: a dictionary or definition of terms; an encyclopedia (an examination of major ideas and concepts); and a cookbook or "a listing of prominent 'recipes' with step-by-step directions for applying techniques to achieve results and outcomes." This resource is comprised of six parts: "Introduction to Financial Risk"; "Accounting, Cash Flow, and Budget Exposures"; "Analyzing Operating Risks"; "Relationship of Risk and Return"; "Nature of a Capital Investment Decision"; and "Factors that Affect the Value of the Firm." Within each part, the author examines specific aspects providing explanations and examples in forms of charts, tables, and budgets and balance sheets. For example, part 6 examines valuation of common stock, capital structure of the firm, and valuation of business combinations.

Using this book, researchers can readily locate data and information including: definitions of specific financial ratios and how to interpret them; how to analyze financial statements; how to conduct a profit-volume analysis; definitions of categories of insurable risk; and how to forecast earnings per share. *The AMA Handbook of Financial Risk Management* is a detailed reference source designed for both practitioners and business students. This book is highly recommended to public libraries and to academic libraries.—**Lucy Heckman**

S

62.   Tucci, Paul A. **The Handy Personal Finance Answer Book.** Canton, Mich., Visible Ink Press, 2011. 317p. illus. index. $19.95pa. ISBN 13: 978-1-57849-322-4; 978-1-57849-389-7 (e-book).

The Handy Personal Finance Answer Book addresses many of the questions that those new to finance and banking will have, including "How do I balance my check book?" and "What is a 401K plan?" Chapter topics include the history of finance, managing one's financial life, and how one's finance and banking needs change over the course of their life.

With over 1,000 questions, the reader is given clear explanations of different principles of finance such as interest, savings, and loans, and then shown how various tactics can be used to save money, get out of debt, or use credit. Clear explanations are given when showing the connection between finance and everyday life occur, such as balancing a checkbook, applying for a loan, or using online banking. The tone of the work and the writing make it suitable for high school students as well as the general reader. Overall, this is a fun and understandable read and this reviewer would recommend this book for a high school or public library reference area.—**Lucy Heckman**

Industry and Manufacturing

Catalogs and Collections

C, P

63. **First Research Industry Profiles. http://www.dnblearn.com/index.php?page=hoover-s-first-research.** [Website]. Parsippany, N.J., Dun & Bradstreet. Price negotiated by site. Date reviewed: 2011.

First Research is a resource with 900 industry profiles. It was acquired by Dun & Bradstreet in 2007. First Research profiles serve the varied needs of the researcher, the business planner, and the business marketer. The reports facilitate market analysis with industry overviews. The report sections include: the competitive landscape, the products, operations and technology, sales and marketing, finance and regulation, human resources, industry indicators, and industry updates. Industry challenges, trends, and opportunities are also covered. The section on executive talking points raises a number of valuable questions that new business owners should consider. Reports end with an opportunity ranking, a list of industry acronyms, and a list of valuable free industry Websites. If small businesses constitute a large part of an industry, data for small business will be displayed apart from the overall aggregate industry data.

Reports draw data from third-party providers: valuation multiples, which are used in business valuations for acquisitions, are provided from business Valuation Resources. Fintel supplies the benchmarking financial ratios for private companies. Inforum provides industry forecasts.

First Research reports appear in ProQuest's ABI/INFORM and in MarketResearch.com. First Research can also be linked to D&B's Hoover's database for libraries that subscribe to the latter.—**Chris LeBeau**

Dictionaries and Encyclopedias

C

64. Blume, Kenneth J. **Historical Dictionary of the U.S. Maritime Industry.** Lanham, Md., Scarecrow, 2012. 581p. (Historical Dictionaries of Professions and Industries). $99.00; $94.99 (e-book). ISBN 13: 978-0-8108-5634-9; 978-0-8108-7963-8 (e-book).

The importance of the role of the maritime industry in shaping the modern world is comprehensively portrayed in the *Historical Dictionary of U.S. Maritime Industry* by Kenneth J. Blume, a professor of history and chair of the Department of Humanities and Social Sciences at the Albany College of Pharmacy and Health Sciences, New York. The bulk of the book is composed of about 400 alphabetically arranged entries that include companies, people, geographical locations, and significant developments over centuries, with particular attention to the period of the mid-nineteenth century to the present. While each entry is self-contained, cross-referencing ties entries together to provide pertinent relationships. The entries show the importance of the maritime industry on the U.S. economy and development and focuses on sail, steam, and power transportation. The dictionary is supplemented by a chronology, an introductory chapter that highlights developments in the maritime industry, four appendixes that summarize significant aspects of the maritime industry, and an extensive bibliography. Although the focus of the book is on history, insights into the future can be drawn from the trends enumerated. The book is recommended as a reference or as a base for further investigation. The nontechnical language should enable readers of various backgrounds to benefit from the presentation.—**William C. Struning**

C, P

65.   **Encyclopedia of Emerging Industries.** 6th ed. Farmington Hills, Mich., Gale/Cengage Learning, 2011. 1025p. index. $520.00. ISBN 13: 978-14144-8687-1.

This encyclopedia reports on growing, new industries, detailing the inception, emergence, and current status of 140 flourishing U.S. industries and industry segments. Each entry (usually 1,500 to 2,500 words) includes most or all of the following sections on its industry: Industry Snapshots, Organization and Structure, Background and Development, Pioneers, Current Conditions, Industry Leaders, Workforce, America and the World, Research and Technology, and Further Reading (bibliographies of 10 to 40 items). An excellent 70-page index is complemented by three specialty indexes: an industry index by SIC, a conversion guide (SIC to NAICS), and a conversion guide (NAICS to SIC) for covered industries. Each chapter provides a wealth of information. Specific examples include microwave applications in medicine as well as communications and cooking; and the use of satellites in communications, broadcasting, the Internet, and navigation.

Writing is uniformly clear, and the presentations are well organized. However, since each of the industries is rapidly evolving, the material becomes rapidly outdated. Antitrust and regulatory issues are mentioned, but little information is offered. There is no attempt at economic analysis, even market shares, although industry leaders are identified and described.—**Richard A. Miller**

Insurance

Directories

P

66.   **Plunkett's Insurance Industry Almanac.** 2012 ed. Jack W. Plunkett, ed. Houston, Tex., Plunkett Research, 2012. 464p. index. $299.99pa. (including online edition). ISBN 13: 978-1-60879-654-0; 978-1-60879-916-9 (e-book).

Plunkett Research is a well-known publisher of industry directories and almanacs. This particular title covers the insurance industry, and is designed for the general reader to compare the top 300 American insurance companies. An overview of the insurance industry trends is provided and graphs and tables are provided for easy interpretation of the information.

The top 300 insurance companies included here are the largest and most successful companies from all areas of the insurance industry. The alphabetic listing of these top companies provides the industry group, types of business, brands, divisions, subsidiaries, plans for growth, current news, contact information for the officers, annual financials, salaries and benefits, and provides an assessment of the company's hiring and advancement of minorities and women. Indexes to the industry, sales, brand names, and the subsidiaries are provided. The information in this book is also available online through the publisher. This work is recommended as a supplement to other insurance ratings guides, due to its very general overview of the insurance industry.—**Kay M. Stebbins**

International Business

General Works

Catalogs and Collections

C, P

67. **Direction of Trade Statistics. http://www2.imfstatistics.org/DOT.** [Website]. $300/year (single user). Date reviewed: 2011.

C, P

68. **International   Trade   Statistics.   http://www.wto.org/english/res_e/statis_e/statis_e.htm.** [Website]. Free. Date reviewed: 2011.

These two sources provide trade data for trade between two foreign countries (not just the United states). The *Direction of Trade Statistics*, from the IMF, in print and as an online subscription database, compiles data on the value of trade between any two countries (not data about the product or commodities involved). The World Trade Organization (WTO), meanwhile, compiles and publishes data about exports and imports of a country by commodity and product, but does not have these data specifically between any two countries. And the *UN Comtrade* database (http://comtrade.un.org) further compiles trade data from several UN sources.—**Eric Forte**

C

69. **IBISWorld. http://www.ibisworld.com.** [Website]. $8,000 (annual subscription). Date reviewed: 2011.

IBISWorld is a good source for market research and industry analysis. The reports are lengthy, use a clear narrative style with many statistical tables and charts, and are updated on a predictable schedule. All reports share a standardized format so that readers can easily compare industries. IBISWorld covers performance and outlook, industry life cycles, products and markets, competitive landscape, and operating conditions. However, the reports include mostly aggregated discussion of consumer demographics and do not include psychographics or segmentation.

IBISWorld systematically analyzes more than 750 industry sectors across the whole spectrum of the economy. This breadth of coverage is invaluable in settings where students' business plans and marketing papers are driven by innovation, green business, or the latest extreme sports craze. With coverage of such topics as "party rentals," "wind power," or "swimming pool construction," IBISWorld fills a gap in available literature.

The database uses the NAICS codes as its primary navigational structure (searching by keywords and SIC Code numbers is also possible). The "drilldown" format makes the code system easy to understand, and thus supports business research skills. IBISWorld also offers an international option that includes China. Although other countries do not have individualized reports, the Global Industry Research series covers worldwide conditions, highlighting relevant countries and major companies.—**Wendy Diamond**

Handbooks and Yearbooks

C, P

70. **CaseBase: Case Studies in Global Business.** Farmington Hills, Mich., Gale/Cengage Learning, 2011. 350p. index. $208.00. ISBN 13: 978-1-4144-8682-6; 978-1-4144-8693-2 (e-book).

This new title from Gale/Cengage presents case studies of international business models and the lessons learned from those models. The work is designed with business students, entrepreneurs, and business owners in mind to help them gain insight in the global business market. Each case study has been written by a business professional or scholar and runs about 5 to 25 pages in length. After an introduction and description of the case study there are sections presented on learning objectives, questions for discussion, and references and bibliographies. Special attention is paid to the organization of the business, compliance to country regulations, and market demand. Examples of the case studies presented here include: a Chinese company's branding strategy for global sportswear; the development of Microfinance in Syria; global regulation of herbal products; and Subway and the international fast food industry in Asia and Latin America. Because this work focuses strongly on international trade and business it will be most useful in undergraduate and graduate libraries offering business programs. It may also be of use in the business resource section of public libraries.—**William C. Struning**

C

71. **World Economic Factbook 2012.** 19th ed. Chicago, Euromonitor International, 2011. 460p. index. $475.00. ISBN 13: 978-1-84264-554-3.

Euromonitor is a respected publisher of international business and marketing reference works. The *Factbook* presents a selection of key economic, political, and demographic data in a standardized format for 204 countries, making it easy to compare countries on these variables. The data in the 2011 edition cover the year 2009 as well as some preceding years. Data sources include national statistical bureaus and multilateral agencies, such as the International Monetary Fund and the United Nations. For each country there is a two-page report. The first page is a textual summary providing the currency unit, the location and area of the country, the Head of State and the Head of Government, the Ruling Party, the Political Structure, the results of the last elections, a quick assessment of political risk, highlights of international disputes, a paragraph summarizing economic developments, a paragraph highlighting the main industries, and an overview of the energy situation.

The numerical data provided are primarily economic measures and population statistics. Economic data include the rate of inflation, the U.S. dollar exchange rate, real GDP growth, GDP in U.S. dollars and the home currency, total and per capita consumption, exports and imports, and tourism receipts and spending. There is also a table listing major trading partners with percentage share of exports and imports and value in U.S. dollars. Population data includes total population, population density, population by age groups, total male and female population, urban population, birth and death rates, male and female life expectancy, infant mortality, and number of households. After a brief introduction that explains the content and layout of the reference work, the first section contains maps of the continents with outlines for individual countries and their capitals. Section 2 contains comparative world rankings with separate tables for rankings by area, population, and economic measures.

Although the price of the volume has gone down considerably (down to $475 from the $650 price tag of the 2010 edition), users may wish to check some of the excellent authoritative sources of data available for free on the Internet such as the CIA's *The World Factbook* (http://www.cia.gov/cia/publications/factbook/) and the *World Development Report* (http://econ.worldbank.org/wdr/).—**Peter Zachary McKay**

Asia

C, P

72. **Plunkett's Almanac of Asian Companies 2012.** Houston, Tex., Plunkett Research, 2012. 450p. index. $29.99pa. (includes online edition). ISBN 13: 978-1-60879-646-5; 978-1-60879-908-4 (e-book).

In the past decade Asia has become a major economic player in the importation and exportation of consumer goods. They have always been known for having competitive pricing in the areas of electronics, apparel, and household item; however, now they are rising in the areas of energy, telecommunications, food products, and pharmaceuticals. This volume profiles 500 of Asia's leading companies, offering statistical data on their business as well as directory-type information. Profiles for manufacturers, major diversified holding companies, financial firms and banks, and technology firms, among others can be found here. There is also comparative data on Asian economies, information on associations and professional societies, and a glossary. Indexes are provided to assist users in locating just the information they are seeking. This book is designed with professionals involved in business development, investments, marketing, and product development in mind. It would also be useful for job-seekers looking for opportunities in the overseas market.—**William C. Struning**

Labor

General Works

Dictionaries and Encyclopedias

C, P

73.   **Survey of American Industry and Careers.** Hackensack, N.J., Salem Press, 2012. 6v. illus. index. $695.00/set. ISBN 13: 978-1-58765-768-9.

The editors of Salem Press compiled essays from 72 contributors who wrote 112 industry profiles for this 6-volume set. The profiles present aspects from the history of the industries to an outlook of their importance over the coming decade. Industries range from large international corporations to small businesses that form the backbone of the North American economy.

The profiles provide information important to students and prospective employees. Each industry has a standard format: industry snapshot, industry market segments, organizational structure and job roles, industry outlook, related resources for further research, author information, and further reading. Readers should pay particular attention to several special features. Five types of descriptive sidebars offer information designed to facilitate decision-making and career choice: contributions of the industry to the economy; inputs—value of the resources commonly used by the industry; occupation specialties— common occupations identified within the industry; occupation profiles that include required education, working conditions, physical exertion expected, and the Holland interest score (personality types associated with vocational choice developed by John L. Holland); and projected employment expectations to 2018.

All six volumes in this set contain a table of contents, a list of contributors, and a list of tables and sidebars. The first volume contains an informational publisher's note, while volume 6 includes appendixes featuring Employment by Industry, 2008 projected to 2018; Fortune 500 Companies by Industry, 2009; a complete bibliography; and a list of electronic resources. In addition, volume 6 ends with three useful indexes: Industries by Career Cluster, Jobs and Careers, and a Subject Index. Volume 1 profiles industries from Accounting Services to Civil Services; Volume 2 profiles industries from Coal Mining to Food Retail; Volume 3 contains industries from Food Services to Local Public Administration; Volume 4 contains industries from Logging to Postal and Packaging Delivery Services; Volume 5 contains industries from Printing to Telecommunications Infrastructure; and Volume 6 features industries from Textile and Fabrics to Water Supply.

Any school or library that purchases this six-volume reference is entitled to free, complementary access to the online version. Registration instructions are included with the purchase of the print version. Administrative sign-up will be required. This valuable resource is easy to use and could prove to be extraordinarily helpful for students, researchers, and job hunters in this difficult economy. It is highly recommended for public, community college, and academic libraries. [R: LJ, Jan 12, p. 138]—**Laura J. Bender**

Handbooks and Yearbooks

P

74.   Beshara, Tony. **Unbeatable Résumés: America's Top Recruiter Reveals What Really Gets You Hired.** New York, AMACOM/American Management Association, 2011. 324p. index. $16.95pa. ISBN 13: 978-0-8144-1762-1.

Using comprehensive coverage of résumé types, content, and style along with cover letters and their use, this handbook is directed to the person who has been on the job hunt for one day, one year, or more. There are many varied examples of résumés and cover letters provided here. Interviewing is more briefly covered with key emphasis on preparation and practice to assure clarity and a solid personal presentation suitable to the situation. The work discusses attention-grabbing language to use on a résumé as well as how to present such liabilities as employment gaps and job-hopping in a favorable light. Behsara, owner of a job recruitment and job placement firm in Texas, also discusses networking (both in person and online), the proper interview follow-up protocol, using Facebook and LinkedIn to your advantage, and how to stand out in a crowded job market. His advice is practical and will apply to many different fields. An index improves access beyond the brief table of contents. The volume would be useful in high school and college libraries as well as in a personal collection.—**Barbara Conroy**

C, P

75.   **Handbook of U.S. Labor Statistics, 2011: Employment, Earnings, Prices, Productivity, and Other Labor Data.** 14th ed. Lanham, Md., Bernan Associates, 2011. 535p. index. $154.00. ISBN 13: 978-1-59888-479-1. ISSN 1526-2553.

Bernan Associates, a noted publisher of federal government agencies reports, has been publishing this title since 1997; prior to this it was published by the U.S. Bureau of Labor Statistics. This 14th edition updates the content of approximately 200 statistical tables contained in previous editions, provides some new features, and has included some tables on income that were derived from the Census Bureau. This work is more that just statistical tables, included are some short articles that reflect events that have impacted the economy impacted statistical data. Additionally, before each set of tables is an article that summarizes what the following tables contain and provide some information regarding the methodology used, relevant definitions, and where more current information can be found. The index provides a quick way to get to specific tables without looking at all the tables in a chapter. Depending on the topic, many tables provide information for 25 years, others for 10 years and some for fewer years because they are new categories of statistics.

This is a one-stop indispensable guide to statistics on a wide variety of labor data, such as employment, productivity, prices, and earnings. While it is true much of this information is available on the Bureau of Labor Statistics Website, it is often easier to find the needed tables by using this book. This very useful compilation of statistics and should be acquired by most libraries with strong business and economic collections and those agencies who deal with labor data at least every other year, but preferably every year.—**Judith J. Field**

S

76.   Hillstrom, Kevin. **Workers Unite! The American Labor Movement.** Detroit, Omnigraphics, 2011. 236p. illus. index. (Defining Moments). $49.00. ISBN 13: 978-0-7808-1130-0.

The Defining Moments series follows a common pattern of narrative, biographies, documents, chronology, terms, and bibliography. The audience is approximately middle school and high school age students. Most of the volumes that I have reviewed have been quite good, with only a few exceptions. This volume provides users with an overview of the rise of labor unions and their impact on the U.S. economy and culture of the United States. The narrative overview provides a history of the labor movement and includes coverage of labor during the colonial time, the nineteenth-century industrial revolution, and rise of free-market capitalism. It concludes with a look at the decline of the labor movement during the past

50 years and what labor organizations may have to do to revitalize themselves. The Biographies section profiles individuals influential in all aspects of the labor movement, such as Samuel Gompers, Jimmy Hoffa, and Walter P. Reuther. The final section provides primary documents that have shaped the history of labor unions. These include excerpts from speeches, debates, trial defenses, and essays. Additional useful materials include photographs, a chronology, a glossary, a bibliography that also includes Websites and videotapes, and a subject index. Each volume in this series now provides a list of research topics that will provide students with a jumping off point for further research. *Workers Unite! The American Labor Movement* is a well-organized, balanced, and approachable reference source for its intended audience, undoubtedly reflective of the composition of the series advisory board (public and school librarians and educators) and hopefully indicative of the quality of other titles in the series.—**Shannon Graff Hysell**

Career Guides

P

77.   Damp, Dennis V. **The Book of U.S. Government Jobs: Where They Are, What's Available, & How to Complete a Federal Resume.** 11th ed. Mckees Rocks, Pa., Bookhaven Press, 2011. 308p. index. $27.95pa. ISBN 13: 978-0-943641-29-4. ISSN 2158-7698.

The U.S. government is the largest employer in the United States. The average salary for a federal employee is $81,258 plus excellent benefits. Currently 50 percent of the federal workforce is eligible for early or regular retirement. All of this makes the 11th edition of *The Book of U.S. Government Jobs* a timely and useful tool.

This edition includes the 2010 hiring reforms and related revised procedures. The book contains 12 chapters that provide job-seekers with very specific information and advice, from the preliminary application and creation of a résumé to special populations who might apply for federal jobs, such as veterans and people with disabilities. Author Dash worked for the federal government for 35 years. He is able to give advice and instruction as an "insider" and someone who hired people for federal jobs.

Each chapter begins with stated objectives. Each topic, from a general description of government employment to skills and education necessary for specific jobs, is thoroughly covered. Also included is a chapter on employment secrets, tips and checklists, an agency directory, and a skills index and networking resources. There is a companion Website (http://www.federaljobs.net) for easy online access to this information. An excellent index provides easy access to specific topics.

The 11th edition includes revised résumé and application guidelines, Civil Service Exam updates, new illustrations, updated agency directories, updated contact information, and the 2010 hiring reforms. This book will be useful to anyone seeking a federal job and those who just want to understand how this massive operation functions. This guide is recommended for all public and academic libraries.—**Joanna M. Burkhardt**

P

78.   **The Top 100: The Fastest Growing Careers for the 21st Century.** 5th ed. New York, Infobase Publishing, 2011. 388p. index. $75.00. ISBN 13: 978-0-8160-8367-1; 978-1-4381-3767-4 (e-book).

The editors of the 5th edition of this title repackage selected information from the U.S. Department of Labor to highlight jobs that are predicted to grow substantially in the next five to six years. The book is geared toward high school students and above. In the introduction to the book the four fields expecting the largest amount of growth are listed: health services, computers and information services, green careers, and the service industry. The statistics offered regarding growth in these areas are not consistent from one category to the next, making their relevance questionable.

The book begins with an introduction giving the general purpose of the work, how it is organized, and what it hopes to do for its readers. The introduction makes clear that all jobs and advancement in any career relies on continuing education and that advanced education allows access to higher paying jobs. The introduction is followed by an alphabetic listing of a wide range of jobs. In this section each job entry includes: an overview, a description of an average day, necessary educational and training requirements, a breakdown of subcategories of jobs in this job title area, types of employers and the number of people who currently work in this type of job in the United States, general job search tips for acquiring this type of job, career path and credentials required for advancement, a salary range including benefits, a description of the work environment for the job, future outlook for the job, and sources of further information about the job. An index completes the work.

There is no indication as to how this edition differs from the previous edition. Because the work relies primarily on U.S. government agency publications, the information in the book is at least two years old. This book will be of most use to the inquiring pre-high school graduate. It is recommended for high school and public library career collections. [R: Choice, Jan 12, p. 844]—**Joanna M. Burkhardt**

Management

Handbooks and Yearbooks

P

79. **Business Plans Handbook: A Compilation of Actual Business Plans Developed by Businesses Throughout North America. Volumes 21 and 22.** Farmington Hills, Mich., Gale/Cengage Learning, 2011. 275p. index. $231.00. ISBN 13: 978-1-4144-6834-1.

These 21st and 22d volumes in the *Business Plans Handbook* series are a collection of actual business plans compiled by entrepreneurs seeking funding for small businesses throughout the United States. This series is designed for those looking for examples of how to structure and compose their own business plans. Each volume presents about 20 sample plans taken from businesses in the manufacturing, retail, and service industries. The types of industries covered vary and cover both established industries and trends in the small business world.

A typical business plan includes the type of business, statement of purpose, summary, industry description, market, product and production, management and personnel, and financial specifics. Along with the actual business plans, these editions also contain two fictional business plans, a directory of venture capital and finance companies, a business template to help users create their own business plan, and a glossary of terminology used by lenders and financial institutions.—**Shannon Graff Hysell**

P

80. Phillips, Joseph. **Project Management for Small Business: A Streamlined Approach from Planning to Completion.** New York, AMACOM/American Management Association, 2012. 294p. index. $21.95pa. ISBN 13: 978-0-8144-1767-6.

This work is designed to help project managers and small business owners learn management skills to see a project from idea to completion in a timely manner. It is written in a straightforward, conversational style that will appeal to those with little extra time. It includes plenty of bullet lists, charts, and sidebars to capture important aspects of project and time management. The work addresses such topics as initiating a project (defining its purpose and creating a time scale for completion), planning for a profit, managing project costs, scheduling, projecting risks, communicating with project stakeholders, managing workflow, and closing out the project. This book will be useful to small business owners as well as those new to project management in larger companies. It may be more useful in the circulating collections of college and public libraries where users can take it home to read it thoroughly.—**Dene L. Clark**

Marketing and Trade

Catalogs and Collections

P

81.   **Business Decision. http://businessdecision.com.** [Website]. CIVIC Technologies. $2,500.00 and up. Date reviewed: 2011.

Business Decision provides a demographic and lifestyles database with map and report functions for public libraries and their small and medium-sized business clientele. It offers thematic graphical displays for essential marketing decisions such as identifying customers, locating retail shops, analyzing competitor locations, and designing media campaigns. The content is derived from the Census Bureau, other authoritative government agencies, and ESRI's Tapestry segmentation system. Data are regularly updated with current-year estimates.

Business Decision enables users to examine the marketing potential of specific geographic locations, including ZIP codes, DMAs, census tracts, and congressional districts. These options provide excellent neighborhood-level coverage. It is also possible to generate maps and reports that cross several standard geographic boundaries. Some examples include "ring studies" with business location information in concentric circles; "drive-time" studies, which measure distance by the time it takes customers to arrive; and "hand-drawn" shapes, which are useful for defining sales territories, service areas, or broadcast zones.

Business Decision offers the data elements and features of more sophisticated systems, yet it is especially easy to use for novices and onetime users. There is a selection guide indicating which map or report is most appropriate for a variety of business situations. Maps are generated by the software according to variables that the user selects in a familiar Web interface. The standard subscription includes remote access for unlimited simultaneous users, and authenticated library patrons can create Web-based reports and maps from any desktop. Subscriptions are affordably structured to meet the needs of public and small academic libraries.—**Wendy Diamond**

P

82.   **WebSite MarketingPlan. http://www.websitemarketingplan.com.** [Website]. Free. Date reviewed: 2011.

This large site contains a wealth of information for small businesses. A large assortment of articles and sample marketing plans are available as well as sample business plans, a newsletter, Internet marketing articles, marketing strategy articles, and more. Featured Directory Categories include articles grouped under Search Engine Marketing, Marketing Strategy, Marketing Plan, and Public Relations. Learn about the four seasons of public relations. Lengthy articles on advertising, using public relations for communicating to customers and finding new ones, and customer retention are outstanding. There are many commercial links here, but plenty of free help for the new entrepreneur can be found as well. Many sample business plans are also available. This site is especially helpful for those interested in e-commerce. Easy to navigate, this site will definitely help entrepreneurs and business owners develop a marketing plan that they can use.—**Susan C. Awe**

Office Practices

P

83.   **The AMA Handbook of Business Documents: Guidelines and Sample Documents That Make Business Writing Easy.** By Kevin Wilson and Jennifer Wauson. New York, AMACOM/American Management Association, 2011. 211p. $19.95pa. ISBN 13: 978-0-8144-1769-0.

The authors Kevin Wilson and Jennifer Wauson have worked with various Fortune 500 companies in providing training guidelines for their administrative assistants and corporate communicators. In this volume they have prepared these guidelines with accompanying samples for today's corporate office communications. The contents of the documents, letters, and reports deal with today's corporate business topics, such as information technology, domestic and foreign employment, human resources, customer service, accounting, and collections. The kinds of documents you will find here are abstracts, annual reports, memos, proposals, e-mails, progress reports, policies and procedures, lab reports, grant proposals, press releases, newsletters, training manuals, speeches and oral presentations, product specifications, sales letters, cover letters and résumés, and surveys. The format of this publication is an alphabetic presentation with bold face entries, definitions with full-page illustrations, and examples of model documents and letters. There are tips and ideas for the improvement of the document with accompanying black-and-white graphics.

This volume is highly recommended for the business collections of public and corporate libraries to help the corporate community with their various reports. This ready-reference tool provides users with guidelines in presenting their personal or corporation's communications with others in a powerful but professional manner.—**Kay M. Stebbins**

5 Education

General Works

Almanacs

C, P

84.   **The Almanac of American Education 2011.** Deirdre A. Gaquin and Sarah E. Baltic, eds. Lanham, Md., Bernan Associates, 2011. 527p. index. $75.00pa. ISBN 13: 978-1-59888-477-7.

Education has always been a contentious public policy issue. Whether it is the role of the federal or state government in public education, the level of funding states should be obligated to provide for public education, the role of private charter schools in public schooling, the accountability of teachers and how to measure it, or outcomes assessment, schooling is under the microscope as never before. Policy debates rage on all of these fronts. To sensibly engage in these debates, one needs to be armed with objective data, and this almanac helps, in part, to meet that need. Data here are drawn primarily from government sources, including the Census and the National Center for Education Statistics, as well as some private sources like the College Board. Tables of data address national education statistics, state and region education statistics, and county education statistics. Within these broad geographic categories, there are data on enrollment, historical and current educational attainment, postsecondary education, and more. These categories are further broken down by such variables as state, age, race, sex, and ethnic origin. There are data on postsecondary enrollments, graduation rates, and earnings by race, level of education, or sex, to name but a few. For many tables, historical data back to the 1960s are presented. Source documents are identified at the end of each of the three major sections. Access to all of these tables is facilitated by a detailed table of contents and list of tables, as well as an extensive subject index. An annotated guide to education resources on the Internet is appended. While interested users can start here, they will no doubt appreciate the truism that, especially in this period where policy is often driven by ideology, data do not speak for themselves.—**Stephen H. Aby**

Dictionaries and Encyclopedias

C, P

85.   **The Greenwood Dictionary of Education.** 2d ed. John W. Collins III and Nancy Patricia O'Brien, eds. Santa Barbara, Calif., Greenwood Press/ABC-CLIO, 2011. 581p. index. $95.00. ISBN 13: 978-0-313-37930-7; 978-0-313-37931-4 (e-book).

This 2d edition of is both a valuable and needed edition to the lexicon of educational terminology, programs, and trends that continue to evolve in the history of American education (see ARBA 2004, entry 238, for a review of the 1st edition). Not unexpected, 850 new terms and revisions have been added by the editors and section editors to this revision. Like any professional field, education continues to change and develop as it serves an expanding diverse population of students. From students found to be autistic, developmentally delayed, gifted, or gender challenged, the over 300 contributors have provided clear and concise entries, along with 46 pages of references that makes this edition a valuable resource for teachers, administrators, and college professors involved in teacher education and research. Parents involved in the at-home education of their children, private school educators, and those in the media reporting on educational topics will benefit from this revised edition. The media and parents especially will appreciate the addition of some of the more esoteric terminology found in the education vocabulary, such as *infusion*, *innumeracy*, *null curriculum*, and *quadrivium*, to mention a few. Even the experienced teacher, not evolved in district and state decision making where such terminology is often used, will find this dictionary to be a valuable resource. Noticeably, some topics require more than one entry. An example is "creative" and its derivative, "creativity" which is found under "creative commons license," "creative discovery area," "creative expression," "creative thinking," and "creativity." For the common user, two changes could be made to this dictionary to make it more user friendly: cross-referencing of topics and listing resources with each entry. Otherwise, this dictionary remains a valuable resource in the education lexicon.—**Joseph P. Hester**

Handbooks and Yearbooks

C, S
86.   **New Literacies: Multiple Perspectives on Research and Practice.** Elizabeth A. Baker, ed. New York, Guilford, 2011. 322p. index. $35.00pa. ISBN 13: 978-1-60623-604-8.

Edited by an associate professor of Literacy Studies in the Department of Learning, Teaching, and Curriculum at the University of Missouri, this work brings together 13 chapters by mostly U.S.-based scholars and practitioners. Exploring the new literacies from a diverse set of perspectives, these chapters look at both theory and practical issues, helping the reader make sense of the complexities of being literate in today's technology-rich cultures both through looking at the new technologies needed to support the more traditional definitions of literacy and the new literacies that are emerging due to the new technologies proliferating. Guiding educators and administrators through understanding the ideas, support needed, and implementation of all types and definitions of literacies for students in K-12 in today's digital society, the volume provides research and how-to information for all, and can be applied in higher level educational settings as well. Whether looking at reading, behaviorist and constructivist applications, language acquisition, cognitive processing, sociological and sociocultural perspectives, feminist perspectives, or other views and interpretations of literacy, this book will provide guidance and support in any endeavor to redefine the term literacy in today's world.—**Sara Marcus**

C, S
87.   Osborne, Allan G., Jr., and Charles J. Russo. **Legal Rights and Responsibilities of Teachers: Issues of Employment and Instruction.** Thousand Oaks, Calif., Corwin Press, 2011. 330p. index. $43.95pa. ISBN 13: 978-1-4129-7546-9.

Authored by a former principal of Snug Harbor Community School in Quincy, Massachusetts, and the Joseph Panzer Chair in Education in the School of Education and Allied Professions and Adjunct Professor in the School of Law at the University of Dayton in Ohio, this work is the first of a two-part set, the second part focusing on the rights of students. Intended to be used as part of the set or alone, this volume is a concise, practical guide to the areas of the law in the United States that are of greatest concern to educators in the K-12 setting.

Organized into nine chapters, the work begins with a discussion of the historical and legal foundations of public education, followed by eight chapters addressing more specific legal aspects. Whether interested in school governance and the teacher, basic constitutional rights and freedoms, employment terms and conditions, collective bargaining, or prohibitions against employment discrimination, the current or future educator and administrator will find information in layperson's terms on the legal aspects and ramifications. Additional chapters address teacher discipline, dismissal and due process, curricular and instructional issues, and tort liability. The authors end the book with three resources: the court systems and the authority of courts, legal resources and references, and a brief introduction to legal research in the ever-changing technological world we live in. Each chapter includes an introduction, summary and recommendations, frequently asked questions and answers, a discussion of what's next, and endnotes. Also included are a glossary of terms, acronyms and abbreviations, and an index. The writing style makes the confusing and convoluted legal world surrounding being a teacher approachable to all, using references and examples to make the knowledge understandable to the nonlegal professional. This is of use not only to practicing teachers and administrators, but also as a text for future teachers to be aware of their rights and responsibilities according to the law.—**Sara Marcus**

Elementary and Secondary Education

Biography

P, S

88.   **PebbleGo Biographies. http://www.PebbleGo.com/.** [Website]. North Mankato, Minn., Capstone Press. Price negotiated by site. Date reviewed: 2011.

This new PebbleGo offering has easy-to-read entries that are categorized by subject topic; several entries are included under more than one heading or subheading. Each entry includes a timeline, short quality video, and information on "early life," "life's work," "later years," and "contributions." Each screen has a read-aloud option. Vocabulary words link to a pop-up definition. Entries include a link to a printable activity. Five educational, age-appropriate games are included, such as "Biography Birthdays" where the user places biographees on a timeline, or "Who Am I?" that asks users to choose the correct person in response to a question. The site also includes Educator Resources, with a link to National Standards, four lesson plans, and three reproducibles. Three of the lesson plans can be used with any biographee, the fourth includes photographs of six specific personalities. This is a very nice resource for even the youngest student.—**Kim M. Belknap**

Catalogs and Collections

S

89.   **Bearport Digital Library. http://www.bearportpublishing.com/ebooks/.** [Website]. Bearport Publishing. Price negotiated by site. Date reviewed: 2011.

This library of digital books allows users to find a book through subject icons or keyword searching. After opening an e-book, a screen offers a summary and bibliographic information. The functionality of the interface is geared to adults, and younger children without an adult guide will find it more difficult. The product would be greatly enhanced if there was a read-aloud function. With some of the books reviewed, the font size is too small, even at full screen. The navigation bar contains icons for several features such a table of contents and bookmarks. This product would be most appropriate for upper elementary students as they are better able to navigate various functions and read the summaries.—**Kay Evey**

S

90.   **Curriculum Resource Center. http://www.factsonfile.com/.** [Website]. New York, Facts on File. Price negotiated by site. Date reviewed: 2012.

Curriculum Resource Center is a database of printable media that can be used in classrooms. This site uses materials from Facts on File's curriculum-supporting looseleaf binder reference materials, which include maps, experiments, timelines, and other visual resources. The images can be printed, e-mailed, saved to one's personal file, or distributed for classroom purposes. These handouts can be used to supplement text and lesson plans in a variety of subject areas. Subjects covered include U.S. and world history (1,300 historical maps), geography (printable U.S. and worldwide maps), government (charts of governing bodies around the world), religion (handouts on various faiths, their leaders, and festivals), math (covering algebra, geometry, and calculus), health and fitness (handouts on sports safety and health topics), and the sciences (covering biology, chemistry, Earth sciences, physics, weather, and space and astronomy). In general, this site is easy to search, with record links making it easy for students to return to previously viewed pages. Like all of Facts on File's sites, this site offers guidance on citing MLA, Chicago, and APA styles. Overall, this database is very useful for teachers and librarians and would be an excellent addition in school libraries.—**Shannon Graff Hysell**

S

91.   **Discovery Education Streaming Plus. http://streaming.discoveryeducation.com/.** [Website]. Silver Spring, Md., Discovery Education. Price negotiated by site. Date reviewed: 2011.

Having access to Discovery Education Online is like having a treasure chest of digital resources at your fingertips. Best known for their video streaming, educators and students can also explore audio clips and photographs. The difficulty with Discovery Education is the wealth of information. When you enter this Website looking for resources, it is easy to get sidetracked. When you find a resource, you are able to add that to your personal content area in "My Discovery." Searches can be done with a variety of criteria. There's also a database of lesson plans using Discovery Education resources. New features are being added regularly. Digital textbooks that support state curriculum are being introduced. The wealth of videos, the ease of searching, and using video clips should be enough for any library to consider this as an option. Staff development about the assignment building, the assignment calendar, and the individual student resources will be important so teachers can learn all that is available.—**Nelda Brangwin**

Handbooks and Yearbooks

S

92.   Bernadowski, Carianne, and Kelly Morgano. **Teaching Historical Fiction with Ready-Made Literature Circles for Secondary Readers.** Santa Barbara, Calif., Libraries Unlimited/ABC-CLIO, 2012. 228p. index. $35.00pa. ISBN 13: 978-1-59884-788-8; 978-1-59884-789-5 (e-book).

Coauthored by an assistant professor of early childhood and elementary education at Robert Morris University and an early childhood and elementary teacher, this work introduces literature circles in general, both the theory and how-to use them, and then provides fourteen example literature circles that focus on historical fiction geared towards students in grades 7-12. Useful for teachers and students, this will also help those who are leading book discussions to find ideas on projects and discussion questions. And while the examples are drawn from historical fiction novels, the techniques and tips can be applied to any piece of writing. Each of the 14 literature circles provided include bibliographic information, an annotation, suggested vocabulary, ideas for a prereading meeting, guided discussion questions, postreading activities, Web extensions, and read-alikes. This will be of use at any level, from elementary through college, for teachers and librarians alike.—**Sara Marcus**

C, P

93.   **Education State Rankings 2011-2012: PreK-12 Education Across America.** Kathleen O'Leary Morgan and Scott Morgan, eds. Washington, D.C., CQ Press, 2012. 469p. index. $75.00pa. ISBN 13: 978-1-60871-728-6.

The 2011-2012 edition of *Education State Rankings* keeps the format that has made previous editions such a useful resource. The content consists of about 440 tables organized into 7 topics (districts and facilities, finance, graduates and achievements, safety and discipline, special education, staff, and students). The table of contents lists all of the table titles for all seven sections. The table titles for each section are listed again at the beginning of each section. The tables are followed by a glossary of terms, a list of sources, and a subject index. The sources used include the National Center for Education Statistics, National Education Association, the College Board, and National Institute for Early Education Research. Each table is labeled by function and date. The original source of the data is listed at the bottom of each table and includes the URL when available. Most of the original data are available online. However, the online data are scattered and researchers would have to work hard to locate all the relevant sources. The value of this book is having information from all the relevant sources organized, indexed, and formatted into consistent tables. Each table is arranged both by rank and alphabetical order. This format allows researchers to quickly locate both comparative and individual state information. The glossary is very helpful for researchers new to the field. The list of sources contains the URL, the street address, and the general contact telephone number. This resource is highly recommended for both public and academic libraries.—**Cynthia Crosser**

P, S
94.   Saccardi, Marianne. **Books That Teach Kids to Write.** Santa Barbara, Calif., Libraries Unlimited/ ABC-CLIO, 2011. 178p. illus. index. $30.00pa. ISBN 13: 978-1-59884-451-1; 978-1-59884-452-8 (e-book).
       Saccardi, an early literacy consultant who has written two related books, has created a work that is more than a recommended list of children's literature for writing teachers: she puts writing topics in context and discusses dozens of children's and young adult books that can be used to teach each topic. Each of the five chapters—"Words," "Taking Some of the 'Chore' Out of Writing," "Making Stories Unique," "Creating Memorable Characters," and "Putting Passion and Voice into Non-fiction Writing"—begins with an introduction, and teaching ideas are included throughout the chapters. Each chapter is divided into subsections related to the topic, and ends with a reference list of the children's and YA books suggested and secondary sources that discuss the literature. Black-and-white cover art for many of the books is included. Appendix A is a collection of 14 reproducible forms that teachers may use or adapt, numbered to correspond to sections of the chapters. Appendix B is a bibliography of books featuring characters who write, but does not contain ideas for their use. All reference lists and bibliographies include one-line descriptions of the titles. The index includes book titles, authors, and concepts. The fluidity of her writing shows the author's expertise, and the layout is pleasing. This work is highly recommended for elementary and middle school library professional collections, and for academic libraries that support teacher preparation programs. Children's librarians in public libraries who do programs on writing may want copies as well.—**Rosanne M. Cordell**

Higher Education

General Works

Dictionaries and Encyclopedias

C
95.   Brooks, F. Erik, and Glenn L. Starks. **Historically Black Colleges and Universities: An Encyclopedia.** Santa Barbara, Calif., Greenwood Press/ABC-CLIO, 2011. 338p. index. $89.00. ISBN 13: 978-0-313-39415-7; 978-0-313-39416-4 (e-book).
       Historically Black Colleges and Universities (HBCUs) have been around since 1837, with the founding of Cheyney University of Pennsylvania. Today the 105 institutions with this designation

enroll approximately 16 percent of black college students and range in size from a few hundred to over 11,000 graduates and undergraduates. This new volume is part handbook and part encyclopedia, based on its arrangement of dividing the colleges into four separate sections depending on the institution's founding date. Every HBCU receives between one and three pages of historical narrative, from the beginnings to the present, but there is no apparent consistency usually between length of an entry and prominence of the college. Fully one-third of the remainder of the volume consists of topics peripheral to the institutional histories, such as paragraphs on select Greek organizations, summations of major court cases, athletics, some statistical charts, a 50-page list of notable HBCU alumni, and excerpts of some central primary federal documents. The authors do not gloss over recent problems befalling these schools (loss of accreditation, for example), and in general treatment of all entries is fair and balanced. A welcome companion volume to Jackson and Nunn's *Historically Black Colleges and Universities: A Reference Handbook* (see ARBA 2004, entry 276), Gasman and Tudico's *Historically Black Colleges and Universities: Triumphs, Troubles, and Taboos* (Palgrave Macmillan, 2008), and Lovett's *America's Historically Black Colleges: A Narrative History, 1837-2009* (Mercer University Press, 2011). This work is recommended for all academic libraries.—**Anthony J. Adam**

Directories

P, S
96.   **Peterson's Four-Year Colleges 2011.** Lawrenceville, N.J., Peterson's Guides, 2011. 1824p. index. $32.95pa. ISBN 13: 978-0-7689-2834-1.

Directory information about higher education can be found in a number of places. A commonly used concise guide to colleges and universities is *Peterson's Four-Year Colleges*. This directory is a single-volume annual publication profiling accredited four-year colleges in the United States and Canada. The college descriptions are arranged alphabetically by state or province, and the college entries contain information such as name, address, telephone number, fax number, Website, acceptance rates, majors, current tuition, student life, and campus safety. A detailed section of inserts provides additional in-depth narrative profiles for more than 400 selected colleges and universities. *Peterson's* includes indexes that are based on entrance difficulty, cost, majors, and a standard alphabetic index. The publisher also provides basic descriptive information about colleges, as well as graduate schools, online degrees, and K-12 private schools, at the company's Website (http://www.petersons.com) at no charge for users.— **ARBA Staff Reviewer**

C, P
97.   **Peterson's Graduate & Professional Programs 2012.** 46th ed. Lawrenceville, N.J., Peterson's Guides, 2012. 1048p. index. $54.95pa. ISBN 13: 978-0-7689-3280-5.

Graduate education is covered comprehensively in *Peterson's Graduate & Professional Programs*. Contact and informational profiles are provided for more than 44,000 graduate programs at more than 2,300 institutions in the United States and Canada. Like *The College Blue Book* (38th ed.; see ARBA 2012, entry 342), this resource is organized around six thematic volumes that can be used as a set or individually. Across all the volumes in this set, three kinds of entries appear: basic profiles, short announcements, and in-depth descriptions. The basic profiles are the heart of each volume, and every program listed has a profile that includes information such as name, address, graduate director, acceptance figures, and a very brief narrative description. Some profiles have a short announcement at the end of their listing containing information that the school or program wants to emphasize to potential applicants. Many profiles also have a cross-reference to an in-depth description of their program, submitted by the schools themselves. These descriptions are found at the end of the subject sections in the individual volumes and appear in a standard format that includes information on programs of study, research facilities, costs, available financial help, and how to apply.—**ARBA Staff Reviewer**

Financial Aid

Directories

C, S

98. Schlachter, Gail Ann, and R. David Weber. **Financial Aid for African Americans, 2012-2014.** El Dorado Hills, Calif., Reference Service Press, 2012. 490p. index. $42.50. ISBN 13: 978-1-58841-217-2.

With the escalating costs of going to college, especially in tough economic times and declining levels of state support for higher education, current directories of financial aid are extremely important. This volume is an update of the 2009-2011 edition of this directory and includes descriptions of nearly 1,300 sources of college funding targeted at African Americans. While 80 percent of the continuing entries had substantial changes, there were only about 50 new sources included in this volume. To be included, funding sources must be open to Americans, focused on African Americans, not overly restrictive in level of support (that is, they must be over $1,000), not centered in particular academic institutions, and free. The entries themselves are lengthy, including the important contact information for the funding source (e.g., address, telephone number, e-mail address, Web address), purpose, eligibility, financial data or level of support, duration, additional information, number of awards, and the deadline for applications. Entries can be searched alphabetically by funding source name within any of five categories: scholarships, fellowships, grants, awards, and internships. The supplementary indexes to these entries include program title, sponsoring organization, residency, tenability (where the funds may be used), subject, and calendar index. Overall, this is an invaluable resource for students seeking financial support for college attendance. It is recommended for public, school, and academic libraries.—**Stephen H. Aby**

C, S

99. Schlachter, Gail Ann, and R. David Weber. **Financial Aid for Hispanic Americans, 2012-2014.** El Dorado Hills, Calif., Reference Service Press, 2012. 446p. index. $42.50. ISBN 13: 978-1-58841-219-9.

This revised edition of *Financial Aid for Hispanic Americans* is part of a four-volume set produced by Reference Service Press, Minority Funding, where each volume is updated biennially. Providing a list of scholarships, fellowships, grants, awards, and internships open primarily or exclusively to Hispanic Americans, this work serves not only students but also researchers as well. The programs for sponsored by 1,100 different private and public agencies and organizations and are open to Hispanic Americans from high school age through the post-doctorate level. Six indexes enable quick location of a desired financial support by program title, sponsoring organization, residency, tenability, subject, and deadline date. Besides the indexes, the work itself is organized into scholarships for undergraduate students; fellowships for graduate students; grants for research, projects and creative activities; awards for achievement and recognition; and internships for work experience. Each entry provides the program title, sponsoring organization, purpose, eligibility, financial information, duration, additional information, number awarded, and deadline. This is a valuable addition to any academic, scholar, or high school where there is a need for financial assistance for Hispanic Americans.—**Sara Marcus**

C, S

100. Schlachter, Gail Ann, and R. David Weber. **Money for Graduate Students in the Physical & Earth Sciences, 2010-2012.** Santa Cruz, Calif., Reference and Research Services, 2011. 276p. index. $40.00. ISBN 13: 978-1-58841-200-8.

Reference Service Press is well known for its directories of financial aid for students. This volume is the guide to financial aid for graduate students in the physical and earth sciences and joins other related volumes, which provide information on financial aid for graduate students in the arts and humanities, the biological sciences, the health sciences, and the social sciences. The result is a listing of nearly 900 grants, fellowships, and awards that assist in funding graduate studies. Included are those needing assistance in the areas of atmospheric sciences, chemistry, computer science, mathematics, physics, and technology. The listings are limited to those funding sources which are "free" (i.e., no repayment or service is required as a prerequisite for receiving the award) and the financial award must be at least $1,000 per year. Each entry gives the name of the award program, the sponsor (including complete contact information such as e-mail addresses and Website), a summary of the award, eligibility requirements, the amount of the award and how it can be used, the duration, additional information, the number of awards available, and the deadline for submitting an application.

Due to the high costs of completing a graduate degree, financial assistance is necessary for most graduate students. Thus, this reference source should receive a high level of use and is recommended for all college and university libraries. It should repay its cost many times over.—**Gregory A. Crawford**

Handbooks and Yearbooks

C, S

101.   **College Financing Information for Teens.** 2d ed. Elizabeth Magill, ed. Detroit, Omnigraphics, 2012. 387p. index. (Teen Finance Series). $62.00. ISBN 13: 978-0-7808-1214-7.

This series from Omnigraphics is similar in format to the publisher's Teen Health Series, only for these volumes the focus is on responsible management of money and finances. The works consist of documents and excerpts written by various government, nonprofit, and for-profit organizations and agencies, including the Department of the Treasury, the United States Securities and Exchange Commission, the American Savings Education Council, the National Association of Securities Dealers, and Visa, Inc.

Joining other titles in the series (e.g., *Cash and Credit Information for Teens* [2d ed.; 2009], *Savings and Investment Information for Teens* [2d ed.; 2009]), *College Financing information for Teens* provides information on preparing financially for college, your role as an education consumer, saving for college, and financial aid resources available from the federal government and other sources. Some of the most valuable information in this book includes discussion of the various ways to finance an education; how to apply for loans and scholarships; special financial aid for athletes and those entering the health care fields; loan cancellation and deferment options for teachers; and financial benefits for those in the armed forces, Peace Corps, and AmeriCorps. This work concludes with a chapter for more information that includes Websites for more information on financial aid resources and state higher education agencies.

This series will prove useful for high school and undergraduate students. Both school libraries and college reference collections should add this work to their collections.—**Shannon Graff Hysell**

Nonprint Materials

S

102.   **TinkerPlots. http://www.keypress.com/tinkerplots/.** [Website]. Emeryville, Calif., Key Curriculum Press. Price negotiated by site. Date reviewed: 2011.

TinkerPlots is a Web-based data analysis program that provides an easy way to manipulate and review data sets. The application can be used by upper elementary or older students to design charts and graphs, and interpret and communicate details about the data. Variables can be dragged and clicked to change chart styles which helps the student organize and examine the statistics. Step-by-step tutorials and videos help the user understand and navigate the program quickly. Group comparisons, relationships, probabilities, and other data dynamics can be analyzed through the use of this application. Sample data sets, access to a help section, and support service are included. The ease of manipulation and visual representation of the data make it a very useful tool in the classroom and will help students analyze, compare, and understand statistics.—**Tom Johnson**

Special Education

P

103.   **Guide to Private Special Education 2011/2012: A Descriptive Survey of Special-Needs Schools and Programs.** Boston, Porter Sargent Handbooks/Alloy Education, 2011. 368p. index. $32.00pa. ISBN 13: 978-0-87558-168-2.

The Porter Sargent handbooks have a long history of providing guides that are helpful to parents and students; this is the first edition of this title and it includes over 450 day and residential programs for elementary and secondary students with special needs. Programs throughout the United States are included. The *Guide* prides itself on the objective nature of the entries. All entries have been included at no cost to the school and all data was collected directly from school administrators to ensure accuracy. The book begins with an introductory essay on how to read the entries, a glossary and a key to abbreviations. Following this is a chart listing all of the schools in the book and information on the types of special needs they cover. Each entry (one-third to one-half page) name of the school, contact information, and program director; conditions excepted; grade range of the school; therapies used; psychotherapy used; enrollment; summer programs offered; year established; and a short paragraph describing key components of the program. School entries are arranged first by state and then alphabetically within each state. The work concludes with a list of associations and organizations arranged by advocacy groups, professional associations, and recreational organizations. An index of programs completes the volume. This is such a wealth of information in a small package that school counselors will want their own copies. This work is highly recommended for public libraries.—**Shannon Graff Hysell**

6 Ethnic Studies and Anthropology

Anthropology

C

104. **The Routledge Encyclopedia of Social and Cultural Anthropology.** 2d ed. New York, Routledge/Taylor & Francis Group, 2011. 896p. illus. maps. index. $375.00; $60.00pa. ISBN 13: 978-0-415-40978-0; 978-0-415-80936-8pa.

Written by a professor of the Anthropology of Southern Africa at the University of Edinburgh, and a professor of the Anthropology of South Asia at the University of Edinburgh, the 2d edition of *The Routledge Encyclopedia of Social and Cultural Anthropology* has been greatly expanded. Although the 1st edition came out as recently as 2000, there have been significant updates in this area of concentration that warrant the new edition. It is essentially a guide to the ideas, arguments, and history of the discipline. It points our controversies and challenges within the field and maps out how the discipline is being practiced today. It complements such other notable reference works as the *Biographical Dictionary of Social and Cultural Anthropology* (see ARBA 2005, entry 319) and *The Encyclopedia of Cultural Anthropology* (see ARBA 97, entry 316). For medium and large academic libraries with collections in anthropology this updated volume is a must purchase.—**Shannon Graff Hysell**

Ethnic Studies

General Works

Dictionaries and Encyclopedias

P, S

105. **Junior Worldmark Encyclopedia of World Cultures.** 2d ed. Farmington Hills, Mich., U*X*L/Gale, 2011. 9v. illus. maps. index. $584.00/set. ISBN 13: 978-1-4144-8671-0; 978-1-4144-8681-9 (e-book).

This new encyclopedia is modeled after of *Junior Worldmark* titles, including *Junior Worldmark Encyclopedia of the Nations* (5th ed.; see ARBA 2008, entry 65) and *Junior Worldmark Encyclopedia of the States* (5th ed.; see ARBA 2008, entry 71). Although the information contained in its predecessor is general in scope, this work focuses on the culture of 315 ethnic groups outside of the United States. Some 25 new groups have been added to the set since the publication of the 1st edition in 1999. It is designed for use by upper elementary students; however, it is suitable for readers of all ages because it contains much information that may not be readily available elsewhere.

The format is attractive. The type is easy to read and there are illustrations, including location maps. There are a reader's guide and a cumulative table of contents at the beginning of each volume, a glossary, and language overview and finder table to specific cultures. A cumulative index can be found in the final volume. The arrangement is alphabetic by country and is continuous in the nine volumes. Within each chapter, cultural groups are treated individually. Information about each group follows the same pattern in 20 subheadings, which include language, religion, holidays, living conditions, and a bibliography. An interesting feature is the inclusion of ethnic recipes. Political problems and ethnic conflicts are addressed only briefly under social problems.

This set is recommended as a worthwhile addition to a children's library collection or a supplement to social studies classes.—**Patricia A. Eskoz**

C, S

106.   Shoup, John A. **Ethnic Groups of Africa and the Middle East: An Encyclopedia.** Santa Barbara, Calif., ABC-CLIO, 2011. 377p. illus. index. (Ethnic Groups of the World). $89.00. ISBN 13: 978-1-59884-362-0; 978-1-59884-363-7 (e-book).

The groups selected for inclusion in this book are based on ethno-linguistic classifications from Africa and the Middle East, defined as the Arab heartlands of the Levant, the Arabian Peninsula, Iraq, Turkey, and Iran. Not all individual ethnicities have been included. Those speaking closely related languages are grouped together with separate entries for those with particular historical or political importance. The entries are alphabetical; each with sources for further readings. There are 117 separate entries such as Afar, Dogon, Fur, Kuba, Taysh and Venda. They include a discussion of who is a part of the group, a short history of the people, a description of life, work and society in the group, and their current location and status. In an introductory essay, the difficulties of determining groups and their sociopolitical organization is set forth. The book is a good resource for the location and understanding the many diverse ethnic groups of Africa and the Middle East.—**J. E. Weaver**

African Americans

Almanacs

C, P, S

107.   **The African American Almanac.** 11th ed. Farmington Hills, Mich., Gale/Cengage Learning, 2012. 1500p. illus. maps. index. $312.00. ISBN 13: 978-14144-4547-2.

The appearance of a new edition of *The African American Almanac* is always welcome. Now in its 11th edition, the present volume follows the same general format as previous versions, covering all topics related to the black experience in the United States, including history, politics, culture and the arts, the sciences and medicine, education, the military, religion, and much more. All material from the 10th edition was extensively reviewed by the editor, with several chapters substantially revised by subject experts. Over half of the biographies are updated, with nearly 50 new personalities added. Cross-references have also been added to the biographical section, as needed. The section titled "African American Firsts" has been updated to include nearly 100 new entries. Of the over 550 black-and-white photographs, illustrations, maps, and statistical charts, over half were not published in the 10th edition (see ARBA 2008, entry 307). The writing is excellent throughout, and all illustrations are clean and often striking. Appendixes of African American award winners (everything from the Olympics to Miss America), an extensive secondary bibliography, and an index complete the volume. Essential for all public, academic, and school libraries.—**Anthony J. Adam**

Biography

C, P

108. **Great Lives from History: African Americans.** Carl L. Bankston III, ed. Hackensack, N.J., Salem Press, 2011. 5v. illus. index. $595.00/set. ISBN 13: 978-1-58765-741-2; 978-1-58765-754-2 (e-book).

Salem Press's Great Lives From History series continues with this 5-volume collection of essays on approximately 770 African American men and women across the span of United States history who have contributed significantly to the nation's culture. Editor Bankston (Tulane University) has assembled a variety of scholars, not all associated with a university or research institute, to cover the range of biographies, and the writing is generally good, although given space limitations depth is impossible. All fields of endeavor are included, the only criteria being that the person have significance in history or culture. Many individuals make regular appearances in other African American reference sources, but even a casual scan will uncover less-familiar names (e.g., Ron Woodson, Norbert Rillieux, Wyomia Tyus). However, perhaps less attention could have been given to musicians and more to business leaders: Herman Cain, Xerox CEO Ursula Burns, and Aetna CEO Ronald A. Williams are all missing. Each signed essay runs between 1,000-2,000 words long and includes the person's name, field of work, area of achievement, early life, life's work, significance, and a brief annotated secondary bibliography. Some 400 black-and-white photographs are scattered throughout the set, but not every biography is so enhanced. Back matter material includes a chronological list of entries, bibliography of nonfiction works, a useful mediagraphy and Website directory, and list of organizations and societies, along with category and subject indices. Print purchasers also benefit from free access to the online version of the set.

Although numerous African-American biographical reference sources are available online and in print, this new Salem Press set will enhance any library's collection and is recommended for all general academic and public reference collections.—**Anthony J. Adam**

Dictionaries and Encyclopedias

C, S

109. **The African American Experience. http://www.abc-clio.com/Previews/index.aspx.** [Website]. Santa Barbara, Calif., ABC-CLIO, 2011. Price negotiated by site. Date reviewed: 2011.

This is a comprehensive research database that provides reliable information on African American life, history, and culture. Users can browse a wide range of subject areas, from "Arts and Entertainment" and "Business and Labor" to "Sports" and "Women." The Resources section includes the following headings: title list, timeline, image index, primary source index, landmark documents, slave narratives, classic texts, and audio files. Altogether there are over 5,000 primary documents provided here, including manuscripts, speeches, court cases, and statistics, as well as a timeline that can be searched by century, decade, or keyword. Lesson plans are included that tie directly to the primary resources and other classroom resources. Content includes the history of blacks in American from the first arrival through the present day and includes some information on African origins. The database has been revamped recently into two formats—one for middle and high school libraries and classrooms, and the second for academic libraries.—**Catherine Barr**

C, P

110. **Black America: A State-by-State Historical Encyclopedia.** Alton Hornsby Jr., ed. Santa Barbara, Calif., Greenwood Press/ABC-CLIO, 2011. 2v. illus. index. $180.00/set. ISBN 13: 978-0-313-34112-0; 978-1-57356-976-7 (e-book).

Hornsby is well known in the field of African American scholarship for his work on Southern history, and here he branches out with a collection of essays by academic scholars noted for their contributions to local histories. Each 10- to 30-page signed essay includes a lengthy chronology of that state's African American history, a historical overview of approximately five pages, brief biographies of three to eight notable African Americans (some individuals appear in more than one state), a multi-paragraph summation of cultural contributions, and a secondary bibliography. Every essay also includes at least one black-and-white photograph or lithographic reproduction, and some essays (Washington State, for example) feature data tables. The length and depth of the articles is primarily dependent upon the historical size of the African American population, with essays on the Southern states and those with significant black populations (e.g., New York, Illinois) predominant. Page limits force most of the essayists to skim over or omit lesser-known events in a state's history, although readers undoubtedly will be surprised by the rich cultural African American heritage of states such as Iowa and Minnesota. As no recent print reference work solely collects state histories in this manner, Hornsby is thus recommended for all public and academic libraries.—**Anthony J. Adam**

C, P, S
111.   **Encyclopedia of African American Popular Culture.** Jessie Carney Smith, ed. Santa Barbara, Calif., Greenwood Press/ABC-CLIO, 2011. 4v. illus. index. $304.00/set. ISBN 13: 978-0-31335-796-1; 978-0-31335-797-8 (e-book).

Distinct cultures exist within the general panoply of American popular culture. Topics such as Muhammad Ali, the Buffalo Soldiers, the Harlem Renaissance, Kwanzaa, and Prince are all part of the distinct African American subset of our general popular culture. The *Encyclopedia of African American Popular Culture* is a four-volume set focusing on this population. Topics are pulled from all areas of everyday life—the arts, business, people, politics, entertainment, religion, sports, fashion, folklore, and cultural movements to name just a few. Each volume contains the same alphabetic list of entries and guide to related topics. Volume 1 contains the introduction, a history timeline dating from 1619, and topics A-C. Volume 2 covers topics D-J. Volume 3 covers topics K-R. Volume 4contains topics S-Z as well as four additional appendixes covering film, radio, television, and popular culture collections. The set also contains a master bibliography.

Overall, the organization is efficient and comparable to most encyclopedia sets. Each entry has a *see also* section for related entries and a further reading section guiding researchers to additional books, Websites, and articles. Entries identified in related articles are highlighted in boldface. The encyclopedia is very comprehensive but admittedly not all inclusive. To aid in the selection process, more than 140 people contributed to writing the entries and an advisory board guided the selection process. Sound choices were made in the selection of entries for this set. The writing is succinct yet extremely informative. Black-and-white pictures, largely of famous people, can be found but are not abundant. Insets of color photographs would have enhanced the user's experience. Academic and public libraries would make a wise choice in purchasing this set. Most people middle school age and up will find this set helpful. Overall, the *Encyclopedia of African American Popular Culture* is an excellent research tool.—**Sue Ellen Griffiths**

Australian Aborigines

C
112.   Rolls, Mitchell, and Murray Johnson. **Historical Dictionary of Australian Aborigines.** Lanham, Md., Scarecrow, 2011. 213p. maps. (Historical Dictionaries of Peoples and Cultures). $75.00. ISBN 13: 978-0-8108-5997-5; 978-0-8108-7475-6 (e-book).

The Aborigines of Australia came to the continent about 60,000 years ago. They settled in the sub-arctic tundra to the south and the tropical rainforest in the north and the arid desert in the mid-section. They are Australia's indigenous people. The entries for this historical dictionary, describe these aboriginal tribes of Australia through the Aborigines' biographies, institutions, traditions, and their culture.

The text has been written by two academics. Rolls is a senior lecturer and co-director at the Riawunna, Centre for Aboriginal Studies, at the University of Tasmania. Johnson has taught numerous courses on Australian history, and is involved in Aboriginal native title claims in Queensland. The authors tell the Aboriginal history by writing down the Aborigine's stories derived from the oral tradition of storytelling. They reveal their history of a vibrant cultural life. Their songs illustrate the relationship between the people and the land, which they call "Dreamtime," while dances and art illustrate the oral tales. The authors have supplemented the text with black-and-white maps, illustrations, and photographs. Chronologies, a note about the orthography of the Aboriginal language and its history, as well as an index are available. The bibliography is a compilation of the reference works and thematic works that cover ethnology, anthropology, politics and race relations, legal and judicial matters, film and media, education, literature, demographics, and the works by indigenous writers.

This reviewer would highly recommend this dictionary from the series. It is a well-written history of the Aborigines that updates their history through 2010.—**Kay M. Stebbins**

Indians of North America

Bibliography

C

113.   Peterson, Herman A. **The Trail of Tears: An Annotated Bibliography of Southeastern Indian Removal.** Lanham, Md., Scarecrow, 2011. 137p. index. $60.00. ISBN 13: 978-0-8108-7739-9.

An impressive advisory board comprised of noted Indian and non-Indian scholars, guides the development and production of the publisher's Native American Bibliography Series. This commendable practice ensures that Native histories and cultures are accurately and appropriately presented. This exemplary practice should be mandatory for publishers of Native-related fiction and nonfiction. This outstanding book is the newest volume in this series.

Regarding accuracy, the author brought considerable knowledge and experience to the research and writing of this book. As the head of Reference and Instructional Services to the Morris Library of Southern Illinois University, he also serves on the national board of directors for the trail of Tears Association and is active in the Illinois chapter of that organization. The reader can be confident of this scholar's accuracy.

In the editor's foreword, he reminds the reader that "In a very real sense, all Native American people have experienced the removal process in the tribal histories. Many of the indigenous nations were repeatedly resettled, each time with the understanding that the newly occupied lands would be guaranteed to them forever." Many people inaccurately believe that the infamous Trail of Tears was limited to the Cherokee; this volume rightly extends the concept and reality of removal to the five tribes of the Southeast that experienced a "Trail of Tears" in differing ways. The chapters are: Choctaw, Creek, Chickasaw, Cherokee, Seminole, Biographical, and Government Documents and Manuscripts. The subtopic in each chapter is adapted to the individual tribe's experience, making it easy for the reader to locate information. There are 818 entries with concise annotations. While researchers will value the convenience, accuracy, and reliability of the comprehensive volume, casual readers and tribal members will find it valuable also.—**Karen D. Harvey**

Dictionaries and Encyclopedias

P, S

114.   **American Indian History Online. http://www.infobase.com/.** [Website]. New York, Facts on File. Price negotiated by site. Date reviewed: 2012.

Facts on File's *American Indian History Online* is a valuable resource for middle and high school age students conducting research on this aspect of American history. The site offers access to more than 15,000 years of history; over 600 tribes are profiled here. The site is compiled from various Facts on File publications and primary source documents.

There are several ways to search this site. Users looking for information on a specific topic can conduct a keyword search or they can browse topics by tribe, culture area, time period, or primary source type. Along with access to primary source documents the site also features a timeline, an image gallery, maps and charts, and a glossary with 1,700 terms. The search results are presented in a clear and readable format and links to related biographies, subject entries, and images are provided. Users can print, copy, or save their results for personal use, which makes this an ideal resource for students using this site for research papers or projects. Along with historical information, subjects covered here include ceremonies and festivals, daily life and customs, economics and trade, land rights disputes, tribal law and government, and assimilation, among others. There is also information on tribal legends, which provides traditional stories from various tribes (accessible through the Primary Sources browse page).

The content is clearly written for middle and high school age students. Although undergraduate students would find this resource useful, it does not offer the depth of information required for their research needs. This database is highly recommended for middle and high school libraries as well as large public libraries. [R: LJ, Jan 12, p. 142]—**Shannon Graff Hysell**

C, S

115.   **Encyclopedia of Native American History.** Peter C. Mancall, ed. New York, Facts on File, 2011. 3v. illus. maps. index. (Facts on File Library of American History). $300.00/set. ISBN 13: 978-0-8160-7250-7; 978-1-4381-3567-0 (e-book).

The *Encyclopedia of Native American History*, a three-volume set published by Facts on File, is a perfect addition to a reference collection that sorely needs current sources on the Indians of North America, mostly north of the Rio Grande. The editor and contributor is Peter C. Mancall, professor of history and anthropology at the University of Southern California and director of the USC-Huntington Early Modern Studies Institute. According to the preface, Mancall has aimed to provide a comprehensive overview of the field, with an emphasis on historical experience. He gives credit to more ambitious works that came before, such as the Smithsonian's *Handbook of North American Indians*, to which all scholars of the Native American experience are indebted.

The *Encyclopedia of Native American History* includes entries on the following topics: tribes, culture (including art, music, religion), laws and treaties, war, medicine, geography, economics, and agriculture. A handy A-Z list of entries appears at the front of each volume. Each entry concludes with citations to further reading. Photographs and a color map insert are also useful. The map is inexplicably placed between letters T and U, and not mentioned in the table of contents or elsewhere in the book. One is left thinking that it was an afterthought. A list of Indian tribes recognized by the U.S. government, a selected bibliography, and an index appear at the end of volume three.

In the preface, Professor Mancall writes that "a work of this magnitude can only succeed through the efforts of the scores of contributors whose work appears here." So true, but why not give credit to these contributors at the front of the book on a dedicated page that includes their credentials and affiliations? A cursory Internet search for several contributors reveals that some are noted scholars in the field of Native American history, some are doctoral fellows or recently minted Ph.Ds, and at least one appears to be an undergraduate in the history program at USC. Editors and publishers would better serve their readers by acknowledging their contributors' backgrounds. Regardless, Mancall has maintained quality control throughout, and students of Native American history will be happy to have this up-to-date encyclopedia.—**John P. Stierman**

C, S

116.   **The Encyclopedia of North American Indian Wars 1607-1890: A Political, Social, and Military History.** Spencer C. Tucker, ed. Santa Barbara, Calif., ABC-CLIO, 2011. 3v. illus. maps. index. $310.00/set. ISBN 13: 978-1-85109-697-8; 978-1-85109-603-9 (e-book).

Even before establishing settlements, North American colonizers clashed with Native Americans—it was an inevitable conflict between cultures. These initial contacts more than often turned into battles and wars, the subject of this new ABC-CLIO three-volume set. An earlier ABC-CLIO book covered much of the same material in one volume and other publishers have distributed their own volumes, but this is the most comprehensive set yet. The first two volumes include the encyclopedia's entries and the third is a collection of 167 relevant documents. An overview and introduction set the scene of Indian-white relations and conflict. The 800-plus alphabetic entries are concise, written by over 200 contributors, and include references. A major strength is the coverage, from settlement to Wounded Knee (1890). Another is the scope of the entries; for example, Civil War veteran and noted Indian fighter George Crook is included, but so is Emmet Crawford, a long-time officer under Crook's command. Entries range from campaigns and battles to leaders on both sides. Broader topics include tribes, weapons, forts, distinct geographic regions, and other related topics. There are 26 maps and 25 tables, covering topics such as a list of Indian massacres and estimated casualties. Other features include a glossary, chronology, 20-page bibliography, and list of contributors. The documents vary from battle accounts to treaties and laws. A comprehensive index concludes the set.—**Boyd Childress**

Handbooks and Yearbooks

C, S

117.   Rielly, Edward J. **Legends of American Indian Resistance.** Santa Barbara, Calif., Greenwood Press/ABC-CLIO, 2011. 341p. index. $85.00. ISBN 13: 978-0-313-35209-6; 978-0-313-35210-2 (e-book).

American Indians have been resisting European hegemony since the cultures collided in the late fifteenth century. In his thoughtful and well-written book *Legends of American Indian Resistance*, Edward J. Rielly, Professor of English at Saint Joseph's college of Maine, explores the lives of 12 Native Americans who are first and foremost remembered for their resistance to this hegemony. His criteria for inclusion is simply that the 11 men and one woman "thoroughly deserve" to be in such a book as this. And who can disagree with such great Native Americans as Philip (Metacom), Pontiac, Tecumseh, Black Hawk, Osceola, Sitting Bull, Crazy Horse, Chief Joseph, and Geronimo? If the book had been longer, he could have easily included others from the American Indian wars that ran through the nineteenth century, but he chose to include three contemporary resistors: Dennis Banks, Russell Means, and Mary Brave Bird. By including them, he makes his book more relevant to today, and students become more aware of the fact that Indian resistance is not just part of the past.

In overlapping chronological order, each of the 12 "legends" is presented as a chapter. Each chapter looks at the method of resistance and the accomplishments, and provides a biographical context. Each narrative concludes with endnotes and a bibliography of recommended reading. A comprehensive bibliography of print and nonprint sources is followed by an index.

Legends of American Indian Resistance is a good starting point for students who are not familiar with the biographees. More sophisticated readers will enjoy reading Professor Rielly's deft and thoughtful treatment of certain controversial events, such as the killings of Sitting Bull and Crazy Horse. This work is recommended for high school and undergraduate students who are beginning to explore Native American resistance.—**John P. Stierman**

Jews

C, P

118. **Great Lives from History: Jewish Americans.** Rafael Medoff, ed. Hackensack, N.J., Salem Press, 2011. 4v. illus. index. $495.00/set. ISBN 13: 978-1-58765-741-2.

This reference set is Salem History's first foray into ethnic categorization of biographies by focusing on Jewish Americans. The publisher's note indicates that planned volumes will cover African Americans, Latinos, and Asian Americans. A problem with any biographical reference to a religious-ethnic heritage such as Jewish Americans is determination of the influence of that heritage on the luminary's life and career. The editor admits that many of the entries cover figures who have "only the most superficial connection to Jewish religious practices or just a fleeting association with the organized Jewish community" (p. xii). The main criteria for inclusion are the impact on American society by the individual, living or dead, and the identification of Jewish background rather than Jewish practice. The entries are arranged alphabetically by last name, but a category index offers a guide to users for the perception of impact. The majority of entries cover contributors to arts and letters, suggesting the connection of the biographical set to American popular culture. To be sure, 18 "educators and scholars" are identified, as are 20 "religious leaders" and 42 "politicians and government officials." but these categories could easily have been expanded compared to the 96 actors and directors. The popular culture profiles, however, are more extensive than entries in the *Encyclopedia of Jewish American Popular Culture* edited by Jack R. Fischel with Susan Ortmann (ABC-CLIO/Greenwood Press, 2009) or *Jewish-American History and Culture: An Encyclopedia* edited by Jack Fischel and Sanford Pinsker (Garland, 1992). Each entry in this work gives a summary of the person's significance, followed by vital data. Sections of the entry cover "early life," "life's work," "significance," and further reading. Cross-references are at the end of each entry. Many entries have sidebars with interpretive information, such as the ways that Woody Allen's Annie Hall was autobiographical and how the film influenced subsequent romantic comedies produced in Hollywood. Entries cover familiar career information but also refer to the connection of the figure to Jewish identity. The fourth volume contains a number of useful appendixes, including a chronological list of entries (not surprisingly, the emphasis is on the first half of the twentieth century). Other appendixes of interest are a bibliography arranged by occupation, Website directory, mediagraphy (productions for television), literary works, libraries and research centers, organizations and societies, category index, personages index, and subject index (where readers might expect more locations than are included). An added value to the reference is that set comes with a complimentary online access to the printed content through the Salem History database. Overall, the set is a useful addition to the Jewish biographical bookshelf and is itself an artifact of ethnic perceptions and American popular culture.—**Simon J. Bronner**

Latin Americans

C, S

119. **The Latino American Experience. http://www.abc-clio.com/Previews/index.aspx.** [Website]. Santa Barbara, Calif., ABC-CLIO. Price negotiated by site. Date reviewed: 2011.

Wide ranging and easy to use, the *Latino American Experience* (LAE) is the first-ever full-text database focusing on the history and culture of Latinos living in the United States. LAE's content spans from the pre-Columbian indigenous civilizations of the Americas through the Spanish and Mexican settlement of much of what is now the United States, to the triumphs and challenges facing present-day U.S. Latinos. It comes in two versions: one for middle and high school users, and the second for academic libraries.

Featuring more than 150 titles (including award-winning titles from Greenwood, Praeger, Arte Público, Columbia University Press, and other imprints), 1,500 images, hundreds of primary documents, Spanish-language content, a timeline, and 225 vetted Websites, LAE is the most comprehensive digital resource to date to focus exclusively on Latinos. In addition, LAE's "Origins" section features both ready-reference and in-depth information about the history, culture, and customs of the people of Latin America, the Caribbean, and the Iberian Peninsula. Due to the fact that this resource is under the guidance of leading scholars in the area of Latin American studies, and is updated regularly, this database is highly recommended.—**Salvador Avila**

7 Genealogy and Heraldry

Genealogy

Directories

P
120. Carangelo, Lori. **The Ultimate Search Book: Worldwide Adoption, Genealogy & Other Search Secrets.** 2011 ed. Baltimore, Md., Clearfield/Genealogical Publishing, 2011. 294p. index. $39.95pa. ISBN 13: 978-0-8063-5515-3.

Again Lori Carangelo has expanded, updated, and enhanced *The Ultimate Search Book*. Superseded editions should be withdrawn from library shelves to avoid the use of outdated information. The author shows her knowledge of the newest government documents that can assist genealogists with their family history research. She introduces court records of cities, states, and national governments. Chapters include: "Search Basics: Forty Search Tips for Starters," "Missing and Runaway Children," "Family Tree, Genealogy, Debtor, Child Support, Heir, Classmate, Old Love, War Buddy, Missing Adults or Anyone," "With or Without a Name, Family Members Separated Due to Adoption, Divorce," and "Internet Searches, Searching the USA, and International Searching." An addendum of state investigator licensing boards, including the 50 states, District of Columbia, and Puerto Rico, concludes the volume.—**J. Carlyle Parker**

P
121. **USGenWeb. http://www.usgenweb.org/.** [Website]. Free. Date reviewed: 2011.

P
122. **WorldGenWeb. http://www.worldgenweb.org/.** [Website]. Free. Date reviewed: 2011.

The USGenWeb Project began in 1996 as a way to coordinate county-based genealogy Websites. At that early period in Internet history, many genealogists were building Websites about particular counties. To help researchers find these sites, a group of genealogists started *USGenWeb*, which has a page for every state and a page for every county within those states. Because different volunteers maintain each page of the project, the content varies from page to page. The state-level pages tend to include a map of the counties in the state, a general research guide for the state, and some user-contributed data. The county-level pages usually include a research guide, links to genealogy societies and libraries in the county, and a surname registry of researchers.

Similar to *USGenWeb* but for international genealogy, *WorldGenWeb* is divided into six continental regions: North America, South America, Europe, Africa, the Middle East and Australia. Drilling down further into the site will lead researchers to Web pages for specific countries and states. For example, for researchers studying Mexico, the NorthAmericanGenWeb page links to a page specifically about Mexico. The Mexico page has links to major research institutions, other Mexican genealogy Websites, personal Websites about specific families, and links to pages about every Mexican state. Some of the state pages are quite detailed, with local histories, record indexes, and research links. Other pages are simply message boards. *WorldGenWeb*, like *USGenWeb*, is volunteer-run, and the quality of any particular page is dependent upon the person maintaining it.—**Jack Simpson**

Personal Names

P, S

123.   **Last Name Meanings Dictionary. http://www.last-names.net/.** [Website]. Free. Date reviewed: 2011.

   This is a commercial site, but it is amazing how much information one can find without incurring any cost. This is how the Website accurately describes itself: "Find the ethnic origin ad meaning of last names. Surname dictionary and genealogy helps include names of Irish, German, English, French, Italian, and Jewish descent." In just a few minutes one can discover such information as the origin of the name, immigration information related to this name, a chart depicting the average life expectancy for one with this name, a Civil War service record, and even link to a message board for those searching this name. This site is a fun way to get started on a genealogical research expedition.—**Greg Byerly**

8 Geography and Travel Guides

Geography

General Works

Atlases

C, P, S

124. **Essential World Atlas.** 6th ed. New York, Oxford University Press, 2011. 176p. illus. index. $24.95pa. ISBN 13: 978-0-19-982982-8.

The latest edition of *Essential World Atlas* is bright and colorful. The atlas provides physical and political maps for every continent, countries, and major regions. An introductory section provides facts on the planet Earth, the Earth's structure, landforms, oceans, climate, water and vegetation, environment, population, the human family, wealth, quality of life, energy, production, trade, and travel and tourism. The atlas includes maps for 69 major world cities and satellite images of 9 major metropolitan areas. Indexes contain the names of all principal places and features shown on the World Maps. National flags, in color, are on the inside front and back covers. Just published in 2011, the atlas is already out of date. The newest country, South Sudan, did not make it into this edition prior to publication.—**Linda M. Turney**

C, P

125. **National Geographic Atlas of the World.** 9th ed. Washington, D.C., National Geographic Society, 2010. 424p. maps. index. $175.00. ISBN 13: 978-1-4262-063-44.

The *National Geographic Atlas of the World* has a long tradition of publication. This latest edition, the 9th, brings the world up to date, including new regional maps for several areas such as Afghanistan and Pakistan, the Korean Peninsula, and Iraq and Iran. Maps include a large number of place names. Arrangement is by continent, including satellite, political, and physical maps, and a section with country summaries, with official flags and demographic and economic data for all independent nations arranged alphabetically. Political maps for regions and specific countries follow. New thematic maps treating environmental issues, natural resources, and human culture have been added as well as maps of space, the ocean floor, and Earth's poles. The index includes more than 150,000 entries for cities and natural features.—**Benet Steven Exton**

Dictionaries and Encyclopedias

C, S

126.   Hanks, Reuel R. **Encyclopedia of Geography Terms, Themes, and Concepts.** Santa Barbara, Calif., ABC-CLIO, 2011. 405p. illus. index. $89.00. ISBN 13: 978-1-59884-294-4; 978-1-59884-295-1 (e-book).

This encyclopedia contains 150 entries of geographic terms and concepts. The broad overviews of generalized topics are designed to cover terms and concepts most likely to be encountered by students and teachers of geography. Some entry examples are: agribusiness, deforestation, linguistic geography, cartography, supranationalism, geopolitics, and middle latitude cyclones. Entries range in length from a few paragraphs to a few pages. Interspersed throughout the text are side boxes of relevant content, as well as illustrations and tables. The work includes an index and selected bibliography for further reading. The brief introductory material in this geography encyclopedia requires some knowledge of scientific terms and concepts. This work is recommended for high school level and above.—**Linda M. Turney**

S

127.   **The Kingfisher Geography Encyclopedia.** Boston, Kingfisher/Houghton Mifflin, 2011. 496p. illus. maps. index. $39.99. ISBN 13: 978-0-7534-6575-2.

When opening this book users will begin to explore the world. They will find concise overviews of the historical, cultural, and geographic highlights of more than 200 independent nations and their dependencies. They will first read informative chapters that explain how the world was formed and how weather and climate continue to reshape the earth we inhabit. Users will then begin to move across the globe continent by continent to learn about the countries within each and how each nation is unique and interesting. Fact boxes give key quick reference information for each country: area, population, capital, languages, religion, currency, exports, and government. At the end of the reference users will find summary material discussing the world's major biological habitats, distribution of water resources, wind and ocean currents, and the effect of pollution on our globe as well as health, economic, energy, trade, telecommunications, industrial production, and educational statistics. Square mileage and population data are also provided for the states, provinces, and regions for each nation. Teachers will find this is a good source to use along with a textbook. School librarians will want to share this beautifully illustrated resource with students to give them a context in which to understand world events and to begin their work on school research projects.—**Adrienne Antink**

Travel Guides

General Works

P

128.   **World Heritage Sites: A Complete Guide to 911 UNESCO World Heritage Sites.** 3d ed. Richmond Hills, Ont., Firefly Books, 2011. 856p. illus. maps. index. $29.95. ISBN 13: 978-1 55407-827-1.

The World Heritage Committee operates under the United Nations Educational, Scientific, and Cultural Organization (UNESCO). It was created in 1972 when the building of the Aswan High Dam threatened the destruction of ancient temples and artifacts. It is charged with identifying and safeguarding cultural and natural locations all over the world that represent value to humanity. To date 911 sites in 151 countries in all parts of the world have been inscribed as World Heritage Sites and more continue to be added. This book profiles each site by date of enrollment with a brief description, criteria for selection, a locator map, and photographs. In addition to expected inclusions, such as the Taj Mahal, Venice, Petra, and the Galapagos Islands, there are lesser-known jewels such as the Biatowieza Forest (Belarus and Poland), which is a primeval forest dating back to 8,000 B.C.E. and the only remaining example of the original forest that once covered much of Europe. Another example is Taxila (Pakistan). This city on the Indus, influenced by Persia and Greece, was an important Buddhist center of learning from the fifth century B.C.E. to the second century C.E. World Heritage Sites are also of more recent origin, such as the White City of Tel-Aviv, built between the 1930s and 1950s in accordance with the urban plan of Sir Patrick Geddes and the organic planning principles of the Modern Movement. Sites are indexed by country and alphabetically.—**Adrienne Antink**

9 History

American History

Atlases

C

129.   Eltis, David, and David Richardson. **Atlas of the Transatlantic Slave Trade.** New Haven, Conn., Yale University Press, 2010. 336p. illus. maps. index. $50.00. ISBN 13: 978-0-300-12460-6.

This ground-breaking work provides the most complete picture currently available of the inhumanity of the transatlantic slave trade as it occurred between 1501 and 1867. During this 350-year time period it is estimated that nearly 12.5 million Africans were displaced due to kidnapping or coercion. This work traces that history through the use of 200 maps that were created specifically for this volume. The maps are based on a scholarly online database (http://www.slavevoyages.org) that records some 35,000 slave voyages during this time period (approximately 80 percent of all voyages made). The maps depict which countries were involved, where the captives came from, how the ships were outfitted, and where they ported and sold the enslaved. Text accompanies each map in the form of letters, diary entries, and poems from the time period. The text greatly enhances the use of the maps and help readers grasp the inhumanity of the time.

This work is highly acclaimed and has won numerous scholarly awards. At the reasonable price of $50 this title deserves to be in all academic libraries and most public library collections. [R: LJ, Jan 11, pp. 123-128]—**Shannon Graff Hysell**

Catalogs and Collections

C, P

130.   **American History. http://www.abc-clio.com/Previews/index.aspx.** [Website]. Santa Barbara, Calif., ABC-CLIO. Price negotiated by site. Date reviewed: 2011.

This electronic resource from ABC-CLIO is designed specifically with teachers and students in mind and can be purchased at the middle and high school level, or at the more advanced academic level. They have recently been revamped to provide an even more student friendly design, allowing user to research assigned topics, search for resources to support a topic, or prepare for a class discussion or debate. This Website focuses on American history from the early exploration (1350) to the American Revolution and the establishment of the 13 original colonies. It covers westward expansion, the Civil War, the Industrial Revolution, and the current threat of terrorism, with much more in between. Entries can be viewed chronologically or thematically, and are linked to references, curriculum studies, and analysis of current events. *American History* features information from nearly 15,000 primary and secondary sources, including biographies, government documents, essays, maps, and statistics. The entries discuss such topics as cultures, events, inventions, religious movements, and personalities that have had an impact on U.S. history. Some 3,300 biographies of important figures, 100 topical overviews that explore connections to past and present events, and 150 thematic essays that discuss major themes are covered here. The essays on each topic are thorough and will be easy for students to understand and the photographs and maps are clear.

Searching this site is straightforward. Along with the option to search by keyword or perform an advanced search, users can also click on Explore an Era to browse various time periods or click on Analyze, a new feature that allows students to find key dilemmas in U.S. history and discover different viewpoints or interpretations from academics. When students find the topic they are researching they will also find related entries located in a sidebar, which will further their research.

The *American History* Website is a remarkable tool that will give learning U.S. history new appeal to young adults. Students will enjoy using it and it will give teachers the opportunity to teach U.S. history in a new and exciting format. The new interface is crisp and easy to use, making it ideal for student use. For all of the topics covered and the use it will have in the library, the classroom, and in students' homes this product deserves careful consideration.—**Adrienne Antink**

Dictionaries and Encyclopedias

C, P

131.   **American Centuries: The Ideas, Issues, and Values That Shaped U.S. History.** Karen Ordahl Kupperman, ed. New York, Facts on File, 2011. 5v. illus. index. $495.00/set. ISBN 13: 978-0-8160-7518-8; 978-1-4381-3708-7 (e-book).

This set presents an interesting combination, or marriage if you will, of a chronology and an encyclopedia. The timeline aspect manifests itself in that each volume focuses on a specific hundred year chunk of American history, from the sixteenth century covered in volume 1 to the twentieth century in volume 5. Within each book an alphabetic arrangement of more or less standardized topics allows readers to follow the historical development of subject like clothing styles or scientific discoveries as the years unfold. Obviously, various periods of our collective saga have unique occurrences, and this is reflected in "one shot" articles, such as "Oral Tradition" in the first volume, which discusses the storytelling customs of Native Americans, but is absent in subsequent books of the set. Typical major headings, from 30 to 40 per volume, include Exploration and Discovery, Health and Medicine, Popular and Folk Culture, and War. On the order of five to ten pages in length, these essay style articles are subdivided with headings that not only break the text up into manageable sections but enable the reader to digest the myriad angles contained within a single topic. Each article is signed by its author and concludes with a generous bibliography for further research.

Another departure from standard reference book publishing is that rather than an overall editor-in-chief, each volume of the series is helmed by an individual expert regarding that particular time period. All five volume editors hold doctoral degrees, are either current or retired professors of history at prestigious universities, and are widely published in their respective fields. It will suffice to say that these are folks who know their stuff; ditto for the 140 plus or minus academics who penned the actual articles.

Generally well written, accessible, and factually accurate, the major concern here is that by the concise nature of this set, important details are necessarily conflated, which could give those less familiar with American history an inaccurate picture of the past. A case in point is the discussion of the American Civil War in volume 4 (nineteenth century). Four years of war is distilled into about two pages and based on just what is presented, one might think that Ulysses Grant won the war from the get go. No mention is given of the laundry list of generals Commander-in-Chief Abraham Lincoln had to appoint and then fire beforehand. While this set as a whole presents an excellent overview of the American story, the reader will nevertheless be forced to "fill in the blanks" in some instances.

Special features include a chronology, introductory essay, and cumulative index in each volume of the set; while not profusely illustrated, the black-and-white photographs, political cartoons, and charts do an adequate job of enhancing the text, while adding visual interest. This set is appropriate for all public and academic libraries and is therefore recommended for purchase.—**Michael Francis Bemis**

C, P, S
132.   **Anti-Immigration in the United States: A Historical Encyclopedia.** Kathleen R. Arnold, ed. Santa Barbara, Calif., Greenwood Press/ABC-CLIO, 2011. 2v. illus. index. $180.00/set. ISBN 13: 978-0-313-37521-7; 978-0-313-37521-7 (e-book).

Immigration and anti-immigration are long-playing themes throughout American history. This two-volume encyclopedia provides brief articles that cover topics from Benjamin Franklin and the Alien and Sedition Acts of the eighteenth century to the amnesty proposals and the Clear Law Enforcement for Criminal Alien Removal Act of the twenty-first century. The articles were written by over 100 different authors, largely academics, are generally only a couple of pages long and are well-written summaries of their topics. The articles are accompanied by select bibliographies on the topic. The "English Only Movement" is a typical one that describes attempts at making English an official language in the United States, beginning with efforts by Benjamin Franklin at reforming the customs of the "Palatine Boors" in 1751. The bibliography accompanying the article refers the reader to the Papers of Benjamin Franklin, edited by Leonard Labaree, for further reading. Following the A-Z arrangement of the encyclopedia articles there is a section entitled "Documents" that contain 53 historical documents covering the period from 1751 to 2009. These documents vary in length from 1 to over 20 pages in length. Typical is one from E. M. Davis to Abraham Lincoln dated 13 June 1860 that relates Davis' opinion about Lincoln's status a proponent of the Know-Nothing party. Following the documents section, there are three term paper type essays. The first covers "Immigration Laws and Policy from 1965-2009," the second is entitled "Colonial Period Up to the 1965 Immigration Act," and the third has the title "The U.S. Political Community: Anti-immigration Sentiment and Issues of Race, Class, Gender, Conscience, and Political Belief." These short papers are around 10 pages in length and are accompanied by notes and sources and further reading. It's not clear what the purpose of these essays are (and the introduction does not mention them), but readers I guess can use them for outlines for getting started with longer term papers. These essays are followed by an appendix that consists of eight tables of data relating to immigration to the United States during the twenty-first century. The encyclopedia concludes with a select bibliography, an index, and a list of contributors.

Overall, the work is well done, with many articles being illustrated by black-and-white photographs. On occasion there are strange lapses such as the article on "Vigilante Movement" that cites a paper by Sylvanna Falcan in Social Justice entitled "Rape as a Weapon at the U.S.-Mexico Border;" the paper is mentioned in the text, but not cited in either the article bibliography nor in the bibliography at the end of the book. This work covers the topic in a well-researched and sensitive manner. The two-volume set belongs in all American libraries.—**Ralph Lee Scott**

C, S
133.   **The Settlement of America: Encyclopedia of Westward Expansion from Jamestown to the Closing of the Frontier.** James A. Crutchfield, ed. Armonk, N.Y., M. E. Sharpe, 2011. 2v. illus. maps. index. $249.00/set. ISBN 13: 978-0-7656-1984-6.

Crutchfield and his co-editors, Candy Moulton and Terry A. Del Bene, have created a workmanlike and traditionally organized encyclopedia of entries on people, places, and events germane to the westward growth of first colonial America and then of the United States. It is an era of U.S. history that does not have a robust bibliography, unlike the eras of colonial and revolutionary America. The latter has seen a great increase in sources lately, with such publications as Paul A. Gilje's *Encyclopedia of Revolutionary America* (see ARBA 2011, entry 388), Rodney P. Carlisle's *The Colonial and Revolutionary Era: Beginnings to 1783* (see ARBA 2010, entry 394), and *Daily Life During the American Revolution*, edited by Dorothy Denneen Volo and James M. Volo (see ARBA 2004, entry 455). This current publication will add to a neglected area.

The entries are usually from half a page to a page and a half, although major topics such as Elections can cover several pages. In addition, several introductory essays on such subjects as railroads, the fur trade, and the gold rush, are more lengthy and help pull the threads of the entries together. Each entry has a brief list of further reading, and also cross-references to other entries. Supplementary material include more than the standard bibliography and index. Helpful in giving a broad picture is the chronology, beginning with the 1607 landing at Jamestown and ending with the 1890 declaration by the U.S. Census Bureau that the era of westward expansion was over. This chronology allows a student to see the progression of westward expansion and its costs as well. One can see how expansion was both aided by and drove technological improvements; for example, the push of railroads further and further west. It also shows the expansion of civil rights; for example, Wyoming was the first territory or state to allow women to vote, and some national initiatives began with the opening up of the west, including the national park system which began with Yellowstone in Wyoming. Also revealed by the chronology is how westward expansion pushed out native peoples; the great cost in lives of various conflicts between settlers and native people; and how the searing issue of slavery was debated within the context of expanding territory.

For the person seeking more information than is contained in the entries, the editors provide a section of primary documents, including official proclamations such as the Northwest Ordinance and the Louisiana Purchase Treaty, interviews with important figures such as Daniel Boone, and first-hand accounts of travels and explorations by fur traders and a survivor of the infamous Donner party. Illustrations are a bit sparse, and more maps might have been included, but this is an encyclopedia that should be considered by both high school and undergraduate libraries.—**Terry Ann Mood**

C, S

134.   Snodgrass, Mary Ellen. **The Civil War Era and Reconstruction: An Encyclopedia of Social, Political, Cultural, and Economic History.** Armonk, N.Y., M. E. Sharpe, 2011. 2v. illus. maps. index. $249.00/set. ISBN 13: 978-0-7656-8257-4.

Battles and leaders, leaders and battles—the Civil War years were marked by tumult and progress far beyond the fields of battle in economics, politics, technology, education, diplomacy, and society, all well documented in this useful two-volume work. Following four brief introductory essays, in excess of 325 entries relate the nonmilitary people, places, and events of the Civil War and Reconstruction era. Other features include 33 documents, a brief chronology, glossary, bibliography, and extensive index. Considering the wide scope of the encyclopedia entries, the index is essential. Finally, a handful of illustrations dot the volumes.

The entries are well written yet concise, with suggested further readings. Examples include developments in the steel industry, the contested election of 1876, New York's draft riots, and the 1871 Chicago fire. Entries on publications and publishing, railroads, Indians, travel, government agencies, and women are reminders that America during the war and tragic era was a vibrant still developing country. Among the documents are two Walt Whitman poems and an excerpt for Geronimo's life story. The chronology is a bonus and should have been placed at the beginning of the work. Overall, this is a model reference work on a subject of critical interest to students designed for the high school and college library.—**Boyd Childress**

Handbooks and Yearbooks

C, S

135.   **Daily Life Through American History in Primary Documents.** Randall M. Miller, ed. Santa Barbara, Calif., Greenwood Press/ABC-CLIO, 2012. 4v. illus. maps. index. $399.00/set. ISBN 13: 978-1-61069-032-4.

Organized chronologically and topically, this four-volume set presents more than 200 selected primary documents drawn from American history to provide insights into how American life in past eras really was. The volumes are arranged according to time period: The Colonial Period through the American Revolution; The American Revolution to the Civil War; The Civil War to World War I; and World War I to the Present. Each volume begins with a historical overview that sets the stage for the period and provides analytical introductions to the selected documents. The documents are varied in that they represent all types of people—men, women, children, free born, slaves, and immigrants. The documents include diaries, letters, memoirs, speeches, sermons, pamphlets, and both public and private writings. Many of the documents have black-and-white illustrations interspersed depicting life during that time period, and each document begins with biographical information about the author. Supplementary materials included in this set include a chronology, lists of suggested readings, and an index.

The nice thing about using primary documents in historical research is that they provide a first-person look at life during a specific time period, depicting true emotions, language used during that era, and varying perspectives of a topic. This set would serve nicely alongside Greenwood Press's other Daily Life series titles and the *Greenwood Encyclopedia of Daily Life in America* (see ARBA 2010, entry 380). *Daily Life Through American History in Primary Documents* would be a useful and worthwhile addition to high school, undergraduate, and large public libraries.—**Brian T. Gallagher**

Asian History

Singapore

C, P, S

136.   Abshire, Jean E. **The History of Singapore.** Santa Barbara, Calif., Greenwood Press/ABC-CLIO, 2011. 179p. maps. index. (The Greenwood Histories of the Modern Nations). $49.95. ISBN 13: 978-0-313-37742-6.

Singapore is a small country, only 3 ½ times the size of Washington, D.C. Yet it has a GDP ranking of 48th out of the 227 countries in the world. How did it go from being one of the world's poorest countries in the 1960s to its current affluence? This book answers the question by tracing the historical, ethnic, political, and economic roots of modern-day Singapore, including how the British colonial experience and the Japanese occupation during World War II influenced today's Singapore. The author shows how the diversity of its people and the globalization of world trade have been constant themes from Singapore's earliest history as a trade crossroads along the Maritime Silk Road, long before the Europeans arrived, to the city's global reputation today for finance, technology, shipping and oil refining. Abshire also explains how Singapore's government-managed economy pursued a strategy of export led industrialization and the use of government-led companies in key industries to build its economic success. Features include a section on notable people in Singapore's history, including Lee Kwan Yew who was the first prime minister of Singapore and considered the father of modern Singapore; a timeline of major events; a glossary; and a bibliographic essay.—**Adrienne Antink**

European History

General Works

C

137.   Rosser, John H. **Historical Dictionary of Byzantium.** 2d ed. Lanham, Md., Scarecrow, 2012. 591p. (Historical Dictionaries of Ancient Civilizations and Historical Eras). $110.00; $109.99 (e-book). ISBN 13: 978-0-8108-7567-8; 978-0-8108-7477-0 (e-book).

Rosser's introduction to this concise volume opens up to the inquirer a wealth of information about Byzantium and the Byzantine Empire (324-1453), the conventional terms for the Roman Empire in this period. Overlooked in most general history studies, Byzantium-contemporary and ancient Constantinople lie at the historic center of the Eastern Orthodox Church (Christian), and the Byzantine Empire represents the Roman Empire as its locus moved east following the founding of Constantinople in 324 during the reign of Constantine. The existence of the Byzantine Empire for over a millennium, even with a short break after its disastrous defeat by the Fourth Crusade in 1204, resulted in a rich culture that flowed historically into the European Renaissance. Nevertheless, visitors to modern Greece, heir to the Byzantine tradition, will find that the tourist industry exhibits little interest in it, catering rather to the ancient rather than the medieval materials and artifacts.

Having given the reader a brief overview of Byzantine history, including a very detailed chronology, the dictionary's author presents the individuals, offices, places, and things that comprised this lesser-known empire. The entries in this 2d edition have been expanded since the publication of the 1st edition (2001) and specific topics such as transportation and gender have been included this time around. As presented, the volume readily lends itself for use in the context of discussions about Byzantine history, culture, artifacts, religion, and related topics; bibliography for which the author provides at the end of the book. This extensive bibliography, more than 75 pages in length, along with related photographs, maps, and site plans, make this volume a valuable asset for any major public library and virtually all college and university libraries as well as for the private libraries of medievalists and medieval aficionados.—**Susan Tower Hollis**

Latin America and the Caribbean

C, P

138.   Jefferson, Ann, and Paul Lokken. **Daily Life in Colonial Latin America.** Santa Barbara, Calif., Greenwood Press/ABC-CLIO, 2011. 222p. index. (The Greenwood Press Daily Life Through History Series). $49.95. ISBN 13: 978-0-313-34070-3; 978-1-57356-744-2 (e-book).

This is one of the latest historical overviews from the Greenwood Press Daily Life Through History Series. The authors capture the 300-year history of Latin America from 1492, when Columbus discovered the Mexican-Aztec-Inca empires ruling in the northern areas of the Americas, and they continue the saga to the Independence-era of 1800-1825. The emphasis here is to show the daily lives of the people of the Latin American colonial period. It covers from Mexico to the colonies of South America, colonies of the Iberian monarchs.

The authors, Ann Jefferson and Paul Lokken, researched archival documents about the Latin Americans, made up of the indigenous people of the Western Hemisphere, the European invaders, and the Africans who were brought against their will as slave laborers, have focused on the African slaves. They found that 60 percent of the African slaves migrated to Latin American and Brazil, the Spanish Caribbean. They found the African slaves played a more integral role in the Inca, Mayan, and Mexican natives' society than had previously been noted. They created their own unique working society, and the authors have provided their stories to illustrate their daily lives in the Latin America.

There is a chronology, glossary, annotated bibliography, and a good index for this interesting updated history of the people of Latin America. This new Latin American history is highly recommended for public and academic libraries.—**Kay M. Stebbins**

Middle Eastern History

P, S

139.   **Ancient Egypt and the Near East: An Illustrated History.** Tarrytown, N.Y., Marshall Cavendish, 2011. 144p. illus. maps. index. $59.95. ISBN 13: 978-0-7614-7934-5.

This slim volume covering eight civilizations of the ancient eastern Mediterranean world presents its materials through clear writing with many illustrations and additional text boxes. It represents part of a series of such volumes, others of which look at ancient Greece and ancient Rome. This volume was developed, according to the author of the foreword, Michele Ronnick, in recognition that knowledge of humanity's achievement predates by far the customary, at least until recently, starting points of Greece, Rome, and the Bible. Thus, this volume examines ancient Egypt with its three major periods, each in separate chapters—the Sumerians; the Babylonians; the Hittites; the Phoenicians; the Assyrians; the Israelites; and the Persians—although it provides little sense of the relation of the Sumerians, the Babylonians, and the Assyrians in the area. By beginning with the Egyptians and then the Sumerians, the reader becomes acquainted with the earliest development of writing, cities, and other aspects of civilization that undergird today's western civilizations. That the focus comes from a western perspective is clear from the second part of the title, "Near East," which works only for those peoples in the countries related to the Atlantic Ocean.

In general, the content is solid and appropriate for its target audience, the middle and high school student. Of some concern, however, is its lack of any bibliography for those young people wishing to explore further. It does include cross-references, a short glossary, and a solid index. In the end the volume should make a valuable addition to the middle and high school library as well as a public library. The publisher indicates that it appears in e-book format as well.—**Susan Tower Hollis**

C, P, S

140.   Kia, Mehrdad. **Daily Life in the Ottoman Empire.** Santa Barbara, Calif., Greenwood Press/ABC-CLIO, 2011. 294p. illus. index. (The Greenwood Press Daily Life Through History Series). $49.95. ISBN 13: 978-0-313-33692-8; 978-0-313-06402-9 (e-book).

As the introduction states, this volume seeks "to provide the general reader with a series of selective representations of daily life in the Ottoman Empire" (p. xiv) rather than an in-depth comprehensive study of the widely varied groups that comprised the Ottoman Empire with their many disparate ways as developed over nearly six centuries. And this it does well in a readable and comprehensive style. Ultimately it provides a solid basis for understanding life in the Ottoman Empire, including far more history than the early "historical" chapter suggests, since history of various sorts appears in many if not most of the succeeding chapters. Ultimately, its importance lies in its presentation of history and daily life in the area as foundational for understanding the modern Middle East.

The first three chapters introduce the reader to the historical, ruling, and governing context of daily life, while the remaining 10 chapters look at the different groups of people and their areas of life. The various people covered include merchants, craftspeople, and peasants in cities, towns, and villages; those in religious communities, addressing such topics as Muslims, Islamic law and education, and Sufi orders and popular culture; and chapters addressing family life and activities related to food and celebrations, games and sport, and sickness and death. The discussions in each chapter are supported by extensive endnotes, and the volume concludes with a selective bibliography including not only print resources but films and documentaries as well as Websites, concluding with a solid index.

Overall, these features make it very accessible to general readers, including students at levels from advanced middle school through the first years of college. Thus this Daily Life volume deserves a place in high school, college, and public libraries, particularly given its reasonable price.—**Susan Tower Hollis**

World History

Atlases

C, P

141.   Haywood, John. **The New Atlas of World History: Global Events at a Glance.** Princeton, N.J., Princeton University Press, 2011. 252p. illus. maps. index. $49.50. ISBN 13: 978-0-691-15269-1.

This book selects some 50 representative dates from prehistory to the present, and provides for each year a short introduction indicating why the time frame is significant in multiple points across the globe, a political map, and a timeline with key political and cultural events around the world leading up to that date. Interspersed in the work are thematic maps on topics such as the world's religions, trade routes, writing systems, migration trends, and more. For each profiled year the five largest cities in the world are given. A few samples of the dates included are 500 C.E., which saw the fall of the Roman Empire and the rise of the first empires in the Andes, 712 and the Arab conquests, and the Treaty of Utrecht in 1715 when Britain emerged as a major power and the height of the Cold War in 1975. For example we learn, in 1650 France became the dominant power in Europe and the Manchus conquered China. Istanbul was the largest city in the world followed by Beijing and Paris. Galileo was being persecuted for heresy and the Baroque architecture style was beginning in Italy. The timelines and maps give the reader digestible snapshots to see recurring themes across continents and time periods. This reference puts historical events in context rather than seeing them only in isolation.—**Adrienne Antink**

Dictionaries and Encyclopedias

C, S

142.   **Ancient and Medieval History Online. http://www.infobase.com/.** [Website]. New York, Facts on File. Price negotiated by site. Date reviewed: 2012.

Ancient and Medieval World History Online pulls all of its information from Facts on File's extensive list of print titles. It is written and designed for use by middle and high school age students and will be particularly useful for teachers and librarians to use as a teaching and research tool. It covers world history from prehistory through the 1500s (users will find information on 1500 to present day in Facts on File's *Modern World History Online* [see ARBA 2012, entry 499]). Coverage includes ancient Egypt, ancient Mesopotamia, ancient Greece, ancient and medieval Asia, and the Islamic Empire. Users will find thousands of subject entries, biographies, maps and charts, primary sources, and timeline entries. As with all Facts on File databases, this one includes an extensive list of videos that will appeal to students as well. A new "Focus on History through Video" feature has recently been added to the homepage to spotlight key videos. A dictionary tool defines some 34,000 words that may be unfamiliar to students. Another key feature in the Facts on File databases are the Topic Centers, which pull interesting entries to help users find a starting point for their research. Each Topic Center and each record has a persistent record link, enabling teachers and librarians to direct their students to specific areas of study.

The site can be searched by keyword, phrase, or person, and can be browsed by topic, era, or region. Biographies can also be browsed by occupation, Primary Sources by type, and the Timeline by year. Full citations are available throughout, and users can print, copy, and save to a folder content for personal use. There is also a special "Focus On" features that provides an in-depth look at relevant topics or figures. This site will be useful to students in the middle and high school grades researching on this topic.—**Shannon Graff Hysell**

S

143.   **Daily Life Through History. http://www.abc-clio.com/Previews/index.aspx.** [Website]. Santa Barbara, Calif., ABC-CLIO. Price negotiated by site. Date reviewed: 2011.

This database, compiled from more than 75 titles in the Greenwood Daily Life series, offers various combinations of access to a wealth of materials on history, culture, religion, economics, people, and so forth. The main components currently are *Daily Life Through History*, *Daily Life in America*, and *World Folklore and Folklife*. Access to the site can be purchased for either the middle and high school audience or the academic audience. The site is designed to promote critical thinking skills through the use of "Analyze" sections that pose intriguing questions and offer various viewpoints. Students will enjoy the video files and multitude of full-color images, while educators will find the lesson plans useful (all lesson plans are correlated to state and National Council for Social Studies standards). Users will be able to study literature, social and religious practices, art, music, language, and more across a variety of time periods. The site also includes content from Greenwood's culture cookbooks, holiday titles, and teen life around the world. It is an invaluable resource for both students and teachers.—**Catherine Barr**

C, S

144.   Horvitz, Leslie Alan, and Christopher Catherwood. **Encyclopedia of War Crimes and Genocide.** rev. ed. New York, Facts on File, 2011. 2v. illus. index. (Facts on File Library of World History). $150.00/ set. ISBN 13: 978-0-8160-8083-0; 978-1-4381-3486-4 (e-book).

The revision to this 2006 encyclopedia updates entries and includes a section of primary documents for ready reference (see ARBA 2007, entry 422, for a review of the 1st edition). There are a total of 8 documents, which range from international documents such as the Geneva Convention to the 1935 Nazi regulation, the Nuremberg Laws on Citizenship and Health. The *Encyclopedia* concludes with an extensive bibliography and information on relevant organizations.

Entries range from half a page to three pages and each include a bibliography. This encyclopedia is mostly focused on the atrocities of World War II to the present, although a few entries do go back to the late nineteenth century. While this encyclopedia explicitly covers war crimes, it also has numerous entries on human rights violations. Many of these entries focus on human rights violations in specific countries. There are some pictures, but it would have been useful if maps had been included as well. This is a very good encyclopedia that introduces difficult topics with concise entries and useful bibliographies for further research. It is recommended for high school and undergraduate collections.—**Allen Reichert**

C, P

145.   **Slavery in the Modern World: A History of Political, Social, and Economic Oppression.** Junius P. Rodriguez, ed. Santa Barbara, Calif., ABC-CLIO, 2011. 2v. illus. index. $189.00/set. ISBN 13: 978-1-85109-783-8; 978-1-85109-788-3 (e-book).

The very title of this book, *Slavery in the Modern World*, would appear to beg anachronism, but, alas, it does not. While we have come a long way, we have not thrown off human nature's seemingly inherent penchant for making slaves of one another, if not in indentured fashion, then something more heinous still. While we may be the most technologically sophisticated creatures ever to have roamed the earth, that sophistication has managed only to make us ever more adroit than ever in capturing and enslaving each other. The Web has further enhanced our skills so at someone in Peoria can, de facto or otherwise, enslave another in Phuket.

A quick look at these two hefty volumes proves in spades your mother's maxim that your sins will find you out. From the earliest "legal" slavery of the Greco-Roman world, to the earliest beginnings of our own country, to today's enslavements in the Arabian Peninsula and Ethiopia, slavery of some kind appeared and shows no signs of vanishing anytime soon. Unfortunately, our tendency to make any sort of routinized duty equivalent to slavery trivializes the all-too real. Make no mistake about: real slavery still exists today, both in the remote and less civilized part of the world, to the most urbane and modernized parts of our own United States. The volume's opening chapter should be required reading of every adult, chronicling as it does past sins and continuing transgressions both here and abroad.

Articles about the main figures, either enslaved or enslaving, pepper the volume: Harriet Tubman, Samuel White Baker, Zafaryab Ahmed, and Marcus Garvey, to name a few. Other articles outline the sex trade, Jim Crow laws, the Dred Scott decision, and the Gulag of the former Soviet Union. Articles on various organizations and/or movements to end various kinds of slavery also inform.

While slavery as most Americans have to come to understand it does not exist within our borders, enslavement of the unprotected remains entrenched: from debt bondage that may have influenced at least some of early Occupy Wall Street participants, to forced prostitution of men, women, and children made easily available via Web, slavery flourishes. Even freedom has enslaved, as some of the poverty-stricken of the disintegrated Soviet Union have come, sadly, to know. These volumes are necessary for many reasons, not the least of which is to remind us that however advanced we have become, we still have a very long way to go. [R: LJ, Jan 12, p. 130]—**Mark Y. Herring**

Handbooks and Yearbooks

C, P

146. **Popular Controversies in World History: Investigating History's Intriguing Questions.** Steven L. Danver, ed. Santa Barbara, Calif., ABC-CLIO, 2011. 4v. illus. index. $380.00/set. ISBN 13: 978-1-59884-077-3; 978-1-59884-078-0 (e-book).

The impetus for this four-volume set was the editor's concern that his students did not always understand the fundamental need for critical thinking when approaching the study of history. This encyclopedia was developed to focus students from a secondary or post-secondary level on evaluating topics that continue to be debated within the field of history. Similar to the popular Opposing Viewpoints series, 53 different historical controversies are presented with short essays in a pro/con format. Twenty-two authors contributed to this set and each argument includes a bibliography. Topics often include black-and-white images or maps, and an occasional side bar to provide more detailed information on a concept germane to the argument. Each volume contains an index for that volume.

The pro and con essays range between ten to twenty pages in length and clearly synthesize the topic and argue the position. However, the main drawback to this encyclopedia is the selection of topics. There does not seem to be any clear criteria, other than representing broad historic eras across four volumes, as to why certain topics were chosen. Even the title doesn't quite match the topics. Popular controversies suggest known issues in history, but topics on ancestral Puebloan communication and the death of Warren G. Harding do not fit this title. A clearer discussion of why topics were included, or even highlighting why particular topics are important, would have strengthened this work considerably. However, even with this regrettable flaw, the topics are well presented and nicely highlight the importance of critical evaluation in the field of history. Recommended for most libraries.—**Allen Reichert**

10 Law

General Works

Dictionaries and Encyclopedias

C, P

147.   **Encyclopedia of Drug Policy.** Mark A. R. Kleiman and James E. Hawdon, eds. Thousand Oaks, Calif., Sage, 2011. 2v. illus. index. $350.00/set; $440.00 (e-book). ISBN 13: 978-1-4129-7695-4; 978-1-4129-7696-1 (e-book).

Drug policy as it pertains to recreational drug use is a hot topic. The United States has been campaigning against illicit drugs for 100 years and waging war against them for 40 years, but people are still using them. This encyclopedia looks at drug policy from many points of view.

The editors and contributors are academics affiliated with universities, medical institutions, and government agencies. They have written 450 alphabetic entries covering all aspects of drug policy. They include articles about court cases (*Gore v. United States*, *People v. Woody*), conferences and conventions (Narcotics Limitation Convention of 1931, 1909 Shanghai Conference), countries affecting U.S. drug policy (Afghanistan, Colombia), drug trade and trafficking (cocaine cartels, drugs and money laundering), laws and policies (criminal justice/enforcement strategies of drug control, drug courts), organizations and agencies (Alcoholics Anonymous, Federal Bureau of Narcotics), people (John Stuart Mill, Myles Ambrose), presidential administrations (Nixon Administration, Clinton Administration), treatment and addiction (12-step programs, Harm reduction), and types of drugs (alcohol, hallucinogens). The first volume includes a chronology of drug policy from 1791 through 2010. Volume 2 has a resource guide, a glossary, and two appendixes containing Richard Nixon's remarks on signing the Comprehensive Drug Abuse Prevention and Control Act of 1970 and an excerpt from the updated Controlled Substances Act.

With broad coverage and diverse points of view, this encyclopedia examines a topic that is both current and important. It belongs in both academic and public libraries.—**Barbara M. Bibel**

C, P

148.   Leiter, Richard A., and Roy M. Mersky. **Landmark Supreme Court Cases: The Most Influential Decisions of the Supreme Court of the United States.** 2d ed. New York, Facts on File, 2012. 3v. index. $250.00/set. ISBN 13: 978-0-8160-6957-6; 978-1-4381-3742-1 (e-book).

This compendium of more than 600 capsule accounts of Supreme Court cases is organized into 23 topical areas (e.g., Death Penalty, Intellectual Property, Privacy) and a catchall section of "Additional Cases." Each entry is segmented as follows: "Case Title," "Legal Citations," "Year of Decision," "Key Issues," "History of the Case," "Summary of Arguments," "Decision," "Aftermath," "Significance," "Related Cases," and "Recommended Reading." A significant change within this set is that the court cases are now listed chronologically rather than alphabetically, making it easier to track the historical progression of the Court's thinking. This edition has also been significant expanded, from 300 legal cases to more than 300, and from one volume to a three-volume set. Most significant that students will be researching are included: *Roe v. Wade*, *Dred Scott v. Sandford*, *Bush v. Gore*, and *Rumsfeld v. Padilla*. The work concludes with a list of cases by title, the Constitution of the United States, a glossary, and a selected bibliography. This work will be a worthwhile addition to academic and public libraries.—**Jack Ray**

C, P

149.   **The U.S. Justice System: An Encyclopedia.** Steven Harmon Wilson, ed. Santa Barbara, Calif., ABC-CLIO, 2012. 3v. index. $294.00/set. ISBN 13: 978-1-59884-304-0.

As Americans we often take our justice system for granted assuming that "liberty and justice for all" is a way of life. In fact, the U.S. justice system is a complicated system that is continually evolving. This three-volume work is an overall resource detailing the structure, people, rights, and legal protections of our country. Volume 1 provides essays on the organization of the justice system at the federal, state, and local level. The essays also cover public law litigation and public interest law, the criminal justice system, the civil justice system, and criminal procedures. Volume 2 is the encyclopedic section of the set that alphabetically lists definitions for hundreds of law-related topics, including major figures in the judicial system, legal statistics, individual laws, and legal terms. The entries often provide cross-references as well as lists of further resources. The third volume is a selection of primary source documents, including statutes, texts of cases relevant in the U.S. judicial system, and specific cases. The set provides a comprehensive bibliography, a glossary, and an index. Overall, this work is written in a way that undergraduates and the educated layperson will understand. It is thorough in that it covers both federal and state issues and the editor has mad every attempt to deliver the material in a way that is nonpartisan and balanced. This will be a useful resource for undergraduate libraries as well as larger public libraries.—**John W. Storey**

Handbooks and Yearbooks

P

150.   Doskow, Emily, and Marcia Stewart. **The Legal Answer Book for Families.** Berkeley, Calif., Nolo Press, 2011. 370p. index. $24.99pa. ISBN 13: 978-1-4133-1373-4.

The Legal Answer Book for Families is ideal for those families struggling with the best way to deal with all aspects of family legal matters, including the areas of couples (e.g., spousal debt, divorce, name changes), children (e.g., foster care, child support, bullying), and seniors (e.g., government programs for residential care, healthcare power of attorney). Nearly every family will have legal concerns or questions at some point in their lifetime and this book is a good starting point for basic information. The book is arranged into 9 chapters: "Marriage," "Divorce," "Child Custody," "Child Support," "Adoption," "Children," "Elder Care," "Wills and Estate Planning," and "Lawyers." Each begins with a comprehensive chapter outline so that the user can go directly to their area of interest. The chapters are written in an easy-to-read and conversational style. The work is designed to be either read through as a text or to be consulted as a reference. Sidebars with interesting facts or scenarios appear throughout the volume. The final chapter discusses when it is most appropriate to get help from a lawyer, how to find low-cost lawyers, and how to help your lawyer to make a successful case. Two appendixes round out the volume: a list of state rules and resources on marriage and divorce laws as well as child support and custody laws; and resources to consult for more information on adoption and elder care questions. Public libraries should have a copy of this work on hand for patrons needing this type of help.—**Shannon Graff Hysell**

Criminology and Criminal Justice

Chronology

C, P

151. Cawthon, Elisabeth A. **Famous Trials in History.** New York, Facts on File, 2012. 463p. index. $85.00. ISBN 13: 978-0-8160-8167-7; 978-1-4381-3709-4 (e-book).

Throughout recorded human history certain trials have achieved iconic status: they are the focus of significant public attention (and fascination), they bring into sharp relief some especially challenging moral and social conundrums with which human societies must grapple, and they become a reference point for historical discussions and debates. These trials most typically feature famous people, sensational circumstances, and significant events, or some combination of these.

The author of the present volume, Elisabeth A. Cawthon, teaches at the University of Texas in Arlington, and has a special interest in legal history. She has published previously on such history, most notably with a book on *Medicine on Trial* (see ARBA 2005, entry 545). She addresses here 100 trials that have occurred during the course of human history, with the first of these the trial of Socrates in 399 B.C.E. and the last of these the trial of Kaing Guck Eav in 2010. Any culturally literate person, at least within the Western tradition, is familiar with the trial of Socrates; the most recent trial addressed in this volume, known as the killing fields trial, was of the commander of the notorious Tuol Sleng prison in Cambodia where huge numbers of innocent citizens were tortured and murdered during the notorious regime of the Khmer Rouge (between 1975 and 1979). As it happens, in 2011—more than 30 years after the horrific crimes committed by the Khmer Rouge—several other surviving leaders of this regime (all in their eighties) were also on trial in Cambodia. In the United States the trials of "tot mom" Casey Anthony, accused of murdering her two-year-old daughter, and Conrad Murray, the physician accused of being responsible for the death of pop singer icon Michael Jackson, were two "famous" trials in 2011. So such trials now occur on a regular basis. As to the balance of the 98 trials here addressed, some are quite universally famous (e.g., the trials of Jesus, Martin Luther, King Louis XIV and Queen Marie Antoinette, John Brown, the surviving Nazi leadership in Nuremberg and Adolf Eichmann in Jerusalem, O. J. Simpson), but many others are far less familiar, other than to students of the history of some time or place (e.g., the trials of John Italos, Bapaji, Vera Zasulich, Aleck Bourne, and in the case of the Ienaga textbook). Each trial is recounted within the following template: key issues; history of the case; summary of arguments; verdict; significance; and further reading. These accounts are well written and informative, and the author admirably draws upon a wide range of documentary sources, in addition to secondary sources and monographs. In her introduction to the volume she notes that the Internet has made trial materials much more widely available, but she limits her reliance upon commentary found on Internet sites. Needless to say, for some of the trials addressed there is a huge literature stretching over many centuries; in the case of some other trials the relevant literature is much more limited.

There are, of course, other reference works on famous or celebrated trials. The author of this review, for example, reviewed Scott P. Johnson's two-volume *Trials of the Century* in 2010 (see ARBA 2011, entry 434), although that work was limited to American trials. But librarians will have to make their own determination on whether the present volume duplicates or complements such reference works they may already have in their collections, and whether they serve a clientele that will be likely to find a hard-copy reference work on famous trials useful for their own purposes. Certainly readers who consult this volume—or choose to read it from cover to cover—will learn much of interest, and will be favored with a pleasurable reading experience.—**David O. Friedrichs**

Dictionaries and Encyclopedias

C, S

152.   **Encyclopedia of School Crime and Violence.** Laura L. Finley, ed. Santa Barbara, Calif., ABC-CLIO, 2011. 2v. illus. index. $173.00/set. ISBN 13: 978-0-313-36238-5; 978-0-313-36239-2 (e-book).

Encyclopedia of School Crime and Violence, edited by Laura L. Finley, presents a significant literary contribution that addresses and acknowledges the severe consequences that school violence generates in modern society. School violence serves as a reminder and disturbing mirror image of the current culture. This powerful two-volume edition represents a vital and comprehensive research tool for understanding troubling social, psychological, and historical implications that impact elementary, high school, and college campus violence. The cover serves as an immediate reminder of the pain survivors and those left behind to grief must endure. It links and contrasts the horror and innocence when revealing a make-shift memorial and stuffed bear that is familiar to readers who peruse library shelves. The content includes notorious acts of school violence, including Columbine and Virginia Tech. However, additional entries examine less serious offenses that may serve as lead-up activities to homicidal attacks including: insidious problems of theft, bullying, cybercrime, violence, sexual assault, and more. The comprehensive approach applies the case study method, a worthy endeavor when examining the factual issues of violence.

Encyclopedia of School Crime and Violence suggests the need for a primary violence prevention strategy that would address the community's public health requirements. Programming strategies would include: emotional intelligence education that promotes empathy, forgiveness, and resiliency skills. Encyclopedic entries examine critical topics that address violence avoidance, and effective policies that encourage peaceful solutions. The Timeline of Significant Events Related to School Crime and Violence immediately captures reader attention. The case study scenarios suggest the need for secondary prevention strategies that identify unstable and potentially vulnerable offenders. In addition, the text recommends tertiary prevention strategies for victim counseling and restorative justice programming.

This set explores a series of explanations and theories in the momentous challenge to examine historic violent incidents. The text also reminds readers how tolerance for lesser offenses constructs a social fabric for violent social climates. The work recommends insightful research and comprehensive crime analysis that serves to initiate and support proactive preventative programming. Micro-level crime analysis of causes creates opportunities for successful remedial actions. For example, bulling and abusive behaviors may lead to rage directed at others, death ideation, or suicide impulse.

The series of over 80 A-Z entries, authored by over 30 professional experts, comprise scholarly presentations that illuminate critical issues. The multi-disciplinary approach examines potential responses and crime prevention strategies. A few representative examples of many exceptional entries include: Bullying in High Schools; Canada and School Crime and Violence; Columbine High School Massacre; Emergency Response Plans; Professor-Perpetrated Crimes; and South America and School Crime and Violence. Each concise entry offers readers the option to supplement subject matter investigation, by documenting further readings, plus a full bibliography of recommended books, journals, and websites at the end of each volume.

Reader-friendly fonts, appropriate line-spacing, and a comprehensive index system enhance research and encourage sustained topic inspection. The recommended readings, extension activities related to school and campus crime and violence, and discussion questions are useful tools for content review, thoughtful deliberation and insightful debate. Moreover, among the most valuable resources are the appendixes: Important Federal Legislation Related to School and Campus Crime and Violence; Primary Source Documents: Sample Legislation: K-12 Public Schools; Primary Source Documents: Sample Legislation: Colleges and Universities; U. S. Supreme Court Cases Related to School and Campus Crime and Violence; and U. S. Supreme Court Decisions Relevant to School Crime and Violence.

Encyclopedia of School Crime and Violence will find widespread acceptance and circulation throughout law enforcement agencies. In addition, library acquisitions will elect to include this text in comprehensive collections that strive to serve private and public needs. Elementary schools, high schools, colleges, and school systems throughout the United States would find the information presented in both volumes essential reading to preventing school crime and violence. International markets will also appreciate the coverage of topics that expand outside the United States. The set illustrates the following reality: School violence and crime are difficult to predict and timely responses to school crime and violence vary. Many remedial responses are seldom evaluated. Case study analysis illustrates difficulties confronted by communities in their efforts to prevent random violence. Offenders vary in their motivation and modus operandi (MO). School crimes and violence can occur at any time and at every level of our educational system: students, former students, random offenders, and even educators may perpetuate the violence. The author, contributors, and publisher offer a superior contribution to assist in the reduction of school crime and violence. [R: BL, Jan 1 &15, 2012, p. 64]—**Thomas E. Baker**

C, P
153.   **Women Criminals: An Encyclopedia of People and Issues.** Vickie Jensen, ed. Santa Barbara, Calif., ABC-CLIO, 2012. 2v. index. $189.00/set. ISBN 13: 978-0-313-33713-0; 978-0-313-06826-3 (e-book).

This two-volume set takes an in-depth look at women who have been arrested and called criminals. It explores the motivation behind women and crime, the psychology, and the various ways society looks at and treats women criminals. Some of the women profiled here are true criminals—committing such heinous crimes as homicide, kidnapping, and assault. Others, like activists, Angela Davis and Dolores Huerta, while considered criminals under the law, are actually motivated by a deeper calling. The first volume discusses the reasons behind female crime, the role race and age play in crime, and the response to females in the criminal justice system. It is arranged into essays written by a wide range of contributors, most of which are scholars in the areas of criminal law, sociology, psychology, and political science. The second and larger volume is a biographical dictionary of women criminals throughout modern history. The entries are several pages in length and provide details of the woman's life, circumstances leading up to the crime, the crime itself, and how it was dealt with by the criminal justice system. Several black-and-white photographs are presented as well as lists of resources for further study. Volume 2 concludes with four appendixes listing arrests, offenders according to victimization data, prisoners and the death penalty, and the death penalty for female offenders. A bibliography and an index round out the volume.

The editor has made every attempt to make this work as broad in scope as possible. The individual stories connect to the larger social-scientific perspective behind each crime. Crime and criminal justice are popular topics in both academic and public libraries and this work is appropriate for both. It is scholarly enough for the undergraduate doing research on the topic but will be easily understood by the general public.—**Lucille Whalen**

C, P
154.   **World Terrorism: An Encyclopedia of Political Violence from Ancient Times to the Post-9/11 Era.** James Ciment, ed. Armonk, N.Y., M. E. Sharpe, 2011. 3v. illus. index. $349.00/set. ISBN 13: 978-0-7656-8284-0.

The recent deaths of Islamist terrorist Osama Bin Laden and Anwar al Awlaki by U.S. strikes illustrates that terrorism remains an integral part of the international political and security landscape. This phenomenon is a historical as well as contemporary development as this exhaustive three-volume encyclopedia demonstrates.

Providing detailed historical and geographical coverage, this compilation covers terrorists, terrorist activities, and governmental and public responses to terrorism on a global scale. It begins by describing the complexities involved in defining terrorism and the differences in such definitions between academics and governmental policymakers. Sections of this book provide detailed articles and bibliographic citations on terrorism through World War II; up to 9/11; and since 9/11. A concluding section in volume 3 describes and analyzes modern terrorism's aims, methods, and tactics.

Examples of subjects addressed within this multifaceted work include Finland: Civil War, 1918; Yugoslavia: Anti-German Resistance, 1941-1945; Iraq: Saddam Hussein Regime, 1968-2003; Nigeria: Anti-Government Violence and Christmas Day Bomber, 1960s-2000s; Sri Lanka: Tamil Tiger Uprising, 1970s-2009; Uganda: Lord's Resistance Army and Other Terrorist Groups, 1996-2001; United States; Ecoterrorism 1980s-2000s; Al Qaeda; Anti-Muslim sentiment; Special Events Security; Internet, Terrorist Use of; Psychology of Terrorists; Suicide Attacks; International Cooperation Against Terrorism; and Special Operations.

This work's strengths are its exhaustive geographic and historical coverage of terrorism and its multifaceted impacts on domestic and international societies and governmental policymaking. Any work of this scope will have weaknesses, with examples of these including fallaciously claiming that the Palestinian Liberation Organization (PLO) is not a terrorist organization (1:4) and citing terrorist apologist Noam Chomsky as a credible scholarly source (3:892) on the subject. These flaws aside, this work will serve as a useful reference for undergraduate research into terrorists and terrorism developments internationally. [R: Choice, Jan 12, p. 860]—**Bert Chapman**

Handbooks and Yearbooks

C, P

155.   **City Crime Rankings: Crime in Metropolitan America.** 18th ed. Kathleen O'Leary Morgan and Scott Morgan, eds. Washington, D.C., CQ Press, 2012. 418p. index. $75.00pa. ISBN 13: 978-1-60871-729-3.

The 18th edition of *City Crime Rankings* delivers well-arranged information and complete-as-possible data available regarding crime in major metropolitan areas and individual cities. It focuses its attention on violent crime, including murder, forcible rape, robbery, aggravated assault, property crime, burglary, larceny and theft, and motor vehicle theft, as well as statistics regarding police officers sworn in to the primary police force in 2010. This title includes a ranking of the safest and most dangerous cities and metropolitan areas. It is worth noting, obviously, that rankings and percentages can change when one considers single cities and metropolitan areas, and this obvious difference carries throughout the title. Appendixes provide population data for cities and metro areas. Indexes include descriptions of metro areas in 2010; a county index for 2010; 20 years of national crimes rates up to 2010; and a summary of national, metro, and city crime statistics.

City Crime Rankings is divided into two major sections: major metropolitan areas and single cities (with populations of more than 75,000 or more). Rankings and percentages pertaining to a particular focus are presented in two forms: alphabetic order and by rankings (lowest to highest) in a particular field. Changes in rankings and percentages are also included. The title does provide description information regarding what constitutes the crimes included, as well as what cities and metro areas are not included and why. Some cities and metro areas did not meet requirements or were unable to provide data due to factors described in the title.

Overall, *City Crime Rankings* delivers what it promises; it provides statistics regarding violent crimes. The material is concise, easy to navigate, and useful. This work is recommended for public and academic libraries, particularly those with sociology, social work, criminal justice, paralegal, pre-law, and law programs.—**Megan W. Lowe**

C

156.   Geis, Gilbert. **White-Collar and Corporate Crime: A Documentary and Reference Guide.** Santa Barbara, Calif., Greenwood Press/ABC-CLIO, 2011. 351p. index. (Documentary and Reference Guides). $100.00. ISBN 13: 978-0-313-38054-9; 978-0-313-38055-6 (e-book).

Gilbert Geis, the author of this new reference volume, is a legendary and hugely admired figure within the world of white-collar crime scholarship. He has made countless seminal contributions to the understanding of white-collar crime and its control over a period of more than a half a century now, and continues to produce a wide range of contributions to the literature at an age when most scholars have long retired from the field, and at a pace that puts his younger brethren to shame. He was the first recipient of the Lifetime Achievement Award of the White-Collar Crime Research Consortium, and the award was subsequently named for him. He has also been the recipient of numerous other well-deserved awards, including the Edwin H. Sutherland Award of the American Society of Criminology, named for the founder of the criminology of white-collar crime. In the interest of full disclosure, the author of this review is indebted to Gilbert Geis for all that he has learned from him over a period of many years, as well as for his warm and on-going friendship. But this would almost certainly be true for any competent reviewer of this volume.

In the wake of the financial crisis of 2007-2009, and the on-going struggles within the economy, interest in understanding white-collar crime and its control is surely on the rise. Massive forms of fraudulent conduct on many different levels, including within the immensely wealthy and powerful Wall Street investment banks, were a key factor in bringing about the economic meltdown. This has been quite widely understood, and is a core thesis of the Oscar-winning documentary "Inside Job" (as well as a number of other recent documentaries), and is also one of the themes of the Occupy Wall Street protests of Fall 2011. Accordingly, it is especially timely to have this documentary guide to white-collar crime authored by the most revered living scholar in the field.

This volume has 13 chapters, with the first devoted to the on-going challenges of defining white-collar and corporate crime and the last to the different options for doing something about it. Two early chapters are devoted to important early developments in relation to American white-collar and corporate crime: the robber barons of the Gilded Age (prototypes for corporate criminals on a grand scale) and the muckrakers of the early twentieth century who pioneered the exposure of crime in high places. A chapter on antitrust crimes addresses a form of corporate crime widely recognized in the late nineteenth century (giving rise to the seminal Sherman Antitrust Act), and still with us today, with recent initiatives directed at Microsoft, Google, and AT&T. A fifth chapter reviews major white-collar crime scandals from the Civil War period to the most recent era. The next chapter addresses a classic form of white-collar crime, insider trading, and related crimes. The recent conviction of a billionaire hedge fund manager is just one high-profile case of the current spate of insider trading prosecutions. Although white-collar crime originally was principally associated with the private sector, a chapter on government white-collar crime addresses the range of corrupt and harmful activities within the public sector that parallel and have intersections with private sector white-collar and corporate crime. A chapter on white-collar crime in the professions (for example, by physicians and lawyers) contends with an especially egregious violation of trust. Environmental and consumer crimes (the topic of the next chapter) have been the focus of much on-going concern, and have received some special attention recently. A chapter on "The Enron Decade of Corporate Debacles" addresses the series of fraudulent corporate accounting cases—with Enron only the highest profile of these—that brought down many major companies in the first decade of the new century, with massive losses. And this decade ended with what has been described as the largest Ponzi scheme in history, that of Bernie Madoff, the topic of the next chapter along with some other large-scale Ponzi schemes of this period. The final substantive chapter, prior to the concluding chapter on prospective ways to address white-collar and corporate crime, reviews the fraudulent dimensions of the "Great Economic Meltdown: 2007-2009." These frauds by some measures produced losses in the hundreds of billions, dwarfing those associated with the corporate debacles and the Ponzi schemes.

Following an incisive preface, each chapter in this volume includes a brief introduction, the reproduction of key documents preceded by some core information: when, where, and the significance of the document; analysis of the documents; informative and interesting "Did You Know?" sidebars; and a very useful list of further readings. The reprinted documents include excerpts from classic contributions to the white-collar crime literature, key legislation or case law, legislative and journalistic reports, and prosecutorial, government agency or public interest, and professional guidelines and press releases. The value of this reference work is also enhanced by a reader's guide to related documents and sidebars, an exceptionally up-to-date and essential bibliography, and an index. But beyond its value as a reference source, this volume can be read from start to finish for its endlessly fascinating narratives and tidbits of revealing information. Quite simply, this superb and immensely timely reference work is sure to be an essential resource for the widest possible range of people engaged in research on or seeking information about white-collar and corporate crime, from high school students and general readers to college and graduate students as well as seasoned scholars in the field. All libraries should order a copy of this indispensable volume for their collection, with alacrity.—**David O. Friedrichs**

C, S

157.   Marley, David F. **Modern Piracy: A Reference Handbook.** Santa Barbara, Calif., ABC-CLIO, 2011. 290p. index. (Contemporary World Issues). $55.00. ISBN 13: 978-1-598-84433-7.

Only 20 years ago, the word "piracy" would have conjured up images of mythical eye-patch wearing sailors or fabled peg-legged, hook-handed caricatures. Indeed, *Hook*, staring Dustin Hoffman, appeared in late 1991, just in time for the Christmas rush, and was exactly 20 years ago. No one thought it would be about anything else other than Tinkerbell and children who don't want to grow up in a place called Never, Never Land. As the saying goes, never say never.

Today, not so much as the word piracy conjures real fears, not mythological ones. We have real pirates roaming real seas again (not to mention those who violate copyright and steal secrets). Contemporary World Issues is a familiar ABC-CLIO series and this one follows it tried and true format. Chapters cover the subject matter's history and background, controversies, special U.S. issues, and various biographical sketches (e.g., Boya, Richard Phillips, Yusuf Mohamed Siad). Chapters on various important documents (e.g., the disappearance of U.S. merchant ships 1955-2005), national and international organizations, and resources are covered. Those looking for quick reminders on the issues surrounding the hijackings of the *Achille Lauro* in the mid 1980s or the *Santa Maria* in the early 1960s are covered. Recent piracies are also covered, such as the *Sirius Star* and the *Maersk Alabama*. While the book may not be exhaustive of the subject, one will be hard pressed to find more information as easily and as quickly.

Those who think that all of this "is on the Web" anyway, so why bother, should be reminded that nowhere on the Web is there this much information in one place. Individual piracies or biographies can be found on the Web, of course, and certain documents as well. But for sheer convenience of subject matter in one place, books such as this not only have a niche, but also fill a very wide audience.—**Mark Y. Herring**

Environmental Law

C, P

158.   Wolf, Michael Allan. **The Supreme Court and the Environment: The Reluctant Protector.** Washington, D.C., CQ Press, 2012. 490p. index. (The Supreme Court's Power in American Politics). $135.00. ISBN 13: 978-0-87289-975-9.

The Supreme Court and the Environment: The Reluctant Protector examines the relationship between the U.S. Supreme Court and current role it is playing regarding environmental issues. With the use of well-written essays and primary documents the text examines the differing interpretations of what the Supreme Court is doing and what it should be doing to ensure our environment is protected. The author explores how the founding of the Environmental Defense Fund and other federal environmental statutes have had an impact on Court decisions and their ability to enforce environmental legislation. The book examines the roles federal administrative agencies, state and local governments, lower courts, environmental organizations, and private corporations have played in the politics of environmental protection. The essays are thought provoking, and the pooling of case and non-case primary documents will prove beneficial to students and researchers finding the links between environmental policy and the actions of the Supreme Court throughout history. In all, this is an excellent resource, appropriate for public and academic libraries.—**Jack Ray**

Human Rights

Dictionaries and Encyclopedias

C, P

159. Condé, H. Victor. **An Encyclopedia of Human Rights in the United States.** 2d ed. Millerton, N.Y., Grey House Publishing, 2011. 2v. index. $225.00/set. ISBN 13: 978-1-59237-209-4.

This set is the 2d edition of *Human Rights in the United States: A Dictionary and Documents*, which Mr. Condé worked on with Rita Cantos Cartwright for ABC-CLIO (see ARBA 2001, entry 567). The page count has increased from 931 to 1,835 pages. The contents have been thoroughly updated and revised to reflect the myriad of changes, events, and legislation since catastrophic terrorist attacks of September 11, 2001. Some 300 terms are defined (such as *rendition* and *grave breaches*), with useful *see* and *see also* references. Each term has a definition, followed by a longer explanation of the significance of the term. There are many quotations and excerpts from various documents. There are also 106 texts of primary documents (up from 59 in the 1st edition) for this controversial subject, such as the Foreign Intelligence Surveillance Act and the USA Human Rights Pledge. Also include are a detailed user's guide, a long introductory essay (48 pages), a list of abbreviations, a chronology, bibliography, and an extensive index. The 18 appendixes include "Charts of the U.N. System for the Promotion and Observance of Human Rights," an explanation of "How an International Human Rights Norm Becomes a U.S. Law," and a discussion of how immigration and aliens are affected by human rights ideas and laws. Condé, an international human rights lawyer and educator, also compiled a related *Handbook on International Human Rights Terminology* (2nd ed.; University of Nebraska Press, 2004). Most of the pages in this set are composed of document texts that should be available free on the Internet, or in *Human and Civil Rights: Essential Primary Sources* from Gale/Cengage (see ARBA 2007, 491), and most of the terms can be found in other dictionaries, so what one is getting with this set is the lengthy expert commentary about the context and importance of the term and documents. This set is recommended for academic and public libraries.—**Daniel K. Blewett**

Handbooks and Yearbooks

C, P

160. Gellman, Robert, and Pam Dixon. **Online Privacy: A Reference Handbook.** Santa Barbara, Calif., ABC-CLIO, 2011. 295p. index. (Contemporary World Issues). $58.00. ISBN 13: 978-1-59884-649-2; 978-1-59884-650-8 (e-book).

ABC-CLIO's Contemporary World Issues series is known for its well-researched topics. This reference handbook about online privacy is no exception. Gellman is a lawyer and expert on privacy matters. He served on the staff of the House of Representatives Subcommittee responsible for the Privacy Act of 1974. Pam Dixon is an author and researcher, and executive director of the non-partisan World Privacy Forum. Together these authors have put together a useful compendium of information that will serve lay persons as well as academic researchers.

The authors are careful to define the scope of the book as it applies to offline versus online privacy. The two are interrelated, but the focus of this volume is the history, concern, debate, and regulation surrounding online privacy. Online activities challenge traditional concepts of information ownership and personal and legal jurisdiction.

The book consists of eight chapters. Chapter 1 sets the scene with a detailed introduction to the concept of online privacy. Chapter 2 talks about the problems identified with the online information explosion and solutions to date. Chapter 3 expands the discussion to international approaches to the problems and how the U.S. perspective differs from that of other countries, especially those in Europe.

Chapter 4 provides a chronology of online privacy from 1791 through 2011 (of course describing origins from offline privacy issues). Chapter 5 features biographical profiles of 38 individuals who have been instrumental in the history and development of online privacy. Chapter 6 highlights important data and documents dealing with online privacy issues, regulations, laws, and agreements. Chapter 7 outlines organizations and institutions that work to define, regulate, and adapt online privacy policies, such as civil liberties groups and consumer groups. Chapter 8 lists resources in various formats, including reports, documentaries, fiction, nonfiction, sound clips, webcasts, and more, all pertaining to online privacy issues. A complete glossary of terms begins on page 263, and a comprehensive index begins on page 271.

This reference is a concise resource that would benefit anyone researching the complex topic of online privacy. It is recommended for public, community college, and university libraries.—**Laura J. Bender**

Immigration Law

P

161.   Bray, Ilona. **U.S. Immigration Made Easy.** 15th ed. Berkeley, Calif., Nolo Press, 2011. 596p. index. $44.99pa. ISBN 13: 978-1-4133-1207-2.

Nolo Press has long been known for its successful self-help law books as well as for its up-to-date legal information online. Although this immigration volume is in its 15th edition, the title now seems somewhat ironic since the view of the American public is generally that immigration should be made more difficult and the government also has moved in this direction. Still, this book continues to make the rules and procedures of immigration as clear and understandable as possible, including such topics as how to get a green card though various means, nonimmigrant and student visas, the naturalization process, and special rules for Canadians and Mexicans. The information is readily accessible through the clear chapter headings and subheading and a detailed index. The text is written in a no-nonsense, easy-to-read style, which usually includes helpful examples.

It is extremely important that users read the introductory chapter on how the text is to be used—particularly since there have been many changes made to the law since recent editions and many of the processing fees have increased. Nolo Press, however, has made the information concerning these changes quite easily accessible. In an insert on the first page of the text, specific information for finding the updates is given. Readers are reminded that the text is reliable up to the date of publication in February 2011, but it is necessary to check the Nolo Website for any updates. Under the section "Legal Updates" summaries of important changes and the date they are to take effect are listed, occasionally followed by links to the government agency involved. It is possible to go directly to the agencies, but without the simplified, step-by-step directions given in the Nolo volume, it would be very difficult to work through all the complicated processes involved.

This book provides information that is sorely needed by those hoping to qualify for immigration to the United States or to remain in the country through one of the various programs available. Not only informative, it also provides advice on the best steps to take in particular cases. For these reasons and for the fact that the updates are made easily available, this volume should be a useful addition to any academic and public library.—**Lucille Whalen**

11 Library and Information Science and Publishing and Bookselling

Library and Information Science

Reference Works

Bibliography

C, P

162.   **The Basic Business Library: Core Resources and Services.** 5th ed. Eric Forte and Michael R. Oppenheim, eds. Santa Barbara, Calif., Libraries Unlimited/ABC-CLIO, 2012. 227p. index. $44.95. ISBN 13: 978-1-59884-611-9; 978-1-59884-612-6 (e-book).

Despite having a team of new editors, the basic objectives of this resource remain unchanged, to serve as a checklist of essential reference tools and provide a set of essays for smaller libraries. It can also serve the needs of library science educators and as a textbook for their students. Although the book was originally targeted for public libraries, the number of academic libraries using the book has continued to increase substantially over the years. The authors broadened the core list to accommodate these market changes. Reflecting the move of reference to electronic databases, this 5th edition includes the available URLs for the print titles selected. This updated edition provides tried and true advice for acquiring and building a business collection in the Web 2.0/3.0 world and includes advice on the best practices for providing business reference help to patrons. The bulk of the volume is lists of bibliographic entries for the core list of reference sources arranged into the following topics: marketing, financial information, government information sources, entrepreneurship, and in-depth academic resources. The essays discuss such topics as accessing the business literature, building a core collection of periodicals, and strategies for serving today's business users.

This essays section is up-to-date, relevant, and an excellent source of specialized resource lists tailored to the essay's topic. Each essay is listed in the table of contents. The index is thorough. This edition is highly recommended for all business, public, and academic libraries.—**Ladyjane Hickey**

P, S

163.   **Children's Core Collection.** 20th ed. Bronx, N.Y., H. W. Wilson, 2010. 2317p. index. $210.00. ISBN 13: 978-0-8242-1106-6.

This work has been a mainstay for almost 100 years (the 1st edition was published in 1909) in supplying authoritative and dependable information on collection evaluation and development for children's libraries in elementary schools and public libraries. The body of the work consists of entries for almost 10,000 in-print titles suitable for readers in kindergarten through sixth grade. They were chosen by the editor in consultation with "an advisory committee of distinguished librarians." Each entry contains full bibliographic and cataloging information plus excerpts usually from two reviews, one descriptive and the other evaluative. The recommended nonfiction titles are arranged by the Dewey

Decimal system and form the first one-third of this book. Noteworthy here are the inclusion of important professional tools (the 010s and 020s), extensive listings of folk and fairy tales (398.2), and section on graphic novels (741.5). Fictional chapter books for grades three through six are listed alphabetically by author in the next section. This is followed by a brief listing of story collections. The individual stories found in these anthologies are given separate entries by title in the main index. A large section follows called "Easy Books." This is an extensive bibliography of recommended picture books for K-3 readers, again arranged by author's name. The first book in a fictional series is given the main entry and additional titles in the series are listed within the entry with publication dates. These internal titles are not included in the index. There are two new annotated sections in this edition: the first contains list of recommended periodicals (about 40 profession-oriented and about 50 children's magazines), and the second gives material on useful Websites and related electronic resources. The remainder of the volume (about 600 pages) consists of a thorough one-alphabet index that exhaustively lists the entries by author(s), illustrators, title, subjects, publishers series, and contents (in the case of story collections). Buyers will receive two (instead of the usual four) annual supplements. The current volume remains an essential professional tool for all libraries serving children. Its only competition in scope and treatment remains *Best Books for Children* (8th ed.; see ARBA 2007, entry 886), which contains more than 25,000 entries arranged by subjects but with shorter annotations and less bibliographic and cataloging information.—**John T. Gillespie**

C, P

164.   **The Medical Library Association's Master Guide to Authoritative Information Resources in the Health Sciences.** Thompson, Laurie L., Mori Lou Higa, Esther Carrigan, and Rajia Tobia, eds. New York, Neal-Schuman, 2011. 659p. index. (Medical Library Association Guides). $295.00. ISBN 13: 978-1-55570-719-4.

  The Medical Library Association's Master Guide to Authoritative Information Resources in the Health Sciences is an essential one-volume collection development tool. Developed on the model of the former Brandon-Hill Selected List, this new AMA guide to the literature provides a standard guide for authoritative and annotated lists of the top resources for the biological and medical subjects covered. The table of contents provides the best method of discovery and navigation. Thirty-four chapters offer a broad subject arrangement of topics such as Dentistry, Anatomy, and Biotechnology. Subsections appear within chapters as needed; for example, chapter 27 covers Genetics and includes two subsections, 27.1 Medical Genetics and 27.2 Genomics. Brief definitions for each topic from either MeSH or *Stedman's Medical Dictionary* appear at the beginning of each section and subsection. Entries include brief bibliographic information, a URL if available, and a "recommended for" designation. Most titles are recommended for academic or hospital libraries. A few are recommended for consumer health collections. Designation as a former Brandon-Hill Selection or a Doody's Core Title is also included with each entry. Cross-references are included if a title is listed under more than one section. Sections are arranged with the top monographs listed first followed by the top journals. Monographs appear to be mostly for print titles. A section for "Databases and Other Electronic Resources" is included as appropriate for each section. Annotations are descriptive and informative. There are a total of 2,011 sources included based on quality and importance to the discipline. Librarians employed in various health sciences settings are the primary contributors. This resource provides a needed collection development tool for health sciences literature and is appropriate for identifying sources for research, practice, reference, study, and review.—**Susan E. Thomas**

P

165.   Saricks, Joyce g. **Read On . . . Audiobooks: Reading Lists for Every Taste.** Santa Barbara, Calif., Libraries Unlimited/ABC-CLIO, 2011. 145p. index. (Read On Series). $30.00pa. ISBN 13: 978-1-59158-804-7.

  Read On...Audiobooks: Reading Lists for Every Taste is a fresh, unique approach to readers' advisory that is part of Libraries Unlimited's Read On series. The author, Joyce Saricks, reveals her vast audiobook experience and creates a list of both fiction and nonfiction works that should enable a reader to find that next good listen. The audiobook format encompasses every book genre, and most important with the audiobook is the presentation. The book selection categories presented for the Read On Series, language/voice, mood, story, characters, and setting, work especially well for audiobooks. Saricks breaks each selection category down into subcategories totaling more than 60. For example, in the language category, Saricks stresses that while writing style is the essence of print, it is the narrator that is most important in setting the tone of an audiobook. She utilizes language subcategories that recommend good examples of full cast readings, the author as narrator, great narrators who have died, female narrators, male narrators, multiple narrators, unique voices, and straight-up virtuoso performances. This book is useful for all audiobook listeners. The scope of the work is broad but not all-inclusive. Saricks explains very well her objectives in the introduction. The work is organized in a simple manner: series foreword, introduction, the five category chapters, and the index. The book is very easy to peruse, and commentary is informative and concise. *Read On...Audiobooks* should be the go-to source to begin exploring the possibilities of this unique format.—**Sue Ellen Griffiths**

P, S
166.   **Senior High Core Collection.** 18th ed. Bronx, N.Y., H. W. Wilson, 2011. 1500p. illus. index. $255.00. ISBN 13: 978-0-8242-1114-1.

This 80-year old standard professional reference work continues to introduce new features that keep it current and relevant, and with the last edition the title was changed from *Senior High School Library Catalog* to more accurately reflect its scope and purpose. The 18th edition includes recommended periodical titles for both students and professionals. Web Resources are called Electronic Resources, listing both free and fee-based resources. The analytical entries for the more than 8,000 book titles form the core of this work, and more than one-half of the titles are new to this edition—reason enough to replace your old edition. Each entry includes complete bibliographic information; subject headings, annotations, grade level recommendations, Dewey classification, and cover art; quotations for select reviews; and book awards, best book lists, and starred reviews. This guide lists only in-print titles and is designed to be used for selection; for reference and readers' advisory; to verify bibliographic, classification, and subject heading information; to aid curriculum support; and as a pre-professional instruction aid. Although this work omits nonprint materials other than Web-based, it remains such an important work for the management of a senior high school library collection that no high school media center of any size should be without it. This work is essential for high school libraries. It is highly recommended for public library professional collections.—**Rosanne M. Cordell**

P, S
167.   Welch, Rollie James. **A Core Collection for Young Adults.** 2d ed. New York, Neal-Schuman, 2011. 417p. index. (Teens @ the Library Series). $75.00pa. ISBN 13: 978-1-55570-692-0.

In 2003 Neal-Schuman published the 1st edition of *A Core Collection for Young Adults* by Patrick Jones, Patricia Taylor, and Edward Kirsten. Now, eight years later, Neal-Schuman has published Rollie Jones Welch's 2d edition of this title. It is almost certain to become a classic. It is larger, deeper, and more useful than the first one.

The 1st edition listed over 1,200 titles. The 2d edition lists 1,386 titles and annotates 877 of them. The listings include author(s), title, pagination, format, publisher, and ISBN. If a title has multiple editions this is also recorded. Rather than noting reader's age ranges, grade ranges are included. Citations of reviews from the following sources are provided: *Booklist, Kirkus, Publisher's Weekly, School Library Journal,* and *VOYA.* Finally, major YALSA awards (e.g., the John Newbury Award and the Alex Award) are listed if the book has won any. Although the annotations list the awards, seven appendixes that record all of the award winners are included. Examples of the awards in these appendixes are the Michael L. Printz Award; Best Book for Young Adults top ten list; Great Graphic Novels for Teens top ten list; and Teens' top ten list. While not all of the books in *A Core Collection for Young Adults* are award winners, these appendixes would be useful to librarians who wish to expand their collection's award winners.

The original edition was divided by author's last name into nonfiction, fiction, and graphic formats. This edition is more finely parsed with the books and their annotations ordered by author's last name and divided into 13 genre categories. These categories are: Adventure Tales, Cautionary Novels, Classic Literature, Coming-of-Age Stories, Fantasy Novels, Graphic Novels, Historical Fiction, Humorous Novels, Inspirational Fiction, Romance Novels, and Science Fiction. To help in locating a specific work there is both a title and an author index. To aid a librarian doing ordering a CD-ROM is included that has four Excel files with all of the books' ordering information included. These files present the books by genre, by author, by title, and by grade level.

If you are a young adult librarian in charge of a collection and own the 1st edition the 2d is a must-buy replacement. If you own neither edition, go out and purchase this one.—**Scott Alan Sheidlower**

Handbooks and Yearbooks

P

168.   **The ALA Book of Library Grant Money.** 8th ed. Ann Kepler, ed. Chicago, American Library Association, 2012. 425p. index. $175.00pa.; $157.50pa. (ALA members). ISBN 13: 978-0-8389-1058-0.

This aptly titled, completely revised, 1-volume compilation provides detailed information on over 2,000 philanthropic programs in the United States. Among these are major private foundations, grant distributors who have contributed at least $100,000, corporate foundations, and hard-to-identify corporate direct givers. All of the funding sources described support libraries and will consider unsolicited proposals.

All entries have been with reliable information from a variety of sources, such as the most recent IRS Form 990-PF, the foundations' annual reports, grants lists, questionnaire responses, press releases, and telephone interviews. Each entry includes the corporation or foundation name, sponsoring company information, content, contact information, giving histories, a financial summary, a contributions summary, corporate officers and directors, application procedures and restrictions, publications, an analysis of grants, and recent grants. This directory provides funding sources for facilities, computers, programs, staffing, initiatives, and other library operations.

Other useful features are four specialized indexes: index to grantors by total grant value, index to grantors by state, named grants, and professional library organization grantors. Although impressive, the usefulness of this big book cannot be judged by size alone. Its true value lies in its information, currency, relevancy, and ease of use for all library fundraisers. The fact that it is in its 8th edition is an indication of its usefulness for libraries of all types.—**ARBA Staff Reviewer**

S

169.   Crews, Kenneth D. **Copyright Law for Librarians and Educators: Creative Strategies & Practical Solutions.** 3d ed. Chicago, American Library Association, 2012. 192p. index. $57.00pa.; $51.30pa. (ALA members). ISBN 13: 978-0-8389-1092-4.

A full revision of the 2d edition of *Copyright Law for Librarians and Educators* tackles issues that have arisen in recent years, in particular digitizing, uploading, downloading, and incorporating materials into Web-based instruction. Crews directs the Copyright Advisory Office at Columbia University and teaches in the Columbia Law School. *Copyright Law* is a brief but informative volume that provides in layperson's terms a distillation of the basics of copyright, including a history of the law, an overview of the rights and the exceptions to the rights of copyright owners, guidelines for determining fair use, special provisions for libraries, and copyright for music and unpublished materials. Practical guides included in the appendix provide checklists for applying the fair use factors and for using copyrighted materials under the TEACH Act, and a model permission letter for those seeking to use copyrighted materials. *Copyright Law* is an indispensable reference tool for the information professional or educator working with copyrighted materials.—**Lisa Kay Speer**

P

170.   Dowell, David R. **Crash Course in the World of Genealogy.** Santa Barbara, Calif., Libraries Unlimited/ABC-CLIO, 2011. 220p. index. (Crash Course Series). $35.00pa. ISBN 13: 978-1-59884-939-4; 978-1-59884-940-0 (e-book).

The preface of this title reads: "This book is intended to be a basic course for library workers who need to absorb an overview of genealogy very quickly in order to help family history researchers who visit the libraries where they are employed." This book will certainly be useful for achieving this goal, but after many years of teaching librarians how to serve genealogists and teaching genealogists how to use libraries and do research, it is also good advice for librarians to study this book and do their own family's genealogical research while assisting genealogists. In general, this is an overall guide that discusses services policies, research principles and top sources, and practical examples of searches. It also addresses special challenges in researching people of color, international research, and adding DNA information to the research. Special features include timelines listing key events in U.S. history that may have created records; illustrations of census records, pedigree charts, and DNA results; maps of Y-chromosome and mitochondrial DNA haplogroups to show the migration of our ancestors; and a glossary. There is one error found on page 41 which reads, "Any item that has been converted to Microfilm or Microfiche in Salt Lake City can be requested for a small fee." In reality, there are a few items that cannot circulate because the institutions that created them also restricted some of them from circulating. Those restricted may only be read in the Family History Library in Salt Lake City, Utah. This book is true to its stated purpose and is recommended for all public and genealogical collections.—**J. Carlyle Parker**

S

171.   Karp, Jesse. **Graphic Novels in Your School Library.** Rush Kress, ed. Chicago, American Library Association, 2012. 146p. illus. index. $50.00pa.; $45.00pa. (ALA members). ISBN 13: 978-0-8389-1089-4.

Authored by a school librarian and reviewer of graphic novels from New York City, this work brings together nine chapters on the concept of graphic novels, a history of the art form, annotated reading lists for grades preK-12, and lesson plans and activities that incorporate graphic novels. The work looks at ways that the graphic novel format has become part of our culture as well as ways that librarians can use them to encourage literacy and a love of reading. It is a guide for those new to graphic novels, describing the symbols and form, and offering basic lesson plans that use graphic novels. The annotated lists will be useful for school librarians building a collection, with each entry providing the title, genre, discussion topics, and a thorough annotation. The author has divided the entries by grades K-8 and 9-12. The lesson plans are a valuable feature that can be applied to various school curricula. Arranged into two sections, the first chapter focuses on activities that deal with the art itself and the second chapter concentrates on the content of the novels. This book is similar in scope to *Graphic Novels Beyond the Basics: Insights and Issues for Librarians* (see ARBA 2010, entry 562). It will be of value not only to the librarian, but also to the educator wishing to incorporate the graphic form into their classroom.—**Sara Marcus**

P

172.   Pearlmutter, Jane, and Paul Nelson. **Small Public Library Management.** Chicago, American Library Association, 2012. 139p. index. $50.00pa.; $45.00pa. (ALA members). ISBN 13: 978-0-8389-1085-6.

Books in the ALA Fundamental Series from ALA Publishing are basic overviews of the best practices to use in any number of library positions. Other books in the series so far include *Fundamentals of Library Supervision* (2d ed.; see ARBA 2010, entry 598) and *Fundamentals of Technical Services Management* (see ARBA 2009, entry 538). This book touches on and explains how best to go about many of the key aspects of managing a small library. It is designed to help the library administrator streamline and improve organization functions so that nothing slips through the cracks and there will be free time for extra activities. Chapters are arranged by topic, including Finance (addressing budget preparation, budget review), Personnel Management (addressing hiring, supervision, discipline, volunteers), Facilities (addressing access to technology, safety issues, renovations), Collection Management (addressing selection criteria, collection evaluation, and challenges), Services and Programs (addressing the proper mix of services, youth and adult services, readers' advisory, and outreach), and the Library as Place (discussing advocacy and developing a community-centered philosophy). The chapters are easy to read, provide many sidebars and bullet lists, and include chapter notes. It will serve as a concise and well-balanced professional guide to managing a small library.—**Gary L. Parsons**

C, P

173.   Tucker, Virginia, and Marc Lampson. **Finding the Answers to Legal Questions: A How-To-Do-It Manual.** New York, Neal-Schuman, 2011. 274p. index. (How-To-Do-It Manuals, no.174). $75.00pa. ISBN 13: 978-1-55570-718-7.

Finding the Answers to Legal Questions: A How-To-Do-It Manual is aimed primarily at librarians who find themselves assisting patrons who are researching legal issues. Authors Tucker and Lampson offer a well-organized and easy-to-use guide for such librarians as well as members of the public who may be researching a legal issue without the guidance of a librarian.

Divided into four parts, the book begins with a summary of the United States' legal system. Part 1 then explains various secondary sources, and details how to find federal law as well as state and local law. Part 2 covers the basics of legal research and what resources may be available outside of the public library setting. Part 3 consists of eight chapters, each devoted to a particular area of the law that a public patron may be involved with—family law, landlord/tenant, and bankruptcy are a sampling of the topics covered. Part 4 is devoted to developing a collection of legal materials, from print sources to creating a Web page.

The information in each chapter is clearly laid out on the page, with white space on either side of the text for easy reading. There is also an "in this chapter" checklist on the first page of each chapter as well as a conclusion or "resources recap" section on the last page. A glossary, appendixes of online resources, and an index complete the volume.

Finding the Answers to Legal Questions is ideally suited for a public library, for use by the librarians employed there. It would also be helpful in an academic library where library and information sciences students would find it of use in preparation for a future position in a public or law library.—**Alicia Brillon**

Publishing and Bookselling

Directories

P

174.   **International Literary Market Place 2012.** Medford, N.J., Information Today, 2011. 1850p. index. $289.00pa. ISBN 13: 978-1-57387-416-8.

P

175.   **Literary Market Place 2012.** Medford, N.J., Information Today, 2011. 2v. index. $339.00pa./set. ISBN 13: 978-1-57387-420-5.

Literary Market Place (LMP) is a good example of a comprehensive directory of publishers in the United States and Canada. In its print form, in two volumes, LMP is an annual publication with more than 12,000 entries for various entities in the publishing industry. Volume 1 is the basic industry directory with information on publishers, literary agents, editorial providers, industry associations, and trade publications. Volume 2 is a directory of supporting services that includes entries for marketers, advertisers, promoters, and suppliers. The entries contain name, address, telephone number, fax number, e-mail address, and Website; key personnel; affiliated offices; and a brief descriptive annotation. Yellow page indexing coverage is provided for companies, personnel, sections, and advertisers at the end of both volumes.

A companion directory to *Literary Market Place* is the *International Literary Market Place*. This annual directory covers the international publishing industry, with nearly 15,500 entries for entities in 180 countries. A single volume in print, *International Literary Market Place* is organized in broad sections: publishing, manufacturing, book trade information, literary associations and prizes, book trade calendar, and library resources. Entries are arranged alphabetically by country and contain basic contact information, key people, and a brief narrative description. An industry yellow pages section covering publishers and supporting companies is available at the end of the directory.

Both publications can be found as a Web-based product called LiteraryMarketPlace.com from Information Today. Subscribers can get complete entries and enhanced searching for publishers by different subject or type of publication. Lists of publishers based on size, sales, city, zip code, and other variables can be generated from this database.—**Shannon Graff Hysell**

12 Military Studies

General Works

Almanacs

C, S

176. Fredriksen, John C. **Middle East Almanac: U.S. Military Action in the Region, 1979 to the Present.** New York, Facts on File, 2011. 728p. illus. index. (Almanacs of American Wars). $95.00. ISBN 13: 978-0-8160-8094-6; 978-1-4381-3390-4 (e-book).

One wonders if the Internet has diminished the value of printed reference books such as this one. Chronologies and biographical capsules are readily available with just a few keystrokes, and for ongoing events such as these conflicts, the printed sources are dated at the moment of publication. Nevertheless, for those who consult printed sources that bring together many pieces of information in one location, this is a good one. The Almanacs of American Wars is a very fine series, and this is a worthy addition. The exhaustive daily chronology, which comprises almost 90 percent of the volume, follows U.S. military events in the region from 1979 to July 2010. This coverage includes activity in Iran, Kuwait, Iraq, Afghanistan, the Horn of Africa, and the war against al-Qadea. The other portion of the main text is very fine biographical selections of sketches of major players in the various countries. Appendixes include casualties in each of the wars, medal of honor recipients, excellent maps, a very good topical bibliography, and an index.

The volume is attractive, well designed, readable, and it includes useful pictures. In sum, for libraries that still purchase this kind of source, it is a good acquisition.—**Joe P. Dunn**

Chronology

C, S

177. Lansford, Tom. **9/11 and the Wars in Afghanistan and Iraq: A Chronology and Reference Guide.** Santa Barbara, Calif., ABC-CLIO, 2012. 349p. index. $89.00. ISBN 13: 978-1-59884-419-1; 978-1-59884-420-7 (e-books).

The events of 9/11 changed the world. The terrorist attacks did define and will further define domestic and international policy and relations for decades to come. The origins, players, and events before and after the terrorist attacks need to be examined in the historical context that Lansford places them in. From the USA Patriot Act to the Wars in Afghanistan and Iraq the world was indeed changed.

This work is divided into 10 well-developed and purposeful chapters. They range from the rise of Osama bin Laden to the planning of Global Terrorism; the September 11th Attacks; Operation Enduring Freedom; Operation Iraqi Freedom; Civil Liberties and the War on Terror; The Global War on Terror; The Insurgencies in Iraq and Afghanistan; The Change in Domestic and Foreign Policies; and the Obama Presidency. A solid preface sets the stage. Also, a list of abbreviations, a glossary, a select bibliography, a set of maps, a solid chronology, several biographies, and numerous primary documents are provided.

Typical examples of biographies include: Barack Obama, Nancy Pelosi, George Bush, Saddam Hussein, and Abu Musab al Zarqawi. Typical examples of primary documents include: the 2003 Bush Ultimatum to Saddam, the USA Patriot Act, and Obama's 2010 National Security Strategy. Overall, this work offers a fair and balanced approach. This work is highly recommended.—**Scott R. DiMarco**

Dictionaries and Encyclopedias

C, S

178. **Conflict and Conquest in the Islamic World: A Historical Encyclopedia.** Alexander Mikaberidze, ed. Santa Barbara, Calif., ABC-CLIO, 2011. 2v. illus. maps. index. $195.00/set. ISBN 13: 978-1-59884-336-1; 978-1-59884-337-8 (e-book).

This work's preface states its main purpose as a "reference source on the major conflicts that have influenced the course of history in the Islamic world since the seventh century" (p. xxix), and geographically covers the Iberian Peninsula, North Africa, the Middle East, South and Southeast Asia, and parts of Sub-Saharan Africa.

Both volumes have an alphabetic list of entries as well as thematic list of entries. The thematic list categorizes entries into concepts, conflicts wars and rebellions, military and equipment, battles, personalities, states and groups, and treaties. Volume 1 also has a chronological list of major conflicts and battles from the seventh century to contemporary times before the alphabetic entries. Volume 2 has a glossary of non-English terms, a list of contributors, and an index after the entries.

The thematic list of entries and chronological list of entries is useful for quick reference. From a geographical perspective, this work does an excellent job of covering the Middle East, North Africa, and Eastern Europe—especially the Ottoman influence in both areas. West Africa and Sub-Saharan Africa are also well covered. South East Asia is not as well covered (and events like the Bali bombings are not mentioned). Notably absent from the entries are those that deal with the rational for conflicts and military tactics.

Entries discussing treaties or battles stick closely to the "mechanics" of the affair without providing much additional background, and hence tend to be brief. Some of the entries are subdivided chronologically (such as the Palestinian Intifada), but other entries, such as the Austro-Ottoman Wars that spanned over two centuries, are not subdivided. Some entries, such as Medieval Islamic Military Medicine, only peripherally cover conflict or conquest. Fortunately such entries are very few. While cross-referencing entries, readers need to be aware that in some cases the same item has variant spellings; for example, Tarsusi is referred to in the main entry, but as "al-arsusi" in Islamic Medieval Siege Warfare.

Concise reference works like this typically suffer from errors of omission. In this regard, this work is no exception (as noted above). More surprising omissions are that some contributors, while acknowledged as contributors of their works at the end of their entries, are not included in the list of contributors before the general index (such as Amy Black and Benjamin de Lee). One can understand the amount of effort required when one considers that the editor contributed about one-third of the approximately 600 entries in this work.

Despite its shortcomings, this reference work does fill a need in that it makes accessible to high school and early college students the rich tapestry of military history in the Muslim world that showcases the Islamic experience from the dawn of Islam to contemporary times.—**Muhammed Hassanali**

C, S

179. **The Encyclopedia of the Vietnam War: A Political, Social, and Military History.** 2d ed. Spencer C. Tucker, ed. Santa Barbara, Calif., ABC-CLIO, 2011. 4v. illus. maps. index. $395.00/set. ISBN 13: 978-1-85109-960-3; 978-1-85109-961-0 (e-book).

The American War in Vietnam involved every aspect of the American experience from the 1960s to the present. It defined a generation. The superlative military encyclopedia editor of over 25 works,

Spencer C. Tucker, again does an impressive job of addressing U.S. involvement in this war with the 2d edition of *The Encyclopedia of the Vietnam War*. He selects topics that go well beyond the actual battlefield and Southeast Asia to, as the subtitle suggests "A Political, Social, and Military History." Truly a scholar, this work is comprehensive and multidimensional in the event from its origins to its long-term consequences.

This work is divided into four volumes arranged in alphabetic format. The first three volumes contain a list of entries; a list of maps; photographs; general maps; the actual entries; and an index. Volume 4 has numerous documents; unit designations; a list of military ranks; an order of battle; a glossary; a chronology; and a selected entry bibliography. A typical example is in volume 1 is on pages 157-161: The Cambodian Incursion. It has solid and helpful information, a useful map, and a black-and-white photograph. This entry was written by a named scholar. Several associated entries are listed as are seven sources. This work is highly recommended.—**Scott R. DiMarco**

C, P

180. Halliday, Fred. **Shocked and Awed: A Dictionary of the War on Terror.** Berkeley, Calif., University of California Press, 2010. 337p. index. $25.95pa. ISBN 13: 978-0-520-26870-8.

If you have ever watched a network newscast on the Iraq war or read a book on terrorism and wonder what some of these words meant than this handy ready-reference volume will answer many of your questions about terminology and the war on terror. Arranged into 12 subject-related chapters (e.g., abduction and torture, wars in Afghanistan, Iraq, Jihad), the terms are listed alphabetically with definitions ranging from a sentence to a page. Most of the terms have current relevance but others present a historical context. A 3-page bibliography and 15-page index conclude the volume. Given the odd nature of chapter arrangement, the index is essential and could have been expanded. There is also the need for a pronunciation guide and there is the perception of a Western bias, but overall the book is a useful, reasonably priced guide to the ever-expanding literature on terrorism. Most public and academic libraries will want to seriously consider its purchase.—**Boyd Childress**

C, P, S

181. Tucker, Spencer C. **Battles that Changed History: An Encyclopedia of World Conflict.** Santa Barbara, Calif., ABC-CLIO, 2011. 655p. illus. index. $95.00. ISBN 13: 978-1-59884-429-0.

Spencer C. Tucker, so eloquently and accurately notes that a few hundred specific conflicts have played critical roles in "defining the direction of history and the evolution of human society." From the May 1479 B.C.E. Battle of Megiddo through the famed 300 Spartans stand at Thermopylae to the Spanish Armada to Culloden and Crecy to Stalingrad and the Ia Drang Valley and finally the 2003 Iraq War, each had its own "historical context and significance to other events." What really matters is these events mattered and Tucker shows the reader exactly why. Sea, air, and land are included.

This work is in chronological format. Each has very useful chart that contains the title; date; the opponents (including a designator for the winner); an approximate of number of troops on both sides; and, most importantly, why the battle was of importance. Some battles have maps and a few even have photographs. A few paragraphs to a few pages of narration follow with a list of references. The volume concludes with a solid index.

A typical example is on pages 279-283: The Battle of Trafalgar on 21 October, 1800 where Nelson and 27 British Ships of the Line engaged and defeated a larger combined French and Spanish fleet in the Mediterranean and effective negates French naval supremacy for decades. A solid and well-written account is provided by Tucker and a map of the battle covers almost a full page. Four good references are also provided. Overall, this is a good one-volume reference work, especially for the price. This work is highly recommended.—**Scott R. DiMarco**

C, S

182. **World War II at Sea: An Encyclopedia.** Spencer C. Tucker, ed. Santa Barbara, Calif., ABC-CLIO, 2012. 2v. illus. index. $189.00/set. ISBN 13: 978-1-59884-457-3.

Spencer Tucker has written a very effective encyclopedia covering the major naval events and figures of World War II. This two-volume set consists for the most part of short articles covering all aspects of the war at sea. Entries cover persons, vessel types, battles, important geographic features, equipment, and popular named events. Typical essays are: Liberty Ships, Z Plan, Norway (Navy), Kaiten, Dieppe Raid, Bab el Mandeb Strait, Battle of the Atlantic, Naval Aviation, Frogmen, Fuchida Mitsuo, Sir Andrew Browne Cunningham (First Viscount Cunningham of Hyndhope), Hell Ships, Wilhelm Franz Canaris, Blockade Running, Panay Incident, and William Francis Gibbs. Each essay ends with a bibliography of further reading on the subject. The set has an eight-page introductory essay entitled "World War II at Sea Overview." The second volume concludes with a "Chronology of Principal Events of World War II at Sea," a glossary, a general bibliography, a list of editors and contributors, a classed subject index (called categorical index), and a general index. The volumes contain a few black-and-white illustrations. Most of the bibliography entries date from 2008 and earlier.

Overall, this is an excellent treatment of naval affairs during the Second World War. It will provide the general reader and the specialist with basic background materials and suggestions for further study. This reviewer noted two notable exceptions, however. The set fails to mention the *M.S. Awa Maru* sinking by the *U.S.S. Queenfish*, and the subsequent court martial of the Captain of the *U.S.S Queenfish*, Rear Admiral Charles Elliot Loughlin. The *M.S. Awa Maru* travelling under a Red Cross flag permit from President Franklin D. Roosevelt, was "accidently" sunk by the *U.S.S. Queenfish* on April Fool's Day in 1945. Only one person of the 2,000 on board survived. This incident significantly colored Japanese/United States relations following the war. Also not mentioned in the set is the sinking of the *MV Wilhelm Gustloff* in January of 1945 by a Soviet submarine resulting in the death of an estimated 9,400 German civilians being evacuated from East Prussia. With the exception of these two significant Allied lacunae, without which the World War II naval story is incomplete, Tucker has compiled a very useful encyclopedia.—**Ralph Lee Scott**

Handbooks and Yearbooks

C, P

183. Fredriksen, John C. **Fighting Elites: A History of U.S. Special Forces.** Santa Barbara, Calif., ABC-CLIO, 2012. 392p. illus. index. $89.00. ISBN 13: 978-1-59884-810-6; 978-1-59884-811-3 (e-book).

Fighting Elites is a reference book providing a series of essays that examine the history and contributions that the U.S. military's Special Forces have provided from Colonial times to the present day. The essays have been arranged in chronological order, beginning with the "special purpose" units used during the Colonial times and followed by the Special Forces units of World War II and the Cold War. The largest section of the work deals with the use of Special Forces since 1992, including Air Force Air Commandos, Airborne Forces, Navy SEALs, Green Berets, Mountain Division (Light Infantry), and Intelligence Support, just to name a few. For each unit represented there is information on their origin, recruitment, training, tactics, and equipment. Defining military engagements are discussed in depth to provide a deeper understanding for the reader on their contributions to the overall military. Biographical entries for 20 noted military members are included as well. The work concludes with a chronology of U.S. Special Forces, a bibliography, and an index. This is a unique guide that will be useful in all sizes of academic and public libraries.—**John Howard Oxley**

C, S

184. Skaine, Rosemarie. **Women in Combat: A Reference Handbook.** Santa Barbara, Calif., ABC-CLIO, 2011. 319p. index. (Contemporary World Issues). $55.00. ISBN 13: 978-1-59884-459-7.

Women in the military is not a contemporary issue—women in combat certainly is. In another ABC-CLIO volume in the Contemporary World Issues series, noted women's issues author Skaine documents women as soldiers—and sailors. Three introductory chapters detail the history, problems and solutions, and international perspective of women in active combat roles. This last chapter on other nations is especially insightful considering how active women have been in military roles worldwide. A chronology, biographical sketches of significant women in uniform, and a data and document section follow. A listing of resources and brief index conclude the volume. This volume, as with the 25-plus others in the series, is aimed more at a secondary school audience and makes a solid addition to school and public libraries. Selectors would be wise to gauge the use of other volumes in the series among their patrons given limited budgets and access to an ever expanding Internet with so much information now available.—**Boyd Childress**

Navy

C, S

185. **The Civil War Naval Encyclopedia.** Spencer C. Tucker, ed. Santa Barbara, Calif., ABC-CLIO, 2011. 2v. illus. index. $180.00/set. ISBN 13: 978-1-59884-338-5; 978-1-59884-339-2 (e-book).

Most military examinations of the Civil War concentrate on land-based campaigns with iconic battles such as Antietam, Gettysburg, Shiloh, and Vicksburg. This work demonstrates that students of this seminal conflict also must examine naval and maritime operations, which played critical roles in its ultimate outcome, if they are to have a satisfactory understanding of this epochal military struggle and how it influenced future U.S. naval activities.

An opening section features a preface, list of entries, list of maps, and an introductory historical overview of key Civil War naval events. The preponderance of this compendium features entries on the individuals, ships, battles, nautical equipment, and strategy that characterized of Union and Confederate naval operations. Examples of entries featured include: Arkansas River; Artillery Projectiles, Naval; Samuel Francis du Pont, Fort Donelson, Battle of; Galena, USS; Guerra de Course; Gulf Blockading Squadron; H. L. Hunley CSS; Sabine Pass; First Battle of; Savannah River Squadron; Submarines; Sultana Disaster; and Charles Wilkes.

Entries are succinctly written and cover oceanic, littoral, and river operations and feature selected maps and pictures. Concluding sections feature a Civil War naval chronology from November 15, 1860-November 6, 1865; a glossary of naval terms, including *astern, coxswain, letter of marquee,* and *windlass*; and a detailed bibliography of primary and secondary sources.

This work is an essential addition to academic, public, and special libraries desirous of having quality U.S. Civil War and maritime/naval history collection. Additional entries on shipping and naval construction workforces and their relationships with commercial managers and the governmental/private sector wartime contracting practices would have strengthened the quality of this compendium further. This work is highly recommended.—**Bert Chapman**

C

186. Fredriksen, John C. **The United States Marine Corps: A Chronology, 1775 to the Present.** Santa Barbara, Calif., ABC-CLIO, 2011. 361p. illus. index. $85.00. ISBN 13: 978-1-59884-542-6; 978-1-59884-543-3 (e-book).

In the genre of chronology, this work dealing with the United States Marine Corps provides a concise and yet thorough treatment of historical events, achievements and personalities associated with this elite fighting force. Following a year-to-year, month-to-month summary of major and minor combat interventions of the Corps, the reader is also provided with photographs, biographical summaries, and other illustrations of value to military historians and history buffs alike. As stated in the introduction: "This chronology attempts to paint a broad picture of Marine Corps achievements." The text also takes care to review noted laws, regulations, weapon systems, and political developments germane to and effecting Marine Corps deployments. For the scholar an extensive bibliography of sources is attached for more in-depth study. This work would be a valuable addition in colleges and research libraries serving an ROTC Program and/or advanced studies in military history.—**Patrick Hall**

Weapons

C, P, S
187. Hays, Peter L. **Space and Security: A Reference Handbook.** Santa Barbara, Calif., ABC-CLIO, 2011. 289p. index. (Contemporary World Issues). $ 55.00. ISBN 13: 978-1-59884-421-4; 978-1-59884-422-1 (e-book).

This well-known and widely available series provides general overviews of important current issues. This title concerns future arenas of warfare and commercial development; the growth potential for both fields seems virtually unlimited. But the current economic crisis severely limits what the federal government is able to do, so more investment will have to come from the private sector. The sections cover the background and history of this human technological endeavor, problems and controversies, worldwide perspectives, missile defenses and space, and the emergence of China as a major player. There are reference notes at the end of the chapters. Also included is the text of 10 relevant documents. Of particular interest for reference work are a chronology (October 3, 1942-June 28, 2010), 45 biographical sketches of important leaders in this field, a list of acronyms, a directory of organizations, and a bibliography of related resources (books, articles, Congressional hearings and reports, and Internet sites). An indication of the scope of this topic can be found in the official Library of Congress subject headings assigned to this work: Astronautics and State, Astronautics, Military, Space Industrialization, Space Surveillance, and Outer Space—Civilian Use—Government Policy. Hays helped edit a related collection of selected essays on this topic entitled *Toward a Theory of Space Power* (National Defense University Press, 2011). This reference work might be considered an almanac as much as a short encyclopedia. It will be most useful in high school, public, and undergraduate libraries for its easy-to-read chapters and wide variety of information about U.S. government policies.—**Daniel K. Blewett**

C, S
188. Robertson, Ann E. **Militarization of Space.** New York, Facts on File, 2011. 394p. index. (Global Issues). $45.00. ISBN 13: 978-0-8150-7873-8; 978-1-4381-3395-9 (e-book).

This research guide provides a clear and even-handed treatment of a complex and controversial subject, well suited to its intended juvenile audience. The well-written text carefully distinguishes between "militarization" and "weaponization" of space, carefully delineating the arguments in this debate. While a wealth of resources are supplied—primary documents, a list of relevant organizations, and an effective annotated bibliography—the aspiring researcher may benefit most from the straightforward and judicious methodology provided, which inculcates a suitably skeptical stance.

The finding aids (table of contents and index) combine with the logical layout of the book to enable rapid and effective investigation in this subject area. Checking the Web addresses and resources resulted in no problems and no other errors of presentation were noted.

The type is crisply printed on archival quality paper in a sturdy hard-case binding. Any library serving a high school or college clientele interested in space militarization issues should find this title worth considering; more senior-level researchers might also consider it a handy reference.—**John Howard Oxley**

13 Political Science

General Works

Dictionaries and Encyclopedias

C, S

189.   **CQ Global Researcher. http://www.cqpress.com/.** [Website]. Washington, D.C., CQ Press. Price negotiated by site. Date reviewed: 2011.

Students looking for international perspectives on global events will find this database a very useful research tool. It contains reports that are written by scholars and experts. Students can search for entire articles, or narrow down the search to specific report sections. Students can also browse the reports by topic, date, or country. Each article includes a pros/cons section, chronology, and Voices from Abroad (a section with international quotes that relate to the topic), all of which are accessible via a sidebar of shortcuts. Topics range from Conflicts in Africa, to the Elderly, to Water Pollution. The interface is well organized with sidebars and the current report on the home page, and utilizing the database is intuitive. How to cite information is also included. The ease of use, coupled with the large amount of information available make this a valuable addition to the reference collections of high school and undergraduate libraries.—**Allison L. Bernstein**

Handbooks and Yearbooks

C

190.   Beary, Brian. **Separatist Movements: A Global Reference.** Washington, D.C., CQ Press, 2011. 370p. illus. maps. index. $142.00. ISBN 13: 978-1-60426-569-9.

One of the ironies of the late twentieth century was the fact that globalization in arts, culture, business, and language and the spread of democratic ideas were accompanied by the growth of ethnocentrism, separatism, and ethnic divisions. *Pari passu* with the centripetal movements in culture, business, and education were centrifugal movement that challenged the artificial nationalisms created and imposed by imperialism and colonialism. Powerful social and religious forces outside government gave rise to colliding ethnic identities, often fueled by religious and linguistic rivalries. As a result, ethnic resentments generated by centuries of subservience led to a surge in irredentism and violence. The very language of politics and the sources of collective identity were recast.

Separatist Movements: A Global Reference describes the state of these irredentist movements at the beginning of the twenty-first century. This is an important study because many of these movements represent potential flashpoints of international conflict posing a threat of a wider conflagration involving major powers. They also represent deep humanitarian concerns about genocide and large scale violation of human rights. Many of these movements represent homeless or stateless people who simply ended up on the wrong side of history.

This book deals with 59 movements. Many of the movements described here are dormant or quiescent, some have petered out like the Tamils in Sri Lanka, South Yemenis in Yemen, and Zanzibaris in Tanzania, some have only formal or historical interest such as the Maoris, Baluchis, Greenlanders, and Northern Italians, some are not strictly irredentist movement at all, such as the Hawaiians, Alaskans, Taiwanese, Puerto Ricans, Turkish Cypriots, Northern Italians, and Afrikaners. In one case the book has been overtaken by events. South Sudanese have gained independence since the book was published. Thus fewer than half the number of entries deal with genuine irredentist movements, such as the Kurds, Chechens, Somalis, and Karens.

Each essay begins with a description of the people and a summary of their history. It is followed by an account of the movement's leadership and a chronicle of recent political developments. A reading section at the end of the essay lists source material. Interspersed throughout the book are biographies of separatist ethnic leaders and their ideologies. An appendix includes key international documents on self-determination. Each essay also explores the roots of ethnic separatism: religion in the Middle East and Africa, and the suppression of indigenous peoples in developed countries. Implicit in this study is the question of what constitutes a people or a nation.

Beary is a veteran journalist and expert in international relations and he has provided a succinct account of the clash of nationalism and ethnic identity. This work is recommended.—**George Thomas Kurian**

C

191.   Chapman, Bert. **Geopolitics: A Guide to the Issues.** Santa Barbara, Calif., Praeger/ABC-CLIO, 2011. 261p. maps. index. (Contemporary Military, Strategic, and Security Issues). $49.95. ISBN 13: 978-0-313-38579-7.

That politics and geography often go hand-in-glove found one of its earliest and most resonant voices in the Baron de Montesquieu's (Charles-Louis de Secondat) Sprit of the Laws. Granted, Montesquieu (more a geographic determinist than subsequent writers) tied his study more to climate than later thinkers did to geography, but he was still in the right ballpark. It has taken us moderns quite some time to understand the importance of geopolitics, but with the globalization of everything else, its inevitability proved a matter of time. Chapman's contribution to ABC-CLIO's Contemporary Military, Strategic and Security Issues is an important one.

Following a brief history of key twentieth-century geopolitical figures, the volume has chapters on selected countries and their geopolitical practices, emerging "hot spots" on the globe, scholarly monographic and periodical literature, and the musing of social networks and blogs and think tanks. A final chapter lists current geopolitical scholars, their biographies, and work. The "hot spots" section includes many familiar and obvious places (e.g., Pakistan, Afghanistan, Iraq, Iran, Palestine) as well as some perhaps less obvious ones (e.g., worldwide drug wars, maritime piracy, the arctic natural resources). The work is current and cutting edge, trite as that phrase might be.

The book tends to the scholarly but remains accessible to anyone interested in the topic. As the world heats up and nations war with each other, while terrorists of every stripe battle everyone, this tool will prove useful for those wishing to know more, or those wanting to broaden their introductory study of the subject in greater depth.—**Mark Y. Herring**

C

192.   **Countries at the Crossroads 2010: An Analysis of Democratic Governance.** Jake Dizard, Christopher Walker, and Sarah Cook, eds. Washington, D.C., Freedom Hous and Lanham, Md., Rowman & Littlefield, 2011. 699p. $89.99. ISBN 13: 978-1-4422-0547-5.

Freedom House is best known for its annual survey *Freedom in the World*, which has been a staple of international studies for over 30 years. But freedom is a complex and composite idea that has many components. It is difficult to measure or quantify it in numbers on a scale without distorting its meaning and scope. There are now 197 sovereign countries in the world and they are as dissimilar as possible in their political behavior, religious traditions, and social makeup. Some nations have a different political karma than others. In many cases, people define the terms liberty, freedom, and democracy differently. It is not possible to make political judgments without first of all defining political terms.

In recent years there have been attempts to establish universally accepted benchmarks for measuring political progress toward freedom and democracy. Freedom House has been a leader in this effort to study the tapestry of freedom on a micro scale rather than in broad generalities and to calibrate the depth of freedom in each country. *Countries at the Crossroads* is a comprehensive assessment of democratic governance in 32 middle-performing countries. This is the second volume in the series. The present volume includes a regionally diverse set of states including Cambodia, Honduras, Kenya, Nicaragua, Sri Lanka, Uganda, and Yemen. A total of 75 separate indicators are used in *Countries at the Crossroads* to measure progress in democratic governance. The conclusions of the study are depressing. They show deterioration in what scholars call "coordination goods," that is, institutions that are critical to the functioning of a viable democracy and transparent and accountable governance systems. Severe impediments have affected civic engagement, freedom of association, media freedom, and ability of citizens to influence public policy. The fragility of state institutions and the growing power of power nonstate actors have created an inhospitable climate for democratic consolidation. Many countries have exchanged freedom for political stability while in others there is neither stability nor freedom.

The effects of the erosion of democracy in these grey zone countries are far-reaching for the future. The regression in democratic governance is such that it cannot be reversed for several generations. The number of countries with a negative trajectory or substandard performance presents a special challenge to policy-makers in developing countries and international organizations who have sought to create inducements for developing countries to improve democratic accountability. The first volume covered 30 countries and the second 32 for a total of 62. We look forward to similar studies for the remaining 70-plus developing countries. This title is recommended.—**George Thomas Kurian**

C

193. **21st Century Political Science: A Reference Handbook.** John T. Ishiyama and Marijke Breuning, eds. Thousand Oaks, Calif., Sage, 2010. 2v. index. $325.00; available as an e-book. ISBN 13: 978-1-4129-6901-7.

This handbook from Sage is designed with political science undergraduate and graduate students in mind. Its editors focus on current topics of interest in the field including hot topics, issues, and debates. The 99 short chapters are arranged into six parts: General Approaches of Political Science; Comparative Politics; International Relations; Political Science Methodology; Political Thought; and American Politics. There are also several chapters that the editors refer to as '"Identity Politics," which discuss such topics as the role politics play in the lives of women, various ethnic groups, various religious groups, and gay and transgendered groups. The chapters are laid out in a way that students and researchers can learn more about interconnected topics or can conduct new research projects. For the most part the editors have tried to keep the chapters as jargon-free as possible, though students will probably need some background in political science to understand the majority of the text. For each entry there are a list of related topics and a list of further readings. All entries are signed and a list of contributors is provided with their credentials mentioned. The electronic version of this work also links to other Sage titles that may be of interest. This is a well-researched and easy-to-use resource that will be of interest to academic libraries with political science studies at the undergraduate and graduate levels.—**Shannon Graff Hysell**

Politics and Government

United States

Biography

S

194.   **The United States Presidents. http://www.abdodigital.com/.** [Website]. Edina, Minn., Abdo Digital. Price negotiated by site. Date reviewed: 2011.

The United States Presidents database includes everything one needs to know about the presidency. Portraits of each president provide an access point to the information. "Fast Facts," a timeline, and a "Did You Know?" section cover childhood, marriage, political careers, elections, and important events during the presidency. Unfamiliar words are highlighted and are hyperlinked to a glossary. For those who wonder about the line of succession to the presidency, it is included all the way down to the eighteenth place—Secretary of Homeland Security. A video with President Obama discusses the letters he receives. Games, on topics such as presidential hobbies and which president is on which monetary denomination, will enhance learning and will be fascinating to young researchers. This site is recommended for school research as well as for independent interest.—**Ellen Spring**

Chronology

C, S

195.   Troy, Gil, Arthur M. Schlesinger Jr., and Fred L. Israel. **History of American Presidential Elections 1789-2008.** 4th ed. New York, Facts on File, 2012. 3v. illus. maps. index. $225.00/set. ISBN 13: 978-0-8160-8220-9; 978-1-4381-3631-8 (e-book).

The *History of American Presidential Elections* was first published by Arthur Schlesinger (Chelsea House) in 1971. Two other eminent historians co-edit this edition, and are joined by several distinguished contributors. The 1st edition had no illustrations or photographs. This edition includes black-and-white Electoral College maps, using various line patterns to differentiate third or fourth party candidates. Political cartoons and caricatures of the day give a flavor of the issues and personalities surrounding each election. The third edition also added overviews, chronologies, electoral statistics, and updated the bibliographies. The three volumes, paged continuously, present election results, both popular and electoral. Historical documents are omitted in this edition, as most are freely available on the Web.

Each election begins with an overview that presents the dates of elections in various states—elections were not uniformly held until 1848, due to an act in 1845 (p. 375). Contributors elucidate on issues, economic status, conventions, complete balloting, platforms, slogans, songs, quotations, and a chronology. Many nominations during the nineteenth-century went far beyond the first ballot. Editors and contributors also illustrate how history repeats itself. In one instance, the Free Soilers in 1848 called candidate Lewis Cass a "doughface" (p. 375), due to his changing positions.

The extensive index has excellent syndetic structure, with cross-references and names of those who influenced elections, even if they were not candidates. It also highlights election years and page numbers relevant to the subjects and persons. Footers within the index also identify the volumes' pagings, easing navigation. These volumes encapsulate the elections with concise information. In-depth essays explore the issues, people, and culture surrounding each election. An appendix lists campaign costs from 1860 to 2008, with the current equivalencies in dollars. Its value goes beyond the political and statistical history of elections to historical geography, presenting each state's border as it was during each election. One can also examine the economy (gross domestic product), populations, number of newspapers, changes in the electoral process (pp. 51-52 on 1804), history, and laws that influenced elections.—**Ralph Hartsock**

Dictionaries and Encyclopedias

S

196.   **The American Presidency.** Chicago, Britannica Educational, 2010. 138p. illus. index. $37.44. ISBN 13: 978-1-6153-5427-6.

S

197.   **The American Presidency Online.** **http://www.britannica.com/presidents/.** [Website]. Chicago, Encyclopaedia Britannica. Free. Date reviewed: 2010.

Britannica's *The American Presidency* print and online sources differ from similar sources on the presidency such as H. W. Wilson's *Facts About the Presidents* (8th ed.; see ARBA 2010, entry 663). The encyclopedia-style entries summarize the president' lives, careers, families, and legacies through descriptive accounts that fill in the outline of dates and facts presented in *Facts About the Presidents*. For example, a student could begin with the facts and then ask questions about what they mean. Or, a student could begin with overviews and follow up with a factual source to explain the details. Whereas *The American Presidency* contains accounts of Obama's college, entry into politics, platform, nomination, and election, it lacks the level of detail found in accounts in *Facts About the Presidency* that provides the exact dates of his father's and mother's marriages, birth dates of all of his siblings, and a clear account of his father's second marriage. *The American Presidency's* multimedia effect are also notable. Multiple photographs are available in both the print and online versions.

Added content in the online version includes U.S. maps of red and blue states showing the electoral vote for each election. There are also articles about all vice presidents and first ladies and special essay about the 2008 election, the White House, the presidency, national monuments, and the role of the first lady. Additionally there are hundreds of primary source documents, 50-plus audio and video clips about presidents, and a memorabilia section in the online version includes a pin or election sign with a slogan for each president. These features and extra articles are not in the print volume of the same titles. The online version is easy to browse, but has no online search function.

The American Presidency is the title of a new print volume and has a featured spotlight in the *Britannica Online School Edition* with a free online Britannica Website. The spotlight version and the free online version are the same product and these online forms of *The American Presidency* are articles taken word for word from *Encyclopaedia Britannica* online articles about presidents, vice presidents, first ladies, elections, and more. Unlike the free online version, the new print volume of *The American Presidency* has text condensed from *Compton's Encyclopedia* by Britannica. About one-third of the text from articles on the presidents in *Compton*'s is included in the print volume about presidents. Thus, the free *American Presidency* Website will be useful especially where a *Britannica Online School Edition* subscription is unavailable. Likewise, the print book of the same title will be useful in school libraries that do not own the most recent *Compton's Encyclopedia*. Libraries having *Compton*'s in print, but not *Encyclopaedia Britannica* would benefit from using the free *American Presidency* Website to supplement the *Compton*'s articles. Those libraries owning *Encyclopaedia Britannica*, but not *Compton's Encyclopedia* would benefit from supplementing their content with the print volume of *The American Presidency* by Compton's.—**Karla Krueger**

C, P, S

198.   Quirk, Paul J., and William Cunion. **Governing America: Major Decisions of Federal, State, and Local Governments from 1789 to the Present.** New York, Facts on File, 2011. 3v. illus. index. $250.00/set. ISBN 13: 978-0-8160-7567-6; 978-1-4381-3547-2 (e-book).

Governing America: Major Decisions of Federal, State, and Local Governments from 1789 to the Present presents and explains significant public policy decisions made by legislative, judicial, and executive branches of federal, state, and local governments. The three-volume set is arranged thematically by broad policy areas: Economic Policies (volume 1); Social Policies (volume 2); Government, Law Enforcement, and Foreign Affairs (volume 3). It is then subdivided by topics and subtopics. Examples of topics include Agriculture, Labor, and Transportation (volume 1); Arts, Health Care, and Moral Regulation (volume 2); and Crime, Elections, and Immigration and Naturalization (volume 3). Each entry is written by an expert in that policy area and provides descriptions of the major provisions of the policies and the actions taken by the responsible governments; the conditions, problems, and politics influencing the adoption of policies; debates of the merits of the policies from different perspectives; and scholarly analysis of the effects of the policies. A selected bibliography and index, plus a list of contributors with their academic and professional affiliations listed, are found at the end of volume 3. The most noteworthy and unique feature of this title is that it is a collection of public policy decisions from all branches of government, and from various levels of government, arranged thematically, and presented in historical context. For its integrated approach to public policy explication, this set is highly recommended for public, high school, and undergraduate academic libraries.—**Polly D. Boruff-Jones**

Directories

C, P

199.   **Washington Information Directory 2011-2012.** Washington, D.C., CQ Press, 2011. 955p. index. $155.00. ISBN 13: 978-1-60426-997-0.

Few works embody the necessity of their existence as well as the *Washington Information Directory*. The directory has been an essential source of information about the federal government and key nongovernmental organizations within the nation's capital since 1975. For those libraries with complete runs of this title, the *Directory* represents a critical research resource for tracing the evolution of the federal bureaucracy and of select organizations that attempt to influence government policy to their benefit. The current volume contains 19 chapters that cover various aspects of government with a final chapter devoted to covering all aspects of Congress. Subject area chapters are organized in a similar fashion. All have been fully updated. For example, the chapter on education begins with a list of general government agencies that support education in the Untied States, followed by a list of key nongovernmental organizations devoted to influencing educational policy. Included are an organizational chart of the Department of Education and a text box of committees and subcommittees charged with addressing education issues in Congress. The remainder of the chapter lists agencies and organizations that address specific areas of education, such as libraries, levels of education, and special topics associated with educational policy (e.g., bilingual education). The final chapter provides a comprehensive listing of resources on Congress, including basic resources on accessing information about Congress, campaign and election data, information about the capital, caucuses, leadership structure, and a list of support groups and political advocacy and party organizations. This is followed by an easily accessible appendix describing each committee of the 112th Congress. Front matter includes a complete list of text boxes and organizational charts and a guide to locating information in the *Directory*. The work concludes with a ready-reference section listing government information found on the Internet, governors and other state officials, a directory of embassies, ambassadors, Department of State country desk offices, and Freedom of Information Act and privacy legislation information.

This edition provides a new chapter devoted to Super Political Action Committees (NEA Fund for Children and Public education, Women vote!—Emily's List, and Working for Us PAC). It also has two new organization charts: one for the national Park service and one for the Centers for Medicare and Medicaid Services. The volume includes name, organization, and subject indexes. The *Directory* remains an authoritative and necessary resource for individuals or organizations interested the U.S. government.—**Robert V. Labaree**

Handbooks and Yearbooks

C, P, S

200.   Baldino, Thomas J., and Kyle L. Kreider. **U.S. Election Campaigns: A Documentary and Reference Guide.** Santa Barbara, Calif., Greenwood Press/ABC-CLIO, 2011. 351p. illus. index. (Documentary and Reference Guides). $100.00. ISBN 13: 978-0-313-35304-8; 978-0-313-35305-5 (e-book).

The title of this work implies, to this reviewer at least, a narrow focus on specific election campaigns in history. However, this is much more than a collection of references related to election campaigns. *U.S. Election Campaigns* explains the superstructure of U.S. politics through an exploration of electioneering laws and guidelines. Beginning with the nineteenth century, this book chronicles the evolution of campaign regulation providing original documents with clear interpretations. Documents are arranged chronologically in each chapter to better illustrate the development and rationale behind America's campaign laws, regulations, and court interpretation of the laws helping the researcher to detect trends and themes over time. The five chapters span more than 200 years: "The 19th Century," "1900 to 1939," "1940 to 1969," "1970 to 1999," "2000 to 2010." The book begins with a "List of Documents and Sidebars" in each chapter, followed by a "Reader's Guide to Related Documents and Sidebars" arranged alphabetically by topic. A chronology of relevant events from 1809 (James Madison's inauguration) to 2010 (the failure of the passing of the DISCLOSE Act) is included. Presented in chronological order in each chapter, a document entry includes the document's title and date of origin with a brief explanation of the significance of the document followed by the original text of the document itself and a substantive discussion of how the document came to be with an analysis of its intent and purpose. Many of the document entries include a list of further reading to aid with additional research. The volume concludes with a bibliography of selected resources and a comprehensive index. A fascinating read, this book is recommended for public, high school, and academic libraries. [R: BL, Jan 1 &15, 2012, p. 74]—**Polly D. Boruff-Jones**

C, P

201.   Barone, Michael, and Chuck McCutcheon. **The Almanac of American Politics, 2012.** Chicago, University of Chicago Press, 2011. 1838p. illus. index. $85.00pa. ISBN 13: 978-0-226-03808-7.

Reviewing this work is a labor of love. It is the kind of reference book that a news junkie like this reviewer reads for pleasure. The work is ordered by state. The organization of each state's data is essentially the same. First, a map of the state by district is provided with a brief statement of demographic and economic statistics, including income and home value breakdowns, employment breakdowns by many categories (e.g., white collar, blue collar, government, veterans, self employed), and education levels. Secondly, there is an extremely well-written essay on the state that includes information on history, economics, and politics—from the state's beginning to the last elections. Then there is a biography of the governor and his or her record as well as a list of the senators and their biographies and records and the congressional representatives with their biographies, histories, and voting records.

With each person, users get information on their voting records on major issues and the results of their latest elections as well as their ratings from the major political NGO's (e.g., ACU, ACLU). Information is provided on their religion, education, and military service. Election results and winning percentages and contact numbers are provided as well. Territorial governors are covered and lists of congressional seniority are given.

For any level of political study, this book is invaluable. Authors Barone and McCutcheon weaved a great blend of prose and hard facts. This series is perhaps among the best works on politics ever published. It is not hard to read and is actually "fun" for those folks interested in these subjects. This is clearly a must book for any library as well as a must for any free citizen wishing to understand his government.—**Gary L. Parsons**

C, S

202.   **Congress Investigates: A Critical and Documentary History.** By the Robert C. Byrd Center for Legislative Studies. New York, Facts on File, 2011. 584p. illus. index. (Facts on File Library of American History). $195.00/set. ISBN 13: 978-0-8160-7679-6.

While we often think of more recent congressional investigations from events like Watergate or 9/11, Congress has been investigating since just a decade or two after this country began. This two-volume set covers the whole history of Congressional investigations from General St. Clair's defeat in 1792 through the Hurricane Katrina investigation in 2006-2007.

Combining lengthy introductory essays with primary source documents, such as speeches, excerpts from testimony, congressional debate and interviews, each of the investigations in the set come to life for the researcher. So much of what and why congress chooses to investigate is dependent upon the political atmosphere and characters in the country at the time that the inclusion of the introductory essay is critical. But the outcomes of investigations frequently hinge on speeches, testimonies, memos, and other primary source documents so those are needed, too, if the conclusions of the investigation are to be fully understood. This set has found a good balance in how to present both primary and secondary material. With appropriate context provided for the primary materials students will be able to make sense of these events and gain an understanding that is greater than they would gain from just the primary or secondary source alone.

Timelines and thorough bibliographies accompany each essay so no matter whether the topic is the Ku Klux Klan, The Teapot Dome Scandal, The Committee on Un-American Activities, Iran-Contra, or 9/11, users of this source will find an excellent combination of context and primary materials to get them on their way.—**Rosalind Tedford**

P, S

203.   Hudson, David L., Jr. **The Handy Presidents Answer Book.** 2d ed. Canton, Mich., Visible Ink Press, 2011. 501p. illus. index. $21.95pa. ISBN 13: 978-1-57859-317-0.

This book showcases over 1,000 questions and answers related to the past and present United States' Commanders in Chief, some 200 more than the last edition (2004). Queries are categorized by topics ranging from the origins of the U.S. presidency to parties and platforms, elections, and individual presidents. For each president such topics as their early life and career, political offices held, presidency, and life after the presidency are addressed. The question-and-answer format that exists throughout the book allows for quick look-ups and makes it convenient for users to leisurely browse by chapter. Those who prefer to search by a specific topic can use the index that is provided. This resource features black-and-white illustrations of presidential photographs, political cartoons, charts, and drawings. Another highlight includes a list of trivia questions at the back of the volume that address such topics as occupations, military service, education, and assassinations. This informative resource will suit public and school library users, especially those who are writing political science or history term papers.—**Maris L. Hayashi**

S

204.   Utter, Glenn H. **Youth and Political Participation: A Reference Handbook.** Santa Barbara, Calif., ABC-CLIO, 2011. 285p. index. (Contemporary World Issues). $58.00. ISBN 13: 978-1-59884-661-4; 978-1-59884-662-1 (e-book).

Youth and Political Participation: A Reference Handbook is a well-researched work on young persons, politics, and encouraging people to vote. After a list of contents and a preface the book includes chapters on the history of youth and political participation, voting after the 26th amendment, and the importance of mass media in the participation of youth. It also addresses the problems that arise from this age group in political participation, including educating this age group to the process of voting, low voter turnout, college elections, and the use of the Internet and other media outlets in reaching this age group. The book provides an international perspective with chapters addressing voter participation in various countries, including Costa Rica, England, France, Germany, Italy, and Japan. The final chapters provide items that will be useful at the reference desk, including a chronology, biographical sketches, data and documents, organizations, print and online resources, a glossary, and an index. Academic and public libraries and scholars researching voting and government and political tendencies of people will find this work to be a complete reference work on the topic of youth and political participation.—**Melinda F. Matthews**

China

C

205.   Sullivan, Lawrence R. **Historical Dictionary of the Chinese Communist Party.** Lanham, Md., Scarecrow, 2012. 361p. (Historical Dictionaries of Religions, Philosophies, and Movements). $85.00. ISBN 13: 978-0-8108-7225-7; 978-0-8108-7470-1 (e-book).

The Chinese Communist Party plays a role as leader of the world's largest country and second largest economy (and growing quickly). The Communist party has had a tumultuous history that includes civil war, the humanitarian catastrophe of the Great Leap Forward (1958-1960), and the death of its main leader Mao Zedong in 1976. The *Historical Dictionary of the Chinese Communist Party* helps to explain the ups and downs of the political party and its role in modern-day world politics.

This volume is well organized and begins with a chronology tracing of events in the year and month order for this period. An introduction puts the events in context and connects people in relation to the events. The main body of information is in dictionary form with information about important persons, movements, institutions, and places. Each of the 400 entries is well researched and offers a good amount of details. The bibliography offers resources for further reading.

Sullivan has taken advantage of the fact that China has opened its doors to the rest of the world and that Communist Party leaders have had more freedom to discuss their politics and opinions. It would be an excellent starting point for research in the Chinese Communist Party and the political history of China in general. This work is highly recommended for academic libraries or any libraries supporting the collection of Asian history or Chinese studies.—**Ma Lei Hsieh**

Europe

C, S

206.   Slomp, Hans, ed. **Europe: A Political Profile. An American Companion to European Politics.** Santa Barbara, Calif., ABC-CLIO, 2011. 2v. index. $189.00/set. ISBN 13: 078-0-313-39181-1; 978-0-313-39182-8 (e-book).

Viewed from the outside, European political systems are remarkably similar but there are historical differences that are sometimes sharper than the ones that divide governments and politics in other continents. As the French would say, *Viva la difference. Europe: A Political Profile* is a two-volume survey of European politics. The subtitle *An American Companion to European Politics* explains the particular angle from which the book has been written. Although European governments are similar each has its own distinguishing signature DNA that serves as a marker in studying its evolutionary characteristics. There is a greater homogeneity among the major European political systems than in any other continent in the world. First, there is an ethnic homogeneity because all of Europe is historically Caucasian. Second, there is a religious homogeneity because most of Europe is majority Christian, with the possible exception of Albania, Kosovo, and Bosnia and Herzegovina where the Turks forced Islam on the population. Thirdly, Europe is the birthplace of democracy and since the eighteenth century of constitutional government the English Parliament is the Mother of Parliaments. The book thus presents a rich tableau of the colliding forces that have shaped European politics.

The book looks at European politics both from the macropolitical and micropolitical perspective. Because almost all of Europe now belongs to the supranational European Union, European governments are less than fully sovereign; they are autonomous but in one sense function as local governments. It is an unusual phenomenon and that is why the study is interesting. Unlike the United States, which has a single national government and is fully sovereign, European governments are relatively circumscribed in their powers, most of which have been ceded to the European parliament. For example, no European government in EU has the right to declare war. Thus, those familiar with U.S. political landscape may find some of the concepts confusing. Comparative political studies can be misleading at times because the lexicon of politics is different in Europe than it is in the United States. The fault line between conservatism and liberalism is less defined in Europe than in the United States. Conservative parties tend to be less socially conservative than in the United States and liberal parties less ideological. Unlike the United States, which has a strict bipolar political party system, European countries have a multipolar system where the power shifts constantly and consensus and compromise are more often the rule than the exception.

Volume 2 presents country profiles of 50 individual countries, including some like Turkey who are not part of Europe in the cultural or political sense. Europe includes the largest country in the world (Russia) and the smallest (Vatican State) and the profiles therefore vary in size and depth of information. Among the most interesting features of the book are the tables that provide a wealth of data on various aspects of European politics. This is a benchmark study recommended for all political science collections.—**George Thomas Kurian**

Ideologies

C, P

207. Atkins, Stephen E. **Encyclopedia of Right-Wing Extremism in Modern American History.** Santa Barbara, Calif., ABC-CLIO, 2011. 345p. index. $89.00. ISBN 13: 978-1-59884-350-7; 978-0-313-36239-2 (e-book).

The *Encyclopedia of Right-Wing Extremism in Modern American History* covers the1930s and onward, reaching before the 1930s only in order to establish the development of white supremacy in the form of the Ku Klux Klan. The title focuses on three types of right-wing extremism: white supremacy/Neo-Nazi movements; Christian identity, Christian reconstructionism, and other right-wing religious movements; and anti-American government extremists.

Although there are too many block quotations for this reviewer, Atkins does a commendable job of writing in an accessible way while maintaining objectivity, despite the highly controversial beliefs of the groups covered in the title. Atkins' synthesis and analysis of the groups and their beliefs, including how they are interconnected, is also objective and professional, although there are some troubling blanket generalizations regarding "white Southerners." This reviewer also thinks that an encyclopedia of any type should contain a visual component, such as illustrations, photographs, or graphics; this encyclopedia does not contain any such component.

However, in spite of too many block quotations, some difficult generalizations, and no visual elements, the *Encyclopedia of Right-Wing Extremism in Modern America* is a good introduction to the topic with some interesting synthesis and analysis. Although a relatively slim volume, it is worth the price. It features an excellent and thorough listing of sources as well as an excellent index. This work is highly recommended for academic libraries supporting history, sociology, psychology, law, criminal justice, and political science programs. It is also recommended for public libraries.—**Megan W. Lowe**

International Relations

C
208.   Kalaitzidis, Akis, and Gregory W. Streich. **U.S. Foreign Policy: A Documentary and Reference Guide.** Santa Barbara, Calif., Greenwood Press/ABC-CLIO, 2011. 331p. illus. index. (Documentary and Reference Guides). $100.00. ISBN 13: 978-0-313-38375-5; 978-0-313-38376-2 (e-book).

This book gives the history of U.S. foreign policy. It contains some introductory material that is a guide to many of the documents and sidebars discussed, followed by nine chapters. It also has an introduction concerning American foreign policy and the theoretical landscape. After this, chapters are given for: George Washington to James Monroe, the origin of realism; Andrew Jackson to Andrew Johnson, Westward expansion and manifest destiny; William McKinley to Woodrow Wilson, beyond realism and isolationism; Franklin D. Roosevelt, from the arsenal of democracy to super power status; Harry Truman to Lyndon B. Johnson, containment; Richard Nixon to Ronald Reagan, toward the end of the Cold War; George H. Bush to Bill Clinton, the new world order; George W. Bush, empire; and Barrack Obama, Liberalism/realism. After this comes an afterword, selected resources index, and information about the author. Chapters are subdivided into articles or sections that give information of the most important foreign policy statements. Each chapter has an abbreviated reference list at the end. Chapters also contain photographs and sidebars that give additional information on the foreign policy environment that occurred during this period of time. The book has an adequate index, the binding and paper are average, and the font size is adequate for the purpose. This work should be of interest to any libraries interested in U.S. foreign policy, foreign policy in general, or U.S. and political history.—**Herbert W. Ockerman**

C
209.   Thompson, William R., and David R. Dreyer. **Handbook of International Rivalries 1494-2010.** Washington, D.C., CQ Press, 2011. 318p. index. (Correlates of War Series). $155.00. ISBN 13: 978-0-87289-487-7; 978-1-60871-841-2 (e-book).

Rivalries between nation-states have been a part of international relations as long as humans have recorded their history. These rivalries can be peaceful or violent and are derived from factors as diverse as economics; religion; the personalities of individual leaders; disputes over territory; ethnicity; access to natural resources; and competition with adjacent countries to gain competitive advantage. This work provides succinct overviews of international rivalries from the Age of Columbus to the present. Chapters provide contextual introductions along with descriptions of European Great Power rivalries; and European nongreat power and Soviet/Russian-United States rivalries; North and South American rivalries; Middle Eastern, North African, and Southwest Eurasian rivalries; Asian rivalries; and Sub-Saharan African rivalries. Examples of profiled rivalries include Austria-Prussia 1740-1870; Portugal-Spain 1494-1580; Soviet Union-United States 1945-1989; Bolivia-Chile 1836-present; Saudi Arabia-Yemen 1990-2000; China-Taiwan 1949-present; China-United States 1996-present; Cambodia-Vietnam 1976-1983; India-Pakistan 1947-present; and Ethiopia-Sudan 1965-present.

Characteristics described within these individual national rivalries include the nature of the rivalry, including whether it is geographical/spatial or positional, whether war has occurred between these competitors, whether external intervention for neighboring powers has occurred, and key events in the ongoing development and evolution of these rivalries. Descriptions of these rivalries include selective bibliographic references, an appendix includes a chronological listing of these rivalries, and the compilation concludes with a significant bibliography.

Despite its somewhat theoretical nature, this is a useful resource for upper-division undergraduates and above desiring to learn more about international political rivalries and quantifying these rivalries. The entries are succinctly written and individual chapters include some maps. This work is limited by just focusing on rivalries between nation-states. While these rivalries remain of critical importance, a comprehensive definition of rivalries must include the roles played by transnational organizations, such as terrorist groups, human traffickers, computer hackers, and drug cartels in influencing bilateral and multilateral relationships between countries.

Examples of current and potential rivalries the authors could examine include the role of sovereign debt and how it influences relationships between countries and international government organizations as demonstrated by the European financial crisis and Greece; the competition for natural resources in the Arctic between countries such as Canada, Denmark, Russia, and the United States; the role of transnational terrorist groups such as Al Qaida and the Taliban in Afghanistan, Pakistan, Yemen, and elsewhere; the role of Mexican drug gangs in influencing U.S. border security, immigration, and counterdrug policies; and the role of human traffickers in numerous areas of the world.—**Bert Chapman**

Public Policy and Administration

Dictionaries and Encyclopedias

C, P, S
210. **Encyclopedia of Disaster Relief.** K. Bradley Penuel and Matt Statler, eds. Thousand Oaks, Calif., Sage, 2011. 2v. illus. index. $350.00/set; $440.00 (e-book). ISBN 13: 978-1-4129-7101-0; 978-1-4129-9406-4 (e-book).

The *Encyclopedia of Disaster Relief* represents a master work. Editor K. Bradley Penuel is the Director of the New York University Center for Catastrophe Preparedness and Response and editor Matt Statler is the Richman Family Director of Business Ethics and Social Impact Programming and a Clinical Assistant Professor of Management and Organizations at NYU Stern School of Business. The two volumes encompass field concepts and essential disaster-related issues. This landmark professional contribution describes an excellent array of professional responses that assist in understanding how communities can become bettered prepared. In addition, this considerable literary achievement discusses strategies and steps that move citizens and communities forward in their efforts for coordinated, timely, adequate, and target-specific responses for disaster relief.

The *Encyclopedia of Disaster Relief* describes how communities can plan for both natural and man-made disasters. The inclusive content illustrates local, national, international disaster relief: mitigation, preparedness, response, and recovery. The encyclopedia entries contain insightful information and practical solutions encountered in disaster scenarios. Relief case studies of major disasters offer explanations on how communities can become more resourceful and resilient to the impact when tragedy strikes. The work is written in a style that benefits students, interested citizens, and professionals. Relief case studies of major disasters overview natural and man-made disasters, and provide a chronology of disaster relief strategies. The contributors offer solutions and facilitate insightful discussions with reference to this vital topic. For example, the entry on Risk Management offers a superior approach to forecasting the probability of risk occurrence. Managing risk offers a proactive approach to saving lives, and reducing the level of risk and potential costs. Analyzing and planning for natural and man-made disasters assists in assessing the "all hazard risk management approach." This requires analyzing a broad spectrum of potential impacts. This type of risk management concerns planning, preparedness, and assesses potential impacts regardless of the cause. This article is one of many fascinating entries. Survivor Guilt is a particularly outstanding contribution. This intriguing and insightful article portrays stress-related syndrome issues suffered by survivors. The content describes the unprocessed guilt that can make recovery difficult and intensifies the grieving process. If guilt is unattended or not treated, chronic depression, self harm, substance abuse, or even suicides represent possible outcomes.

This two-volume encyclopedia offers 425 highly accessible entries and exceeds the standard for quality encyclopedia production. Readers are immediately drawn to a cover highlighting the globally recognized Red Cross symbol that serves as a source of comfort and support for disaster relief operations. The set's developers and designers took extreme care to offer readers a superior product that includes heavy, weight-bound pages. The large fonts, text organization, appropriate illustrations, index system, and appendixes enhance readability and understanding. Readers will find the September 2007 National Preparedness Guidelines, definitions of terms, and acronyms and abbreviations helpful. The well-organized and comprehensive entries offer further readings and cross-references to supplementary topics of interest that encourage additional research opportunities.

Various type of readers and libraries will be interested in the *Encyclopedia of Disaster Relief*: first responder agencies and police, fire, and rescue services would find the volumes useful for training programs. In addition, high schools, community colleges, universities, and private libraries would find this two-volume set a valuable educational resource.—**Thomas E. Baker**

C, S

211.   **Encyclopedia of the U.S. Government and the Environment: History, Policy, and Politics.** Matthew Lindstrom, ed. Santa Barbara, Calif., ABC-CLIO, 2011. 2v. illus. index. $180.00/set. ISBN 13: 978-1-59884-237-1; 978-1-59884-238-8 (e-book).

The two-volume set begins with three essays: "The U.S. Government and the Environment before 1960," "The U.S. Government and the Environment, Contemporary Issues," and "The U.S. Government and the Global Future." A broad spectrum of people, issues, societies, agencies, and legislation are presented. These include people on all sides of environmental issues (e.g., John Muir, Al Gore, James Inhofe), places (e.g., Glen Canyon Dam, Wetlands, Yosemite National Park), international activities (e.g., Antarctic Treaty, Nuclear Test Ban Treaty, Migratory Bird Treaty Act of 1918, Vienna Convention for the Protection of the Ozone Layer), nongovernmental societies (e.g., Environmental Defense Fund, International Whaling Commission), industries (e.g., Alaska Oil Pipeline, Coal Mining), environmental disasters (e.g., Exxon Valdez Spill, Love Canal), issues (e.g., Acid Rain, Climate Change, DDT), laws (e.g., National Environmental Protection Act of 1969, both a narrative and the primary document), and court cases (e.g., *Massachusetts v. EPA of 2007*). Content of each article is useful, particularly in the history of various departments and divisions. For court cases, authors give the number of the case, and a narrative about it, both of which are very useful. Most articles include a brief bibliography and references to related entries. The book concludes with a useful chronology, mostly from 1798 to the present.

Two structural changes would greatly improve this set. First, since this is titled the *Encyclopedia of the U.S. Government and the Environment* it should be assumed that all agencies are part of the federal system unless otherwise noted. For consistency, all should be entered under U.S. (U.S. Environmental Protection Agency), or all should be under the direct name (Environmental Protection Agency). Those not part of the federal government can be qualified, such as the Food and Agricultural Organization (International organization), Environmental Defense Fund (Nonprofit organization).

A second addition could be a chart listing the structure, confusing at best, of the agencies, as EPA is independent, but BIA, BLM, and Fish and Wildlife are in the DOI, while Forest Service is in Department of Agriculture, and FEMA is in Homeland Security. This is partially done in the entry for "Stream Corridor Restoration Program." No user's guide exists to explain placement of entries. The index needs to be viewed in multiple locations to ascertain all information. EPA is indexed three times, as Environmental Protection Agency, EPA, and U.S. Environmental Protection Agency. Each of these index entries lists differing page locations for information. The article on the EPA is entered under U.S. Environmental Protection Agency. The same can be said for Fish and Wildlife service, also indexed as U.S. Fish and Wildlife Service, and printed in the latter position. In spite of these navigation problems, the content of will serve students well in academic libraries.—**Ralph Hartsock**

C, P

212.   **Encyclopedia of Water Politics and Policy in the United States.** Steven L. Danver and John R. Burch Jr., eds. Washington, D.C., CQ Press, 2011. 510p. illus. index. $175.00. ISBN 13: 978-1-60426-614-6; 978-1-60871-760-6 (e-book).

In July 2010, the United National General Assembly passed without opposition a resolution stating that safe and clean drinking water and sanitation is a fundamental human right essential to the full enjoyment of life and supports all other human rights. This encyclopedia reminds us that many of the key issues concerning the right to safe drinking water and basic sanitation have been and continue to be regularly debated in the United States. Entries are organized into four parts. Part 1 contains chapters that review regional water issues, including describing specific historical characteristics and geophysical features and noting hydrological concerns unique to the region. Of particular note is the chapter on the Northeast because it reminds the reader that water politics is not unique to the western United States. Part 2 contains entries about key issues and topics with regard to water politics and policy-making. Examples of topics covered include acid rain, dam building, and recreational water rights. These entries help lay a foundation for understanding the underlying issues in parts 3 and 4 of the encyclopedia. Part 3 addresses the legal aspects of water rights and politics. Included are entries that describe important court cases that have defined the legal boundaries of government regulation of activities involving water and the rights of specific groups, such as Native Americans, to access water resources. Part 4 describes specific water projects, such as the Hoover Dam, that were implemented to control water flows in our nation's rivers, lakes, and coastal areas or projects intended to provide better access to water in areas of rapid urbanization and farming communities.

Considered collectively, the entries about specific projects offer insight into the significant resources that have been allocated during the past 125 years to control water distribution. Entries are arranged alphabetically within each chapter and include *see also* cross-references and a bibliography of further readings. Pictures and text boxes are included throughout the work. Front matter includes alphabetic and thematic tables of contents and lists of featured topics (text boxes) and contributors. A comprehensive index is included. This work is highly recommended for anyone interested in understanding historical and contemporary water politics and policy issues in the United States. [R: Choice, Jan 12, p. 855]—**Robert V. Labaree**

Handbooks and Yearbooks

C, P

213.   Hillstrom, Kevin. **U.S. Health Policy and Politics: A Documentary History.** Washington, D.C., CQ Press, 2012. 717p. index. $185.00. ISBN 13: 978-1-60871-026-3.

Contained within this one volume is a very comprehensive overview of U.S. health policies. Subtitled "A Documentary History," the readers is presented with a concise and yet thorough review of the history of health policies and medicine in Colonial America beginning in the early 1600s. From pandemics such as the Boston smallpox epidemic of 1721, to a description of early state supported colonial hospitals, a snapshot of what health care was like in early America is presented. The book also traces the professionalization of American medicine and how doctors, nurses, and other health professionals were trained. In the section entitled "Charlatans, Quacks and the Patent Medicine Trade," the ubiquitous environment that served as the precursor for government regulation over various drugs and medicines is place into its historical context. Through primary source materials taken from the Congressional Record and other federal documents, the background and politics leading up to Obamacare concludes this health policy survey. The work also contains a chronology of major historical events and people who helped shape health policies in the United States. An extensive bibliography and a thematic table also aid the researcher with furthering their knowledge in this area. This works is highly recommended for both academic and public libraries wishing to build their health and medical collections.—**Patrick Hall**

14 Psychology

Psychology

Bibliography

C, P

214.   **PsycINFO. http://www.apa.org/pubs/databases/psycinfo/index.aspx.** [Website]. Washington, D.C., American Psychological Association. Price negotiated by site. Date reviewed: 2011.

PsycINFO is the online version of *Psychological Abstracts*. The online database provides journal indexing back to 1806. *PsycINFO* is the preeminent index to some three million psychology literature, and covers journals, books, book chapters, technical reports, dissertations, published conference papers, bibliographies, and more. Sources are international. Using *PsycINFO* through the Ovid interface takes advantage of the Ovid "Map to Subject Heading" functionality, which automatically provides a list of suggested terms from the *PsycINFO* Thesaurus for any word or phrase typed into the search field. Specialized functions in the Subject Heading Mapping Display are Auto Explode (i.e., automatically search the indicated term and all narrower subject headings) and Focus (i.e., restrict the search to records where the indicated term is a major aspect ["focus"] of the article). The optimal search style to use in the Ovid interface is to build a search one concept at a time, and then combine sets from the search history. This is very different from most other databases. The most commonly used Limits appear in the Advanced Search interface, and many more are accessible via the Additional Limits button. In addition, options for narrowing a search by subject, author, or journal are available in the results interface.—**Suzanne S. Bell**

Dictionaries and Encyclopedias

S

215.   Streissguth, Tom, and Heath Dingwell. **The Truth About Stress Management.** New York, Facts on File, 2011. 160p. index. (The Truth About Series). $35.00. ISBN 13: 978-0-8160-7647-5.

The Truth About series from Facts on File is a multivolume series that discusses situations that are relevant to teens today. Each volume is devoted to a specific topic, with this volume focusing on the topic of stress management, focusing specifically on the consequences of stress, the different types of stress, and healthy ways of coping with stress. The volumes are each organized in an A-Z format. This volume provides entries on: emotional stress, the benefits of using exercise to cope with stress, the use of medication and meditation in dealing with stress, and stress management techniques. Each entry is like a mini-essay on the topic. Each entry concludes with a list of resources for further reading. Entries are supplemented with sidebars that provide "Questions and Answers," "Fact or Fiction?", and "Did You Know?" segments. Supplemental materials include a list of hotlines and help sites where teens can go for further information, a glossary, and an index.

This series is generally useful for teens and young adults. This title may be of particular interest since the teenage years can bring considerable stress and often times set the stage for how people learn to cope with it in the future. Those interested in this title may also want to consider Omnigraphics' *Stress Information for Teens: Health Tips About the Mental and Physical Consequences of Stress* (see ARBA 2009, entry 1251), which at $58 is more expensive but provides more detailed information on the topic. The text of this title is straightforward and the advice is generally useful.—**Shannon Graff Hysell**

Handbooks and Yearbooks

S

216.   Levy, Joel. **Phobiapedia.** Danbury, Conn., Scholastic Library Publishing, 2011. 80p. illus. $8.99pa. ISBN 13: 978-0-54534-929-1.

Kids will be amazed to learn that there is a name for nearly every fear they can imagine. This book clearly outlines 50 phobias that will be of interest to children, from the very common (arachnophobia—the fear of spiders) to the truly puzzling (lutraphobia—the fear of otters). The author describes what each fear means, the science behind the phenomena, and the etymology of each phobia's name. The book is filled with facts and photographs that children will find interesting; oftentimes the photographs are a very graphic, which will probably delight this age group if not their elders. The book begins with an A-Z of phobias and then goes on to describe them. Kids will enjoy learning more about the phobias of germs, snakes, and bats, and also learn why having a little fear of some things is not a bad thing. This book will be popular in elementary and middle school libraries as well as the children's collections of public libraries.—Shannon Graff Hysell

C

217.   **Social Psychology.** Richard J. Crisp, ed. New York, Routledge/Taylor & Francis Group, 2011. 4v. index. (Critical Concepts in Psychology). $1,140.00/set. ISBN 13: 978-0-415-49940-8.

Defined as "an attempt to understand and explain how the thoughts, feelings, and behavior of individuals are influenced by the actual, imagined, or implied presence of others," social psychology has undergone significant changes since it was first recognized in the 1940s and 1950s. This four-volume reference work, edited by Richard Crisp, a recognized leading authority in the field, attempts to make sense of the incredible amount of literature and research done in the field of social psychology. Crisp has organized the volume into four parts: "Self and Social Cognition," "Attitudes and Social Influence," "Group Processes and Intergroup Relations," and "Aggression and Love." The volume begins with an in-depth essay written by the editor on the history and intellectual context of the study of social psychology. The essays in the volume will help the reader understand the evolution of the discipline's study and understand better how new developments in the study of psychology are changing the way we understand it (e.g., computerized methodologies, MRIs). This set is written in a scholarly tone that will be most useful to graduate students of psychology, researchers in the field, and practitioners knowledgeable about the fundamental concepts behind social psychology.—**Shannon Graff Hysell**

P

218.   **Stress-Related Disorders Sourcebook.** 3d ed. Amy L. Sutton, ed. Detroit, Omnigraphics, 2011. 621p. index. (Health Reference Series). $85.00. ISBN 13: 978-0-7808-1148-5.

The subtitle of this title tells it all: "Basic Consumer Health Information about Stress and Stress-Related Disorders, Including Signs, Symptoms, Types, and Sources of Acute and Chronic Stress, the Impact of Stress on the Body, and Mental Health Problems Associated with Stress, such as Depression, Anxiety Disorders, Bipolar Disorder, Obsessive-Compulsive Disorder, Substance Abuse, Posttraumatic Stress Disorder, and Suicide, Along with Advice about Getting Help for Stress-Related Disorders,

Managing Stress and Coping with Trauma, a Glossary of Stress-Related Terms, and a Directory of Resources for Additional Help and Information." Omnigraphics's tradition of including long subtitles enumerating content may help librarians and readers choose this book.

This is a compilation of articles on stress and stress-related diseases collected into one volume. Each article has been reviewed by David A. Cooke, Omnigraphics' medical consultant, assuring readers of its reliability and authority. Authors, dates, and Web addresses are given for each article when possible. The writing level of the book varies from chapter to chapter due to the variety of sources used. Most articles are written for the lay person, defining stress, explaining diseases caused or worsened by stress, or treatments and alternative measures for managing stress. For readers unfamiliar with medical terminology, a glossary is included. Some articles may be too technical for a general audience.

The 3d edition has been reorganized by long-time editor, Amy L. Sutton, incorporating new research about stress. One-third of the articles are dated 2010, one-third are dated 2008 or 2009, and one-third are older than 2008. The book is divided into five parts: Introduction to Stress and Stress-Related Disorders; How Stress Affects the Body; How Stress Affects Mental Health; Treating Stress Related Disorders; and Stress Management. New research on veterans returning from Iraq and Afghanistan and research from post-9/11 trauma are incorporated into this volume. This edition provides more information on alternative and complementary therapy and stress management than the 2007 volume (2d ed.; see ARBA 2008, entry 693).—**Sally Bickley**

15 Recreation and Sports

General Works

Atlases

C, P, S

219. Tomlinson, Alan. **The Atlas of Sports: Who Plays What, Where, and Why.** Berkeley, Calif., University of California Press, 2011. 144p. illus. maps. index. $21.95pa. ISBN 13: 978-0-520-26824-1.

This text is an informative resource that provides a well-written overview of sports. The text is likely to be of interest to individuals that are a sports fan or an athlete. Unlike other sports books, this touches on the topics of the "who, what, when, where, and why" of sports.

This paperback text spans just over 130 pages. The cover includes a well-designed layout that incorporates high-quality color photographs of sport scenes, including football, basketball, tennis, golf, and equestrian sports. There are several color photographs of sport spectators and fans, including pictures of fans displaying their team spirit. The book's content begins with an introduction, acknowledgements, and "National Sports." The body of the text follows, including: International Sports Politics; An A to Z of Sports; The Economics of Sports; and Country Profiles. International Sports Politics includes a variety of topics such as the Olympic games, the football world cup, the commonwealth games, drugs in sports, tackling disability, gay games, and development and peace. A to Z of Sports includes more than 20 sports ranging from American football to cue sports, multisports, and wrestling. The Economics of Sports includes international federations, media, sponsorship, consuming sports, merchandising, gambling, and sports tourism. Part 4 includes County Profiles, ranging from Afghanistan to Morocco and Zimbabwe. Part 4 includes a useful glossary of country names. The Sources section is comprehensive and includes Website information.

This text is well written, easy to follow, and user friendly. Numerous color pictures, tables, and illustrations are included throughout. The layout and design of this text is effective, providing the reader with useful and easy-to-understand information. Adult readers and children may enjoy reading this together. This text could complement a variety of libraries including personal, school, and recreation centers.—**Paul M. Murphy III**

Dictionaries and Encyclopedias

P

220. Blevins, Dave. **The Sports Hall of Fame Encyclopedia: Baseball, Basketball, Football, Hockey, Soccer.** Lanham, Md., Scarecrow, 2012. 2v. index. $200.00/set. ISBN 13: 978-0-8108-6130-5.

The Sports Hall of Fame Encyclopedia is a complete list of all athletes and behind-the-scenes-personnel that have been inducted into one of the major sports hall of fames: The Baseball Hall of Fame, The Basketball Hall of Fame, The Soccer Hall of Fame, the Football Hall of Fame, and the Hockey Hall of Fame. In all, it is a biographical listing of nearly 1,500 of the greatest athletes to play U.S. sports. The book is arranged in alphabetic order by last name and each biography includes information on their contribution to their sport, position(s) played, career statistics, and biographical information. The best of the best are listed here, including: Yogi Berra, Joe Gibbs, Mia Hamm, Earvin "Magic" Johnson, Joe Montana, Robert "Bobby" Orr, and Jerry Rice. Most of these players will have been written about extensively in other resources that libraries will already own. This work is unique in that it ties the players in with their Hall of Fame contemporaries and includes information on how they were selected for the honor and the Hall of Fame selection process in general. Appendixes include lists of each sport's Hall of Fame with an inductee list by year and in alphabetic order.—**Shannon Graff Hysell**

C

221.   **Encyclopedia of Sports Management and Marketing.** Linda E. Swayne and Mark Dodds, eds. Thousand Oaks, Calif., Sage, 2011. 4v. illus. index. $695.00/set; $875.00 (e-book). ISBN 13: 978-1-4129-7382-3; 978-1-4129-9415-6 (e-book).

Available in print and online, this encyclopedia is destined to be the major reference work on sports management and marketing in the United States for years to come. The four-volume set covers all aspects of sports marketing including trends, issues, concepts, economics, law, and human resources practices. It covers both the marketing of the sports themselves and their related products as well as marketing nonsport material goods using sports and athletes as a platform (e.g., celebrity endorsements). It does not, however, include articles on individuals, although the careers of many prominent people in the industry can be traced through other articles. Over 800 alphabetically arranged articles are included, with each article being between 1,000 and 4,000 words in length and written by a noted expert. To aid in accessing the needed information, volume 1 includes Reader's Guide, which arranges the articles by 21 broad subject categories such as customer/fan, facilities/operations, management, news media, price, sales promotion, and social marketing. The style of writing is consistent across articles and each article includes *see also* references to other articles and a bibliography of further readings. The work includes full-color photographs throughout. A complete index rounds out the set.

This encyclopedia is currently the best resource available for introductory information on all aspects of sports marketing and management in the United States. It should be acquired by larger public libraries and by all academic libraries serving students in this specialized area of business and marketing.— **Gregory A. Crawford**

Handbooks and Yearbooks

S

222.   **Science Behind Sports Series.** Farmington Hills, Mich., Lucent Books/Gale/Cengage Learning, 2011. 7v. illus. index. $33.35/vol.

This multivolume series on the scientific principles behind many popular sports is aimed at 6th through 10th grade students. Recently published volumes are on ice hockey, gymnastics, snowboarding, and basketball. The series aims to provide basic scientific concepts, such as kinetics, acceleration, and velocity, by describing how these principles work in athletics. All of these volumes achieve that aim through clear writing, comprehensive, age- and grade-level information, and attractive and colorful illustrations that bring each topic to life.

The authors are writers of books for young people. Each volume provides an overview of the sport, its history, changes to its rules over time, equipment needed, and techniques. Throughout users will find information on the biomechanics and physiology of playing the sport and well as common injuries and medical conditions associated with the sport. All volumes have sidebars, numerous photographs and illustrations, a glossary, and resources to consult for further information. Because young adults have a natural interest in sports that at times supersedes their interest in science, this set will provide a good link between the two subjects.—**Shannon Graff Hysell**

C, P, S

223.   **Sports in America: From Colonial Times to the Twenty-First Century.** Steven A. Reiss, ed. Armonk, N.Y., M. E. Sharpe, 2011. 3v. illus. index. $349.00/set. ISBN 13: 978-0-7656-1706-4.

This three-volume encyclopedia is the first to cover all areas of sports in North America from an academic historical and sociological view. The bulk of the encyclopedia is roughly 400 brief essays of 1,000-8,000 words, arranged alphabetically. The essays cover all types of sports, biographies of individuals involved in sports, and many related sports issues, such as psychological, legal, racial, business, media, events, venues, teams, etc. Subheadings and black-and-white photographs add value to the entries. The authors of each essay include list of further reading that increases the academic content. A list of all contributors with their institutions follows the table of contents.

Preceding the A-Z entries is an in-depth examination of sports in America divided into seven historical periods: Colonial Era, Early Republic, Gilded Age, Progressive Era, Interwar Period and World War II, Postwar Era 1946-70, and After 1970. These longer essays are interesting and attract readers to further details in the shorter topic entries which follow. This summary and analysis of sports in America is well written and an important contribution to sports history.

A "topic finder," detailed index, and cross-references make the volumes easy to use. The third volume includes two other useful listings besides the general bibliography and index. First, a chronology that starts in 1618 when King James I of England issued a ruling on what recreation was permitted on the Sabbath to settle a conflict between Puritans and Catholics and ends in 2011 with Super Bowl XLV and Barry Bonds' mistrial. Second, an annotated alphabetic listing of more than 130 sports institutions, organizations, and governing bodies with Websites.

Editor, Steven A. Reiss, of Northeastern Illinois University, is a prime mover in sports history. This encyclopedic set will be a valuable addition to most libraries since sports is a defining part of American life, occupying much of its citizens' time as participants or spectators in what has become a $200 billion per year enterprise. [R: BL, Jan 1 &15, 2012, p. 73]—**Georgia Briscoe**

Baseball

P

224.   Bortolotti, Dan. **Baseball Now!** 2d ed. Richmond Hills, Ont., Firefly Books, 2011. 160p. illus. index. $24.95. ISBN 13: 978-1-55407-826-4.

The newly revised 2d edition of *Baseball Now!* takes a popular rather than scholarly approach to covering baseball's history and place in popular culture. It is less focused on statistics and more focused on the players themselves and their roles they play within their teams. The book focuses on 70 stars of the National and American Leagues focusing on the highlights (and lowlights) of their careers, the successes (and failures) of their teams, and how they got to be at the top of their careers. It includes up-to-date coverage of the 2010 regular season, the league playoffs, and the World Series. The book is filled with more than 100 full-color photographs that will appeal to fans of all ages. Although it is not comprehensive enough to serve as an all-purpose resource on the topic of baseball, this book would serve nicely as a supplementary resource to other reference baseball titles already available in a public library's collection.—**Paul M. Murphy III**

Basketball

P

225.   Grasso, John. **Historical Dictionary of Basketball.** Lanham, Md., Scarecrow, 2011. 497p. (Historical Dictionaries of Sports, no.2). $80.00. ISBN 13: 978-0-8108-6763-5.

To the casual fan names such as James Naismith and terms like March Madness are part of the language of basketball. For those more interested and experienced, this 2d volume in Scarecrow's new historical sports dictionaries is a welcome addition to reference literature. Arranged in alphabetic order, more than 600 names, places, terms, organizations, leagues and conferences, teams and schools, and events chronicle the history of the game. Included are players (men and women), teams, and even brief entries on countries where basketball has become such an internationally popular game. Terms like power forward and D-league are briefly documented. An interesting chronology and introduction precede the well-written entries and 12 appendixes trace Olympic and international basketball, NBA championships, the NCAA and NIT tournaments, and basketball halls of fame inductees. Cross-references in bold lead the user to other relevant entries. Nearly 40 pages of bibliography conclude this useful ready-reference book where names like Connie Hawkins, Bob Pettit, and John McLendon come to life again.—**Boyd Childress**

Bodybuilding and Weight Training

P

226.   Ramsay, Craig. **Anatomy of Muscle Building: A Trainer's Guide to Increasing Muscle Mass.** Richmond Hills, Ont., Firefly Books, 2011. 160p. illus. $24.95pa. ISBN 13: 978-1-55407-816-5.

This volume is like having an X ray of each exercise or stretch one uses in their bodybuilding program. The full-color, detailed illustrations show users how a change in position can alter the muscle emphasis or improve safety or effectiveness. After a quick introduction to choosing the right gym and two pages of muscle definitions and illustrations, the work is arranged into six main chapters: Cardio Workouts; Chest & Abdominals; Back; Shoulders; Arms; and Legs. For each exercise users will find a detailed illustration listing the muscles in use; step-by-step instructions on how to execute the exercise; a list of the muscles used; and "Trainer's Tips" that explain proper technique and breathing exercises. The illustrations are beautifully executed and well labeled. The layout provides a lot of whitespace and lends itself to either browsing or finding specific information. There is no index, but there is a glossary located at the end of the volume. This title would be useful in public libraries, in academic libraries with sports medicine programs, and in the personal libraries of fitness trainers.—**Shannon Graff Hysell**

Cycling

P

227.   Heijmans, Jeroen, and Bill Mallon. **Historical Dictionary of Cycling.** Lanham, Md., Scarecrow, 2011. 415p. (Historical Dictionaries of Sports). $95.00. ISBN 13: 978-0-8108-7175-5; 978-0-8108-7369-8 (e-book).

The *Historical Dictionary of Cycling* appears to be compiled as a labor of love by the authors, Bill Mallon and Jeroen Heijmans, both who are avid cyclists. It covers a wide variety of topics. The beginning provides a brief chronology of cycling from 1493 to the present, followed by short introductions to seemingly random topics: road cycling, women in cycling, bicycle technology, popularity of cycling, track cycling, and more. A majority of the book consists of definitions of equipment, individuals, and events. Most entries are short, generally one or two paragraphs. Occasionally there will be longer entries for famous bicyclists or events like the Tour de France. Even these, however, rarely exceed two pages. About one-third of the book is dedicated to appendixes, which offer lists of winners from various races or tours, the Olympics, and world championships. World record holders in the hour and speed categories are also provided. The book concludes with a 20-page bibliography, organized into topics, in order to encourage further reading.

The problem with print reference sources like these is that they are infrequently used anymore. Google searches are faster and more convenient. The *Historical Dictionary of Cycling* does not provide extensive entries that might encourage purchase by public libraries for their patrons. Although compiling past winners of various races in one place is helpful, this information can be often retrieved quickly online, as this reviewer confirmed with the Tour of Fitchburg and Tour of Somerville. This source may be of interest to cycling aficionados. However, for a retail price of $95, the cost is likely too prohibitive.—**Kevin McDonough**

Football

P

228.   Page, Joseph S. **Pro Football Championships Before the Super Bowl: A Year-by-Year History, 1926-1965.** Jefferson, N.C., McFarland, 2011. 224p. index. $35.00pa. ISBN 13: 978-0-7864-4809-8.

Author Joseph Page notes that his childhood reading of Jerry Izenber's book *Championship* (Scholastic Book Services, 1971) fueled his interest in football. This new book might well attract an eager audience of younger football fans as well as students of the history of the game seeking key dates, names, or statistics. Page systematically treats championship games from 1926 through 1965, the pre-Super Bowl era. For each year and game he identifies the teams involved, the score, data, location, attendance, weather conditions, and field condition. He then provides a short narrative description of each contest plus a scorecard, starting lineups and player substitutions, head coaches, game officials, and team statistics, where available. Page clearly has labored to gather factual information and present it in a clear, straightforward fashion. Football trivia buffs will encounter many unusual and interesting tidbits, including the fact that the 1932 NFL championship game was played in Chicago, indoors, on a shortened field used the previous week for a circus. A list of "Professional Football Champions Prior to the 1933 Title Game," brief chapter notes, a short bibliography, and the index follow the game descriptions. The lack of photographs is disappointing.

Fans interested in more in-depth coverage of particular games or broader histories of the AFL and NFL will have to look elsewhere. For example, several books have been written about the 1958 NFL Championship game as a turning point in both the history and popularity of professional football, but Page's account scarcely suggests the importance of this overtime contest. Still, the crisply written, reasonably priced book should find a home in public and academic library sports collections.—**Julienne L. Wood**

Golf

P

229.   Mallon, Bill, and Randon Jerris. **Historical Dictionary of Golf.** Lanham, Md., Scarecrow, 2011. 797p. illus. (Historical Dictionaries of Sports, no.3). $99.00. ISBN 13: 978-0-8108-7197-7.

Golf is traditionally thought to have originated in the fifteenth century, although even earlier versions of a similar game have been recorded as far back as the thirteenth century. Through the years it has grown in popularity and evolved even more so. This 3d volume in Scarecrow's new historical sports dictionaries is a welcome addition to reference literature on the history and culture of golf. Arranged in alphabetic order, more than 300 names, places, terms, organizations, and events chronicle the history of the game. After an extensive introduction highlighting the history and current situation of the game as well as a chronology that runs from 1297 to 2009, the book provides cross-referenced entries on players (men and women), terms used in the game, top golf courses, and key tournaments. The book provides 11 appendixes that cover such topics as the World Golf Hall of Fame, lists of professional champions, amateur champions, and awards. Cross-references in bold lead the user to other relevant entries. Nearly 75 pages of bibliography conclude this useful ready-reference book.—**Shannon Graff Hysell**

Ice Skating

P

230.   Hines, James R. **Historical Dictionary of Figure Skating.** Lanham, Md., Scarecrow, 2011. 375p. (Historical Dictionaries of Sports). $85.00; $84.99 (e-book). ISBN 13: 978-0-8108-6859-5; 978-0-8108-7085-7 (e-book).

Hines, a Ph.D. musicologist, seems to be making a second career studying and writing about the history of figure skating. No wonder he was enlisted to author this volume in the new Scarecrow Press Historical Dictionaries of Sports series. Hines, a retired college professor who taught for 35 years and who is currently an elector to both the United States Figure Skating Hall of Fame and the World Figure Skating Hall of Fame, has now written this dictionary, his second authoritative book on the topic. His first, the 2006 *Figure Skating: A History*, is a comprehensive, well-researched monograph on the history of the sport. This dictionary gleans from Hines' first book, adding statistical data and listing information about international figure skating organizations and governing bodies. An introductory timeline-arranged chronology spanning from 1220 to 2010 includes "15 pivotal points in the history of figure skating," such as the scandal during the 1994 U.S. Championship games involving Nancy Kerrigan and Tonya Harding, which focused public attention on the upcoming Winter Olympics and helped gain a whole new audience for the sport. The 800-plus entries comprising the body of this dictionary offer well written, cross-referenced paragraphs that address both the art and sport of figure skating. A nice balance of historical and biographical entries is achieved and the items chosen for inclusion make for interesting reading. Finally, 11 informative appendixes and a thorough bibliography round out the work.

Historical Dictionary of Figure Skating is available in either print or e-book format and is recommended for public libraries, for academic libraries supporting sports and/or performing arts curricula, and for figure skating aficionados, who will likely wish to include both of Hines' books in their personal libraries. A publisher's postscript indicates that Dr. Hines is currently researching a third book on the history of ice dance and pairs skating, which should fill yet another gap in the figure skating literature.—**Linda D. Tietjen**

Soccer

P, S

231.   **The Complete Book of Soccer.** 2d ed. Chris Hunt, ed. Richmond Hills, Ont., Firefly Books, 2011. 384p. illus. index. $39.95. ISBN 13: 978-1-55407-688-8.

The Complete Book of Soccer has now been updated to include many new photographs and statistics, including those from the World Cup 2010 and post-Cup results. The author provides a comprehensive history and overview of the game, including its top players, most recognized players, key tournaments, club histories, and tons of statistics. There are biographies for 200 of soccer's top players of all time, 100 of which are top contemporary players. Hunt provides histories on the World Cup and European championships as well as inside stories on coaches and teams. He also covers rules of the games and the evolution of its play. The text is supplemented with more than 500 color photographs. The 2d edition has updated sections that include controversial topics in the sport today, such as the increasing power of clubs and international scandals. And, although they do not get as much coverage as the men, Women's Soccer is included as well along with the statistics and results from the Women's World Cup. This book is written with general readers and soccer enthusiasts in mind and will be useful in high school and public library collections.—**Paul M. Murphy III**

P

232.   Dunmore, Tom. **Historical Dictionary of Soccer.** Lanham, Md., Scarecrow, 2011. 312p. (Historical Dictionaries of Sports). $70.00. ISBN 13: 978-0-8108-7188-5; 978-0-8108-7395-7 (e-book).

For those more interested and experienced in soccer and its history, this volume in Scarecrow's new historical sports dictionaries is a welcome addition to reference literature. Arranged in alphabetic order, more than 400 names, places, terms, organizations, leagues and conferences, teams and schools, and events chronicle the history of the game. Included are players (men and women), teams, and even brief entries on countries where soccer has become such an internationally popular game. Terminology used in the game is briefly documented. An interesting chronology and introduction precede the well-written entries and 20 appendixes trace presidents of the federation of soccer, FIFA World Players, Olympic games, various national cups, and intercontinental cups. Cross-references in bold lead the user to other relevant entries. Nearly 20 pages of bibliography conclude this useful ready-reference book. This is an excellent reference source for students, researchers, and the general public needing facts about soccer on an international level.—**Boyd Childress**

Tennis

P

233.   Grasso, John. **Historical Dictionary of Tennis.** Lanham, Md., Scarecrow, 2011. 419p. (Historical Dictionaries of Sports). $75.00. ISBN 13: 978-0-8108-7237-0; 978-0-8108-7490-9 (e-book).

In the Internet Age, with Google and Wikipedia, one wonders how long publishers will publish and consumers will buy reference books such as the *Historical Dictionary of Tennis*. Although many of the basic facts regarding the game of tennis, such as who won what major tournament, or who is in the International Tennis Hall of Fame, are accessible online, the tennis enthusiast will enjoy simply sitting down and thumbing through pages that reflect a love for the game.

The bulk of the dictionary is the hundreds of cross-referenced, A-Z entries on tournaments, terminology, players, and contributors. John Grasso, a historian of the Olympics and author of the *Historical Dictionary of Basketball* (see entry 225), writes these in an accessible, conversational style. The entries are accompanied by a historical overview of tennis from its origins in the twelfth century, a list of acronyms used throughout, a chronology, appendixes (winners/champions of the major events), and a bibliography subdivided by topic. Although academic librarians may not consider this an essential purchase, public librarians and tennis historians will want to add the *Historical Dictionary of Tennis* to their collections.—**John P. Stierman**

16 Sociology

Death

P

234.   Grover, Robert J., and Susan G. Fowler. **Helping Those Experiencing Loss: A Guide to Grieving Resources.** Santa Barbara, Calif., Libraries Unlimited/ABC-CLIO, 2011. 233p. index. $50.00pa. ISBN 13: 978-1-59884-826-7; 978-1-59884-827-4 (e-book).

This book introduces librarians, mental health counselors, teachers, and parents to resource that they can use to help people, both adults and children, in dealing with loss and the emotions that accompany that situation. It is divided into eight chapters. The first is an introduction to the work, explaining the rational and criteria used in selecting the books, e-books, CD-ROMs, and videos included in the resource section of each subsequent chapter. The second chapter discusses grief. Chapter 3 deals with children and how they handle loss. Chapter 4 discuses young adults and how they handle grieving. Chapter 5 discusses loss of a child, while chapter 6 deals with the loss of a spouse. Chapter 7 deals with grieving as we age and chapter 8 talks about grief and religion.

Each of the chapters, except the first, start out with a detailed discussion of the topic and present a good outline of the subject citing very relevant studies dealing with the topic. The resources are then listed. They are listed alphabetically by author in all the chapters, except chapters 3 and 4 which deal with the way children and youth handle loss. In those chapters the resources are arranged by topic. In both these chapters there are works of fiction that are designed to help the young person, while all the resources for adults are nonfiction. The resources have good annotations that were either written by the authors or taken from credible review sources.

This book will be a valuable resource for those that will be dealing with a significant loss. The thoughtful discussions of each topic at the beginning of the chapters set this book apart from those that simply list some helpful resources. It will be useful in most libraries.—**Robert L. Turner Jr.**

Disabled

C, P

235.   **The Complete Directory for People with Disabilities, 2012.** 20th ed. Millerton, N.Y., Grey House Publishing, 2011. 993p. index. $165.00pa.; $300.00 (online database); $400.00 (print and online editions). ISBN 13: 978-1-59237-758-9.

Intended for individuals with disabilities, service providers, and family members and friends, this directory is a massive guide to a wide variety of resources and services. Some 9,009 directory entries are arranged under 27 chapters and more than 100 subchapters. Section 1 contains 24 chapters arranged by topic, including assistive devices, camps, computers, travel and transportation, veteran services, foundations and funding resources, independent living, and rehabilitation facilities. Many of these chapters include subcategories, appropriate to the topic, that aid in locating resources. For example, the chapter for assistive devices includes automobiles, hearing aids, chairs, kitchen and eating aids, ramps, scooters, wheelchairs, beds, and much more. Section 2 includes nine chapters for various disabilities, including aging, blind and deaf, cognitive, dexterity, hearing, mobility, specific disorders, speech and language, and visual. These, too, include subcategories for associations, camps, print and nonprint resources, and support groups, among others. The entries themselves are brief, usually including an address, telephone and fax numbers, e-mail and Website addresses, names of a few top personnel, and a very brief description of the resource or service. There are also three extensive indexes, including an alphabetic entry and publisher index, a geographic index arranged by state, and a disability and subject index that is quite detailed. This work can also be accessed as an online database through the publisher (http://gold.greyhouse.com). By using the database users can conduct subject-specific searches and find direct links to listee's Websites and e-mail addresses. Overall, this directory would be a valuable resource for public and academic libraries as well as for social service professionals in related fields. [R: LJ, Jan 12, p. 140]—**Stephen H. Aby**

Family, Marriage, and Divorce

P, S

236.   Barnes, Amber, and Julia A. Watkins. **The Truth About Family Life.** 2d ed. New York, Facts on File, 2011. 240p. index. (The Truth About Series). $35.00. ISBN 13: 978-0-8160-7641-3.

The Truth About series from Facts on File is a multivolume series that discusses situations that are relevant to teens today. Each volume is devoted to a specific topic, with this volume focusing on the topic of family life, focusing specifically on the changing dynamics of family life in modern America and how the definition of "normal" is changing. The volumes are each organized in an A-Z format; however, the volumes can be considered neither dictionaries nor encyclopedias. For example, this volume provides entries on: communication styles in families, blended families, racially mixed families, birth order, teenage parents, and gay parenting. Each entry is like a mini-essay on the topic. Each entry concludes with a list of resources for further reading. Entries are supplemented with sidebars that provide "Questions and Answers," "Fact or Fiction?", and "Did You Know?" segments. Supplemental materials include a list of hotlines and help sites where teens can go for further information, a glossary, and an index.

This series is generally useful for teens and young adults. This title may be of less interest to them given the fact that most teens are familiar with the topic of family life and have been raised seeing a variety of different types of families both in their day-to-day lives and in the media. Other books in the series that cover more cutting-edge and controversial topics may be of more interest for this age group, such as those on violence, suicide, sexual behavior and unplanned pregnancy, and drugs. The text is straightforward and the advice is generally useful.—**Shannon Graff Hysell**

Gay and Lesbian Studies

C, P

237.   *The New York Times* **on Gay and Lesbian Issues.** By Susan Burgess. Washington, D.C., CQ Press, 2011. 512p. illus. index. (TimesReference from CQ Press). $49.00. ISBN 13: 978-1-60426-593-4; 978-1-60871-754-5 (e-book).

This excellent book belongs in every social science collection. Numerous articles and editorials are reproduced from *The New York Times* that address the paper's coverage of gay and lesbian issues from 1851 until 2010, accompanied by a narrative written by Susan Burgess, a professor of political science and women's and gender studies at Ohio University that provides a context and analysis of the documents.

The book's 12 chapters are organized thematically, with the first chapter, "The Stonewall Uprising and Its Aftermath," offering a baseline to understand how issues related to gays and lesbians were treated by *The New York Times* before, during, and after this catalytic event. The following chapters address the paper's treatment of seminal issues for gays and lesbians. Chapter 2, for instance, "Gay Civil Rights Laws and the Emerging LGBT Community," documents and analyzes various pro and con legislative initiatives (e.g., Anita Bryant's Dade County campaign in 1977, NYC's City Council approval of a homosexual rights bill in 1986), and chapter3, "Sexuality, Gender, and Science," includes fascinating documentation and analysis of issues such as the APA's declassification of homosexuals as psychopaths, brain research, and transsexuality. Subsequent chapters address AIDS, Coming Out, The Right to Privacy, Military, Youth and Education, Violence against LGBT People, Same-Sex Marriage and the Family, Religion, and Sexuality and Gender in the Workplace. Each chapter is finely crafted, with the reproduction of the original *New York Times* pieces and Burgess's outstanding narratives working in tandem to make for a reference book that is both erudite and accessible. Its thorough index enhances *The New York Times on Gay and Lesbian Issues*'s tremendous value by facilitating tracking down information in a superb reference book that is packed with it.—**G. Douglas Meyers**

Philanthropy

Catalogs and Collections

P
238.   **Catalog of Federal Domestic Assistance. http://www.cfda.gov/.** [Website]. Free. Date reviewed: 2011.

A great deal of information about grant-giving organizations is freely available on the Internet. Perhaps the largest source of grants is the U.S. government, and the essential resource for finding federal funding is freely available online. The Web-based *Catalog of Federal Domestic Assistance* (www.cfda. gov) provides access to all federal funding programs that are available to individuals, state and local governments, private organizations, and nonprofit groups. This directory can be searched by functional area, agency, program title, applicant eligibility, deadlines, program number, grant, and keyword. Of course, foundations, government agencies, and other grant makers can be identified directly using a search engine, and many of their Websites provide detailed information about available funding opportunities. Many potential funding sources have key application documents linked directly from their Websites. Libraries should be cognizant of the kind of grant opportunities their users might pursue and be ready to highlight available directory resources from their own collections and the open Web. This is a key source to be aware of due to its broad content area and that it is free.—**Shannon Graff Hysell**

Directories

P
239.   **Foundation Grants to Individuals.** 20th ed. New York, Foundation Center, 2011. 1600p. index. $75.00; $19.95/month (online edition). ISBN 13: 978-1-59542-374-0.

Foundation Grants to Individuals is one of the most extensive resource covering private grant-giving to individuals. In its print form, this annual single-volume publication profiles nearly 9,000 U.S. granting institutions that have ongoing programs geared to individuals. The entries are listed geographically by state and alphabetically by the name of the grant maker. Elements of the entries include full contact information, assets, expenditures, total giving, grants to individuals, loans to individuals, fields of interest, types of support, program information, and application details. Access is facilitated by indexes arranged by geography, international giving, company name, specific school, type of support, subject, and grant-maker name. Online access to this information is available through the publisher at http://gtionline.fdncenter.org/. The organization closely follows the arrangement of its print counterpart. For users seeking less comprehensive information, the "Foundation Finder" section of the Foundation Center Website offers free basic information on grant makers in the United States and can be searched by grant-maker name as well as geographical location to identify grant makers in a given city, state, or ZIP code (http://foundationcenter.org/findfunders/foundfinder/).—**ARBA Staff Reviewer**

Handbooks and Yearbooks

C, P

240.   Miner, Jeremy T., Lynn E. Miner, and Jerry Griffith. **Collaborative Grantseeking: A Guide to Designing Projects, Leading Partners, and Persuading Sponsors.** Santa Barbara, Calif., Greenwood Press/ABC-CLIO, 2011. 215p. index. $65.00; $35.00pa. ISBN 13: 978-0-313-39193-4pa.

Based on over 40 years of experience as grant-seekers, leaders of national grant workshops, reviewers of grant proposals and critiquing guidelines for grants, this work is a companion volume to the two other books by these authors, for introductory and advanced grant writing—*Proposal Planning & Writing* (4th ed.; see ARBA 2009, 754) and *Models of Proposal Planning & Writing* (Praeger), respectively. This book is about different types of collaboration and the characteristics that make for a successful collaboration project. Including details, examples, and subheadings to guide the reader, this work will benefit grant-seekers or considering seeking a grant that is collaborative in nature, as well as those currently or considering the sponsoring of a collaborative grant, and those evaluating or reviewing grant applications that are collaborative. Separated into 3 parts, the 10 chapters address the fundamentals of collaborative grant-seeking, provide examples of successful collaborative grants, and explore evaluation strategies for collaborative grant-seeking. This is not focused specifically towards librarians, but is beneficial to anyone seeking guidance on collaborative grant writing. This book will not stand alone, but is a valuable addition to any collection where grant writing is supported as the content is specific to the needs and characteristics of collaborative grant-seeking, a unique type of grant-seeking not often covered in depth in other manuals and books.—**Sara Marcus**

Poverty

C, S

241.   Hombs, Mary Ellen. **Modern Homelessness: A Reference Handbook.** Santa Barbara, Calif., ABC-CLIO, 2011. 289p. index. (Contemporary World Issues). $55.00. ISBN 13: 978-1-59884-536-5; 978-1-59884-537-2 (e-book).

The author, who has served as the deputy director of the U.S. Interagency Council on Homelessness from 2003 to 2009, has updated her 2001 work titled *American Homelessness: A Reference Handbook* (3d ed.; see ARBA 2002, entry 842). This work deals with homelessness in the last decade and highlights the improvements that have been made in the United States and other countries to decrease homelessness. It is divided into 8 chapters with the first being a good introductory overview of the problems and obstacles associated with homelessness. The book mainly focuses on America, but mentions a few other countries.

The second chapter looks in detail at the problems, controversies, and solutions to homelessness. The first topic is how does one define and measure homelessness.

Chapter 3 gives the reader a worldwide perspective on homelessness by briefly examining how the United Kingdom, Ireland, Denmark, other countries in Europe, Canada, and Australia are dealing with homelessness and some of the policies that have worked in those localities. Chapter 4 is a chronology.

It covers events, legislation, and movements from 2001 to September 22, 2010. Chapter 5 contains biographical sketches of people who have advanced the cause of eliminating homelessness by doing research, writing policy, and creating partnerships. Most are of contemporary people with a few historically important people. Chapter 6 gives a documentary overview of homelessness. It highlights key data, speeches, government documents, and reports that highlight the issue, while chapter 7 is a directory of organizations, associations, and agencies involved in helping homelessness with the contact information and Websites. The final chapter lists resources, including some print publications, nonprint media, Websites, and databases. Special issues of journals dealing with homelessness are mentioned, but the many articles found in the popular and scholarly journals are not. There is a glossary and index as well as extensive notes and good bibliographies in most chapters.

This book gives a good overview of the progress made in the last decade and the issues involved around homelessness. It is a good starting point for understanding the problem.—**Robert L. Turner Jr.**

Sex Studies

C, P

242.   Ditmore, Melissa Hope. **Prostitution and Sex Work.** Santa Barbara, Calif., Greenwood Press/ABC-CLIO, 2011. 201p. index. (Historical Guides to Controversial Issues in America). $55.00. ISBN 13: 978-0-313-36289-7.

Prostitution and Sex Work consists of nine chapters. The first two chapters discuss the key players in the sex trade, including prostitutes and sex workers, clients, management (pimps, madams), advertising, attorneys, and reformers and outreach workers. Also discussed are the places where the sex trade takes place, including hotels, brothels, the street, strip clubs, and the Internet. The work discusses the problems associated with the sex trade, most specifically the spread of sexually transmitted diseases and the violence oftentimes associated with the sex trade. Following chapters cover the legal aspects of the sex trade, including human trafficking, the history of sex trade in the Wild West, and the legal rights of prostitutes and sex workers. Several supplementary materials round out the volume: a timeline; three appendixes providing historical accounts, documents by sex workers, and legal documents and commentary; a list of online resources; a select bibliography; and an index.

For centuries the sex trade and prostitution has been one of the most controversial legal and social issues. This book provides a cogent and systematic analysis of the issue. Arguments against the sex trade as well as those supporting it are well presented here.—**Tze-chung Li**

Substance Abuse

Dictionaries and Encyclopedias

C, S

243.   **Alcohol and Alcohol Problems Science Database. http://etoh.niaaa.nih.gov/.** [Website]. Free. Date reviewed: 2011.

The National Institute on Alcohol Abuse and Alcoholism (NIAAA) has created this portal to support researchers and practitioners searching for information related to alcohol research. This page includes links to a number of databases, journals, and Websites focused on alcohol research and related topics. This database also includes a link to the archived ETOH database, which is the premier Alcohol and Alcohol Problems Science Database. It was produced by NIAAA from 1972 through December 2003. Although it is a fairly academic site, there are parts of it that can be of value to high school teachers and students as they discuss and research the topics of alcohol abuse and alcoholism in their classes.—**William O. Scheeren**

C, P, S

244.   **Drugs of Abuse.** Tarrytown, N.Y., Marshall Cavendish, 2011. 320p. illus. index. $59.95. ISBN 13: 978-0-7614-9973-2; 978-0-7614-7944-4 (e-book).

This is concise and well-written description of the properties, physical and psychological effects, and medical consequences of the use of 124 drugs of abuse. Some of these drugs are controlled substances, while others are more readily available to the public with fewer restrictions. In any case, each drug included in this volume is thoroughly but succinctly described, including its background, pharmacological effects, health effects, and social effects, among others. All entries also include a Key Facts section describing the drug's classification (in the United States, Canada, United Kingdom, and by the International Narcotics Control Board), street names, short- and long-term effects, and dangers. A number of entries include a diagram of the chemical structure of the drug, a feature that may be of use to high school chemistry classes. While the signed entries range from one to seven pages, most are between one and three pages, with *see also* references to related entries. Despite their length, they are not superficial in their descriptions of the features of the drugs. A few of the entries provide overviews not of drugs but of related topics, such as the Central Nervous System or Drug Laws. Additional features can include photographs of brain scans of normal and drug-effected brains, color diagrams of receptors, and tables of data. A glossary and drug table is provided, as is a detailed index to topics, diagrams, and illustrations. Overall, this volume would be a valuable addition to reference collections in public, school, and academic libraries.—**Stephen H. Aby**

C, P, S

245.   **Substance Abuse, Addiction, and Treatment.** Tarrytown, N.Y., Marshall Cavendish, 2012. 352p. illus. index. $59.95. ISBN 13: 978-0-7614-7943-7; 978-0-7614-9972-5 (e-book).

Although not classified as handbook, this one volume provides the reader with a thorough overview, descriptive and proscriptive narrative germane to the issue of substance abuse and other forms of addiction. Each signed article is highly systematic and yet concise in its treatment of a topic. For example, in the chapter entitled, Heroin Addiction Treatment, the reader is presented with a description of the problem, followed by a diagnosis of heroin addiction, suggestions for treatment, along with information to aid the addict in his or her full recovery. For the researcher interested in more quantitative data, many of the chapters provide statistics on the success rates of various substance abuse programs. In the appendix, a table listing various drugs is included, which not only defines the common name for a particular drug, but gives the street name of the narcotic. Heroin, for example, is also known as antifreeze, brown sugar, china white, or horse. This volume also provides an excellent bibliography of monographic as well as Internet sites related to substance abuse. In short, this work is a necessary addition to any comprehensive collection dealing with drug abuse and its treatment.—**Patrick Hall**

Handbooks and Yearbooks

P, S

246.   **Drug Information for Teens: Health Tips About the Physical and Mental Effects of Substance Abuse.** 3d ed. Elizabeth Magill, ed. Detroit, Omnigraphics, 2011. 468p. (Teen Health Series). $62.00. ISBN 13: 978-0-7808-1154-6.

Although teen substance or drug abuse fluctuates over time and with different drugs, the overall pattern of abuse is alarming. The physical, mental, emotional, and behavioral effects of hallucinogens, inhalants, tobacco, ecstasy, cocaine, steroids, and others can be substantial. This handbook, written for a teenage audience, provides information on the causes, effects, and preventive measures related to drug and substance abuse among teens. Overall, there are 56 chapters grouped into 9 sections or parts: general information about addiction and substance abuse; alcohol; tobacco; marijuana; abuse of legally available substances; drug-related health concerns; treatment for addiction; and resources for more information.

The chapters in section 1 explain the science of addiction, risk factors, how drugs effect the brain, peer pressure, and statistics on drug use among teens. Sections 2 through 4 address alcohol, tobacco, and a range of other common drugs and substances that are abused. The section on related health concerns deals with such topics as teen suicide, mental illness, sexual health and pregnancy, abuse and violence, and other problems that are drug-influenced. There are an additional number of chapters dealing with treatment, statistics, and policy controversies. All chapters are excerpted or adapted from other sources, which are cited. Chapters also include definitions of technical terms, things to remember, quick tips, and important facts. A final section of the book provides directory information on state and national organizations that provide additional information or assistance as well as hotlines and helplines. There are also suggestions for further reading, as well as a combined subject/name/title index.

Except for the chapter on the physiology of the brain, the chapters are quick to make a connection to their teenage reading audience. The prose is straightforward and the book lends itself to spot reading. It should be useful both for practical information and for research, and it is suitable for public and school libraries.—**Stephen H. Aby**

17 Statistics, Demography, and Urban Studies

Demography

Catalogs and Collections

C, P

247.   **DemographicsNow. http://library.demographicsnow.com.** library ed. [Website]. Farmington Hills, Mich., Gale/Cengage Learning. $3,528.00 and up. Date reviewed: 2011.

DemographicsNow is another desktop database that gives libraries basic access to census data and geospatial mapping. Demographic data is supplied from Experian/Applied Geographic Solutions. *DemographicsNow* is a user-friendly application incorporating 1,000 demographic variables with Census-defined geographic variables including state, county, census tract, block group, place, Metro CBSA, and ZIP code plus DMAs. Areas can be ranked based on a selected demographic or income-based variable. Consumer expenditure data have been added to show consumption for the basics such as apparel, auto and transportation, food and beverage, health care, furnishings, restaurants, and shelter.

The interface guides the novice user through a search beginning with geography and followed by the choice of map type: summary, comparison, ranking dynamic map. Comparison reports are helpful to compare market areas, and *DemographicsNow* allows comparisons of up to 16 geographical areas. A business owner can compare the percentage change in demographics, the average, median, and per capita income in geographic areas, and the percentages of ethnic groups in the selected cities. A business owner can find numbers of households and five-year projections to guide new store locations or to help determine product lines. It is possible to compare the retail potential for household items based on geography. Demographic trend data give business owners indicators of growing or shrinking market areas.

For the times when superimposed geographic borders do not satisfy a user's needs, ring mapping might be just the thing. With ring mapping, user can plot specific variables in a given radius centered on an address. Results are downloadable into Excel, Word, HTML, or .pdf. This product may be best suited for site analysis, economic development, and researching disposable income. Libraries may purchase national- or state-level data.—**Chris LeBeau**

Dictionaries and Encyclopedias

C

248.   **Encyclopedia of the U.S. Census: From the Constitution to the American Community Survey (ACS).** 2d ed. Margo J. Anderson, Constance F. Citro, and Joseph J. Salvo, eds. Washington, D.C., CQ Press, 2012. 456p. illus. maps. index. $175.00. ISBN 13: 978-1-60871-025-6.

The *Encyclopedia of the U.S. Census: From the Constitution to the American Community Survey (ACS)* represents the collective expertise and insights of 83 contributors—each knowledgeable in some aspect of population or census matters. The book is comprised of some 140 articles on a broad variety of topics related to census taking. Each article is presented alphabetically and is cross-referenced and followed by a bibliography to facilitate further investigation. A list of articles and an index enable readers to locate subjects of particular interest. The articles are rich in historical background, but treatment of recent innovations also provides an up-to-date look at census taking in the United States today. For example, considerable space is devoted to the recently introduced American Community Survey, which provides interim to the traditional decennial census. The text is complemented by tables and figures as well as a section of pictorial highlights. Complex topics, such as sampling, are discussed in understandable terms without sacrificing rigor, thus making the encyclopedia meaningful to a broad range of readers. [R: LJ, Jan 12, p. 136]—**William C. Struning**

C, P

249.   Gitlin, Martin. **The Baby Boomer Encyclopedia.** Santa Barbara, Calif., Greenwood Press/ABC-CLIO, 2011. 231p. illus. index. $55.00. ISBN 13: 978-0-313-38218-5; 978-0-313-38219-2 (e-book).

This is a historical reference encyclopedia of the 80 million Americans born between 1946 and 1965 (p. vii) and consists of the impact these individuals had on U.S. history up to the present. The introduction stresses that many adhered to traditional political and religious beliefs despite the prevalence of lifestyle radicalism receiving widespread media coverage (p. ix).

An opening chronology lists key events in the life spans of baby boomers covering from the 1946 publication of Benjamin Spock's *Baby and Child Care* and including events such as the Food & Drug Administration's 1960 approval of the birth control pill; the 1968 assassinations of Martin Luther King Jr. and Robert Kennedy; the 1973 Supreme Court decision *Roe v. Wade* legalizing abortion; Ronald Reagan's 1980 election; the 2001 terrorist attacks; Barack Obama's 2008 election; and the first baby boomers reaching retirement in 2010.

Entries are arranged alphabetically and broken down into topical areas such as arts and culture, economy and jobs, family, health, literature, politics and activism, religion, sports, and others. Examples of entries include the television series *All in the Family*; James Baldwin; civil rights movement; environmental movement; Internet; the rock group Led Zeppelin; parenting; religion and spirituality; and the women's movement. Entries are one to three pages long and contain succinct bibliographies.

This work could be strengthened further by including entries on Evangelical Christianity and economic globalization. Nevertheless, it is an adequate introduction to the history of this time period and is recommended for public and undergraduate academic libraries.—**Bert Chapman**

Handbooks and Yearbooks

P

250.   **American Buyers: Demographics of Shopping.** Ithaca, N.Y., New Strategist, 2010. 384p. index. $125.00. ISBN 13: 978-1-935114-93-2.

American Buyers: Demographics of Shopping provides information on the proportion of U.S. households that purchased individual products and services, as well as how much money they spent on those purchases. That information should be useful in estimating the size of market segments together with the corresponding amount of expenditures. Comparisons in spending among categories and items can also be made. Using supplementary data available from syndicated services, estimates could be made of brands and types. Products and services are grouped into 10 categories, each comprising a chapter in which household buying is tabulated by demographics (e.g., age, income, high-income, type, race region, education), and by percent buying and amount spent. Data are given for an average quarter and an average week in 2008 (latest available). Quarterly buying is more appropriate for items purchased infrequently, while weekly data capture purchases made more often. Tabulations made by New Strategist offer readily useful information derived from raw data gathered by the U.S. Bureau of Labor Statistics. Tables in each chapter are preceded by a brief summary of highlights and a graph depicting the most important items. Since data are for 2008 only, an appendix shows annual data from 2000 through 2008 in order to indicate trends. A second appendix gives further details on BLS data collection. A list of tables, explanatory introduction, glossary, and index are included. This is a companion volume to *Household Spending: Who Spends How Much On What* (2008 data offered in the 15th edition), which contains further details on the demographics of U.S. consumer buying. [R: LJ, Dec 10, p. 140]—**William C. Struning**

P

251.   **The American Marketplace: Demographics and Spending Patterns.** 10th ed. Ithaca, N.Y., New Strategist, 2011. 611p. index. $120.00; $89.95pa. ISBN 13: 978-1-935775-27-0; 978-1-935775-28-7pa.

The American Marketplace provides tables of Americans' salaries and income, and what they are purchasing, whether it is food, a home, or a college education. The editors of New Strategist have gathered most of their statistics and numbers from U.S. government sources. The introductory chapter entitled "Attitude Trends" discusses Americans' attitudes about their lives, such as happiness, success, religion, families, gays, how they get their news, and right to have guns—topics that influence the numbers. The editors believe that by gathering these numbers and organizing them into helpful tables they will help the American consumer find his way out of the "Great Recession" we are experiencing since 2008, enable them to track the current economic trends, and, hopefully, recover and prosper.

The additional sections describe the current trends of education, health, housing, income, labor force, living arrangement, population, spending, time use, and wealth. There are helpful descriptions of the tables on the preceding page for each section. There is a glossary, a bibliography of government and organization Websites, and an index. This reviewer would highly recommend this title for all academic and public library collections as well as for corporate libraries for their consumer marketing research. This current *American Marketplace* covers the years 2007-2009. [R: LJ, Jan 12, p. 140]—**Kay M. Stebbins**

P

252.   **Americans and Their Homes: Demographics of Homeownership.** 3d ed. Ithaca, N.Y., New Strategist, 2011. 603p. index. $120.00; $89.95pa. ISBN 13: 978-1-935775-29-4; 978-1-935775-30-0pa.

Housing is clearly a major factor in the national economy as well as being an important indicator of the quality of life. Therefore, information on trends in the housing market is of significant importance to researchers and others who are associated with the nation's housing. A reliable and comprehensive source of information on housing in the United States can be found in *Americans and Their Homes: Demographics of Homeownership*. The book is built around some 466 tables that provide detailed data on the demographics of owners and renters, characteristics of homes (e.g., size amenities), characteristics of the home location, satisfaction of owners and renters, and motivation for moving/buying. Special attention is paid to new housing units and to mobile homes. Amounts spent by item in 2009 by home owners, home owners by mortgage status, and home renters provide insights into the influence of housing on spending patterns. Tables are easy to read and include explanations of the data, sources of the data, and a brief summary statement of major trends found in each table. The book can be used as a reliable, comprehensive, and recent (2009) source of data on housing as it is based on U.S. government data. It can also be used to provide interesting and useful insights into the current state of, and notable trends in, housing in the United States—largely by reading chapter introductions and table summaries. [R: LJ, Jan 12, p. 140]—**William C. Struning**

Statistics

General Works

C, P

253.   Crow, Ben, and Suresh K. Lodha. **The Atlas of Global Inequalities.** Berkeley, Calif., University of California Press, 2011. 128p. maps. index. $21.95pa. ISBN 13: 978-0-520-26822-7.

Inequalities in the distribution of world resources and amenities have been well documented, but quantified estimates of the amounts of inequality are less available. Moreover, a comprehensive overview of all inequalities is difficult to locate. *The Atlas of Global Inequalities* by Ben Crow and Suresh K. Lodha, both of the University of California at Santa Cruz, dos much to correct both shortfalls. Since inequalities are most apparent on a national or country basis, the authors utilize country as a basis for presentation. Following an introductory chapter that defines inequality and identifies its causes, broad types of inequality are portrayed and discussed in the first seven chapters. Steps toward reducing inequality are next presented, with the caution that much remains to be done to ease extreme disparities. Colorful graphs, charts, and tables that help to highlight basic data are spread throughout the book. Supporting data can be found in tabular form in a final chapter, along with a key to definitions, a list of data sources, and an index. Text is limited but adequate to provide explanation and cohesiveness to the numerous graphics.—**William C. Struning**

United States

Catalogs and Collections

C, P

254.   **FedStats. http://www.fedstats.gov/.** [Website]. Free. Date reviewed: 2011.

The official Website of the Federal Interagency Council on Statistical Policy is a gateway to statistics from over 100 U.S. Federal agencies and is well organized and easy to use. Users can find under Links to Statistics, "Topic Links A-Z," "MapStats," and "Statistics By Geography from U.S. Agencies." MapStats provides statistical profiles of states, counties, cities, Congressional Districts, and federal judicial districts. The "Statistical Reference Shelf," a bit further down on the homepage, is a large collection of online reference sources like the *Statistical Abstract of the United States* (131st ed.; see ARBA 2012, entry 866). You will find a variety of other sources such as the *State and Metropolitan Area Data Book* and *Digest of Education Statistics*, which will provide statistics on many topics of interest to entrepreneurs. On the other half of the page, Links to Statistical Agencies, under "Agencies by Subject," click Economic on the drop down arrow to lead you to a list of Periodic Economic Censuses. Below this area, you'll find "Data Access Tools," which link users to agency online databases.—**Susan C. Awe**

Handbooks and Yearbooks

C, P

255.   **State Rankings 2011: A Statistical View of America.** Kathleen O'Leary Morgan and Scott Morgan, eds. Washington, D.C., CQ Press, 2011. 604p. index. $110.00; $75.00pa. ISBN 13: 978-1-60871-731-6; 978-1-60871-733-0pa.

Now in its 22d edition, and now published by CQ Press but edited by the same editors as previous editions, this series continues to provide a wealth of data from a wide variety of sources focused entirely on the individual states. As the editors state, the mission of the work is to translate complicated and often convoluted statistics into meaningful, easy-to-understand state comparisons. This they have done in an admirable fashion.

The organization of the 2011 edition remains the same as in previous editions, although most of the statistics have been updated to reflect newer data. The work is organized into 15 sections: agriculture; crime and law enforcement; defense; economy; education; employment and labor; energy and environment; geography; government finance: federal; government finance: state and local; health; households and housing; population; social welfare; and transportation. Each section contains a variety of related topics with each one presented using two different tables. The first table gives the states in alphabetic order and the other gives the states in rank order on that particular topic. Full source information is given for each chart. The work also includes a listing of additional sources of information along with relevant Websites and a sparse but useful index.

For libraries that seek to provide current statistical comparisons for the states, this is a useful purchase. The main advantage of this work compared to standard reference sources such as the *Statistical Abstract of the United States* (131st ed.; see ARBA 2012, entry 866) is its presentation of data at the state level, especially of comparative information. No other work provides such a wide variety of information in such a straightforward manner.—**Gregory A. Crawford**

Urban Studies

Handbooks and Yearbooks

P

256. **America's Top-Rated Cities, 2011: A Statistical Handbook.** 18th ed. Millerton, N.Y., Grey House Publishing, 2011. 4v. index. $65.00pa./vol.; $225.00/4-vol. set. ISBN 13: 978-1-59237-545-5.

This 18th edition of *America's Top-Rated Cities* provides statistical information on 100 cities in the United States that have ranked high in business and environmental conditions by surveys and editorial reports, in interviews, and through personal visits to the cities by the staff writers. Each volume represents a specific geographic region of the country (Southern, Western, Central, and Eastern), and lists chapters alphabetically by city name. The chapters include background essays that offer brief historical facts and current news followed by rankings related to areas such as cultural arts, health, and women and minorities. Statistics are presented in two categories: "Business Environment" and "Living Environment." "Business Environment" covers topics such as economy, employment, and income, while "Living Environment" features information on housing, cost of living, and education. The volumes conclude with five different appendixes that offer comparative statistics, contact information for chambers of commerce, and county names. The appendixes are repeated in each of the volumes for easier reference. Two new cities have made the list of top-rated cities in this edition: Gainesville, Florida, and Cambridge, Massachusetts. The publisher also notes that three cities are included due to their popularity even though they do not meet the population requirement: Boulder, Colorado; Edison, New Jersey; and Fargo, North Dakota.

Users who are thinking of relocating to a different city, or individuals who would like to see if their businesses have the possibility of thriving in a new location will find that this provides valuable information that could help them in the decision-making process. This resource is suitable for large public libraries, academic libraries whose institutions include business schools, business libraries, and corporate libraries.—**Maris L. Hayashi**

C, P

257. **Cities in American Political History.** Richardson Dilworth, ed. Washington, D.C., CQ Press, 2011. 760p. illus. index. $165.00. ISBN 13: 978-0-87289-911-7; 978-1-60871-801-6 (e-book).

Urban studies have long languished in the shadow of area studies and country studies. But there has recently been a resurgence of scholarship in this field and *Cities in American Political History* is an example. It is quite limited in scope, covering only 10 U.S. cities in 10 different eras in American history. The selection of these 10 cities is in itself a commentary on the dynamics of urban growth. Of the 10 cities that appear in the first era between 1776 and 1790 only two appear in the last era between 1989 and 2011. On the whole 29 cities make the list and the rise and fall of these cities itself makes an interesting study. At the time of the first census in 1790 the majority of the big cities were located in New England, the largest being New York with a population of 33,133. In 2010, seven of the biggest cities were located in Texas, Arizona, and California but the largest city remained New York with a population of over 8 million.

The book looks at some major themes in the history of American cities under three rubrics: Government and Politics; Industry; Commerce and Labor; and Race, Ethnicity, and Immigration. All these themes appear in national history but metropolitan studies give the historian the advantage of a powerful zoom lens into the way the local melds into the national to create a tableau of colliding interests and shifting identities. The history of American city government runs parallel to the constitutional development of the United States but is marked by constant experimentation. The charters of the cities mimicked the national Constitution in broad outline but contained many innovations that have no parallel in the national government. The second theme deals with industry, commerce, and labor where the cities had more leeway to establish their own protocols and maximize their resources and natural advantages. The third theme relates to ethnicity and immigration. The racial composition of the cities has been radically altered in favor of non-white minorities. Most new immigrants settled in cities rather than in the countryside and rural areas. Thus, immigration has played a larger role in the development of cities and urban quality of life and in the decline of rural areas.

Richardson Dilworth has assembled an impressive roster of contributors to create a valuable addition to urban studies. In addition to the entries, the book has a number of useful features, including sidebars of useful facts, extensive bibliographies, maps, statistics, lists of mayors, and a chronology. This work is highly recommended. [R: BL, Jan 1 &15, 2012, p. 64]—**George Thomas Kurian**

P

258.   **Companion to Urban Design.** Tridib Banerjee and Anastasia Loukaitou-Sideris, eds. New York, Routledge/Taylor & Francis Group, 2011. 714p. index. $220.00. ISBN 13: 978-0-415-55364-3.

This work provides core, foundational ideas and concept found in modern-day urban design. This is a hot topic in contemporary public policy, bridging the gap between the concepts of multiculturalism, environmentalism, economic development, community living, and public health and urban development. The *Companion to Urban Design* provides more than 50 original essays from international scholars and authorities on such concepts as the ideas behind the concepts that shape modern urban design; current innovations relevant to urban design; debates and conflicts in the theories behind urban design; the modern-day challenges of climate change and sustainability on urban design; and the various disciplinary influences on the theory and practice of urban design today.

This is a hot topic among urban developers, policymakers, architects, and landscape professionals. As such it will be useful in academic libraries serving undergraduate and postgraduate students studying these field as well as larger city public libraries that provide services to these groups.—**Herbert W. Ockerman**

P

259.   **The Comparative Guide to American Suburbs 2011/2012.** 6th ed. Millerton, N.Y., Grey House Publishing, 2011. 1956p. index. $150.00pa. ISBN 13: 978-1-59237-834-0.

The 6th edition of *The Comparative Guide to American Suburbs* is described as a one-stop resource to over 2,700 suburban communities (also known as bedroom suburbs) that serve as the buffer between rural areas and the metropolises. This edition includes 232 more suburbs than the 5th edition and covers 75 metropolises, 10 more than in the 5th edition (see ARBA 2010, entry 818, for a review of the 5th edition). The book is arranged in alphabetic order from Akron, Ohio, to Worcester, Massachusetts, and by individual suburbs within each metro area. Each metro area contains a state map. The data are presented under six major rubrics: geography, climate, population, income, housing, and education. Each of these sections is then divided into 44 subcategories (5 more than the last edition). Surprisingly, the book focuses only lightly on quality of life indicators, such as health, environment, and crime. Following the suburb profiles are rankings charts on 35 data points that fill 300 pages. The rankings justify the title, *Comparative Guide*, and provide a handy road map to the best suburbs in certain areas. There are two indexes.

Like most Grey House publications, this guide is well researched and organized. There are a number of relocation directories, but none specifically for suburbs rather than cities. Most of the basic information in this book is easily available online; however, it would be time consuming to gather it together as this book has done. The information has a short shelf life making it necessary for libraries to purchase each new update, which appear to come out every two years. The book is recommended for all public libraries with data collections.—**George Thomas Kurian**

C, S

260.   **U.S. Infrastructure.** Paul McCaffrey, ed. Bronx, N.Y., H. W. Wilson, 2011. 200p. index. (The Reference Shelf). $55.00pa. ISBN 13: 978-0-8242-1108-0.

H. W. Wilson's The Reference Shelf series addresses topics of current interest by providing a collection of reasonably balanced and varied articles as a starting point for research. In this, the series is much like the Grolier Pro/Con and Chelsea House Point/Counterpoint series and seems designed to appeal to much the same audience—high school students and, perhaps, college freshmen and the general public. *U.S. Infrastructure* contains 30 short articles (most 2-4 pages with the longest around 7 pages in length), divided into 4 broad collections, including breeched levees and fallen bridges; transportation infrastructure; the train debate; power and communication networks; and waterworks. The vast majority of the articles are drawn from newspapers and magazines, rounded out with a few pieces originally printed in trade publications and special interest magazines. There is no scholarly material in the collection (although some articles draw on peer-reviewed research), which ends with a further reading bibliography and a short index. While all policymakers agree this is something that needs to be kept up, how it should be maintained and who should pay (federal, state, or local governments or private industry) is a hot and controversial topic that this book does a good job addressing.—**Peter Larsen**

18 Women's Studies

Dictionaries and Encyclopedias

S

261.   **American Women's History Online. http://www.infobase.com/.** [Website]. New York, Facts on File. Price negotiated by site. Date reviewed: 2012.

Designed for use by middle school and high school aged students, this resource is an authoritative database on American women's history. All of the material has been pulled from Facts on File's extensive list of historical reference sources. It provides biographies, historical entries, maps and charts, images and videos, and timelines for the past 500 years of women's history. The site is filled with Topic Centers that handpick entries within each era, which can serve as starting points for research. Users can search by keyword or phrase, or they can browse by topic or era Biographies can be browsed by occupation and primary sources can be searched by type. Some other useful features for students doing research are persistent record links and tabbed search results that show relevant results. Four special timelines have been included: a general timeline for the past 500 years in women's history; a timeline of the history of women's reproductive rights; a timeline of women in politics; and a timeline of the women's suffrage movement. (All timelines are updated monthly.) Along with biographies, users can also find relevant information on key topics and historical events, such as legal cases, social issues, and organizations. Special features include an "Editor's Selection of the Month" section that highlights an event tied to each month and a "Focus On" feature that spotlights a specific topic, such as women in politics. The more than 60 historical videos cover topics that will be fascinating to students, including fashion, the history of working women, and women in politics. Overall, this database is very useful for students, teachers, and librarians.—**Shannon Graff Hysell**

C, P

262.   **Encyclopedia of Women in Today's World.** Mary Zeiss Stange, Carol K. Oyster, and Jane Sloan, eds. Thousand Oaks, Calif., Sage, 2011. 4v. illus. index. $495.00/set; e-book available. ISBN 13: 978-1-4129-7685-5.

The three editors of this, all of which have an extensive background in women's studies, set an impressive task with this encyclopedia, explaining the changes that have occurred in the situation of women worldwide in areas as vast as poetry, politics, the economy, and education. The goal of the work is to provide authoritative entries and broad coverage on women's history topics making the information accessible to a general audience. This work contains hundreds of signed entries contributed by more than 400 specialists. Contributors come mainly from academia with a few exceptions of experts in the field. While the entries are displayed in alphabetic order there is a Reader's Guide that provides greater context for the individual entries. There are 15 thematic areas and they range from Activism and the Arts to Media/Popular Culture and War and Conflict. Even though the same entry may be displayed in multiple topic areas this section is very useful in collocating related items. Entries range from a couple of pages to several pages. All entries contain a *see also* section and a brief bibliography of further readings.

The e-book version of this resource was reviewed and it offers several additional features, including a chronology of women in today's world, a glossary, a resource guide, and the Beijing Declaration and Platform for Action. The e-book version offers full-color photographs with most entries and includes *see also* and related title lists with each entry. The editors plan to update the online edition with 500 new entries in the next two years that will cover anything missed in this original version and update users on the latest trends in contemporary women's studies. Overall, the text is jargon-free and understandable. This is a must have for all academic and public libraries.—**Shannon Graff Hysell**

Handbooks and Yearbooks

C, P, S

263.   **Celebrating Women in American History.** Elizabeth Rholetter Purdy, ed. New York, Facts on File, 2011. 5v. illus. index. $315.00/set. ISBN 13: 978-0-8160-7878-3.

The five-volume *Celebrating Women in American History* is a great collection for any high school or public library serving a young adult demographic. The author, Elizabeth Rholetter Purdy, of this set has a Ph.D. in political science and publishes articles on political science and women's studies. This set includes comprehensive coverage from colonization of the United States to contemporary issues. Each volume is broken down into different time periods: Colonization, Revolution, and the New Republic: Beginnings to 1860; Industrialization and Political Activism: 1861-1899; The Progressive Era and the Great Depression: 1900-1937; Expanding Social Roles and Postwar Activism: 1938-1960; and Modern Feminist Movement and Contemporary Issues: 1961-Present. The chapters in each volume cover specific cultural sections including arts and literature, business, education, entertainment, family, health, politics, science and medicine, and society. Each book introduces the time period and the changes in women's roles during the time. The books are well documented with a comprehensive bibliography. The set is very engaging with inset photographs and images as well as pertinent sidebars. Further reading opportunities are listed at the end of each chapter. Each book comes with its own subject index.—**Michelle Martinez**

C

264.   **Gender and Women's Leadership: A Reference Handbook.** Karen O'Connor, ed. Thousand Oaks, Calif., Sage, 2011. 2v. index. $325.00/set. ISBN 13: 978-1-4129-6083-0.

Gender and Women's Leadership is part of a series of two-volumes sets related to leadership. Editor O'Connor states: "It is my hope that student, faculty, researchers, and reference librarians will benefit from this series by discovering the many varied ways that leadership permeates a wide variety of disciplines and interdisciplinary topics."

Gender and Women's Leadership consists of a series of essays by experts in the field—primarily the authors are university professors and among other contributors are a syndicated columnist; the founder of a consulting firm, Women Online; and a senior researcher with the Girl Scout Research Institute. The essays are arranged within the following categories: Feminist Theories of Leadership; History of Women's Public Leadership; Women's Leadership in Social Movements; Women's Leadership in the Global Context; Women's Leadership in the Business and Profit Sector; Women's Leadership in Religion and Religious Organizations; Women's Leadership in Academia; Leadership in Women's Health; Women's Leadership in the Media; Women's Leadership in Sports; Women's Leadership in the Arts; and Women's Leadership in Public Policy. Each entry contains references and further reading and the resource is indexed . Specific entries within the main categories focus on subject-specific topics, which include: women as leaders in the digital age, women's leadership in sociology, women's leadership in professional sports (including a profile on Billie Jean King), and women's leadership on fashion design. Each essay includes a summary.

This two-volume set is an essential source for academic libraries supporting a women's studies program. It is also recommended to university libraries in general since it contains a treasure trove of scholarly articles focusing on women in various fields and provides some historical contexts. It also cuts across many subject disciplines; for instance, a biology student might want to read the essay "Women's Leadership in Biology."—**Lucy Heckman**

C, P

265.   Kinnear, Karen L. **Women in Developing Countries: A Reference Handbook.** Santa Barbara, Calif., ABC-CLIO, 2011. 348p. index. (Contemporary World Issues). $55.00. ISBN 13: 978-1-59884-425-2; 978-1-59884-426-9 (e-book).

Women in Developing Countries: A Reference Handbook is an exploration of females in less-well-off countries containing a preface, list of developing countries, background and history, controversies and solutions, concerns, a chronology, biographical sketches, facts and data, a useful directory of organizations, a list of selected print and nonprint resources, a glossary, and an index.

   Forty-eight pages of statistics on various topics are invaluable to researchers of poor countries. For example, table 6.3 "Literacy, School Enrollment, and Government Policies" supplies data on literacy rate (women ages 15-24), female children not enrolled in primary school, ratio of female to male primary school enrollment, ratio of female to male secondary school enrollment, and government education program on 126 countries from the continents of Africa, East Asia and the Pacific, South and Central Asia, Near East and North Africa, and South and Central America. The lowest literacy rate of females 15-24 is 23 percent in Niger. Brunei, Democratic People's Republic of Korea, Samoa, Singapore, Tonga, Bahrain, Libya, Trinidad, and Tobago have a 100 percent literacy rate on women ages 15-24. A chronology on the countries runs from 1914-2011. This work is a useful reference on females from poorer countries for researchers and belongs in most academic and public libraries. [R: Choice, Jan 12, p. 856]—**Melinda F. Matthews**

C, S

266.   Moon, Danelle. **Daily Life of Women During the Civil Rights Era.** Santa Barbara, Calif., Greenwood Press/ABC-CLIO, 2011. 241p. illus. index. (The Greenwood Press Daily Life Through History Series). $49.95. ISBN 13: 978-0-313-38098-3; 978-0-313-38099-0 (e-book).

   In *Daily Life of Women During the Civil Rights Era*, Moon (San José State University) examines the experiences and roles that women played in the role of the civil rights movement in the United States. The work examines civil rights reform during the progressive era, victory of the suffragist vote, World War I, World War II, the Cold War, the feminist movement, antiwar movements, and political movements. The author describes the complex problems faced by each group and how women rallied to support their cause. A variety of themes are discussed in-depth within the volume, including rights to citizenship, domestic violence, birth control and reproduction rights, labor and employment, racism, human rights, and peace movement. The book contains chapter source notes, a chronology from 1865 through 2004, an extensive bibliography, historic black-and-white photographs, and an index. The text provides worthwhile insights into the important subject of the civil rights movement and the influential and consistent role that women have played in its unfolding.—**William C. Struning**

C, S

267.   Sloan, Kathryn A. **Women's Roles in Latin America and the Caribbean.** Santa Barbara, Calif., Greenwood Press/ABC-CLIO, 2011. 226p. illus. index. (Women's Roles Through History). $59.95. ISBN 13: 978-0-313-38108-9; 978-0-313-38109-6 (e-book).

   Kathryn Sloan explores how women have shaped today's Latin America, from Queen Isabella who sent Columbus to the New World to Chile's Michelle Bachelet, the first woman elected to a Latin American presidency who was not the widow of a prominent man. The author takes a thematic approach, sketching out in broad strokes how Latin American women lived during the major eras of its history, looking at the difference social class and life stage made on their every-day experiences. The author covers the formative themes of work, family relationships, culture, religion, politics, and the law. This is not a country-by-country survey of notable women, although the arts and politics chapters include a few more individual profiles.

One of Sloan's major themes is how religion infused Latin American society. For example, in colonial times, having a daughter become a nun brought honor to her family while providing her respect and protection. According to the custom of the time, a girl needed a sizeable dowry to make a suitable marriage. If her parents could not afford the necessary dowry, rather than be forced to marry beneath her status, she could join a convent as an alternative. As a nun, she often had more freedom to pursue intellectual pursuits. This was the case with Sor Juana Ines de la Cruz. This seventeenth-century nun chose the convent over marriage as means to pursue her scientific and philosophical studies. Sor Juana was well known in her time as a literary figure. In the chapter on women's roles in politics we learn that although women won the right to vote later than in other regions of the world, starting with Ecuador in 1929 and ending with Paraguay in 1961, women have wielded significant influence by working in education, social reform, and even fighting in the region's revolutions. Recently six Latin American women have been elected president of their country. Latin America has a diverse history and the contributions of its women are equally diverse.—**Adrienne Antink**

Part III
HUMANITIES

19 Humanities in General

General Works

C

268.   **The Classical Tradition.** Anthony Grafton, Glenn W. Most, and Salvatore Settis, eds. Cambridge, Mass., Harvard University Press, 2010. 1067p. illus. index. $49.95. ISBN 13: 978-0-674-03572-0.

The Classical Tradition is a scholarly guide to the many ways classical Greek and Roman culture have influenced subsequent cultures up through the present. The book opens with an alphabetic list of approximately 500 articles on topics ranging from the academy to zoology, and covering both concepts like liberty and individuals like Jacques-Louis David. The language is engaging and sophisticated and seems most appropriate for a college educated audience. Articles about concepts such as republicanism discuss how it has been defined over time in a very fluid way that weaves disparate eras into a larger narrative rather than in a straight chronological format: an article's discussion is just as likely to start in the twentieth century as in the first, always with an eye of course on its relevance to classical origins. There is a bibliography included at the end of each article and documentation is also included for all illustrations as well as references within the text of an article itself. Each article is attributed to a specific author utilizing the author's initials. There are three inserts of images, most of them in color, each consisting of approximately 30 pages. Illustrations are of both ancient sources as well as more modern sources influenced by classical sources. Unfortunately there are no clear cross-references between these images and the articles they are related to in the text. The book closes with a list of contributors and a comprehensive index replete with see also references. This volume is highly recommended for academic libraries. [R: LJ, Jan 11, p. 123; Choice, Mar 2011, p. 1261]—**Philip G. Swan**

20 Communication and Mass Media

General Works

C, P
269. **The New Encyclopedia of Southern Culture: Media. Volume 18.** Allison Graham and Sharon Monteith, eds. Chapel Hill, N.C., University of North Carolina Press, 2011. 439p. index. $47.50; $26.95pa. ISBN 13: 978-0-8078-3401-5; 978-0-8078-7143-0 (e-book).

This is volume 18 of the ongoing publication of *The New Encyclopedia of Southern Culture*, a work which seeks to present the "powerful historical and mythical presence" of the American South. Focusing on the broadly defined world of "media," the editors present 40 thematic essays and 132 topical articles. After an excellent introduction to Southern media cultures, the thematic essays address major forms of mass media including film, the Internet, journalism, radio, and television. Film, represented by 21 separate essays, takes center stage with topics as varied as censorship of film, civil rights in film, and specific genres such as horror, musical, prison, and good ole boy films. The topical articles cover authors, book titles, film titles, magazines, and people. These articles are in no means comprehensive and there does not seem to be great logic in their selection. For example, Southern evangelists, who often use the media to help put out there message, are well represented with separate articles on Jim and Tammy Faye Baker, Jerry Falwell, Billy Graham, Pat Robertson, and Jimmy Swaggert. But Southern musicians and musical performers (some of whom are covered in other volumes of the encyclopedia) are noticeably absent. Tennessee Ernie Ford, Dolly Parton, and Elvis Presley are included, but there is no mention of Loretta Lynn, Bill Monroe, or any of the Carter Family. The selection of television shows is also haphazard with *Hee Haw* and *The Dukes of Hazard* included, but not *Dallas* or *The Andy Griffith Show*, although both are mentioned in thematic essays. Several interesting entries, such as "The Beatles and Jesus Controversy," should be included in more general articles such as one on The Beatles. Similarly, there are articles on film adaptations of works by Pat Conroy and John Grisham, but no entries on the authors themselves.

Although the work does have some flaws, it is an interesting addition to the wide array of topics covered in other volumes of *The New Encyclopedia of Southern Culture*. Most academic and larger public libraries, especially those that own other volumes of the encyclopedia, will definitely want to add this title.—**Gregory A. Crawford**

Authorship

General Works

C

270.   Day, Robert A., and Barbara Gastel. **How to Write and Publish a Scientific Paper.** 7th ed. Santa Barbara, Calif., Greenwood Press/ABC-CLIO, 2011. 300p. illus. index. $55.00; $29.95pa. ISBN 13: 978-0-31339-195-8; 978-0-313-39197-2 (e-book).

Scientists new to the paper writing process will find *How to Write and Publish a Scientific Paper* to be a relevant, informative, and practical guide. Comprehensive in scope, the work discusses how to approach a writing project, ethical principles in scientific publishing, writing grant proposals, working with other media, and preparing oral presentations to go along with your paper. The information given is effectively supported by examples which are relevant and up to date. Not only does this book contain valuable information about the field of scientific writing, it also contains detailed information on appropriate writing styles, words and expressions to avoid, and words and expressions to use in their place. The book is arranged into 41 chapters that basically cover two tasks—how to write a scientific papers and how to get it published. Common errors in grammar are also addressed. Users can easily access this information through a cross-referenced, comprehensive index at the back of the book. They can also find resources for further study through a selected bibliography at the end of the book. On the whole, students and practicing scientists will find this title to be a valuable reference for academic writing in general.—**Helen Margaret Bernard**

C

271.   Mallette, Leo, and Clare Berger. **Writing for Conferences: A Handbook for Graduate Students and Faculty.** Santa Barbara, Calif., Greenwood Press/ABC-CLIO, 2011. 229p. index. $29.95pa. ISBN 13: 978-0-313-39408-9; 978-0-313-39407-2 (e-book).

Graduate students and faculty new to the process of writing papers on their research projects for conferences will find *Writing for Conferences* to be a relevant, informative, and practical guide. Comprehensive in scope, the work discusses the step-by-step process of conference publishing, ethics in publishing, and presentation tips. The information given is effectively supported by examples which are relevant and up to date. Not only does this book contain valuable information about writing conference papers, it also contains detailed information on preparing the presentation, presenting a presentation, and how to successfully network at a conference. The book is arranged into 16 chapters that basically cover two tasks—how to write a conference paper, and the best way to present it and make the most of your conference time. Users can easily access this information through a cross-referenced, comprehensive index at the back of the book. The work provides a glossary at the end of the book and scheduling options to get everything done on time. On the whole, graduate students and faculty will find this title to be a valuable reference for academic writing in general and conference writing in particular.—**Helen Margaret Bernard**

S

272.   **Nonfiction: Writing for Fact and Argument.** By Valerie Bodden. Mankato, Minn., Creative Education/The Creative Company, 2010. 4v. Index. $23.95/vol.

Although the author of these volumes does a commendable job with a dry subject, it is hard to image a student sitting down and reading through or referencing these titles. Each book is written in narrative style with historical backgrounds on the evolvement of the writing style. The books are nicely illustrated with photographs and drawings, but students who need help organizing their writing styles will look for a style manual with short concise directions rather than reading through these. Each volume provides a bibliography and a glossary.—**Kyla M. Johnson**

C, P

273.   Norton, Scott. **Developmental Editing: A Handbook for Freelancers, Authors, and Publishers.** Chicago, University of Chicago Press, 2009. 238p. index. $22.50pa. ISBN 13: 978-0-226-59515-3; 978-0-226-59516-0 (e-book).

This title serves as both a guidebook for the role of editor as well as a career tool for the editor needing advice on how to make the most out of their career. The author uses a realistic, yet often-times humorous, approach to dealing with a wide range of authors, editors, and publishers. The book is divided into chronological chapters that follow the path a manuscript takes to becoming a book: shaping the proposal, finding the hook, building the narrative, and then executing the style. As examples of how to execute these rules, the author uses a variety of nonfiction styles, including popular science, travel guides, and memoirs. Alongside the text users will find sidebars highlighting key points to remember and advice for the editor (e.g., career advice, editing techniques). The book is now available in a less expensive paperback edition (useful for those using it at their desk) as well as an inexpensive e-book version (the e-book edition runs $7.00 to $22.50). This guidebook will work best as a desk reference for acquisition and production editors; however, it would be useful in the reference collections of academic and public libraries where writers and editors can access it for clear writing advice.—**Lori D. Kranz**

Style Guides

C, P, S

274.   Lipson, Charles. **Cite Right: A Quick Guide to Citation Styles—MLA, APA, Chicago, the Sciences, Professions, and More.** 2d ed. Chicago, University of Chicago Press, 2011. 213p. index. $14.00pa. ISBN 13: 978-0-226-48464-8.

Cite Right bills itself as a quick guide to multiple style guides—and it delivers. Addressing more than just the traditional big three—MLA, APA, and Chicago—*Cite Right* explains the purpose and the basics of citations before launching into the book proper. The book is divided into two parts: an overview of citations and the quick guide for citations in every format. The quick guide section provides the citation formats for a variety of sources in 11 general areas: Chicago/Turabian; MLA; APA; AAA; CSE; AMA; ACS; physics, astrophysics, and astronomy; mathematics and computer science; Bluebook legal citations; and ALWD legal citations. Each section provides examples of a variety of formats, from traditional print sources to electronic and Web formats. Each chapter provides an index to the types of citations provided. *Cite Right* also includes a chapter for frequently asked questions pertaining to all reference styles, providing quick answers to general questions like "Do I need to cite everything I use in the paper?", and questions about bibliographies and quotations. This 2d edition has been updated with new styles for the IEEE and ASCE, which are often used in engineering. There is also a new discussion on the usefulness and problems with citation software, which is growing in popularity. Probably the most important addition to this 2d edition is information on how to cite new forms of media, including video blogs, social networking cites, and instant messages. Overall, *Cite Right* is an easy-to-use resource that provides its users with easy-to-find answers pertaining to citations and their formats. This resource is highly recommended for public libraries, school libraries, and academic libraries. [R: C&RL News, Jan 12, p. 53]—**Megan W. Lowe**

C, S

275.   **Writer's Reference Center. http://www.infobase.com/.** [Website]. New York, Facts on File. Price negotiated by site. Date reviewed: 2012.

Facts on File's new *Writer's Reference Center* database provides high school and undergraduate users with key tools for writing effective papers. The resource is designed to be a one-stop source for those needing information on such topics as the mechanics of writing, word definitions, grammatical questions, and how to write and rewrite papers. It will not completely replace the benefits that students would find by actually visiting a campus writing center and getting one-on-one help from an advisor; however, for those who will not step foot into a writing center it is a good alternative. The resource provides more than 100,000 definitions from Fact on File's array of dictionaries and reference books, including *The Facts on File Encyclopedia of Word and Phrase Origins* (4th ed.; see ARBA 2009, entry 885) and *Dictionary of Literary and Thematic Terms* (2d ed.; see ARBA 2007, entry 882). It also includes some 150 essays on grammar, style, and research as well as specific word usage and style questions. Special features include highlighted topics for writers and featured words and phrases that will help users expand their vocabulary. Users can use a basic search feature or browse by subject. Full citations in MLA and Chicago formats are available throughout and users can print, copy, or save their searches to a folder for personal use. This is a solid source for high school media centers and undergraduate libraries and may be just what young readers need to become more proficient in their writing craft.—**Shannon Graff Hysell**

Journalism

C
276.   Applegate, Edd. **Journalism in the United States: Concepts and Issues.** Lanham, Md., Scarecrow, 2011. 164p. index. $45.00. ISBN 13: 978-0-8108-8185-3; 978-0-8108-8186-0 (e-book).

Applegate has written several single-authored books on journalism topics, has published in multiple academic journals, and has taught graduate and undergraduate journalism courses. *Journalism in the United States* is best suited to undergraduate journalism courses as it covers multiple topics of interest in varying depth. The eight chapters focus on topics such as theories of the press and media, freedom of the press, objectivity and balance, and treatment of minorities in the media. Each chapter ranges in its depth; for instance, Applegate's discussion of the purposes of media is 12 pages not including references, while the closing chapter on the history and current critiques of journalism education is over 40 pages long. Thus, some chapters provide the undergraduate with a brief introduction of a topic and varied subtopics while others, most notably the final chapter, show a depth of understanding perhaps more appropriate for the upper-level undergraduate or even graduate student. Although Applegate begins by citing multiple statistics (from 2009) about the state of the media in a digital world, he does not devote a chapter to the shifts that online journalism has wrought. For example, in the chapter on media and minorities, a discussion of photograph manipulation in the news during Hurricane Katrina would have been fitting. Similarly, Applegate's recommendations for journalism programs in chapter 8 should have included some consideration of ethics in a digital age. This book would be well suited to an introductory undergraduate journalism course, particularly at a liberal arts institution.—**Stephanie Vie**

Newspapers

S
277.   **World News Digest. http:/www.infobase.com/.** [Website]. New York, Facts on File. Price negotiated by site. Date reviewed: 2012.

This database brings together nearly 70 years of news from *Facts on File's World News Digest* into an easy-to-search database. It provides archived articles on a wide range of topics, including political, social, and economic events since the *World News Digest* began in November 1940. It is updated twice a week and includes a newsfeed. The site features primary source documents and special features on high-interest topics, newspaper editorials, editorial cartoons, coverage of current events, and content from the *World Almanac*. The political, economic, and cultural stories are linked to handpicked (by Facts on File's editors) to primary sources, essays, illustrations, and other related articles. Useful to teachers and school library media specialists are the teaching resources in the areas of government civics, economics, history, and social studies. Useful to students is the "Need a Research Topic?" feature that offers suggestions for research topics based on the student's search. The site provides hyperlinks from articles to related materials so that students can research the history behind each topic. This database provides a wealth of information and will help students researching for a multitude of assignments.—**Shannon Graff Hysell**

Radio, Television, Audio, and Video

S

278.   Grover, Sharon, and Lizette D. Hannegan. **Listening to Learn: Audiobooks Supporting Literacy.** Chicago, American Library Association, 2011. 188p. index. $55.00pa.; $49.50pa. (ALA members). ISBN 13: 978-0-8389-1107-5.

The authors of this book make a convincing case that audiobooks can play an important role in advancing literacy in grade K-12. Audiobooks not only present another outlet for learning but also can engage students by encouraging literature comprehension. In 10 chapters the authors present such topics as the history of the audiobook, tips to harness their library's audiobook collection and form a useful collection, provide thematic lists of quality titles and suggest group activities that can by used by teachers and librarians, and show ways to encourage parents to use audiobooks as a way to help their children develop literacy skills. The majority of the book is an annotated bibliography of audiobooks, organized by grade level. For each audiobook the authors have provided: title, author, narrator, publisher, an annotation, the subject it falls under, and a suggestion for how the audiobook can be used in an activity or discussion. The work concludes with appendixes on how to evaluate an audiobook, an audiobook lexicon, and Websites of audiobook publishers. For those new to using audiobooks in their collection or to promote literacy, this book will provide a lot of useful tips. If using for collection development or readers' advisory purposes, it should be noted that it is not as comprehensive as *Read On ... Audiobooks: Reading Lists for Every Taste* (see entry 166), which offers more titles and has useful tips on readers' advisory and audiobooks.—**Sara Marcus**

21 Decorative Arts

Collecting

Coins

P

279. Cuhaj, George. **Standard Catalog of World Coins 1601-1700.** 5th ed. Iola, Wis., Krause Publications, 2012. 1560p. illus. index. $85.00pa. ISBN 13: 978-1-4402-1704-3.

The newest edition the *Standard Catalog of World Coins*, this current work covers coins minted between the years 1601 and 1700. Extensive coverage of coins struck by countries, principalities, states, and provinces is included. For example, Germany and Austria are arranged alphabetically by state. Each political division begins with a brief paragraph description, locating it geographically and historically. Sufficient coverage of non-Western coins for this time period is also included; Chinese empires and Vietnam are but two such listed entries. The data has been gathered by the author, an experienced and accomplished numismatist, along with the assistance of more than 200 experts worldwide.

Each entry has at least one black-and-white photograph for visual comparison with the coin in hand. Distinguishing marks or features are listed. Pricing information is as current as possible, although with any work of this nature, it must be used as a guide and not as an exact guideline. An extensive introduction discusses unique points to consider when collecting and trading coins of this time period. Dating, identification, and privy marks are three examples of the items in the introduction. A legend abbreviations table with numerical item references rounds out the volume.

This work will find use in any collection supporting interests in numismatics, general collecting, or the history of the seventeenth century. As noted earlier, currency of the pricing information is always a concern in any collector's catalog, and so it is with this volume. This can easily be solved by further revisions of the present volume.—**Gregory Curtis**

P

280. **North American Coins & Prices CD.** 2012 ed. [CD-ROM]. Iola, Wis., Krause Publications, 2012. $14.95. ISBN 13: 978-1-4402-1867-5.

The 2012 *North American Coins & Prices* is the CD-ROM version of this popular title. It is a typical coin price guide, arranging coins in increasing denominations by country of issue. An illustration of the obverse and reverse accompany each coin and, in a few cases, include a close-up detail. The illustrations are as clear as the original coin will allow. Physical particulars, mintages, and various grades, along with projected prices, are provided for each coin. The prices are merely to be used as guidelines.

The CD-ROM is organized by country, denomination, and then date of issue. Users will find information on coins from the United States, Canada, and Mexico using the index, or a simple word search can be performed. The CD-ROM can be used to confirm the details you know about your coins, such as weight, diameter, and year of issue; authenticate coins from the seventeenth century to the present; or find closer inspection of 3,000 high quality coin illustrations. The resource also provides detailed information and insightful commentary on top coin picks and the history of U.S. coin minting, all within the introduction. The knowledgeable collector might find some of this preliminary information instructive, but will use this guide primarily for coin identification and pricing.

This resource is particularly useful because it brings together the coinage of all three countries of North America in one handy volume. The CD-ROM can be used on a PC or Mac platform. The trend of many coin collectors of North America is to collect coinage from two or all three countries, not just that of their own homeland. This resource is highly recommended for public library collections.—**Margaret F. Dominy**

Firearms

P

281. **Gun Digest, 2012.** By Dan Shidler. Iola, Wis., Krause Publications, 2012. 568p. illus. index. $32.95pa. ISBN 13: 978-1-4402-1447-9.

The most recent edition of this standard work continues the tradition of comprehensive coverage of guns and gun topics for all shooters—hunters, handgunners, collectors, handloaders, and those interested in the history of firearms. The volume is broken into three sections: feature articles, departments, and the catalog itself. The feature articles include both articles on the history of firearms and their production as well as current topics of interest to today's shooters. Biographies of several individuals are also included in this section. In the departments section, users will find informative articles on the current state of the shooting industry with product development discussions concerned with presenting information needed by the consumer in making purchasing decisions. Articles include such topics as scopes, handloading, and a blackpowder review.

The main section of the volume is the catalog of currently produced and available guns of all types—rifles, handguns, shotguns, blackpowder, and air rifles. Each entry in this section includes an illustration of the firearm listed as well as other useful information: caliber, barrel length, weight, overall dimensions, stock composition, type of sights, any special features, and an estimated price. If there is an alternate price for added features, models, or left-handed version, that price is listed as well. The work is filled with black-and-white and color photographs, more than 1,300 in all. The volume concludes with several indexes and appendixes, among those listed are periodicals devoted to firearms, books on the subject, and a manufacturer's directory.

This work will find many users in public libraries and libraries specializing in firearms, hunting, or collecting topics. To be most useful to researchers, this volume needs to be purchased for each edition published because of the changing nature of the subject matter. This will not present a burden to most libraries because of the reasonable price of the work.—**Gregory Curtis**

P

282. **Standard Catalog of Firearms, 2012: The Collector's Price & Reference Guide.** By Jerry Lee. Iola, Wis., Krause Publications, 2012. 1472p. illus. index. $39.99pa. ISBN 13: 978-1-4402-1688-6.

This ready-reference guide to firearms provides pricing information for new and used civilian firearms and comes from a recognized subject authority. (Purely military firearms have their own separate volume, although "civilianized" variants of military weapons are covered here.) Coverage is thorough and comprehensive, with over 25,000 different weapon models (ranging from palm-sized derringers to the 35-pound Barrett Model 82 sniper rifle) being treated in a clear, accurate presentation of the salient facts. Most of the illustrations are in monochrome, with a small color insert displaying some particularly noteworthy specimens; all of the illustrations are clear and enable easy recognition of significant detail. In addition to the carefully categorized pricing information, introductory essays provide an illuminating summary of the collecting environment, and the main text is interspersed with collector advice and individual reminiscences concerning particularly popular examples of the gun maker's art. A table of contents, running heads, and an index make finding any specific item fast and easy. A high standard of accuracy is maintained throughout.

This volume is sturdily perfect-bound in a lay-flat binding, and clearly printed on good-quality newsprint, deserving consideration from any library serving a firearms collection clientele. Worth noting is the capacity of this book to serve as a reasonably effective tool for firearms identification in addition to its primary function as a pricing guide.—**John Howard Oxley**

Crafts

P

283.   Duerr, Sasha. **The Handbook of Natural Plant Dyes.** Portland, Oreg., Timber Press, 2010. 169p. illus. index. $19.95pa. ISBN 13: 978-1-60469-071-2.

This book is ideal for those who love the artful side of both gardening and crafting. The author is an artist and designer that approaches her craft with a naturalistic approach that involves being accountable, deliberate, and aware of the process as well as the product. The book is arranged into five basic chapters that discuss how to get started (materials needed, basic fibers and dyes to use), recipes for nontoxic color, gathering and growing your own plants for dyes, sample plants and dye, and various types of projects and gifts you can make by doing these processes. The author provides thorough definitions of plants that can be used, concise instructions for how complete each project, and brilliant full-color photographs throughout the volume. The work concludes with a glossary, list of resources, a list for further reading, and an index. For those interested in a more holistic and natural way of crafting, and those looking for unique gift ideas, this book will be a useful resource. It would be of use in most public libraries.—**Shannon Graff Hysell**

P

284.   **Firefly's Step-by-Step Encyclopedia of Needlecraft.** Richmond Hills, Ont., Firefly Books, 2011. 320p. illus. index. $29.95pa. ISBN 13: 978-1-55407-925-4.

P

285.   Seward, Linda. **The Complete Book of Patchwork, Quilting & Appliqué.** Richmond Hills, Ont., Firefly Books, 2011. 184p. illus. index. $24.95pa. ISBN 13: 978-1-55407-804-2.

Firefly's Step-by-Step Encyclopedia of Needlecraft is a wealth of information for the person interested in needlework. The work is a how-to reference that does not bog down but gives just enough information to tantalize the needle worker whether novice or experienced. It provides comprehensive, step-by-step instructions for learning how to knit, crochet, quilt, appliqué, embroider, and sew by machine or by hand. Included are creative, doable projects that put these skills to use. The table of contents consists of: an introduction; project index (with superior color photographs of the more than 50 projects); techniques; each of the six main crafts with colorful examples; templates; yarns used; and an index and acknowledgments. Additionally, there are extensive stitch glossaries and specialized techniques that are explained and illustrated in detail. Both British Imperial and U.S. Customary measuring systems are used making this reference accessible to most countries. At the beginning of each section there is a clear synopsis of that section by a cheery author. The authors' (all accomplished craftsmen in their specific craft) objectives are to give each reader the confidence and mastery of new skills to create new items. The instructions and techniques give all the information you need to start and finish these projects and to use this reference as a stepping-stone to new skills and new interests.

The Complete Book of Patchwork, Quilting & Appliqué covers every quilting process and answers what will be many quilters technical questions. Along with a detailed history of quilting around the world, the work offers 1,000 step-by-step illustrations on how to complete detailed designs and techniques. The work includes information on equipment and techniques, colors and fabrics, cutting and pressing fabrics, joining and setting pieces, reverse and shadow appliqué, hand quilting, and special techniques (e.g., curved seams, tie quilting). The author includes several patterns and templates that cover both beginning and advanced quilt patterns as well as an A-Z glossary to terms.

These volumes both are both the ultimate straightforward crafting reference and they will appeal to all skill levels and most public libraries.—**Nadine Salmons**

Fashion and Costume

Dictionaries and Encyclopedias

P

286.　Lewandowski, Elizabeth J. **The Complete Costume Dictionary.** Lanham, Md., Scarecrow, 2011. 579p. illus. index. $125.00. ISBN 13: 978-0-8108-4004-1.

The Complete Costume Dictionary by Elizabeth Lewandowski is an impressive reference book. The main 325-page dictionary defines terms from ancient to modern time periods and from cultures and geographic areas worldwide. Nearly 200 additional pages organize the terms in three appendixes: "Garment Types," "Garment by Country," and "Garment Types by Era." A selected bibliography and author and illustrator notes complete the volume. The author's stated intent was to share the hundreds of costume terms she has collected throughout the years of her research. This she admirably does with definitions ranging from one word to a few sentences. Most terms indicate country or area associated with a term.

The appendixes attempt to complement the main dictionary by re-sorting the terms into three general categories. Appendix A, "Garment Types," lists pages and pages of terms (four columns per page) under categories as broad as Accessories (nearly 800 terms) and Fabric (almost 3000 terms). Fewer terms are listed under specific terms, such as Apron (about 100 terms) and Straw (30 terms). Appendix B is "Garment by Country." Appendix C, "Garment Types by Era," offers lists of words from the Cradles of Western Civilization cultures, focusing on the Western European tradition. The earliest is Egyptian (4000-30 B.C.E) and Biblical (Unknown-30 C.E.) Approximately 50 more pages move through standard historical eras, such as Early Gothic (1200-1350 C.E.,) Charles I and the Commonwealth (1625-1660 C.E.,) Crinoline (1849-1865 C.E.), and 1950-1960 C.E. The difficulty with all three appendixes is lack of context for a reader without the wide-ranging knowledge as the author's. There is little use in seeing long lists of words for which one must go to the main section of the dictionary to obtain a definition.

The center section of color illustrations is disappointing, as they are primarily full-page illustrations of western women's wear and selected accessories, primarily taken from Dover publications. Sketches of dress and costume from various world cultures and time periods labeled with dictionary terms would have offered added value.

In spite of falling short with the appendixes and illustrations, this volume adds to the reference works available on clothing. A closely written eight-page bibliography lists standard and lesser-known costume and fashion sources (mostly books, but a few articles) for cultures worldwide. No references date later than 2000. This reference book is interesting to browse as well as to look up single terms. It is comprehensive across many cultures and areas. Given the price and narrow focus of the topic, however, the list price is probably too high for current library budgets.—**Lizbeth Langston**

Directories

P

287.   Baugh, Gail. **The Fashion Designer's Textile Directory: A Guide to Fabrics' Properties, Peculiarities, and Garment-Design Potential.** Hauppauge, N.Y., Barron's Educational Series, 2011. 319p. illus. index. $35.00pa. ISBN 13: 978-0-7641-4628-2.

In the title Baugh clearly states her target audience; however, the subtitle is what defines the book. Its topic will interest readers with either a casual or professional interest in the many different fabrics on the market today.

A brief section 1, Responsible Design, is a short discussion about the fabric industry and how designers can make choices that promote sustainable practices. The 20 pages of section 2, The Language of Textiles, covers such topics as the supply chain, fiber, yarn, and color. The 200-plus page section 3 is The Textile Directory. Section 4, The Charts, contains tables organized down the pages by weave (e.g., plain, pile, basket weave) and various factors across the page, such as fabric names, weights, advantages and disadvantages, and end use. A glossary and index complete the book.

The Textile Directory is the heart of the book. Specific fabrics are categorized into five chapters: Structure, Fluidity, Ornamentation, Expansion, and Compression. Within the chapters, fabrics are listed from heaviest weight to lightest. I think that conceptualizing the chapters by topic is a successful way of presenting similarities and differences. Baugh's presentation guides a reader to think about the properties and potential uses of each fabric within the categories she chose.

Within the structure of each entry, the left-hand side of the page describes a fabric and the general use. Photographs of fabric swatches (showing front and back) run along the bottom. The right-hand side of the page presents a fashion shot. Also on the page are facts and figures and a brief description of how the fabric is used in the garment illustrated. The introduction stresses the importance of environmentally friendly practices in an industry sometimes perceived as frivolous or concerned with status. To counter that perception many of the entries contain a "Design Responsibly" box that describes the production practices or recyclabilty of a fabric, and requests designers to choose producers that choose safer, less exploitive, or environmentally friendly practices.

Baugh packs a lot of information in her book. The intricacy of the layout results in an easy-to-use and delightful directory that reflects the effort needed to successful design a fashionable garment. My only quibble is that there is no information on the garment designers and date of creation.

This book will be useful to a wider audience than those within the fashion industry. Home sewers and costumers can learn a lot from Baugh's research. *The Fashion Designer's Textile Directory* is definitely a dynamic work rather than a dictionary or encyclopedic listing of hundreds of fabrics. Her clear prose and consistent entries will delight and educate the reader. This book could belong equally well in a reference or circulating collection of a library whose patrons are interested in fine fabrics, garment design, and construction.—**Lizbeth Langston**

22 Fine Arts

General Works

Dictionaries and Encyclopedias

C, P, S
288.   **The Grove Encyclopedia of American Art.** Joan Marter, ed. New York, Oxford University Press, 2011. 5v. illus. index. $750.00/set. ISBN 13: 978-0-19-533579-8.

The Grove Encyclopedia of American Art is a five-volume work that is based, in part, on entries found in *Grove Art Online* (see ARBA 2002, entry 993). The content covers prehistoric art through works of the twenty-first century. Articles are well written and are meant for a nonspecialist audience. Black-and-white images of artwork are incorporated throughout the text with a small insert of color images included in each volume. There is an effort to include work by African, Asian, Latino, and Native American artists. The definition of art encompasses painting and sculpture as well as architecture, computer art, design, film, collage, printmaking, and photography. Contemporary movements, such as conceptual art, environmental art, and performance art, get a good degree of attention. Prominent art critics, patrons, and collectors get biographical articles, as do prominent art educators and the institutions they work for. Significant museums also receive entries as well as the cities in which they are located.

The entries are arranged in alphabetic order, with the volumes divided at approximately 600 pages a piece. A typical biographical entry includes the dates of birth and death, the main mediums and themes explored by the artist, and an examination of key works followed by a bibliography. Non-biographical articles covering a style or a movement give an overview of dates and the names of key figures and concepts along with a comprehensive bibliography. The author of an article is always included. One significant weakness in the text is a dearth of cross-references: there are a few *see also* references at the close of articles but it would be helpful if terms within the article were bolded to indicate articles available elsewhere in the encyclopedia. Volume 1 opens with a list of articles and a note on use and abbreviations. Volume 5 closes with a topical outline, a directory of contributors, and an index. This set is recommended for public, high school, and college libraries.—**Philip G. Swan**

C
289.   Milam, Jennifer D. **Historical Dictionary of Rococo Art.** Lanham, Md., Scarecrow, 2011. 307p. (Historical Dictionaries of Literature and the Arts). $80.00; $79.99 (e-book). ISBN 13: 978-0-8108-6183-1; 978-0-8108-7952-2 (e-book).

This book is part of a larger series titled Historical Dictionaries of Literature and the Arts. It is a fairly comprehensive dictionary on the Rococo art period, which is associated with the reign of Louis XV in France in the eighteenth century, but continued to spread into other countries as late as 1885. It was a reaction against the Baroque splendor and the Classicism conservatism that dominated art in seventeenth-century France. The book has an excellent annotated chronology of Rococo history, as well as a significant essay on the entire Rococo period and its various styles and variations throughout Europe. A review of the literature and an extensive bibliography frame over 350 cross-referenced entries on significant artists, patrons, critics, painters, sculptors, architects, theorists, and major centers of artistic production. This book is highly recommended as a reference work in this specialized area of art history, and will be of use to the beginning as well as the expert researcher of art history.—**Bradford Lee Eden**

C

290.   Palmer, Allison Lee. **Historical Dictionary of Neoclassical Art and Architecture.** Lanham, Md., Scarecrow, 2011. 288p. (Historical Dictionaries of Literature and the Arts,). $80.00; $80.00 (e-book). ISBN 13: 978-0-8108-6195-4; 978-0-8108-7474-9 (e-book).

Neoclassicism emerged in the mid-eighteenth century and lasted through the late nineteenth century. While looking back to the classical eras of Greece and Rome, the movement was a vibrant recognition of the belief that "the art of this time cannot be separated from the historical events in Europe." As such, it brought together art, philosophy, and political reality, and cannot be meaningfully extricated from the political upheavals and revolutions of the time.

This resource provides a short chronology of both artistic and social events, a thorough introduction to the subject matter, and 30 pages of rich bibliography arranged historically, topically, and by artist. The relevance of the topic is also brought to light, as it is noted that we see a revival of neoclassicism in the arts. However, to say that while this revival is a reaction to the "spare functional modernism," it began with postmodernism is perhaps to marry two ideas too different in function and scope. Entries contain bolded cross-references, with a substantial number of *see also* suggestions at the end of many entries. This is both standard to the series, and exceedingly helpful. The timeline of the included entries makes for pleasing overlaps; the discussion of Romanticism is expected and well written. It is good to see the intertwining of the world of ideas continue in this vein, with a short entry for Schopenhauer. This is a fine work that is essential for all universities that support majors in art, architecture, and history.—**Stephen J. Shaw**

C

291.   Palmer, Allison Lee. **Historical Dictionary of Romantic Art and Architecture.** Lanham, Md., Scarecrow, 2011. 286p. (Historical Dictionaries of Literature and the Arts). $80.00. ISBN 13: 978-0-8108-7222-6; 978-0-8108-7473-2 (e-book).

Beginning in the late eighteenth century and lasting well into the 1850s, Romanticism as a philosophical and artistic movement embraces the awakening of modernism while at the same time reinterpreting the classical tradition that came before it. Many of the works of art and artists we associate with the nineteenth century find their roots in romanticism. The work, by an art historian noted for her work in the artistic period, has a lengthy introduction discussing the roots, changes, and influences on the future that Romanticism brought to the world. The major portion of the work is an alphabetically arranged listing of artists, tools, methods, philosophies, countries, and movements associated with Romanticism. Each entry is from a half-page to one and one-half pages in length. In the case of individuals birth and death dates are given where known. Each entry discusses the importance to the Romantic idea with bold typeface referencing other topics in the dictionary. Black-and-white illustrations accompany several of the entries adding visual interest to the work. An extensive bibliography for further reading and research completes the volume. No index appears at the end of the volume, but with the alphabetic arrangement and the cross-referencing of topics little value is lost by it being left out.

This volume will find ready use in collections supporting art history, philosophy, cultural studies, and history. Well bound in hardcover format and with its easy to use alphabetic format, the work should stand up to years of use in the library setting. Any library with collecting interests in the arts, philosophy, or the history of the eighteenth and nineteenth centuries will find this a useful addition.—**Gregory Curtis**

Handbooks and Yearbooks

P, S

292.   **Eye on Art Series.** Farmington Hills, Mich., Lucent Books/Gale/Cengage Learning, 2011. $33.45/ vol.

Written for middle school to high school age students, the Eye on Art Series from Lucent Books provides an in-depth look in to the various art movements. New titles in the series include: *Manga, Ancient Egyptian Art and Architecture*, and *Art Deco*. The works discuss various art movement, artists, and important works. Also discusses are efforts used to restore artwork. The works begins with an informative introduction and then go on to chapters that discuss details of the trade. For example, the volume on manga has chapters on the roots of manga, Shonen manga, the girls of Shojo manga, and American manga and anime (also known as Amerimanga and Americanime). The volumes include detailed notes, lists for further reading, and an index and picture credits. What makes this series special for students, however, are the beautiful full-color pictures that appear on nearly every page and the sidebars that discuss important aspects of the arts in further detail; for example, the volume on manga has sidebars on how manga is neither a comic nor a novel, the School of Manga at Kyoto Seika University, and Comic-Con (the popular 40-year-old comic book convention). This set is highly recommended for school and public libraries.—**Shannon Graff Hysell**

Architecture

C

293.   **Archinform Index of Persons. http://eng.archinform.net/archli/index.htm.** [Website]. Free. Date reviewed: 2011.

This database for international architecture, originally emerging from records of interesting building projects from architecture students, has meanwhile become the largest online database about worldwide architects and buildings from past to present. Included in this database, students will find over 29,000 mostly twentieth-century building projects both built and planned from architects and planners. The database can be searched by architect, town, or keyword. The indexes use a query form. For most of the entries, teachers and students will find the name, address, keywords, and information about further literature. Some entries include images, comments, links to other Websites, or internal links. This database delivers more than the title would imply. This is a valuable resource for several areas in a technology curriculum.—**William O. Scheeren**

C

294.   **Cities and Building Database. http://content.lib.washington.edu/buildingsweb/index.html.** [Website] Free. Date reviewed: 2011.

The *Cities and Buildings Database* is a collection of digitized images of buildings and cities drawn from across time and throughout the world, available to students, researchers, and educators on the Web. When this database was begun in 1995, it was to provide a multi-disciplinary resource for students, faculty, and others in academia. Since then, it has grown steadily with contributions from a wide range of scholars, and contains images ranging from New York to Central Asia, from African villages, to the Parc de la Villette, and conceptual sketches and models of Frank Gehry's Experience Music Project. Because these images were scanned from original slides or have been pulled from documents in the public domain, students and teachers with access to the Web can use them freely in the classroom. This would be helpful for students who need to illustrate their research projects.—**William O. Scheeren**

23 Language and Linguistics

General Works

C, S

295. Lems, Kristin, Leah D. Miller, and Tenena M. Soro. **Teaching Reading to English Language Learners: Insights from Linguistics.** New York, Guilford, 2010. 256p. index. $30.00pa. ISBN 13: 978-1-60623-468-6.

Authored by three educators in the ESL/Bilingual Education Program at National-Louis University, this work provides theory, research, and practical examples to assist educators and students of ESL and reading education, whether in special classes or as part of a general education program in expanding their knowledge base for working with English-language learners at all levels to improve their literacy. The information provided within these seven chapters can assist educators at any level, from kindergarten to post-graduate, who are working with students whose native language is not English. Each chapter begins with a list of new vocabulary that is defined in the glossary at the end of the book, and ends with two sections: how does this look in the classroom, and questions for further study. Whether used as a textbook in a reading or ESL classroom in an education degree program or as a reference for those already in the field, this work explains the processes involved in second-language acquisition from a linguistic and literacy field. Looking not only at reading, but also listening, speaking, and writing, the case studies and examples help illustrate the theory and research presented.—**Sara Marcus**

C

296. **The World's Major Languages.** 2d ed. Bernard Comrie, ed. New York, Routledge/Taylor & Francis Group, 2011. 912p. index. $75.00. ISBN 13: 978-0-415-60902-9.

The 2d edition of this well-received title provides information on more than 50 of the world's languages, two of which are new to this edition—Amharic and Javanese. The editor has chosen the languages based on their cultural and historical significance as well as on the number of speakers using it worldwide. The languages are looked at in depth, focusing on grammatical features, phonology and syntax, its role in history, and its role in culture. This is a book designed for specialists in linguistics and will serve as a research tool for those learning more about languages they are studying. A bibliography and an index are provided to aid research. This work will be useful in academic collections in larger universities.—**Shannon Graff Hysell**

English-Language Dictionaries

General Usage

C, S

297. **Webster's Dictionary & Thesaurus for Students.** 2d ed. Darien, Conn., Federal Street Press, 2011. 825p. $12.98pa. ISBN 13: 978-1-59695-107-5.

This dictionary is apparently intended for American grade school and middle school children. At 37,000 words, and with no derivations or illustrative sentences (although it does have illustrative phrases for a minority of the terms), it is not a serious dictionary for the high school student or beyond, but is rather essentially a dictionary to help young children know how to spell words and define them. The font is big and clear, and the definitions are clear also, although they may be in some cases beyond the understanding of the intended audience.

There is literally no discussion of the database or editorial background of the dictionary, other than a statement on the back cover that it is "authoritative," and "created with students in mind by the editors of Merriam-Webster and Encyclopaedia Britannica, America's premier reference publisher." The only editorial apparatus whatsoever is a one-page preface discussing how to tell the main entry from other things, and discussing "defined run-on phrases," "run-in entries," and "undefined run-on entries," terms which one would guess will still mystify all but the most determined young would-be lexicographers and users of this work.

The dictionary, with no illustrations, occupies the first half of this enormous paperback volume—499 of this volume's total of 825 pages. The entire dictionary portion is accompanied by the grey legend "dictionary" in the upper right-hand margin of every right-hand page (probably to differentiate it from the lengthy thesaurus at the back). Some 5,000 new words have been added to this 2d edition. Omitted from this edition are the "encyclopedic entries" that were included in the original edition; these probably will not be missed since the majority of the encyclopedic entries can easily be found in other sources or online.

Perhaps the most useful portion of this volume is a 48-page inserted color atlas of the world in the middle of the volume. It covers the entire world, including one plate of the United States, but does not include maps of the individual states. Each plate is a shade larger than 5 ½ by 7 ¾ inches. A map of this size, covering the entire United States, is not very useful to adult eyes, but perhaps for the intended audience, it would be. The same may be said for all of the other plates, but they do have the advantage of being current and could give a child a sense of where specific countries and major cities are, in relationship to other areas.

The final 300-plus pages of this volume are a thesaurus. Normally, a thesaurus is the worst thing to give to an unsophisticated young student, who, without a wide experience with reading and the language, does not understand the shades of meaning between synonyms and as a result uses the various alternatives interchangeably, with a generally jarring or comic result. To give them their due, the creators of this work recognize this problem and offer a relatively short thesaurus in which every alterative term is defined, in an attempt to distinguish each from the other, a laudable effort.

All in all, this is a giant, economy-size version of a paperback dictionary that students carry around to help them spell words, and which professors generally tell college students to abjure. Given its physical size (larger than 7 x 9 inches), it is not the kind of thing that a child will lug around in a backpack, so it is presumably intended for home use. It is not a particularly good purchase for a library that already owns a decent dictionary, atlas, and thesaurus, and it is certainly not the one dictionary to have if a household could have only one, given its limited vocabulary and lack of word derivation information, but it might be useful as a household reference tool, in concert with other works, especially given its current atlas and thoughtful attempt at a thesaurus.—**Bill Miller**

S

298. **Webster's Dictionary for Students: Special Encyclopedic Edition.** 4th ed. Darien, Conn., Federal Street Press, 2011. 533p. $4.49pa. ISBN 13: 978-1-59695-125-9.

Webster's Dictionary for Students is an excellent addition to any library, anywhere. Extremely user-friendly, as well as being more than just a dictionary, the *Student Dictionary* is a versatile and easy-to-use resource. Handy features include sections on general spelling rules, rules for forming plurals, world maps, countries of the world, U.S. capital and U.S. territories, the branches of government, laws and how they are made, presidents of the United States, and important events in American history. The dictionary section itself is easy to use. The dictionary is kid-friendly, with words included that are appropriate for ages 8 and up; it does not contain any unusual words or subject-specific jargon. The definitions are adequate without being too lengthy. New to this edition is the addition of special Canadian and British spellings, which the publisher hopes will give the work a wider appeal. This small volume is updated on a regular basis (the 3d edition was published in 2010); users can probably skip buying each new edition and select new editions based on their personal needs.

Multi-purposed and effortless to use, *Webster's Dictionary for Students* is an ideal resource for any library. It is recommended for public and school libraries and is inexpensive enough to recommend for home use as well.—**Megan W. Lowe**

Rhyming

C, P, S

299. **Webster's Rhyming Dictionary.** Darien, Conn., Federal Street Press, 2011. 214p. $3.99pa. ISBN 13: 978-1-59695-112-9.

Webster's Rhyming Dictionary, created in cooperation with the editors of Merriam-Webster, contains more than 40,000 entries of words based entirely on their similarities in rhyme. It is intended for use by anyone of any age who writes poems, song lyrics, greeting cards, or anything else requiring words that rhyme.

The main entry words are placed alphabetically according to their rhyming sounds. All main entries are listed by the way the rhyming sound is most often spelled. Alternate spellings for the rhyme are listed as cross-reference entries that take the user to the appropriate main entry. All main entries and cross-reference entries, regardless of the number of syllables in the rhyming sound, are alphabetized by the boldface form in a single sequence, with one-syllable words listed first, followed by two syllable words, and so forth. To find a rhyme for a given word, the user needs to know the spelling of the word and its rhyming sound. For example, "apple" lists several choices, including "dapple, scrapple, chapel, mayapple, and pineapple."

Webster's Rhyming Dictionary is probably more suited for use by the individual or single classroom, rather than a library's reference section. Persons in the throes of writing are not likely to rush to the nearest library to find a rhyme, especially since this volume's modest cost and reasonable value make it accessible for individual purchase.—**Kay O. Cornelius**

Terms and Phrases

C, S

300. Ammer, Christine. **The Facts on File Dictionary of Clichés: Meanings and Origins of Thousands of Terms and Expressions.** 3d ed. New York, Facts on File, 2011. 556p. index. (Facts on File Library of Language and Literature). $60.00. ISBN 13: 978-0-8160-8353-4; 978-1-4381-3705-6 (e-book).

The fact that language constantly changes is reflected in this collection of both old and new clichés. Some older clichés that are no longer used have been left out, although some curious choices remain (e.g., "according to Hoyle," "grow like Topsy"). Newer expressions include "soccer mom" and "Ground

Zero." The expressions are arranged alphabetically, mostly by keyword, with initial articles sometimes left at the front and sometimes put at the end after a comma (i.e., "acid test, the"). The choice of keyword access points is sometimes confusing, but there are *see* references both within the text and the index that lead from one version to another. Even though the alphabetic arrangement is sometimes questionable (i.e., "forbidden fruit" is placed between "for better or for worse" and "for crying out loud") the scope of coverage is broad. The information on each phrase includes etymology, derivation, and history and was gathered from diverse sources, including Erasmus, Jonathan Swift, *The Oxford English Dictionary*, John Ciardi, William Safire, and *Bartlett's Quotations*. Purported to have around 4,000 entries, this selection would serve as a quick reference or a starting point for language research. [R: Choice, Jan 12, p. 846]—**Martha Lawler**

Thesauri

C, P

301.   **Historical Thesaurus of the Oxford English Dictionary.** New York, Oxford University Press, 2009. 3984p. index. $395.00/set. ISBN 13: 978-0-19-920899-9.

The *Historical Thesaurus of the Oxford English Dictionary* is far more than your typical thesaurus. This work is an original work 40 years in the making. It is being touted by the publisher as the first historical thesaurus of the English language—of any language for that matter. This thesaurus is really a historical inventory of the history of the English language, showing how words have evolved over time and in relation to one another.

This work is a huge undertaking. It includes more than 920,000 words and nearly 4,000 pages. The terms are listed in alphabetic order, with the synonyms listed in chronological order (with the earliest synonym first). The work provides detailed information on how terms evolved and how the English language developed over time. The work uses a thematic system of classification that distinguishes between true synonyms and closely related words. A comprehensive index provides complete cross-referencing between all of the terms in the resources, and a color chart is enclosed that shows the top levels of the classification structure. This two volume work is a hefty resource by any standard. Volume 1 is the thesaurus, organized by semantic categories, while volume 2 is the alphabetic index listing the synonyms. This organization makes it possible to use the resource by searching the index for a specific word, or by browsing by category in volume 1 to find a word's historical development.

This advanced thesaurus will be most useful in the hands of language and linguists students and scholars. This will be a leading resource in the study of the history of the English language for years to come.—**Shannon Graff Hysell**

Non-English-Language Dictionaries

French

C, P, S

302.   **Larousse Unabridged Dictionary: French-English/English-French.** New York, Larousse/Houghton Mifflin, 2010. 2368p. $64.50. ISBN 13: 978-203-5410382.

This newest contribution to French-English lexicography has made a big splash, with the emphasis on big. In terms of physical size, with almost 2,400 pages and weighing in at close to 7 pounds, it is a massive tome that inhibits portability. In terms of entries, its claim of over one million entries and the comprehensiveness of its content justify the moniker of unabridged.

Most important, of course, is the dictionary itself; the French to English part is designed for French speakers and vice versa. A word of caution: the entries often cover so many possible uses that the uninitiated may have a hard time distinguishing meanings and determining which translated word is the best one they are looking for. The common English word "get" takes up 11 columns and the French word "faire" 10; one would hope the user has the patience to assimilate all the possible definitions before deciding on the appropriate one. Thus, the audience is definitely advanced students, language professionals, and translators. Those less familiar with the language should opt for a desk or pocket dictionary.

In addition to the regular terms one might expect, the dictionary is very strong on slang and even includes instant message terms. The dictionary accommodates the 1990 French-language spelling reforms by including both forms of the word as the headword (e.g., connaître, connaitre), with the new form marked by an asterisk. Comprehensiveness, though, at times verges on silliness; "le web" is defined in English as "Web," "le Web 2.0" as—you guessed it—"Web 2.0," though there is no entry for "World Wide Web." Likewise call-outs on the respective cultures of the two countries are described using terminology of the opposite language. This policy makes sense in light of the bilingual nature of the work, but if English speakers should stumble across the definition of "Bob's your uncle" in the English section, they will find it described only in French. Definitions are usually appended with usage notes (like specialty field or regional usage) and illustrative sentences. Another useful feature is the inclusion of irregularly conjugated verbs among the entries (e.g., "vais" directs the user to "aller"), not a common practice.

The supplemental material is both a blessing and a bane. The communication portion, with writing tips like how French and English differ in punctuation and capitalization, and color plates, with illustrations and bilingual labeling of such objects as car engines and boats, are very useful, even though the terms are also defined in the dictionary proper. One questions, however, the need for the cultural supplement and the cursory maps of English and French-speaking countries, both of which can be found in better resources elsewhere.

As the new kid on the block, the dictionary has to prove itself against the competition, a feat it accomplishes if only in the sheer number of entries alone. The *Oxford Hachette French Dictionary* (see ARBA 2008, entry 872) may be more practical for the general user. The highly respected and equally labeled "unabridged" Collins Robert *French Dictionary* (9th ed., 2010) is only a year old but it actually has 200,000 fewer entries than the *Larousse*. And certainly the *Larousse* pedigree is synonymous with high quality. The only thing not big about this dictionary is the price; at about $65, it is certainly affordable for most academic and large public libraries.—**Lawrence Olszewski**

German

C, S

303.   **Larousse Concise Dictionary: English-German/German-English.** New York, Houghton Mifflin, 2010. 1293p. $14.95pa. ISBN 13: 978-2-03-541052-8.

This new edition of the *Larousse Concise Dictionary: English-German/German-English Dictionary*, although concise, is likely one of the most up-to-date German dictionaries available today. Its 90,000 words and 120,000 translations include words users would expect to find in any dictionary, but also a number of terms of a recent vintage. The English translations give both British and American spellings and usage, and the category each word belongs in is clearly indicated. In view of the fact that a new spelling system has been used in Germany since the late 1990s, this dictionary adheres to it, but it also gives the older version of each altered word.

Throughout the dictionary, there are boxed entries for several terms that receive special treatment. Among the boxes in the English/German section, featured items include "Open University," "Grammar School," "Great Britain," "Whitehall," "Senate," and "Pentagon." The German/English part includes boxes on the "Wirtschaftswunder," "Wurst," "Loveparade," "Nummernschild," and many others. Brief facts about political and cultural life in Germany, Austria, and Switzerland and entries that answer a number of questions usually treated in world almanacs are also included. At the end of the book is a list of English and German irregular verbs. This dictionary would be a very good choice for a student of the German language.—**Shannon Graff Hysell**

Spanish

C, P, S

304.   **Webster's Everyday Spanish-English Dictionary.** Darien, Conn., Federal Street Press, 2011. 423p. $3.99pa. ISBN 13: 978-1-59695-117-4.

This resource is a compact dictionary to more than 40,000 words translated first from Spanish to English and then from English to Spanish. The work follows a strict letter-by-letter alphabetization and each word has a guide to pronunciation. The definitions are very concise and no examples of common uses of the words are presented. The work does, however, provide synonyms for words when appropriate as well as cross-references to unusual words (e.g., *mouse* leads the user to *mice* for its plural form). Supplementary materials include a chart explaining the conjugation of Spanish verbs and a chart depicting irregular verbs in English, a list of abbreviations used in the book, a guide to pronunciation, common Spanish abbreviations, and list of numbers in both English and Spanish.

This dictionary is most appropriate for use by students of Spanish or Spanish-speaking persons learning English. Larger libraries will want a more comprehensive Spanish volume on hand at the reference desk, such as *The University of Chicago Spanish Dictionary* (see ARBA 2002, entry 986) or *Oxford Spanish Dictionary: Spanish-English, English-Spanish* (4th ed.; see ARBA 2009, entry 901), but this volume will be useful as a supplemental volume or for small libraries and personal use.—**Shannon Graff Hysell**

24 Literature

General Works

Bibliography

P

305.   Dilevko, Juris, Keren Dali, and Glenda Garbutt. **Contemporary World Fiction: A Guide to Literature in Translation.** Santa Barbara, Calif., Libraries Unlimited/ABC-CLIO, 2011. 526p. index. $85.00. ISBN 13: 978-1-59158-353-0.

This is a guide to more than 1,000 authors of fiction whose works have been translated into English in the years 1980-2010. Authors whose works were extensively published and translated before 1980 have not been included. Entries are arranged in nine chapters devoted to regions of the world, then by country or language group. Each author gets one entry, which usually contains the following items: author, title, translator, place of publication and publisher, genre/literary style/story type, annotation, related titles by the same author, one or two subject keywords, original language, a list of other translated books written by the author, and sources credited. The mostly descriptive annotations range in length from a sentence or two to several hundred words. Each chapter contains a bibliographic essay that contextualizes some of the major non-English traditions. Also included are author, title, and subject/keyword indexes and several bibliographies devoted to additional reference sources, anthologies containing works in English translation, and print and electronic sources that keep readers abreast of the latest translations. The authors of *Contemporary World Fiction* are academics from the University of Toronto.

Contemporary World Fiction is an excellent reference, readers' advisory, and collection development tool for academic libraries (especially those located in colleges and universities with world literature courses), large public libraries, and individuals, who will find its readable contents well suited for browsing. This title will supplement sources such as *The Oxford Guide to Literature in English Translation* (see ARBA 2002, entry 1059) and the World Authors series from H. W. Wilson.—**Jonathan F. Husband**

Bio-bibliography

C, S

306.   **21st Century Novels: The First Decade.** Farmington Hills, Mich., Gale/Cengage Learning, 2011. 3v. illus. index. $420.00/set. ISBN 13: 978-1-4144-8761-8; 978-1-4144-8762-5 (e-book).

Designed with high school students and undergraduates in mind, this 3-volume set focuses on fiction literature from the past 10 years, the first decade of the twenty-first century. The book has a wide scope, focusing on international authors and those with a multicultural perspective. Therefore, users will find a wide variety of literature represented here, including Patricia Santana's *Ghosts of El Grullo*, Junot

Diaz's *The Brief Wondrous Life of Oscar Wao*, and Aravind Adiga's *The White Tiger*. Alongside these multicultural authors, there are the expected successful novels including the Harry Potter series, Steig Larsson's Millennium trilogy, book-to-movie favorites (e.g., *Atonement*, *The Secret Life of Bees*), and popular book club titles (e.g., *Life of Pi*, *Prodigal Summer*). For each entry there is an introduction to the story and author, literary and historical context, themes, major characters, biographical information about the author, information on the style, and the work's critical reception. Other features of the set include: fact boxes, a bibliography, Web sources, further reading lists, 270 photographs and illustrations, and a title index. The work is laid out in a way that will make it ideal for student research. It is recommended for high school and undergraduate libraries where it can be used for literature assignments and course work.—**Shannon Graff Hysell**

Dictionaries and Encyclopedias

C

307. Auger, Peter. **The Anthem Dictionary of Literary Terms and Theory.** New York, Anthem Press, 2010. 389p. $22.95pa. ISBN 13: 978-1-84331-871-2.

The *Anthem Dictionary* defines literary terminology using modern examples with which twenty-first century students will relate. The entries listed in the A to Z section of both familiar terms and new are models of clarity. Etymology, a brief history, explanation of the term, and examples of its use are given. These have been updated; for instance, the term *song* in the A-to-Z listing includes Bob Dylan, while the Beatles "Yellow Submarine" is the example for *mondegreen*. Technical terms used in each definition are printed in all capital letters to enable quick reference to other parts of the volume where they are defined.

A thematic index is especially valuable as it enables students to match or compare familiar terms with new ones that they may not know. Divided into three sections, the first two, Technical Terms and Types of Writing, provide the vocabulary necessary for intelligent discussion of reading and writing. The third section on Literary Theory provides terminology for critical thinking about literature. In addition to such general terms as *aesthetics*, *avant-garde*, and *zeitgeist*, there are also lists of concepts associated with particular writers and schools of thought.

A timeline of all the works mentioned in the entries with authors, dates, and the critical terminology which may apply to each, extends from Classical Literature beginning with Homer's *Iliad* to 2009. This is followed by a list of recommended books and online resources with a brief discussion of what can be found in each.

Although primarily for the serious use of students, the examples in the entries are frequently lively and entertaining. Seasoned scholars will benefit from not only updated words like *gynocriticism*, *ecocriticism*, and *kitchen sink drama*, but also by the new directions of terms such as disability studies. This volume is a highly useful research tool for everyone involved in literary criticism. [R: Choice, Mar 2011, p. 1252]—**Charlotte Lindgren**

C, S

308. **Encyclopedia of Themes in Literature.** Jennifer McClinton-Temple, ed. New York, Facts on File, 2011. 3v. index. (Facts on File Library of World Literature). $195.00/set. ISBN 13: 978-0-8160-7161-6; 978-1-4381-3268-6 (e-book).

Designed with high school students and undergraduates in mind, this three-volume set provides a unique look at the most common and reoccurring themes found in literature. The first part, which is about one-third of volume 1, provides entries on 50 specific themes, including their definition, how it relates to other prominent themes, and how it has evolved over time. Themes covered include the expected (e.g., death, family, freedom, pride, violence) as well as a few unexpected (e.g., science and technology, social class, tradition). The entries are thorough and include *see also* references to titles and authors listed in the volume as well as a list of further reading.

The bulk of the volume provides essays on specific themes in 300 individual pieces of classic literature. The works are listed alphabetically by author and provide detailed information on how specific themes are treated within the book. For example, in the essay on Margaret Atwood's *The Handmaid's Tale* there are detailed essay on the use of gender, heroism, and oppression within the book. The titles selected for inclusion will be known and popular in most high school and undergraduate literature classes and include: *Pride and Prejudice*, *The Great Gatsby*, *Hamlet*, and *The Crucible*. The list of themes and titles at the beginning of volume 1 and the helpful cross-references within the volumes will aid in using this work as a reference title. This three-volume set will be a useful resource to have on hand in high school and undergraduate libraries and will serve the reference needs of a variety of students.—**Shannon Graff Hysell**

C, S

309.   **Encyclopedia of World Writers: 1800 to the Present.** Marie Josephine Diamond, ed. New York, Facts on File, 2011. 605p. index. (Facts on File Library of World History). $85.00. ISBN 13: 978-0-8160-8204-9; 978-1-4381-3650-9 (e-book).

The *Encyclopedia of World Writers*, now in its 2d edition and targeted at high school and undergraduate college students, admirably fulfills its stated goal of covering authors and literary movements outside the United States, Great Britain, and Ireland. (These countries are covered by other encyclopedias in the Facts on File Library of World Literature series.) According to the edition notes, major additions include numerous authors from Eastern Europe and the Balkans who have come to prominence since the fall of the Soviet Union. The "most significant" new writers from Latin America, Canada, Africa, the Caribbean, Asia, the Middle East, and Australasia have also been added, although authors who have not yet been translated into English are generally excluded.

The entries are clearly written and well detailed, although contributors are not listed anywhere in the volume. Many entries on major authors (that is, authors that students are most likely to encounter in the classroom) include critical analyses of selected works, and virtually all entries include bibliographies of longer secondary works. Cross-references within the *Encyclopedia* are indicated, and the entries are prefaced by a short history of world literature since the 1800s, a timeline with the birth and death dates of each author covered, and a list of the authors grouped by geographical region. The helpful index lists individual works as well as authors, and the selected bibliography for the entire volume comes to nearly 20 pages. High school and college libraries will certainly want to consider adding the *Encyclopedia* to their collections. [R: Choice, Jan 12, p. 847]—**Maren Williams**

Children's and Young Adult Literature

Bibliography

P, S

310.   **Bridges to Understanding: Envisioning the World Through Children's Books.** Linda M. Pavonetti, ed. Lanham, Md., Scarecrow, 2011. 521p. index. $55.00pa. ISBN 13: 978-0-8108-8106-8; 978-0-8108-8107-5 (e-book).

As the world shrinks and cultures clash, it is increasingly important for up-and-coming generations to become conversant with cultures other than their own. American children are expected to explore worlds beyond their cultural heritage—finding commonalities with other ways of life while learning also to recognize inaccurate depictions in international literature. So, a major premise of this bibliography is that young readers must learn to read globally—but also critically.

This book is the fourth in a now formally recognized series of annotated bibliographies (henceforth known as Bridges to Understanding) conceived in 1997 by the United States Board on Books for Young People (USBBY). It is intended to be a window on the world of "international literature," meaning English-language books set in foreign lands or cultures, created by foreign authors or illustrators, or originally published outside of the United States. Pavonetti and her team of 28 contributors describe over 700 books published between 2005 and 2010, thereby continuing the work of the previous edition, *Crossing Boundaries with Children's Books* (see ARBA 2007, entry 888). Part 1 consists of two short guest essays highlighting the importance of both preserving cultures in translation and reading global children's literature with a critical eye. Part 2, the bibliography itself, comprises seven chapters that explore every major region of the world outside of the United States (including "Canada and the Far North"). Not surprisingly, the chapter on Europe is the lengthiest. An additional chapter covers global and multinational books. Related information, such as relevant Websites, journals, celebrations, organizations, and awards, is also woven into each geographical chapter's listing. Part 3 consists of several chapters of supporting resources.

New to this bibliography is a separate list of outstanding international books (OIB) recognized by the USBBY since 2006; most are also cross-listed within the annotated entries. While this bibliography is fully indexed it is mildly disappointing that the subject indexing does not extend to the entries themselves (as was done for the previous three bibliographies). Instead, each entry is clearly footnoted with suggested subject headings.

This latest edition in the USBBY-sponsored series continues to serve as an unrivaled reference resource to guide the reading needs of preschool children through young adults in a global learning environment. Compare perhaps to Libraries Unlimited's *Window on the World: International Books for Elementary and Middle Grade Readers* (see ARBA 2010, entry 923), which is narrower in scope and geared more toward classroom teachers than librarians.—**Lucy Duhon**

P, S

311. **Database of Award-Winning Children's Literature (DAWCL). http://www.dawcl.com/.** [Website]. Free. Date reviewed: 2011.

This database includes 8,400 records from 96 awards presented in six English-speaking countries— the United States, Canada, Australia, New Zealand, England, and Ireland. The purpose of the database is to create a tailored reading list of quality children's literature or to find out if a book has won one of the indexed awards. The expected users are librarians or teachers intervening for a child-reader; however, anyone may make use of it to find the best in children's literature, including parents, book store personnel, and children and young adults themselves. When one clicks the link "Explanation of Awards," they will find a list of awards, their countries, and a brief explanation. Books are indexed so researchers can find them using either the form search or the keyword search. Because most awards are given every year, DAWCL remains a work in progress with addition of any new awards and new award-winners. This will be a valuable site to school and public librarians for collection building and instruction.—**William O. Scheeren**

P, S

312. Gillespie, John T. **The Family in Literature for Young Readers: A Resource Guide for Use with Grades 4 to 9.** Santa Barbara, Calif., Libraries Unlimited/ABC-CLIO, 2011. 470p. index. (Children's and Young Adult Literature Reference). $60.00. ISBN 13: 978-1-59158-915-0.

What is family, if not the most basic social foundation for all children? But what defines a "family" has indeed changed over the centuries and across cultures. Perhaps surprisingly, the traditional "nuclear family" of the recent past has now been surpassed by a myriad of other arrangements and is no longer the predominant one for home life in the United States. Its decline has been hastened in the last half-century by factors such as increasing divorce rates, cohabitation replacing marriage, working mothers, widespread birth control resulting in smaller families, and the mainstreaming of once questionable social norms and lifestyles. A typical "family" now includes those groups of people living together under homosexual unions, in mother-only households, or in blended (step-family) and extended family arrangements. Children's literature has both reflected and helped to reinforce this trend toward a multitude of accepted models.

Gillespie, probably the leading bibliographer and scholar in the field of children's literature, has assembled a resource that addresses the need to navigate this growing and changing category of children's literature involving what we now consider "family." Intended as a companion volume to his *Historical Fiction for Young Readers* (see ARBA 2009, entry 922), this three-part book opens with an extensive introductory chapter on both family life and family as depicted in children's literature, from pre-history extending through the last century. Part 2 outlines the components necessary for a good children's book, lists basic techniques for stimulating children to read, and gives advice on how to organize booktalks. Gillespie analyzes over 40 specific "family books" considered ideal for such events. Each three- to five-page synopsis includes a plot analysis, a listing of principal characters, the major theme and family issue discussion points, and individual passages suggested for booktalks. Part 3 consists of a briefly annotated bibliography of over 1,200 currently available family stories grouped by general topic. Adequate indexing is provided.

This book is intended for public and school librarians, teachers and homeschoolers, but would also benefit academic library collections supporting schools of education. Similar resources might include: *Best Books for Children* (see ARBA 2007, entry 886) and the somewhat dated, *Our Family, Our Friends, Our World* (see ARBA 93, entry 1127). In truth, there are plenty of children's literature bibliographies— both general and specialized—that touch on the subject of family and might be a fair substitute, but this book will likely become the single landmark guide for years to come.—**Lucy Duhon**

P, S

313. Herald, Nathan. **Graphic Novels for Young Readers: A Genre Guide for Ages 4-14.** Santa Barbara, Calif., Libraries Unlimited/ABC-CLIO, 2011. 188p. index. (Genreflecting Advisory Series). $40.00. ISBN 13: 978-1-59884-395-8.

Reading is fundamental to ultimate success in life. What better way to interest reluctant readers than to tempt them with books of a visual nature? Modern comics have for roughly a century entertained and even educated readers. Although the debut of the longer graphic novel cannot be traced to a single moment, it has become increasingly commonplace since the late 1970s, and the medium has surged in popularity over the last decade due to the Japanese manga invasion. A format rather than a genre, graphic literature encompasses at least as many genres as mainstream literature. There has been a resulting need to codify lists of graphic books specific to and appropriate for children.

Like any good reference resource, this slim hardback organizes its entries by topic, genre, and by grade or reading level. A true advisory tool, it "seeks to connect young readers with the books they will enjoy." Herald, a lifelong aficionado and son of the series editor, briefly introduces the reader to the idea of the graphic novel as a legitimate literary format and lays out the arrangement of the book. Eight chapters cover major genres, from educational to science fiction. They reference over 600 title entries spanning the last century, from *Tintin* to *Dragon Ball*. Emphasis is on the last decade. Each entry consists of a short annotation, a suggested grade level, full bibliographic details, and award information when available. Parental advisories are provided. The appendix lists helpful supporting resources.

This book will undoubtedly undergo future revisions, as it covers a rapidly expanding medium and there is much format crossover in children's popular literature. Improvements might include a subject index and a glossary, since many terms will be foreign to readers unfamiliar with graphic novels. One technical error noted is the lack of a designation for award-winners per entry (despite the introduction's reference to such a symbol). Compare this resource to the smaller, illustrated, and more efficiently designed *Getting Graphic! Comics for Kids* (Linworth, 2004), or the larger, more general *Graphic Novels: A Genre Guide to Comic Books, Manga, and More* (see ARBA 2008, entry 886). Graphic novels are not as universally appreciated as conventional literature, but they are here to stay. Any interpretive guide that can keep up with voracious young readers is thus welcome. This book is an imperative addition to school and public libraries and will be very useful to parents of reluctant readers as well.—**Lucy Duhon**

P, S

314.   **The Newbery & Caldecott Awards: A Guide to the Medal and Honor Books.** 2011 ed. By the Association for Library Service to Children. Chicago, American Library Association, 2011. 172p. index. $28.00pa.; $25.20pa. (ALA members). ISBN 13: 978-0-8389-8569-4.

Since its first publication in 1990, this annual paperback has supplied useful, basic information on America's two most prestigious annual literary awards in the field of children's literature: the Newbery Medal for the author of the most distinguished contribution to literature for children and the Caldecott Medal to the artist of the most distinguished picture book. Like its predecessors, the current volume begins with a brief introduction on these awards, giving basic information about history, criteria, and administration. The body of the work is, again, divided into two parts, the first on the Newbery and the second on the Caldecott. Each is arranged in reverse chronological order and covers the award from the present (2011) to its beginnings (1922 for the Newbery, 1938 for the Caldecott). For each year both the medal winners and the Honor books are listed, each with a four- or five-line concise, descriptive annotation. Bibliographic information is basic. There is, for example, no indication of in-print status, editions, price, or ISBN numbers, but the Caldecott section contains a valuable directory listing the media used in each of the winners (e.g., gouache, watercolor). There are also author/illustrator and title indexes. Each edition contains at least one special feature related to the awards. This year, it is an excellent nine-page essay by Barbara Z. Kiefer on the art of the picture book. Although this information is available from other sources (both print and online), this handy, inexpensive reference has justifiably been a mainstay in school and public libraries children's rooms for years. Because 95 percent of its contents are holdovers from last year's edition, very small libraries may wish to stagger its purchase. Otherwise, most libraries will find this a fine, necessary addition to their reference collection.—**John T. Gillespie**

C, P, S

315.   **Outstanding Books for the College Bound: Titles and Programs for a New Generation.** Angela Carstensen, ed. Chicago, American Library Association, 2011. 164p. index. $50.00pa.; $45.00pa. (ALA members). ISBN 13: 978-0-8389-8670-0.

Outstanding Books for the College Bound, which began in 1959 and is compiled every five years, is a standard list for school and public librarians. Unlike the last edition, this one only covers the three most recent lists: 1999, 2004, and 2009. It also includes a history of the lists; chapters on the use of the lists by school, public, and academic libraries; and a chapter on their use by nontraditional students and lifelong learners. The 2009 list includes five academic disciplines: arts and humanities, history and cultures, literature and language arts, science and technology, and social sciences. This edition has a section that combines the three lists into the same genre groups used in the 2009 list. An appendix of the selection committee's policies and procedures and a title/author index complete the volume. Since the 1999, 2004, and 2009 lists are available on the Young Adult Library Services Association (YALSA) pages of the American Library Association Website and this slim paperback may seem pricey in a time of constrained budgets, librarians will have to decide whether the convenience of the print lists and the short chapters suggesting uses are worth the cost. This work is recommended for school and public libraries and academic libraries supporting teacher preparation programs; it is an optional purchase for other academic libraries.—**Rosanne M. Cordell**

P

316.   Rabey, Melissa. **Historical Fiction for Teens: A Genre Guide.** Santa Barbara, Calif., Libraries Unlimited/ ABC-CLIO, 2011. 324p. index. (Genreflecting Advisory Series). $45.00. ISBN 13: 978-1-59158-813-9.

The Genreflecting Advisory Series is a popular library tool in aiding both patrons and librarians in finding and selecting genre-specific books, and *Historical Fiction for Teens* is a timely addition. Teen librarian Melissa Rabey does a wonderful job in introducing the historical fiction genre particularly with regards to young adult historical fiction. Rabey uses broad categorizations to break down historical fiction, which I think does some disservice to the genre given the wide scope of historical fiction in multiple countries wherein Rabey lumps the books into a landmass. For example, she does this with Europe—all historical fiction across Europe is grouped here with Britain pulled out into its own section. The sections are further subdivided into time periods and the books are listed alphabetically by author with a brief synopsis of the book, and useful information such as awards the book has won, possible read-alike books, and the title's grade level are listed when available. The genre of historical fiction is further divided, after the countries, into Historical Mysteries, Historical Adventures, Historical Fantasy, and Time Travel, each of which are subdivided by type, such as historical adventures regarding pirates. The final chapter includes other guiding resources, including both online and print. The indexes at the end include award-winners, thematic book lists, author index, title index, and keyword index. This is an essential item for public libraries or those that have many teenage historical fiction fans.—**Michelle Martinez**

P, S

317.   Reid, Rob. **Reid's Read-Alouds 2: Modern-Day Classics from C. S. Lewis to Lemony Snicket.** Chicago, American Library Association, 2011. 145p. index. $45.00pa.; $40.50pa. (ALA members). ISBN 13: 978-0-8389-1072-6.

Rob Reid is an author of books about children's literature. He also teaches courses on children's literature and literature for adolescents at the University of Wisconsin—Eau Claire. There he is a senior lecturer in the library science program.   In addition, since 2007, he has written a monthly column, "The Reid-Aloud Alert," for *Book Links* magazine. This column, which forms the basis for this book, basically gives the librarian a 5- and 15-minute section from a novel written for children from K-12 to read aloud to them. In this book Reid has collected 200 titles from which the librarian can choose. All of the titles date from 1950 to 1999 and Reid has chosen some of the best writers in the fields of children and young adult literature, such as Laurence Yep and Judy Blume.

The books that Reid covers are organized alphabetically, and, to help the reader find the book(s) they are looking for, Reid includes three indexes. The first index arranges titles by decade and year. The second index categorizes the 200 books by general subjects and genres, such as friendship or fantasy/ science fiction. The third index arranges the titles by various grade levels, dividing the books into four levels: early elementary (grades K-2); upper elementary (grades 3-5); middle school (grades 6-8); and high school (grades 9-12).

Reid's Read-Alouds is recommended for all school library media specialists in a K-12 setting and all public children or young adult librarians who are trying to get their students or their patrons to read more. Library school students could also use it to help get a feel of what makes a good read-alouds for children.—**Scott Alan Sheidlower**

Dictionaries and Encyclopedias

C, P

318.   O'Sullivan, Emer. **Historical Dictionary of Children's Literature.** Lanham, Md., Scarecrow, 2011. 341p. (Historical Dictionaries of Literature and the Arts, no.46). $80.00; $80.00 (e-book). ISBN 13: 978-0-8108-6080-3; 978-0-8108-7496-1 (e-book).

In the field of children's literature, dozens of "best books" exist, as do many children's book award reference sources. Most bibliographies focus on subject areas or age groups, or highlight specific geographical areas or ethnicities. Few cover children's literature as a whole. Fewer still do it concisely. Multivolume sets, such as *The Oxford Encyclopedia of Children's Literature* (see ARBA 2007, entry 909), have covered children's literature beautifully, as have slightly less voluminous works such as *The Continuum Encyclopedia of Children's Literature* (see ARBA 2002, entry 1068). O'Sullivan's new dictionary concisely covers essential children's authors and illustrators as well as basic terminology, genre, form, and theme. And it does so from a unique perspective.

This handy hardback of over 500 entries opens with a brief list of acronyms and abbreviations, followed by a chronology outlining milestones in children's literature, and an introduction explaining the origins and purpose of children's literature, its unintended western bias, and its likely future course. Entry topics range from "anthropomorphism" to "science fiction," and include basic (e.g., "easy reader") and lesser-known (e.g., "penny dreadful") terms. A treasure of a book, especially for those familiar with long-forgotten European literary giants, this dictionary includes an eclectic international sampling. O'Sullivan is Irish but is an eminent scholar in German; this has resulted in some unique name entry contributions, such as Wilhelm Busch (the progenitor of the modern comic strip) and the groundbreaking cautionary tale writer, Heinrich Hoffmann. The latter's wonderful *Struwwelpeter* (or Slovenly Peter) thus occupies text alongside *Pollyanna*. Terms, names, and titles are cross-referenced in bold typeface within entries in this economically designed resource. An appendix lists medals and awards. The work closes with an extensive and authoritative source list.

This dictionary is a small goldmine. In terms of coverage, its closest single-volume competitor remains Anita Silvey's *Essential Guide to Children's Books and Their Creators* (see ARBA 2003, entry 1022). Slightly larger, Silvey's sparingly illustrated book concentrates solely on American authors and illustrators (or those highly acclaimed in the United States), and contains more expansive, chapter-like entries to O'Sullivan's telescopic, more utilitarian approach. One shortcoming of O'Sullivan's book, however, is the lack of indexing (without which it is difficult to confirm, for example, whether illustrator Roger Duvoisin was completely omitted from the work), but its expeditious use of cross-references generally makes up for this. Overall, this book's size belies its value. It is highly recommended for almost any library shelf.—**Lucy Duhon**

Handbooks and Yearbooks

C

319. Bodart, Joni Richards. **They Suck, They Bite, They Eat, They Kill: The Psychological Meaning of Supernatural Monsters in Young Adult Fiction.** Lanham, Md., Scarecrow, 2012. 268p. index. (Scarecrow Studies in Young Adult Literature, no.43). $45.00. ISBN 13: 978-0-8108-8227-0; 978-0-8108-8228-7.

Bodart's summation of scary stuff in young adult reading cuts to the heart of Gothicism. Her introduction, a gem of a lecture on otherness, connects the dots between the literary no man's land and the unstable, unknowable path between the teen age and adulthood. Her bibliographies present classic and recent sources from Maurice Sendak to Anne Rice and Stephen King. On the down side, commentary on literary models strays from sturdy analysis ("Rot & Ruin") to thin retelling of the plots, a fault of "The Raised by Wolves Series." A troubling aspect of Bodart's writing is the predominance of the verb to be, evidence of her tendency to state the obvious rather than comment. Missing from her survey are gender differences and the classic entrapment of the female. Overall, this is a worthy book for the public and school library and for psychology and young adult education shelves of teacher's colleges. [R: SLJ, Jan 12, p. 148]—**Mary Ellen Snodgrass**

Fiction

General Works

P

320. Honig, Megan. **Urban Grit: A Guide to Street Lit.** Santa Barbara, Calif., Libraries Unlimited/ ABC-CLIO, 2011. 251p. index. (Genreflecting Advisory Series). $55.00. ISBN 13: 978-1-59158-857-3.

Honig provides an introductory survey of the new, fast growing genre of street lit—also referred to as urban fiction, hip-hop lit, and gangsta lit. It is made up of edgy stories focusing on personal relationships and survival of the fittest. Making its appearance in the 1990s, the genre draws readers who tend to be young, African American, and female. Urban fiction is characterized by stories of life on the streets and in the projects using brutal descriptions of drugs, violence, sex, abuse, and prison. The author explores the subgenres of street lit with annotated bibliographies of recommended titles. The subgenres include: players and hustlers; coming of age; "drama" (which in street lit means outrageous female characters fighting over men); crazy in love stories and "ride or die chicks"; erotica (both heterosexual and homosexual); thrillers and tales of vigilantes; hard times; prison life and life after prison; family relationships (good and bad); friendships; and poetry, memoir, and nonfiction. Just like your favorite heart-healthy restaurant, each book is rated with 1 to 3 "guns" for violence and 1 to 3 "chili peppers" for sexuality. Special features include a glossary of street lit terms for those new to the genre; a list of street lit publishers; recommended titles for collections for young adults and adults; and resources for keeping up-to-date on new releases. This reference is targeted to librarians unfamiliar with this genre, answering the questions: why should you have a street lit collection, what should be in it, and how to address the concerns you will be sure to get from older library users about these works. Honig helps you remain relevant to your younger audience while being sensitive to clients who may be uncomfortable with these authors.—**Adrienne Antink**

P

321.   Morris, Vanessa Irvin. **The Readers' Advisory Guide to Street Literature.** Chicago, American Library Association, 2012. 138p. index. (ALA Readers' Advisory Series). $48.00pa.; $43.20pa. (ALA members). ISBN 13: 978-0-8389-1110-5.

This is a guide, concentrating on street fiction (or urban literature), for librarians doing readers' advisory service. Although controversial in some libraries, it continues to be wildly popular among many patrons. Narrative chapters describing the conceptual groundwork for street fiction readers' advisory service, methods of working with street, and how to incorporate those theories into readers' advisory service, are followed by nine chapters on street literature subject areas with lengthy, generally unannotated bibliographies of suggested book titles in these areas. The work covers a variety of subgenres in terms of scope, popularity, style, and major authors and works. The work concludes with an appendix of street literature publishers, works cited, literature cited, and an index. Vanessa Irvin Morris is an Assistant Professor at the College of Information science and Technology at Drexel University, and founder of a teen book club focusing on street literature, working with inner-city teens at a Philadelphia library.

Most libraries do not have readers' advisory specialists, and the function is generally included with reference services or under the "public service" rubric. While there is no substitute for librarians who know, love, and keep up with books, this guide, with its current reading list, might have some use for collection development and readers' advisory in public libraries and school libraries as a substitute for the outdated reading lists usually supplied by teachers and educational administrators, along with Megan Honig's *Urban Grit: A Guide to Street Lit* (see entry 320), and regular perusal of reviewing media such as *Booklist* and *Library Journal*.—Jonathan F. Husband

C, S

322.   Sollars, Michael D. **Dictionary of Literary Characters.** New York, Facts on File, 2011. 5v. index. $400.00/set. ISBN 13: 978-0-8160-7379-5; 978-4-4381-3289-1 (e-book).

This five-volume work incorporates and updates Facts on File's earlier volumes on American and British literary characters while adding many from non-English-language sources. More than 40,000 characters from novels, stories, and plays are included, with 2- to 12-line descriptions of each. While there is no index, there is an author list that includes all the works by an individual writer and all the characters in each. For users who cannot recall an author's name, there is a separate title list with such entries as *Burr* (Gore Vidal). Such users would then have to go to the author list to find the characters in Vidal's novel. This method seems cumbersome, although the electronic version may be more flexible. As with any such endeavor, there are many oversights and inconsistencies. While 86 characters, even minor ones, appear from *Jane Eyre*, there are only 12 from *The Great Gatsby*, omitting Myrtle Wilson's sister, party guests, servants, and others. All the Sherlock Holmes novels are included but only four of the stories. There are only two Miss Marple novels and no Agatha Christie stories at all. Martin Amis is represented by four novels but not *London Fields*, generally considered his masterpiece; and Caryl Churchill by two plays but not *Top Girls*, her best-received work. Michael Sollars and his dozens of contributors are to be commended for including several works by such figures as Isabel Colegate, Wright Morris, and Robert Surtees, but where are William Boyd, Elmore Leonard, and Bernhard Schlink? Any users expecting comprehension or consistency will be frustrated.—**Michael Adams**

Crime and Mystery

Bibliography

P

323.   Haynes, Elizabeth. **Crime Writers: A Research Guide.** Santa Barbara, Calif., Libraries Unlimited/ ABC-CLIO, 2011. 204p. index. (Author Research Series). $40.00pa. ISBN 13: 978-1-59158-914-3.

In order to save space, this selection of authors was limited to 50 names, representing various categories and time periods. The introduction discusses the crime fiction genre (along with a timeline of current events) and explains the organization of entries and definitions of abbreviations. A section on "How to Use this Book" suggest approaches for students, teachers, librarians, book club leaders, and researchers who wish to go beyond the scope of this book. An alphabetic list of authors seems superlative. Since the individual author entries are arranged alphabetically. Each entry lists the name by which the author is best known, along with their original name and any other aliases. These are followed by a sample quote from one of the author's works, a biographical sketch and applicable categories within the crime fiction genre (e.g., amateur detective, police procedural, legal, humorous, English setting). The most helpful aspects are the lists of awards received, major works (with the first date of publication), and research sources for further information. At the end are lists of authors by categories, a general bibliography, a descriptive of the major crime fiction awards, and an index of titles, authors, characters, and categories. The writing and editing in parts of the text could have been better and the need to restrict the number of authors has left out such authors as Ellis Peters and Lillian Jackson Braun. However, the representative choice of authors and the large amount of concise and helpful information serve well as an excellent starting place for further research.—**Martha Lawler**

P

324.   Niebuhr, Gary Warren. **Make Mine a Mystery II: A Reader's Guide to Mystery and Detective Fiction.** Santa Barbara, Calif., Libraries Unlimited/ABC-CLIO, 2011. 292p. index. (Genreflecting Advisory Series). $55.00. ISBN 13: 978-1-59884-589-1.

This second volume of *Make Mine a Mystery* focuses only on novels that use a serial fictional character to solve crimes. Books described in the 1st edition are here listed with dates, but those written since the beginning of the twenty-first century are fully annotated. The over 700 titles are separated by the kind of investigators: amateurs, traditional and eccentric, and detectives, public and private, and ex-cops and rogues. Each entry provides publisher, date, ISBN, and symbols indicating awards and whether the novels are considered soft boiled, traditional, or hard boiled. Authors' Websites are given when available.

Entries are listed alphabetically by author, but the same author may appear under different headings; for example, Elizabeth Peters' character Amelia Peabody is under Eccentric Amateurs, while her Vicky Bliss is under Traditional. The introduction to each series ends with suggestions of other writers of similar mysteries that readers may enjoy and a list in bold face of subjects: Cats under Lillian Braun's

Jim Qwilleran/ Koko and Yum Yum, or Native Americans under Tony Hillerman's Joe Leaphorn and Jim Chee. The appendixes are useful and extensive. In addition to a lengthy bibliography, which includes CD-ROMs, conventions, filmography, guides, and online resources, there are also an author index, title index, a 26-page subject index, a character index, and a location index.

Designed primarily for librarians, bookstore owners, and teachers who advise readers, the book will please all mystery fans wanting to find a good read in their favorite genre, and perhaps even discover a whole new series.—**Charlotte Lindgren**

Biography

P

325.   Drew, Bernard A. **100 Most Popular Contemporary Mystery Authors: Biographical Sketches and Bibliographies.** Santa Barbara, Calif., Libraries Unlimited/ABC-CLIO, 2011. 439p. index. (Popular Author Series). $65.00. ISBN 13: 978-1-59884-445-0; 978-1-59884-446-7 (e-book).

In the seventh volume by Drew in Libraries Unlimited's Popular Author Series, each entry consists of a brief biography and overview of the writer's work, usually supplemented with quotations from interviews and an extensive bibliography. The bibliographies separate series titles from stand-alone novels and also include story collections, contributions to other collections, edited books, film and television adaptations, and secondary sources (mostly magazine and online articles). There are photographs for about half the subjects. In addition to a title and author index, an appendix groups the writers into such categories as historical mystery and police procedural. Drew points out that many popular figures, including Elmore Leonard and P. D. James, are not present since they appear in volumes devoted to genre fiction and thriller and suspense writers. As with any such endeavor, however, quibbles can be made, as with the inclusion of Charlaine Harris and the exclusion of Craig Johnson, among others. Drew frequently offers interesting tidbits: Jeff Lindsay attended mime clown school, and Peter Lovesey's childhood home was destroyed by a bomb during World War II. He does not mention that Lawrence Block is an excellent audiobook reader or Anne Perry's involvement in the events forming the basis of Peter Jackson's *Heavenly Creatures*, but the included information is always interesting.—**Michael Adams**

Science Fiction, Fantasy, and Horror

C, P

326.   **21st-Century Gothic: Great Gothic Novels Since 2000.** Danel Olson, ed. Lanham, Md., Scarecrow, 2011. 675p. index. $75.00. ISBN 13: 978-0-8108-7728-3; 978-0-8108-7729-0 (e-book).

21st-Century Gothic: Great Gothic Novels Since 2000 accomplishes exactly what its title proclaims. By way of polling over 180 specialists in the gothic field, such as critics, writers, and professors, Olson has compiled a collection of essays about 53 gothic novels published globally between 2000 and 2010. Far more than 53 gothic novels were published during that time, but Olson has chosen to present detailed analyses of over 5,000 words for each of the included novels rather than a brief overview of a larger number.

Although each included essay is specific to the author's intentions and opinions, they attempt to convey similar information about why the novel is considered gothic and how the novel has helped traditional gothicism grow and evolve. Some examples include, "From Asperger's Syndrome to Monosexual Reproduction: Stefan Brijs' The Angel Maker and its Transformations of Frankenstein," "Death and *The Book Thief* by Markus Zusak," and "Raised By the Dead: The Maturational Gothic of Neil Gaiman's *The Graveyard Book*." The essays are well written and are probably best-suited for college audiences. *21st-Century Gothic* also includes appendixes with information about consultants and contributors, honorable mentions that were not included in the book, publication details for the included novels, and an excellent index.

Because of the nature of the volume and its inclusion of topical, but not micro-managed, essays, this text will allow readers and researchers to gain a feel for the field of gothic literature as well as serve as a specific resource for any of the included texts. The content does serve a rather niche audience, but the content does refer to historical gothicism and provides critical research for recent publications that may be difficult to find.—**Tyler Manolovitz**

National Literature

American Literature

General Works

C, S

327.   Evans, Robert C. **The American Novel.** New York, Facts on File, 2011. 2v. (Understanding Literature Through Close Reading). $150.00/set. ISBN 13: 978-0-8160-7675-8.

This close examination of various passages from 150 of the most frequently taught novels in high school and college classrooms serves as an introduction to the study of literature and the importance of novels. The choices of titles are arranged alphabetically and range from James Fenimore Cooper's *Last of the Mohicans* (1826) to Cormac McCarthy's *The Road* (2006). Some authors are represented by more than one work and some entries are longer than others, with more discussion and more passages chosen. Each entry includes the title, author, year of publication, and a brief synopsis of the plot. Each passage is preceded by a brief introduction and summary and followed by an analysis of various elements from the passage and questions for discussion. An introduction discusses the purpose and layout of the listing and is followed by a list of authors and their works included in the entries and by a chronological listing of the titles. The selection of titles is very broad and sometimes curious. The summaries and discussions are written in a style that is functional and simple. The purpose of this listing is to examine the techniques and elemental features that make certain literary works classics.—**Martha Lawler**

C, S

328.   **Icons of African American Literature: The Black Literary World.** Yolanda Williams Page, ed. Santa Barbara, Calif., Greenwood Press/ABC-CLIO, 2011. 519p. index. (Greenwood Icons). $100.00. ISBN 13: 978-0-313-35203-4; 978-0-313-35204-1 (e-books).

Part of the Greenwood Icons series on popular culture, *Icons of African American Literature* is both entertaining and provocative. Some of the best chapters are the general essays on forms such as Blues, Jazz, Slave Literature, and Signifying, or movements, which include Black Aesthetic, Black Arts, and the Harlem Renaissance.

Organized alphabetically, the black writers range from Maya Angelou to August Wilson. Introduced by a photograph and brief identification, there follows a biography and critical discussion of works. Inserts within the chapters summarize Important Data and Information or Little Known Facts. Some of the contributing writers also have added a section of notes. Each essay concludes with a bibliography, which may be subdivided into other genres such as videography, discography, and filmography; and finally suggestions for further reading.

The volume has been designed to foster discussions and this is aided by the excellent index, which in addition to names, titles, places, journals, and awards, also lists topics from Ageism and Alienation to Women. Topics for further discussion are listed under individual works; for example, *Beloved* has

(Morrison) themes of community and motherhood, and author James Baldwin has the theme of African American masculinity.

One of the strengths of the volume is its meaningfulness to readers of all colors and backgrounds. The explanations of vocabulary, music, literature, history, and life styles help to define all American culture, not just the black literary world. Although designed primarily for classroom and libraries in high schools and undergraduate colleges, its readable style, broad range of information, and lists of primary and secondary sources make it a natural resource for anyone interested in American society.—**Charlotte Lindgren**

Individual Authors

Maya Angelou

C, S

329.   Thursby, Jaqueline S. **Critical Companion to Maya Angelou: A Literary Reference to Her Life and Work.** New York, Facts on File, 2011. 430p. illus. index. (Facts on File Library of American Literature). $75.00. ISBN 13: 978-0-8160-8093-9; 978-1-4381-3610-3 (e-book).

This highly useful volume on Maya Angelou is a reliable, up-to-date resource intended for high school and undergraduate students. Following the introductory guide to its uses, the book is divided into three major sections plus a number of appendixes. Part 1 contains biographical information from her birth throughout her life and includes pictures of her from infancy to later in life and a listing of published biographies. Part 2 provides alphabetically arranged discussions of all Angelou's writings, including her autobiography *I Know Why the Caged Bird Sings*, with commentary on the works themselves, information about publication, a description of characters, and contemporary reviews. Part 3 describes friends, places, and ideas connected to Angelou, such as Harlem, racism, and San Francisco.

Serious scholars will find the appendixes especially helpful. A chronological bibliography includes all Angelou's own books, translations, and published letters. There are listings for both Websites and periodicals and a lengthy bibliography of essays in scholarly journals and biographical and critical books. A chronology lists the facts about Angelou and the events in her life that affected her work. Although the volume claims to be designed for the nonspecialist, its extensive bibliographical references and ease of use make it a valuable work for Angelou scholars and students of African American literature on every level of expertise. [R: Choice, Jan 12, p. 848]—**Charlotte Lindgren**

Mark Twain

C, S

330.   **The Routledge Encyclopedia of Mark Twain.** J. R. LeMaster and James D. Wilson, eds. New York, Routledge/Taylor & Francis Group, 2011. 866p. index. $65.00. ISBN 13: 978-0-415-89058-8.

As one of America's most beloved authors, Mark Twain is frequently studied in high school and college literature courses and a popular topic of research among those students. This volume provides more than 700 A-Z entries that cover all aspects of Twain's life, including his literary career, achievements, and family and friends. The work pays in-depth attention to the author's works, which include his travel narratives, essays, letters, sketches, and autobiography as well as his best-known literary works. The entries often show the ties between Twain's real life and his fictional works, showing where his ideas came from in his life experiences. Along with entries for his specific works, users will find in-depth entries on significant characters, places, landmarks, and themes (e.g., humor, language, race, politics). The work is supplemented with a chronology, a genealogy of the author, and a thorough index. The entries are scholarly yet still written in an accessible style that will be useful for students, researchers, and teachers. It would be a useful addition to many high school libraries and most academic libraries.—**Charlotte Lindgren**

Walt Whitman

C

331.   **The Routledge Encyclopedia of Walt Whitman.** repr. ed. J. R. LeMaster and Donald Kummings, eds. New York, Routledge/Taylor & Francis Group, 2011. 862p. index. $65.00pa. ISBN 13: 978-0-415-89057-1.

It only seems right that the American poet who wrote "I am large, I contain multitudes" should deserve an encyclopedia. This work is a reprint of the well-received 1998 edition of this title. Editors LeMaster and Kummings have assembled a formidable array of Whitman critics and biographers to contribute to this hefty reference book. The work provides broadly drawn entries treating Whitman's poems, editions, friends, critics, influences, landscapes, themes, subjects, and the cultural milieu. Each entry is signed, and most have bibliographies.

The largest part of the encyclopedia is the alphabetic arrangement of proper names, places, poems, and subjects. More than 800 pages of double-column text cover contemporaries such as Ralph Waldo Emerson, Henry David Thoreau, and Bronson Alcott, and later writers such as Allen Ginsberg and Jack Kerouac, who carried on a dialogue with Whitman within their own works. Among the larger subjects treated here are transcendentalism, romanticism, Abraham Lincoln's death, phrenology, mysticism, individualism, racial attitudes, popular culture, and influences on Whitman. The entry for transcendentalism alone, by noted scholar Roger Asselineau, runs 1,500 words, has a 13-item bibliography, and contains 11 *see also* references. There are individual entries for each edition of *Leaves of Grass* and for dozens of the major and not-so-major poems. The poetry explication and literary biography sections outline the changes in theory and criticism over the course of the century. This alone could make the book a worthy purchase for students encountering Whitman's paradoxical work for the first time.

The editors supplement the volume with a genealogy of the Whitman family; a chronology of the poet's life; his publishing history through 1993; and a detailed index of names, places, and subjects. The book is attractively illustrated with examples of his poems in manuscript, newspaper columns, and nineteenth-century studio photographs. This is a scholarly work that provides context to the life and works of this American poet who is rediscovered by each generation. For those that do not have a copy of the original 1998 edition or would like to supplement their collection with the much less-expensive paperback edition now available, this resource is still a valuable addition to American literature collections.—**ARBA Staff Reviewer**

British Literature

Individual Authors

William Shakespeare

C, P, S

332.   Cousins, A. D. **Shakespeare: The Essential Guide to the Plays.** Richmond Hills, Firefly Books, 2011. 256p. illus. index. $24.95pa. ISBN 13: 978-1-55407-928-5.

This work discusses the themes, language, imagery, and context of each of Shakespeare's popular plays. It covers every history, comedy, tragedy, and romance in Shakespeare's array of works, including the well-known (e.g., *Hamlet*, *A Midsummer Night's Dream*) to the lesser-known (e.g., *Pericles*, *Cymbeline*). The text provides plot summaries and character lists for each play, as well as sources, settings, and famous quotations. The layout will appeal to young adults and general readers with its inclusion of sidebars, diagrams, charts, and illustrations. The charts and tables depict the characters and interrelationships within the plays and serve as an interesting way to study the plot. Also included are images of stage and film reproductions from various historical periods and cultures. Edited by Cousins, a fellow at the Australian Academy of the Humanities, the work has contributions by an international team of Shakespearean scholars, making it an authoritative source of information on these plays. This, along with its accessible writing style and abundance of illustrations, makes it appropriate for high school, undergraduate, and public library collections.—**Shannon Graff Hysell**

P

333.   Tanner, Tony. **Prefaces to Shakespeare.** Cambridge, Mass., Harvard University Press, 2010. 825p. $39.95. ISBN 13: 978-0-674-05137-9.

Critics will never tire of offering their summary assessments of Shakespeare's entire dramatic output. Tony Tanner's book takes its place alongside volumes stretching back at least to William Hazlitt's essay on Shakespeare's characters (1817), A.C. Bradley's on the tragedies (1904), Harley Granville Barker's studies in the 1930s, and Harold C. Goddard's two volumes in 1951. Similar overviews again seem in fashion, as evidenced recently by Harold Bloom (1999), Marjorie Garber (2005), A. D. Nuttall (2008), and Jonathan Bate (2008). Tanner, whose title recalls Samuel Johnson's eighteenth-century *Preface to Shakespeare*, offers a thoughtful, literate, and provocative consideration of the plays (but not the poetry) arranged by genre. Originally written for the Everyman's editions (1992-1996) and averaging about 20 pages each, the essays address for a general audience the major themes and techniques of each work. Tanner's approach is a more literate reflection than academic critique; closer to Goddard and Bate than to Bloom's sweeping generalizations or Garber's theoretically nuanced analysis. This is a reference book in a unique sense; the book lacks an index, bibliography, or cross-references and rarely offers footnotes, making it hard to track most of Tanner's borrowings, which are usually identified only by the critic's name. Not a handy compendium, it is a book users will have to read, not raid. Each essay can be enjoyed in one sitting, and the combination of Tanner's insights and the confident, casual flow of his prose is a delight.—**Christopher Baker**

J. R. R. Tolkien

C, S

334.   Ruud, Jay. **Critical Companion to J. R. R. Tolkien: A Literary Reference to His Life and Work.** New York, Facts on File, 2011. 658p. index. (Facts on File Library of World Literature). $75.00. ISBN 13: 978-0-8160-7794-6; 978-1-4381-3684-4 (e-book).

J. R. R. Tolkien has been heralded as one of the most popular writers of the twentieth-century. His is best-known as the author of the fantasy works *The Lord of the Rings* and *The Hobbit*, but he was also a professor at Oxford University and writer of critical scholarship.

The volume is divided into four major sections. Part 1 is an illustrated brief biography, which shows how Tolkien's personal life blended with his ideas. Part 2 consists of alphabetically arranged discussions of novels, stories, poems, scholarly essays, and lectures; first date of delivery or presentation (usually a summary); and each followed by a separate section on critical commentary or interpretation and brief list of further readings. Also included in this section are his works published posthumously, including the 12 volumes of *The History of Middle-earth*, which was edited by his son between 1983 and 1996. Part 3 introduces people (e.g., Christopher Tolkien, C. S. Lewis); places (both real and fictional); and influential literary works (e.g., the epic *Beowulf*) and how they relate to Tolkien's ideas.

Part 4 is made up of appendixes: a chronology of Tolkien's life and times, a bibliography of Tolkien's works, a bibliography of secondary sources, and a list of Internet sources on Tolkien. An extensive index makes material easy to find. This literary reference is a vital source for understanding the role of Tolkien in the history of twentieth-century and fantasy literature. [R: LJ, Jan 12, p. 130]—**Charlotte Lindgren**

Canadian Literature

C, P

335.   Reznowski, Gabriella Natasha. **Literary Research and Canadian Literature: Strategies and Sources.** Lanham, Md., Scarecrow, 2011. 210p. index. (Literary Research: Strategies and Sources). $39.95; $39.95 (e-book). ISBN 13: 978-0-8108-7769-6; 978-0-8108-7769-6 (e-book)..

Tenth in the series Literary Research: Strategies and Sources, this volume examines research methodology, strategies, and tools with reference to the literary heritage of Canada. Previous volumes have focused on other predominantly English-speaking countries and specific literary eras. Canada's unique multilingual as well as multicultural experience makes researching its literary history a special challenge. As with previous volumes in the series, the chapters cover the basics of online searching and typical types of literary reference sources—catalogs, bibliographies, indexes, reviews, journals, and other periodicals and newspapers. Subsequent chapters focus on microform and digital collections as well as more specialized archival and manuscript collections. Also included is a chapter discussing the somewhat ephemeral Web resources and the particular challenges of these sites as well as some principals of Website evaluation. The final chapter presents a unique research scenario focusing on the controversial Canadian writer Morley Callaghan with respect to his literary reception both at home and abroad. A useful appendix of resources in related disciplines is included as well as a short bibliography. A detailed index concludes the volume. For both novice and seasoned researchers of Canadian literature, this guide will be most relevant.—**Virginia S. Fischer**

Spanish Literature

C, P

336.   **World Literature in Spanish: An Encyclopedia.** Maureen Ihrie and Salvador A. Oropesa, eds. Santa Barbara, Calif., ABC-CLIO, 2011. 3v. index. $350.00/set. ISBN 13: 978-0-313-33770-3; 978-0-313-08083-8 (e-book).

This three-volume encyclopedia is a mixed bag. On the one hand, its broad geographic breadth includes not only Spain and the New World but also areas like Equatorial Guinea, the Canary Islands, and the Philippines, which are normally ignored in works of this type; however, it virtually omits U.S. Hispanic writers. The 2011 publication date gives it a currency such that fairly recent prominent writers, like Javier Marías and Laura Esquivel, are included, along with death dates of recently expired authors, like Josefina Aldecoa. The team of more than 200 contributors have academic pedigree on both sides of the Atlantic. One of the editors, Maureen Ihrie, was a co-editor of the *Dictionary of the Literature of the Iberian Peninsula* (see ARBA 94, entry 1289) as well as of the *Feminist Encyclopedia of Spanish Literature* (see ARBA 2005, entry 1089). The other editor, Salvador A. Oropesa, is a distinguished professor of modern language and American ethnic studies. More than one-third of the 848 signed entries are cultural or thematic topics rather than biographical, widening the purely literary intent of the work by including introductory and rather lengthy essays on the history, culture and literature of every Spanish-speaking country. Most the topics of these essays are fairly conventional (e.g., Gaucho Literature), but some are less so (e.g., Amazon Theme in Spanish American Literature). Cross-references within the text are indicated by the standard (*) and by *see* references at the end of articles. Translated titles in English are indicated as such with italics with the publication year; those not translated are in bold type with an approximate English equivalent. Each of the volumes is preceded by an identical table of contents and a guide to 57 related topics under very broad headings (e.g., Absurdism, Essay). Appendixes provide access by century and by country, and also include a glossary of literary and cultural terms and a bibliography of recent print resources in English. A truly outstanding feature of these supplementary materials is a list of free publicly available electronic resources and e-journals. An extensive index of almost 150 pages, comprising about 11 percent of the text, concludes the set.

So what's lacking? Unlike the topical entries, the biographical entries are surprisingly short; for example, Nobel Prize winner García Márquez merits one page, Cervantes a little more than two. Most writers are given less than a page, regardless of prestige. Entries are followed by two or three primary sources, often moot choices since they are not always the author's most crucially acclaimed or important works; for example, the only two listed for Camilo José Cela are *Christ versus Arizona* and *San Camilo, 1936*, two of his more recondite works. The write-ups conclude with secondary sources intended to serve as a springboard for further research; however, many seem to be beyond the reach of the intended audience because of their highly scholarly publication in academic journals and the surprising large number in Spanish, which seems contrary to the emphasis on accessing English-language material and when in fact other appropriate English-language materials exist. Perhaps the greatest concern is the idiosyncratic nature of the selections. One could belabor the specific examples of what's included or not, but let a few examples suffice. The entry on Roberto Bolaño omits *2006*, probably his most highly acclaimed work. Muñoz Molina's *Beatus ille* and *Sefarad* have both appeared in English (*A Manuscript of Ashes* [2008] and *Sepharad* [2003], respectively), despite the entry's indication that they have not (page 657). A 1972 "translation" of Pereda's *Peñas arriba* (page 834) is not an English translation at all; Skármeta's *The Poet's Wedding* (page 909) did not get beyond galleys. One also questions the inclusion of names not normally associated with literature, such as Ramón y Cajal, Selena, Che Guevara, for which this source would not normally be the most obvious one to consult. The unsuspecting high school, undergraduate college, and general public audience for whom this source is intended will be caught off guard if unaware of these occasional potholes of potentially misleading, if not erroneous, information.

So what is the user to do? For decent overviews of the culture and themes of the countries comprising the Spanish-speaking world, brief biographical information on current writers, and guides to electronic resources, this encyclopedia will suffice. But for historical figures or more in-depth coverage, the user should be directed elsewhere.—**Lawrence Olszewski**

Nonfiction

P

337. O'Connor, Maureen. **Life Stories: A Guide to Reading Interests in Memoirs, Autobiographies, and Diaries.** Santa Barbara, Calif., Libraries Unlimited/ABC-CLIO, 2011. 723p. index. (Real Stories Series). $60.00. ISBN 13: 978-1-59158-527-5; 978-1-61069-146-8 (e-book).

The fourth title in Libraries Unlimited's Real Stories series, *Life Stories* is a selective, annotated guide to autobiographies, memoirs, and diaries. An introduction describes the author's aims and methods in putting together this book, including her views on the differences between autobiographies and memoirs. Some 655 titles receive paragraph-long annotations, while some 2,800 other books, including fiction titles and biographies written by other people, are described in conjunction with these titles. Arrangement is by broad categories, further divided by subcategories (e.g., The Creative Life includes the subcategories of Artists, Humorists, Writers). Appendixes list classics, controversial titles, awards, and resources. Author/title and subject indexes are included. Canadian Maureen O'Connor, who worked 35 years as a public librarian, is also the co-author of *Canadian Fiction: A Guide to Reading Interests* (Libraries Unlimited, 2005).

Although O'Connor consulted many sources, as described in the introduction, *Life Stories* is a very personal book that reveals her love of reading. It will reward readers and browsers who can start with one annotation, get information about the title and author, and discover many other titles of interest. Reader's advisors and collection developers, particularly in public libraries, will find *Life Stories* very useful.—**Jonathan F. Husband**

Poetry

C, P, S

338.   **Greek Poets.** Rosemary M. Canfield Reisman, ed. Hackensack, N.J., Salem Press, 2012. 235p. index. (Salem Singles). $29.95pa.; $44.95 (e-book). ISBN 13: 978-1-42983-660-9; 978-1-58765-911-9 (e-book).

C, P, S

339.   **Russian Poets.** Rosemary M. Canfield Reisman, ed. Hackensack, N.J., Salem Press, 2012. 206p. index. (Salem Singles). $29.95pa.; $44.95 (e-book). ISBN 13: 978-1-42983-665-4; 978-1-58765-916-4 (e-book).

These two volumes are part of a new series from Salem Press called Salem Singles that provide selected articles from the publishers acclaimed *Critical Survey of Poetry* (4th ed., see ARBA 2012, entry 1018). *Russian Poets* provides essays on 16 Russian poets, including Sergei Esenin, Mikhail Lermontov, Alexander Pushkin, and Marina Tsvetayeva. Each entry contains a list of principal poetry and other literary forms, achievements, a biography, and an up-to-date bibliography of often times more than 10 sources. Black-and-white photographs of the poets are provided when available. The work begins with an overview entry on Russian poetry that includes the history of poetry in the region, its influences, and the role key poets played in social, literary, and artistic circles.

Greek Poets provides 19 biographical essays on influential Greek poets, including Archilochus, Odysseus Elytis, Homer, Pindar, and Sappho. This volume provides three introductory essays: Greek Poetry in Antiquity, Greek Poetry Since 1820, and Macedonian Poetry. It also includes a checklist for explicating a poem, bibliography, list of online resources, and geographical, category, and subject indexes.

These two volumes are not necessary purchases for the reference departments of those owning *Critical Survey of Poetry* since it is all repeated information. However, those libraries unable to purchase the 14-volume set ($1,295) may want to add these smaller, lower-priced titles as needed to supplement their literature collections. Other subject-specific volumes are to follow in the next year, including those on Spanish poets, war poets, surrealist poets, and visionary poets, just to name a few.—**Shannon Graff Hysell**

25 Music

General Works

Bibliography

C, P

340.   **Film and Television Music: A Guide to Books, Articles, and Composer Interviews.** Warren M. Sherk, comp. Lanham, Md., Scarecrow, 2011. 667p. index. $75.00. ISBN 13: 978-0-8108-7686-6; 978-0-8108-7687-3 (e-book).

There are very few bibliographic resources on film and television music currently available. This work attempts to fill that gap. It is a fairly comprehensive listing of books and articles on this topic from 1906 through 2005. Only books and articles in English are included, which provides overall coverage for the film industries in the United States, Canada, the United Kingdom, Australia, and India. The book is divided into 11 chapters, with a good introduction and guide to the book at the beginning. The chapters are: "Books on Film and Television Music," "Academic Dissertations and Theses," "Composer Biographies," "Songwriter and Lyricist Biographies," "Books with Material on Film and Television Music," "Music for the Accompaniment of Silent Films," "Film Music Periodicals," "Composer Society Journals and Newsletters," "Film and Media Periodicals," "Music Periodicals," and "General Interest and Other Periodicals." Overall, this is a huge and timely reference work that covers a largely unmined topic in twentieth-century music history.—**Bradford Lee Eden**

Dictionaries and Encyclopedias

P

341.   **Encyclopedia of African American Music.** Emmett G. Price III, Tammy L. Kernodle, and Horace J. Maxile Jr., eds. Santa Barbara, Calif., Greenwood Press/ABC-CLIO, 2011. 3v. illus. index. $224.00/set. ISBN 13: 978-0-31334-199-1; 978-0-31334-200-4 (e-book).

This is an impressive three-volume set useful for scholars and practitioners interested in African American music. Executive editor Emmett G. Price III, author of *Hip Hop Culture* (see ARBA 2007, entry 1010), draws on his extensive scholarly and practical background with black music and musicians in this series, as do associate editors Kernodle (PhD in Music History, The Ohio State University) and Maxile, Jr. (associate director of research at the Center for Black Music Research, Columbia College, Chicago). Each volume offers both an alphabetic and topical list of entries for ease of access; the first volume provides an introduction and a timeline of significant moments in African American music. The appendixes in volume 3 discuss significant compositions, music videos, archives, research centers, and Websites as well as a selected bibliography of resources and reference works and a genre-specific bibliography of African American music. The more than 400 entries included in these three volumes were composed by over 100 contributors; each entry is clear, easy to understand, and cross-referenced to other entries or songs/videos. While many entries are brief, these volumes serve well as companions to earlier reference works by Greenwood Press, including Eileen Southern's *Biographical Dictionary of Afro-American and African Musicians* (Greenwood Press, 1982).—**Stephanie Vie**

C, P

342. McGuire, Charles Edward, and Steven E. Plank. **Historical Dictionary of English Music ca. 1400-1958.** Lanham, Md., Scarecrow, 2011. 341p. (Historical Dictionaries of Literature and the Arts). $90.00. ISBN 13: 978-0-8108-5750-6; 978-0-8108-7951-5 (e-book).

Jon Woronoff, Series Editor, points out in the foreword of this work that it "deals with just that— English music over the ages, here focused on music from the early Renaissance to the mid-20th century, ending with the death of Ralph Vaughan Williams." The dictionary begins with a list of acronyms and abbreviations, a chronology beginning in the 1335 Robertsbridge Codex, and ending with the death in 1958 with the death of Vaughan Williams. In an introduction the authors provide an interesting overview of English music, which can stand alone in its historical depth. The main part of the bibliography is alphabetically arranged and annotated. It provides the name, dates of birth and death, the person's involvement with music, and a brief biography. No individual discographies or bibliographies are provided. In addition there is a selected bibliography that begins with an interesting essay and contains about 500 items. The bibliography begins with references and general works, and then lists composers, conductors, critics, journalists, and assorted writers, musical instruments, and miscellaneous. While this work duplicates a number of other bibliographies that include English music, the work is recommended for public and academic libraries.—**Robert L. Wick**

Handbooks and Yearbooks

P

343. **Encyclopedia of National Anthems.** 2d ed. Xing Hang, comp. Lanham, Md., Scarecrow, 2011. 2v. maps. index. $150.00/set. ISBN 13: 978-0-8108-7662-0.

This work was originally printed in 2003 and consisted of 704 pages in one volume (see ARBA 2004, entry 1084). This revised and expanded edition represents 193 countries in two volumes (1060 pages). Included are the texts in the country's official language and in English, and the sheet music required for performance. Non-Latin scripts have original lyrics with Romanization and translations.

This edition also includes maps that show geographic neighbors, basic demographic data, flags, and enhanced historical background about the country and its anthem, all in black and white; much of this geographic, and up-to-date demographic data are also available on the Web, with color images (https://www.cia.gov/library/publications/the-world-factbook/).

The new edition also contains anthems of international organizations (European Union, United Nations). At the conclusion of this source are anthems of non-members of the United Nations (e.g., Formosa, Western Sahara, Kosovo), or extinct states (e.g., USSR, East Germany, Orange Free State). These are without maps so the users will need to consult historical atlases.

Since the maps and flags are black and white, only the shading of the flag is shown. The colors of the flag need to be listed if users are to know what the design of each flag represents. Cartographic reproduction reflects low budgeting. Nevertheless, this encyclopedia serves as a quick and useful source for nearly 200 national songs. [R: LJ, Jan 12, p. 140; BL, Jan 1 &15, 2012, p. 64]—**Ralph Hartsock**

C, P

344. Zager, Michael. **Music Production: For Producers, Composers, Arrangers, and Students.** Lanham, Md., Scarecrow, 2012. 422p. index. $60.00pa. ISBN 13: 978-0-8108-8201-0; 978-0-8108-8202-7 (e-book).

This updated, 2d edition of *Music Production* focuses on the topics of the role of music supervisors, new production techniques, and the updated terms being used in modern-day music contracts. It still includes many of the same valuable tips and tricks of the trade that the author focused on in the 1st edition (Scarecrow Press, 2006), but includes new information that will keep music producers up-to-date in today's fast-changing industry. After an introduction and a chronology of the music recording industry, the work is broken down into three sections: Music Production; Recording Technology; and The Music Business. Music Production, the lengthiest of the sections, focuses on creative concepts, songwriting, arrangement and orchestration, mixing and mastering, music videos, and the production process. It concludes with two chapters on the history of popular music. Recording Technology provides two chapters on working in the studio and audio engineering. The final section, The Music Business, discusses marketing and promotion, creating a business plan and album production budget, and music contracts. The work concludes with a bibliography and an index.

This well-researched volume touches on all aspect of the music production business and would be useful as a reference work in music libraries or a textbook in the classroom. It should be in all university music reference collections.—**Shannon Graff Hysell**

Instruments

Piano

P

345.   **The Pianist's Craft: Mastering the Works of Great Composers.** Richard Paul Anderson, ed. Lanham, Md., Scarecrow, 2012. 291p. index. $65.00. ISBN 13: 978-0-8108-8205-8.

The Pianist's Craft is a collection of 19 essays discussing the teaching, preparation, and performance of some of the most accomplished piano composers. Included are works by Bach, Haydn, Gershwin, Brahms, Liszt, and Chopin. The contributors are all recognized contributors to piano composition and include artists, teachers, recording artists, and clinicians. They discuss in depth such topics as the composer's tempo, articulation, dynamics, lyricism, and instrumentation. This book is meant for those studying piano at the advanced level, including pianists, instructors, and music scholars.—**Shannon Graff Hysell**

Violin

P

346.   Nardolillo, Jo. **The Canon of Violin Literature: A Performer's Resource.** Lanham, Md., Scarecrow, 2011. 217p. index. (Music Finders Series). $65.00. ISBN 13: 978-0-8108-7793-1.

Written with performing violinist, violin instructors, and college music professors in mind, this volume lists works that are regularly performed and recorded in concert halls and studied by students in conservatories. The work is organized alphabetically by composer and includes the work's title, date of composition, the date and performer of its premier, key, duration, instrumentation, and movements of the work. There are notes included for each piece that address historical, technical, and performance information that will be helpful to performers. Each listing concludes with bibliographic information on publishers, editions, the editors of the sheet music, and a list of recordings and books for further study. Overall, the information is comprehensive for each listing and will provide those interested in further study a jumping off point for further research. The work concludes with a chronological list of works, a list of works by genre, indexes by piece title and performers, and a bibliography. This work will be useful in music collections in music libraries as well as in the hands of violin instructors and music directors.—**Shannon Graff Hysell**

Musical Forms

Classical

C, P

347.   Gagné, Nicole V. **Historical Dictionary of Modern and Contemporary Classical Music.** Lanham, Md., Scarecrow, 2012. 367p. (Historical Dictionaries of Literature and the Arts). $80.00. ISBN 13: 978-0-8108-6765-9; 978-0-8108-7962-1 (e-book).

Covering the field of classical music from 1890 to the present, this dictionary, compiled by a musicologist, librettist, and composer, focuses primarily on composers and musicians (quite often they are both) but also includes methods, styles, and techniques (but not individual works). Granted that the demarcation between modern and contemporary is fluid, but most of the names and styles included by definition fall under the broad rubric of modernism; hence the exclusion of Elgar, Puccini, Rachmaninoff, and Sibelius, who, though belonging chronologically, stylistically do not. Although one wonders how Ralph Vaughan Williams and Frederick Delius made the cut, two examples of composers whose total body of work one does not normally associate with atonal music.

The dictionary provides basic information about each topic, with bolded cross-references in each entry. The emphasis on biographical fact, not music criticism, provides in a nutshell the essence of the contribution of the composer to the development of twentieth-century music. The entries do not include a complete work list, rather just those works that the compiler deemed the most representative, important, or well-known. Some entries are also followed by a list of cross-references, on occasion very extensive (some run to a half a page or more). The 57-page bibliography is comprehensive and well organized; it is particularly outstanding in the number and quality of print and Web resources for individual composers. The dictionary is preceded by an introduction that sets the framework for the historical development of the period and by a useful chronology, which even includes occasionally premiere dates for the works tracked. The work is commendable for its coverage of women, minority, and international figures as well as the inclusion of performers in the related fields of jazz, pop, and rock, like Duke Ellington and the Beatles, whose influence impacted the realm of classical music.

This dictionary is an appropriate addition to both public and academic music reference collections as an introduction to the composers and movements for the general public and undergraduates as well as a jumping-off resource for further investigation. [R: LJ, Jan 12, p. 134]—**Lawrence Olszewski**

C, P

348.   McVicker, Mary F. **Women Composers of Classical Music: 369 Biographies from 1550 into the 20th Century.** Jefferson, N.C., McFarland, 2011. 253p. index. $45.00pa. ISBN 13: 978-0-7865-4397-0.

Women Composers of Classical Music provides a chronological survey of women composers beginning with the Renaissance and continuing through 1970. There are several limitations built into the book. For instance, the Renaissance period is limited to only women composers in Italy, and the "choice of what section a woman should be included within is based on the time period of their first major composition" (p. 3). An interesting aspect of the book is the introductions, which provide a look at the musical culture of each country or area represented by a composer in that section. These introductions are interesting and provide some insights into the culture that allowed or provided roadblocks to the success of women composers. In addition to the biographies the author has provided a timeline of women opera composers, a brief bibliography (76 items), a discography of both LPs and CDs, and an index. While it does not attempt to be a complete list, this work provides an interesting overview of women composers through the centuries. While designed as a reference work, the book is also interesting to simply read through to obtain an overview of many women composers who have been forgotten or have been overlooked. This book is recommended for all public and academic libraries, and for the personal collections of composers, musicians, and teachers.—**Robert L. Wick**

Orchestral

P

349.   Meyer, Dirk. **Chamber Orchestra and Ensemble Repertoire: A Catalog of Modern Music.** Lanham, Md., Scarecrow, 2011. 426p. $75.00. ISBN 13: 978-0-8108-7731-3.

Music is in as much transition as my own profession, librarianship. From the first flagitious salvo fired by the erstwhile Napster to the ubiquitous iTunes of today, music continues to create and re-create itself, almost with each passing year. The once omnipresent 8-track tapes of my youth gave way to cassettes, then to CDs, and now to earbuds for iPods and other handheld devices. Blink and you are likely to miss the next iteration of music in our times.

Switch the channel to classical music and the story changes again. Find anyone under 30 (or heads without gray hair) at a classical concert or opera these days and it is like winning the lottery: glorious, extremely rare, but the odds are decidedly against it. Narrow that yet again, to chamber music, and the chances of counting the stars may prove more successful. Having said all that, for those of us who live to hear it, German Conductor Derek Meyer's book strikes a hopeful chord (pun intended).

While Meyer's book is a catalog to chamber music after 1900, it has everything the Euterpe in us all longs to see. Patterned after David Daniel's *Orchestra Music* (4th ed.; see ARBA 2006, entry 1093), Meyer catalogs chamber orchestra and ensemble pieces. The main part of the catalog is arranged alphabetically by composer, and each entry contains information needed to know what instruments and their number are required to play it—flutes, oboes, clarinets, horns, strings, and more—and the duration of each piece. The appendixes prove even more valuable. Arrangement here is first by solo voices, then solo instruments, string orchestras, ensembles by string count, followed by compositions that use no percussion, no harps or pianos, and so on. A twenty-first century repertoire comes next rounded out by a listing by duration. Publishers and other resources, such as Websites, are also included.

Doubtless such tools will go the way of all digital flesh, but for now this is a must-have tool for any serious musical endeavor in any community regardless of size. After all, music is the food of life, to paraphrase, and now there's a way to have it play on and on.—**Mark Y. Herring**

Popular

General Works

P

350.   Webb, Robert. **The Ultimate Playlist: 100 Great Cover Versions.** Northumbria; distr., Chicago, Independent Publishers Group, 2012. 168p. illus. index. $15.95pa. ISBN 13: 978-0-8571-6019-5.

This book features 100 popular songs that began as cover songs. Cover songs are interesting in that they were not always immediate hits when they originally came out but due to a more popular artist covering the song or due to an original take by a new artist the song takes off and gains a new or larger audience. For each song selected users will learn of the original artist that sang the song and the writer, as well as stories of how a new artist came to cover the song and how its popularity then took off. The author, a British journalist and author of other popular music titles, writes in an engaging style and has done his research to uncover some surprise artists and hit. He suggests key tracks from a variety of popular artists, including the Beatles, David Bowie, Florence & the Machine, Jimi Hendrix, Elvis Presley, and U2. The book does have a slight British flair to it, but the playlists will appeal to many American music lovers as well.—**R. K. Dickson**

Hip-Hop

C, P

351.   Rausch, Andrew J. **I Am Hip-Hop: Conversations on the Music and Culture.** Lanham, Md., Scarecrow, 2011. 213p. index. $29.95. ISBN 13: 978-0-8108-7791-7; 978-0-8108-7792-4 (e-book).

This book is more of a recollection of early innovators, musicians, poets, and music groups within the hip-hop culture, than a reference work on hip-hop. The author interviews and discusses 25 influences and major figures within this music genre, including Chip Fu, Daddy-O, dream hampton, Kool Keith, Paradime, Sadat X, and Spinderella, among many others. Each interview includes the questions asked along with the answers, and a discography of that artist. For those who are interested in personal recollections of early hip-hop artists and their opinions related to various topics within this musical genre, this book would be of interest.—**Bradford Lee Eden**

26 Mythology, Folklore, and Popular Culture

Folklore

C, P, S

352. **Encyclopedia of Asian American Folklore and Folklife.** Jonathan H. X. Lee and Kathleen M. Nadeau, eds. Santa Barbara, Calif., ABC-CLIO, 2011. 3v. illus. index. $265.00/set. ISBN 13: 978-0-31335-066-5.

Asian American studies is a relatively new field of scholarship. Not only does it bridge Asia to America, it also shares a deep connection with Asian studies. Research on various aspects of Asian America has flourished in recent years, with each in-depth study a welcome addition to the field. This comprehensive three-volume encyclopedia is the first of its kind, covering 23 Asian American ethnic and cultural groups, including lesser-researched Mongolian Americans and Nepali Americans as well as mixed heritage and mixed race Asian Americans. The volumes contain more than 600 entries contributed by nearly 180 scholars, one-half of whom are teaching faculty and the others are Ph.D. candidates and independent scholars. A survey of the history, people, and culture of each group precedes shorter essays on alphabetically arranged topics, such as arts and crafts, festivals and holidays, folk music, religion, and rites and passage reflecting different communities. Each entry is accompanied by a list of further readings; some entries also include black-and-white illustrations that could be enhanced with color to demonstrate the colorful images of cultural activities. The table of contents and a dictionary index are replicated in all three volumes for easy reference. The encyclopedia is intended for users in high school, college, the general public, as well as professionals to support and enhance the cross-cultural and cross-disciplinary study of Asian American folklore and folk life. This set is recommend for readers at all levels.—**Karen T. Wei**

C, P

353. **Folklore: An Encyclopedia of Beliefs, Customs, Tales, Music, and Art.** 2d ed. Charlie T. McCormick and Kim Kennedy White, eds. Santa Barbara, Calif., ABC-CLIO, 2011. 3v. illus. index. $280.00/set. ISBN 13: 978-1-59884-241-8; 978-1-59884-242-5 (e-book).

Expanded from two volumes to three since the 1st edition of 1997 (see ARBA 99, entry 1180), this set admirably tackles an extremely broad subject. The co-editors have gathered contributions from more than 160 authors who specialize in a wide variety of theoretical approaches to the study of folklore. Articles cover not just folktales, but also folk music, art, medicine, and foodways. Others explore concepts vital to the field of study, such as cultural relativism, tale types, and diffusion. Each article begins with a succinct definition before delving further in depth. The writing style varies widely, as one might expect considering the number of authors involved; nevertheless, further standardization of articles would have been helpful. For instance, the number of references provided at the end of an article varies from just a few to almost a full page. In addition, the list of contributors at the beginning of the first volume provides only names and institutional affiliations, not the titles of each authors' article(s). This could have easily been solved by providing an index by author, or by including the information in the main index. The encyclopedia also seems to exhibit a certain bias towards European, North American, and

East Asian traditions; coverage of Africa, South America, Australia, New Zealand, and the islands of the South Pacific is scant at best. Despite these shortcomings, however, *Folklore: An Encyclopedia of Beliefs, Customs, Tales, Music, and Art* is one of the most comprehensive reference works available on the topic, and should certainly be included in any academic library supporting programs in folklore, anthropology, or related disciplines.—**Maren Williams**

C, S

354.   Guiley, Rosemary Ellen. **Encyclopedia of Vampires and Werewolves.** 2d ed. New York, Facts on File, 2011. 430p. illus. index. $85.00. ISBN 13: 978-0-8160-8179-0; 978-1-4381-3632-5 (e-book).

In the *Encyclopedia of Vampires and Werewolves*, Facts on Files has produced a volume seemingly intended to cash in on the current popularity of supernatural creatures, but has instead created a nicely conceived publication that also includes more historical, literary, and cultural information. Rosemary Ellen Guiley serves as an authority in fields relating to the paranormal, and certainly adds a great deal of quality and insight into this work.

The *Encyclopedia* includes over 500 entries relating to vampires and werewolves. The volume expectedly covers popular culture topics such as television shows and movies (e.g., *True Blood*, *Twilight*), literature (e.g., *Dracula*, the Sookie Stackhouse series), and writers and actors (e.g., Anne Rice, Robert Pattinson). Of more academic interest, though, are the entries that delve into factual topics relating to cultural legends and lore (e.g., akhkharu, skinwalkers) and real-life topics (e.g., New England vampires, Spaulding family vampires).

The entries vary a great deal in length depending on the topic, but each is well written and provides the most pertinent information necessary. The volume also includes a bibliography, an index, and a smattering of color graphics and images to help illustrate the writing. Although some of the more current popular culture topics may lose some of their timeliness, the *Encyclopedia of Vampires and Werewolves* provides enough value in its cultural and historical topics that it should prove beneficial to many collections.—**Tyler Manolovitz**

P, S

355.   Steiger, Brad. **The Werewolf Book: The Encyclopedia of Shape-Shifting Beings.** 2d ed. Canton, Mich., Visible Ink Press, 2011. 368p. illus. index. $19.95pa. ISBN 13: 978-1-57859-378-1; 978-1-57859-376-7 (e-book).

The Werewolf Book: The Encyclopedia of Shape-Shifting Beings is a 368-page work fully dedicated to the werewolf and its significance in history, literature, mythology, and popular culture. This 2d edition has been complete updated, encompassing several hundred entries and many black-and-white photographs. The entries vary from strict discussions of objective facts, to relatively in-depth subjective scholarly essays. The topics discussed include fictional characters (e.g., Teenage Werewolves), actors, authors (e.g., Stephenie Meyers, author of the Twilight Series), historical figures (e.g., Adolph Hitler), movies, geographic regions, significant objects, and other important topics related to werewolves.

The text is organized alphabetically by topic name to help in locating specific entries. Additionally, a table of contents, chronology, and index are included. The index specifically, is extremely detailed and valuable in navigating the text. Virtually anything werewolf related is either given its own entry, or discussed within another entry and discoverable via the index. The entries are easily comprehended and organized in a way that is both easy to navigate and understand.

The Werewolf Book is certainly exhaustive up to the point of publication, but the popularity of werewolves an the supernatural may cause some of the content to become quickly outdated. Despite this possible drawback, *The Werewolf Book* is wonderfully thorough, exhaustively detailed, and affordable enough to be part of most collections.—**Tyler Manolovitz**

Mythology

P, S

356.   **Gods and Goddesses of Greece and Rome.** Tarrytown, N.Y., Marshall Cavendish, 2012. 320p. illus. index. $59.95. ISBN 13: 978-0-7614-7951-2; 978-0-7614-9980-0 (e-book).

Gods and Goddesses of Greece and Rome accomplishes exactly what its title suggests by offering an encyclopedic description of the 76 major gods and goddesses of the ancient Greek and Roman cultures. The entries range in length depending on the article, but the length appears to be appropriate for each subject. Each article concludes with a bibliography and, of particular use, a cross-reference list of related articles within the volume.

The text of *Gods and Goddesses of Greece and Rome* is written to a high school audience, and as a result is easy to understand and could be easily picked up by a general audience. The writers do an admirable job of describing the important aspects of the gods and goddesses without losing focus or confusing the reader. The volume does not have the space to go into painstaking detail, but the overview provides enough information to offer a useful introduction.

Not to be overlooked, *Gods and Goddesses* is very dense with beautiful color images and photographs of paintings, sculptures, landscapes, structures, and artifacts relating to each deity. These images serve an important role of conveying the ways in which men and women interpreted and incorporated each myth into their lives. The images also help to break up the text and, in addition to helping encourage the reading of what could become dry subject matter.

Gods and Goddesses of Greece and Rome is a great introductory work to the topic, especially for high school audiences and is recommended for collections supporting research into ancient religions, myths, Greece, or Rome. [R: LJ, Jan 12, p. 130]—**Tyler Manolovitz**

Popular Culture

Dictionaries and Encyclopedias

P

357.   Cavalier, Stephen. **The World History of Animation.** Berkeley, Calif., University of California Press, 2011. 416p. illus. index. $39.95. ISBN 13: 978-0-520-26112-9.

This book is a composite picture of historically and culturally significant animated films and shorts across the globe. Various genres and styles, such as Claymation and CGI are included. Selections are not limited to Hollywood blockbusters, but also include arthouse, cult favorites, experimental, and stylized films. Each selection includes some commentary that combines plot summaries with social history and industry innovation. Breakout boxes explore terms and subjects in more detail, and biographies spotlight innovators in the field. While the book has more of a coffee-table feel with its large photographs and short text, the chronological order of films helps to deliver a story of animation's global history. The screenshots in the book act as a visual timeline, which help detail the evolution of each country's animation industry. The chronological arraignment of the book is broken up into periods of time, each of which is preceded by a description of the changes that took place to mark the advent of each new era in animation history. This book is recommended for casual readers as well as film students.—**Brian J. Sherman**

P, S

358.   **Religious Celebrations: An Encyclopedia of Holidays, Festivals, Solemn Observances, and Spiritual Commemorations.** J. Gordon Melton, ed. Santa Barbara, Calif., ABC-CLIO, 2011. 2v. illus. index. $189.00/set. ISBN 13: 978-1-59884-205-0; 978-1-59884-206-7 (e-book).

This two-volume reference work documents a wide variety of religious celebrations by a number of major religions, including a number of festivals, holidays, commemorations, and observances. There are more than 600 entries, including major entries for many of the world's religions: Baha'i Faith, Buddhism, Chinese Religion, Christianity, Hinduism, Islam, Jainism, Judaism, Shinto, Unbelief, Wicca/Neo-Paganism, Liturgical Calendar, and Zoroastrianism. Each entry has a short description, a list of *see also* references, and a short bibliography. There is a large index at the end, and all entries are listed in the table of contents in the front of each volume. Illustrated with many black-and-white photographs and various charts, this book is one of many available works documenting the feasts and holidays of various religions and religious practices. [R: BL, Jan 1 &15, 2012, p. 72]—**Bradford Lee Eden**

Handbooks and Yearbooks

P, S
359.   Fagan, Bryan D., and Jody Condit Fagan. **Comic Book Collections for Libraries.** Santa Barbara, Calif., Libraries Unlimited/ABC-CLIO, 2011. 162p. illus. index. $45.00pa. ISBN 13: 978-1-59884-511-2.

Authored by the creators and maintainers of the popular comic book collection at James Madison University, this work is for those seeking to start a collection, seeking support for such a collection, and those interested in a history and overview of the form. Separated into nine chapters, the work begins by discussing comic books, graphic novels, and popular culture, followed by the structure of the comic book. Next the players, such as publishers and creators, and other industry terms and organizations are defined and discussed. The fourth chapter focuses on the genres that are found in comic book collections. The remainder of the work is geared for the library professional, addressing the creation and maintenance of a core comic book collection, cataloging these materials, guidelines for promoting the collection, comics in other parts of the library, and Web resources. A glossary and index make this work useful as a reference and approachable to the novice, while the writing style encourages reading selected chapters from start to finish as indicated by the information need. Three appendixes present an initial graphic title list and inclusion criteria, comic book characters and their titles, and a list of further readings on comics, graphic novels, manga, and anime. The notes and references in each chapter assist the avid researcher in finding more information, while a collection development, cataloging, or public services librarian or future librarian will benefit from reading this cover to cover.—**Sara Marcus**

P, S
360.   **Graphic Novels and Comic Books.** Kat Kan, ed. Bronx, N.Y., H. W. Wilson, 2010. 195p. illus. index. (The Reference Shelf, v.82, no.5). $50.00pa. ISBN 13: 978-0-8242-1100-4.

It is not groundbreaking news that comic books and graphic novels have experienced a surge in popularity in the past 10 years, in both bookstores and the classroom. However, those who wish to use the material in the classroom or those who are lost on how to develop a collection of this sort still exist. This Reference Shelf publication is a great way to start researching. A majority of the articles are reprinted from national newspapers with only a handful from professional literature. Regardless of the source, the articles come from industry insiders and scholars in the field, as well as librarians incorporating comic books into the collection. The book explores the genre in segments, first delving into the history of comics and graphic novels. Further chapters get into the crux of the matter and discuss how the genre has become a serious literature and is being introduced into the classroom on all levels. Librarians can draw their own attention to the chapter of including comics into the stacks. Interviews with comic book and graphic novel creators are also included in this material. Although the material in this book is just reprints of previously published material, this collection of articles is a great practical handbook on how others have used the genre as well as for historical information and collection development advice.—**Brian J. Sherman**

C, S

361.   Leslie, Larry Z. **Celebrity in the 21st Century: A Reference Handbook.** Santa Barbara, Calif., ABC-CLIO, 2011. 272p. index. (Contemporary World Issues). $55.00. ISBN 13: 978-1-59884-484-9.

Geared for high school students, but of equal value to college students interested in the culture of celebrity and its changing impact on our society, the eight sections in this work provide an updated comprehensive view of resources available on all aspects of twenty-first century celebrity. Beginning with the background and history of celebrity status, Leslie next addresses problems, controversies, and solutions related to celebrity culture in our society. A worldwide perspectives section discusses the impact on celebrity status on politics, the arts, and business, while a chronology chapter covers the significant events that have led to the evolution of celebrities and their elite status. There are 30 biographical sketches presented in the next chapter that highlight top celebrities of our day (e.g., Oprah Winfrey, Tom Cruise, Britney Spears), followed by a chapter of data and documents relevant to celebrities, including magazines and television programs, celebrities and the movies, and highest-earning celebrities. A directory of organizations and Websites covers such topics as celebrity-sponsored charities, speakers bureaus, and fan clubs. A list of selected print and nonprint resources is provided at the end that includes books, journal articles, magazines video, video games, and Internet sites. Written so a high school student can understand but also at an interest level for college students, the brief entries are an excellent overview or starting point for further research on any aspects of celebrity and its affect on culture.—**Sara Marcus**

27 Performing Arts

General Works

P

362.   Frasier, David K. **Show Business Homicides: An Encyclopedia, 1908-2009.** Jefferson, N.C., McFarland, 2011. 410p. illus. index. $75.00. ISBN 13: 978-0-7864-4422-9.

According to the author, who has written a number of books on suicide and murder in the entertainment industry, this encyclopedia is a companion to his 2002 book *Suicide in the Entertainment Industry* (see ARBA 2003, entry 815), which recorded 840 instances of suicide among celebrities. This work documents almost 300 cases of instances where celebrities were the murderer or a celebrity was murdered. For each entry, an M (murderer), V (victim), or M-S (murder-suicide) follows the name. Other notations such as M-acquitted, M-not charged, V-suspected are also appended. As much detail then follows about the person's life, death, and police report information. There are black-and-white photographs of various celebrities interspersed throughout the volume. Two appendixes at the back of the book provide information on narcocorridos (ballads recounting the exploits and travails of drug kingpins) and a notes section containing more detailed published information on certain celebrities. There is also an extensive bibliography and index. This book is targeted to two audiences: the general reader fascinated with celebrity deaths, and the serious researcher looking for more detailed information.—**Bradford Lee Eden**

P

363.   **The Grey House Performing Arts Directory 2011/2012.** 7th ed. Millerton, N.Y., Grey House Publishing, 2011. 1102p. index. $185.00pa.; $375.00 (online database; single user); $475.00 (print and online edition). ISBN 13: 978-1-59237-551-6.

The 7th edition of this enormous and information-rich tome offers in-depth and comprehensive listings on performing arts in the United States. Seven major categories are represented: Dance, Instrumental Music, Vocal Music, Theatre, Series and Festivals, Performance Facilities, and Information Resources. Entries in the first five categories are broken down by state and city, with detailed contact information, budget, income sources, annual attendance, and more. Under Performance Facilities, 2,752 venues are listed, organized by state and then city. Under Information Resources, 715 sources are listed under associations, newsletters, magazines and journals, trade shows, directories and databases, and industry Websites. There are six large indexes to access the above data quickly and efficiently: entry name index, executive name index, facilities index, specialized field index, geographic index, and information resources index. This reference volume is a treasure trove for anyone looking for information on the performing arts in the United States.—**Bradford Lee Eden**

Film, Television, and Video

Biography

C, P

364.   Van Riper, A. Bowdoin. **A Biographical Encyclopedia of Scientists and Inventors in American Film and TV Since 1930.** Lanham, Md., Scarecrow, 2012. 323p. illus. index. $75.00. ISBN 13: 978-0-8108-8128-0; 978-0-8108-8129-7 (e-book).

This volume chronicles the portrayal by actors of 78 scientists, engineers, and inventors in American films and television shows from 1930 (roughly the advent of sound in films) to 2009 (the depiction in 2010 of Mark Zuckerberg, the inventor of Facebook, in the movie *The Social Network* is not included). Otherwise the coverage by Van Riper, a historian who specializes in science and technology, is amazingly thorough and complete. For example, obscure television shows in which the subject is portrayed only by a brief voice over are included. The entries are arranged chronologically by the birth date of the subject and divided into four time periods: before the nineteenth century (e.g., Aristotle, da Vinci, Benjamin Franklin), the nineteenth century (e.g., Mores, Pasteur, Bell), the twentieth century to 1945 (e.g., Freud, Einstein, Kinsey), and the twentieth century after 1945 (e.g., Oppenheimer, Bill Gates, Steve Jobs). Entries average about five pages in length but range from two to twelve pages. The entries for Edison and Einstein are the longest, because each has been portrayed by 30 times in the media. Each entry consists of three parts. The first is a brief essay that includes biographical information on the subject and coverage on why he or she is important. This is followed by material on each screen portrayal that includes a critical analysis. The second part lists chronologically each screen presentation of the subject including the actor involved and title, date, length of screen time, and series note where applicable. Lastly, in narrative form, there is a brief bibliography of important books and articles about he subject. A few black-and white stills from shows are scattered throughout the text and a 10-page introduction orients the reader to the book and its contents. The book ends with an index that includes the names of subjects, the people who portrayed them, and titles of films and shows. It is helpful in spite of some omissions. This unusual but excellent book is recommended for film and science collections.—**John T. Gillespie**

Catalogs

P

365.   Hyatt, Wesley. **Television's Top 100: The Most-Watched American Broadcasts, 1960-2010.** Jefferson, N.C., McFarland, 2012. 196p. index. $55.00pa. ISBN 13: 978-0-7864-4891-3.

This is an entertaining and historical look back on some of the most popular and memorable events that generated the largest American television audiences. The author reviewed weekly ratings in every issue of *Variety* from 1960 through 2000, as well as those from *The Los Angeles Times* and *The Washington Post* to determine the top 100 highest television rankings. He admits that only the top 25 can be verified—the remaining 75 are based on his personal research and best estimates. Here users will find popular television finales (e.g., M*A*S*H), popular episodes (e.g., the "who shot JR" episode on *Dallas*), sporting events (e.g., Super Bowl XVI), television interviews (e.g., Oprah's interview with Michael Jackson), and holiday specials (e.g., *The Bob Hope Christmas Special*). For each entry the author has provided the name of the show and its episode title, date it aired, rating, competition, and a synopsis and backstory of several pages. The author writes in an entertaining manner that will appeal to the general public. The work concludes with appendixes listing the top 100 in chronological order, providing a list of top-rated shows prior to 1960, top 100 facts and figures, a bibliography, and an index. This book could be used for research as well as for entertainment in public libraries.—**Anita Zutis**

P

366.　Marill, Alvin H. **Movies Made for Television 2005-2009.** Lanham, Md., Scarecrow, 2011. 179p. index. $60.00. ISBN 13: 978-0-8108-7658-3; 978-0-8108-7659-0 (e-book).

Movies Made for Television 2005-2009, the fifth and latest volume in a series, begins with a foreword by Ron Simon championing the scholarly talents of this book's author Alvin Marill and his important contribution to documenting this genre.

The book then follows, as with the previous volumes, with an introduction reflecting the film's history of this period. Entries are numbered and listed alphabetically by the title.

Each entry includes: title, network and date aired, length, a well-researched and succinct summary, production companies, and cast. After the entries are the following lists: "Chronological List of Titles, 2005-2009"; "Television Movies Adapted from Other Sources" (including information on the sources); actor index; and director index. As with the previous volumes, made for British television movies and direct-to-video movies are excluded.

Movies Made for Television 2005-2009 is a very well-written, well-researched, and well-chronicled listing of all television movies from this period. This would be a great reference book for any media library or as part of a trivia collection at a public library.—**Linda W. Hacker**

Dictionaries and Encyclopedias

C, P

367.　Booker, M. Keith. **Historical Dictionary of American Cinema.** Lanham, Md., Scarecrow, 2011. 477p. (Historical Dictionaries of Literature and the Arts). $85.00. ISBN 13: 978-0-8108-7192-2; 978-0-8108-7459-6 (e-book).

This dictionary examines the over 100-year-old American film industry. It is intended to be a broad view of that industry. It begins with a chronology that covers the years 1878 to 2010 highlighting events, films, and technologies of the film industry. The introductory essay looks at each stage of development of the industry. It includes brief discussions on the silent film era, the sound era, the golden age of Hollywood, the 1950s and the end of the golden age, and, finally, brief looks at the subsequent decades and the major trends featured in each.

The main part of the work is the dictionary itself. The entries are well written with most being less than a page long. It has entries for people (e.g., actors, directors, composers, studio bosses); studios (e.g., MGM, United Artists, Universal Studios); film types (e.g., musicals, comedy, action film, horror); individual films and awards (e.g., Academy Awards, the Razzies). The words in boldface type in the entry refer the user to another entry in the dictionary. There are also a few *see also* references. Each entry gives a good summation of the topic. This is a very browsable book. Reading one entry and following the boldfaced words allows one to take a leisurely stroll through American films.

This work ends with an extensive bibliography. Included are references to general film studies, genres and film modes, individual films, personnel, reference works, and Internet resources. This is very useful for those patrons who desire a more in-depth treatment of American film history. The book is well done. It will be useful to patrons who desire to learn about the American cinema.—**Robert L. Turner Jr.**

C, P

368.　Booker, M. Keith. **Historical Dictionary of Science Fiction Cinema.** Lanham, Md., Scarecrow, 2010. 333p. $80.00. ISBN 13: 978-0-8108-5570-0.

Jules Verne, H.G. Wells, and Mary Shelley are three writers that are the inspiration for a multi-million dollar film industry that continues to push the envelope on how filmmakers can translate the human imagination onto film. Booker delivers a concise chronology and introduction of the evolution of science fiction cinema beginning with Mary Shelley's *Frankenstein*, often labeled as the first science fiction novel. Directors, actors, and films are listed in 300 entries alongside monsters, aliens, and other terms. Most entries provide descriptive or biographical information rather than critical commentary, although key terms such as feminism and gender do explore the topics in further detail. All the terms are cross-referenced and a lengthy bibliography is included. Booker is the author of several science fiction books and is a professor of English at the University of Arkansas.—**Brian J. Sherman**

P

369.   **Encyclopedia of Religion and Film.** Eric Michael Mazur, ed. Santa Barbara, Calif., ABC-CLIO, 2011. 644p. index. $85.00. ISBN 13: 978-0-313-33072-8; 978-0-313-01398-0 (e-book).

Created to reflect a recent increased interest in the religious aspects of film, this encyclopedia contains 90 entries. Many of these are in-depth essays, averaging four to six pages each. Subjects include religions (e.g., Buddhism, Voodoo), events (e.g., Holocaust, holidays), people (e.g., Frank Capra, Martin Scorsese), aspects of religion (e.g., angels, mysticism, rituals), film genres (e.g., horror, Bible films, silent film, westerns), issues (e.g., censorship, women), and places (e.g., Japan, Latin America). While the film medium today has a broader connotation, in several modes (e.g., analog, digital, internet, made-for-television), the encyclopedia emphasizes traditional films, mostly with English language for dialogue. An extensive, yet selective filmography (pp. 471-561) references those films mentioned in the text, a user's guide, but not an inventory of religious films. The encyclopedia proves quite functional here, in that each filmography entry locates the subject entries that discuss that film. Even is addressed in the essay on Westerns. Most entries are written from the scholarly point of view to discover spiritual insights from the films. Most entries direct readers to similar entries in the work.—**Ralph Hartsock**

C, P

370.   **Movies in American History: An Encyclopedia.** Philip C. DiMare, ed. Santa Barbara, Calif., ABC-CLIO, 2011. 3v. illus. index. $280.00/set. ISBN 13: 978-1-59884-296-8; 978-1-59884-297-5 (e-book).

This 3-volume set, which contains a total of over 450 articles is divided into 3 parts that are unequal in length. The first, which covers all of volume 1 and half of volume 2, contains information on about 250 films. The second, which involves the rest of volume 2 and about one-third of volume 3, has entries on about 130 film people. The third, the remainder of volume 3, contains approximately 70 topical articles. Scattered throughout the text are over 200 black-and-white photographs, chiefly of stills from movies discussed. Although the editor, a faculty member at California State University at Sacramento and author of books on American history and religion, has written an impressive 40-page introduction (complete with a fine bibliography) that succinctly outlines American film history, warts and all, he, nowhere, states the rationale behind the set, or gives an indication of its intended scope or criteria for selection of material. One, therefore, must resort to the dust-jacket blurb that says that the set "focuses on the relationship between American society and movies and filmmaking in the United States."

The articles in part 1 are arranged alphabetically by film title and average about a page or two in length. Very important films get longer treatment (e.g., *Citizen Kane* weighs in at six pages). The coverage extends from *The Great Train Robbery* of 1903 through titles from early 2000 like *Brokeback Mountain* and *Crash*. The classics and popular favorites are well represented; however, given the work's purpose, it seems difficult to justify the presence of such titles as the Harry Potter series, or the French films *Breathless* and *The 400 Blows*. In a narrative form, these entries outline the film's history, mention key personnel involved, give a brief plot summary, and describe the film's significance. All of the entries in the set end with a brief, current bibliography (books only) and the author's name. Contributors are listed in volume 3, with, unfortunately, only an academic institution for identification—no mention of rank, department (one assumes they are faculty), or other qualifications.

The profiles included in part 2 are also about 1 or 2 pages in length with key personnel given longer entries (Hitchcock gets seven pages). They are equally divided in number between stars like Garbo, Keaton (both Buster and Diane), Gable, and Monroe and important producers and directors from both the past (e.g., Griffin, DeMille, Cukor) and the present (e.g., Scorsese, the Coen Brothers, Ang Lee).

These director entries also include a selective filmography. Movie moguls like the Warner Brothers, or production members (e.g., film composers) are not included. The last, and perhaps the most interesting part of the set, explores Hollywood history through a variety of topics that include articles on various genres (e.g., westerns, gangster films, coming of age films, sports films), treatment of various minorities (unfortunately, Hispanics are not included), technical topics (e.g., color, cinematography, screenplays), social topics like politics and religion in film, and such general topics as the Academy Awards, the Hays Office, and the Sundance Film Festival. There are no entries for the depiction of various aspects of American family life or specific historical events in film.

Obviously, however, this set contains a number of strengths in coverage. These are marred somewhat by a lack of user-friendly organization. For example, the cross-referencing among the parts is incomplete or often absent; the thorough, 86-page subject/title/person index (which is for some reason is completely repeated in each of the volumes) gives page numbers but not volume numbers; and the table of contents (again repeated in each volume) does not indicate the beginning and end of each volume. Much of the material covered in this set is already available in less expensive formats. Two examples, Scott Siegal's *The Encyclopedia of Hollywood* (see ARBA 2005, entry 1199) and Robert Sklar's less current *Movie-Made America: A Cultural History of American Movies* (Vintage, 1994). Nevertheless, this set is recommended for large reference collections and those specializing in film studies.—**John T. Gillespie**

P

371.   Robinson, Mark A. **Encyclopedia of Television Theme Songs.** Jefferson, N.C., McFarland, 2011. 199p. index. $95.00pa. ISBN 13: 978-0-7864-6517-0.

Robinson has a lot to offer for those interested in television trivia and, especially, nostalgic for the television of their youth in his descriptions of nearly 1,000 television themes, both with and without lyrics. The entries, arranged alphabetically by program title, consist of network, years aired, name, composer, and, sometimes, performer of theme, cast of program, and brief description of program and what is most notable about its theme music. *Absolutely Fabulous*, for example, opens with "This Wheel's on Fire," composed by Bob Dylan and the Band's Rick Danko but performed by Julie Driscoll and Adrian Edmundson. The tune, Robinson explains, captures the protagonists' flower-power youth and their penchant for destructiveness. He also mentions other performers who have recorded the song. *Have Gun—Will Travel* is interesting because it has two themes: opening with an instrumental piece by the great film composer Bernard Herrmann and closing with "The Ballad of Paladin," sung by Johnny Western and written by Western, Sam Rolfe, the program's creator, and Richard Boone, its star. Robinson offers many such tidbits, but his title promises more than he delivers. He claims his encyclopedia includes "most of the classics," but among the missing are Rolfe Kent's ironically peppy introduction for *Dexter* and Alabama 3's "Woke Up This Morning," which gave *The Sopranos* one of the most famous theme songs of all time. Robinson describes the themes of many less-well-known cable shows. There is a short appendix of compilations of television themes on CD, an eight-title bibliography, and a name and title index.—**Michael Adams**

P

372.   Terrace, Vincent. **Encyclopedia of Television Shows, 1925 Through 2010.** 2d ed. Jefferson, N.C., McFarland, 2011. 3v. index. $145.00pa./set. ISBN 13: 978-0-7864-6477-7; 978-0-7864-8641-0 (e-book).

Television historian Vincent Terrace's current title, *Encyclopedia of Television Shows, 1925 through 2010*, is an update of his *Encyclopedia of Television Shows, 1925 through 2007* (see ARBA 2009, entry 1065). Now in three volumes and slightly larger in size, this title remains the most comprehensive resource for information regarding American television programs.

The 10,500 alphabetically arranged entries of varying lengths contain the following details for each show: running dates, genre (e.g., comedy, crime drama, talk, adult, reality), channel, brief plot summary, and cast (e.g., announcers, assistants, hostesses and models typically used in game shows such as *The Price is Right*). Some entries contain the specific air dates for pilots, opening lines, background for setting and characters, and music; original titles are listed with *see* references for new titles and spin-offs are identified. Unaired programs are also included as well as selective international programs rebroadcast on U.S. channels (e.g., *The Benny Hill Show*, *Absolutely Fabulous*). Noteworthy entries include experimental programs broadcast from 1925 through 1946 and original programming aired on the Internet. A name index concludes volume 3.

Terrace's research and dedication to American television programs are illustrated in his attention to detail. Serious researchers in the field of television studies who require specific and reliable data as well as the average television viewer who enjoys a nostalgic look at television programs of olden days will consult this resource. Every library needs this title on its reference shelf.—**Alice Crosetto**

C, P

373.   Webb, Graham. **The Animated Film Encyclopedia: A Complete Guide to American Shorts, Features and Sequences, 1900-1999.** 2d ed. Jefferson, N.C., McFarland, 2011. 509p. index. $125.00pa. ISBN 13: 978-0-7864-4985-9.

There are over 7,000 entries in this encyclopedia that focuses on animated shorts, sequences, and feature films. A very brief introduction details the updated material since the book's first publication in 1979, briefly mentioning the inclusion of CGI films as well as films that have been rediscovered. Each entry contains production information, date, running time, and a very short synopsis. Voice credits are included where possible. Most entries are brief with the exception of modern films and shorts, which tend to feature larger production crew listings. The entries cover not only hand drawn animated works, but live films that have animated components. This update also encompasses CGI animated films that were introduced in the 1980s. It should be noted that this reference work focuses on cinematic animation and not productions for television.—**Brian J. Sherman**

Handbooks and Yearbooks

C, P

374.   Eckhardt, Ned. **Documentary Filmmakers Handbook.** Jefferson, N.C., McFarland, 2012. 196p. illus. index. $49.95pa. ISBN 13: 978-0-7864-6043-4.

This handbook could serve as a textbook or a reference for student filmmakers, those trying to break into the film industry, or professional documentary filmmakers. The author, a documentary filmmakers and founder of the television and documentary programs at New Jersey's Rowan University, has organized the book into three logical parts: Preproduction; Field and Studio Production; and Postproduction. The book covers such topics as project organization and design, film shooting techniques and aesthetics, production equipment, effective storytelling, ethics and fair use law, and funding. The author has included interviews with several leading documentary filmmakers, including Arnold Shapiro (*Scared Straight*) and Paul Gallagher (*Behind the Music*). Along with conversational text and plenty of white space and bullet lists, the author has provided sample proposals; log sheets; black-and-white photographs; and a bibliography of books, documentaries, Websites, and more. This work will be a useful addition in college and academic libraries with film schools as well as public libraries needing this type of information for their clientele.—**Anita Zutis**

C, P

375.   **Magill's Cinema Annual 2012: A Survey of the films of 2011.** Farmington Hills, Mich., Gale/ Cengage Learning, 2011. 600p. index. $198.00. ISBN 13: 978-1-55862-833-5.

The 2012 edition of *Magill's Cinema Annual* continues to offer an in-depth retrospective for over 250 domestic and foreign films released in the United States. Designed for film enthusiasts, students, and the entertainment industry as a single source of information on the theatrical releases of 2011, these guides' features include extensive credits, awards and nominations (including the Golden Raspberries), obituaries, nine indexes each, a bibliography of selected film books for the year, and most importantly critical reviews with author bylines.

Entries are alphabetically arranged by film title and each review contains up to 16 items of information, ranging from taglines and film reviews to trivia and film quotes. A number of separate indexes allow the reader to quickly scan through the guide for specific directors, screenwriters, or subject matter. Of particular strength is the cumulative title index, including all of the films reviewed in the previous volumes of the series.

The guide's only weakness comes from the list of contributing reviewers, many of whom are listed as freelance reviewers or publishing professionals. Analysis from noted film reviewers such as *Chicago Sun-Times* film critic Roger Ebert, among others, are cited in the individual film entry, but the full review is left to the series contributors. Although many of the contributing reviewers will not be well known to even the most dedicated of moviegoers, the newest installment in the ongoing series is still a valuable overview of the year in film. This volume is recommended for any academic library supporting a film studies program.—**Josh Eugene Finnell**

C, P

376.   Pool, Jeannie Gayle, and H. Stephen Wright. **A Research Guide to Film and Television Music in the United States.** Lanham, Md., Scarecrow, 2011. 174p. index. $50.00. ISBN 13: 978-0-8108-7688-0.

The study of film and television music history is a relatively recent phenomenon. The authors indicate that the most significant research in this area has happened in just the last 20 years. Existing reference guides for film music research are few and far between, and this book attempts to fill that gap. A number of important areas are discussed: a brief history of film music research, sources for the study of music in silent films, the complex issues of early sound film studies, the primary sources for cue sheets and scores of film music, the cue sheet and its importance for film music research, recordings and their challenges (what a composer wrote is not always what ends up heard in the film), film music preservation and composer estates and legacies, and a comprehensive review of film music collections and archives in the United States. A very detailed and up-to-date annotated bibliography is included, along with an index. This work deserves to be placed in the reference area of all academic music libraries.—**Bradford Lee Eden**

Theater

Chronology

P

377.   Bordman, Gerald, with Richard Norton. **American Musical Theatre: A Chronicle.** 4th ed. New York, Oxford University Press, 2011. 1017p. index. $125.00. ISBN 13: 978-0-19-972970-8.

This 1,017-page reference work is the gold standard in the area of musical theater history in America. It is a season-by-season, show-by-show chronological report of the events occurring on the musical state in America. The chronology is organized into important historical eras. The prologue section deals with origins and events prior to 1866. The next section, called "Act 1," carries the reader to 1892 and eventually to "Act 7," which ends with the year 2010. Each of the eras begins with an orienting essay that leads to the show-by-show detail. There are over 1,000 musicals present in this work. Unfortunately, a certain number mentioned have completely disappeared leaving only their names.

The major known works presentations follow a pattern of name, plot synopsis, principal players, short biographies of participants, scenery and costume descriptions, and critical reactions. This history also mentions many musical and nonmusical events such as opera, review, punk rock, television, film, and more, which influenced and effected musical theater. Most of the major musical events discussed are of necessity that of Broadway and off-Broadway venues, although other cities, especially Chicago, are cited.

One useful and entertaining aspect of this chronological history is the sprinkling of many short sidebar biographies of the major players in musical theatre. The reference work opens with interesting introductions to the 1st and present 4th edition. The book contains four indexes. The first deals with citations to over 2,000 musical cited in the text. The second index references nonmusical and musical events that were the progenitors of American musicals (i.e., the opera *Carmen* is the source for the musical *Carmen Jones*). The third index cites songs, and the final index refers to people.

This volume is certainly *the* reference work that is a necessity for scholars, and a joy for all lovers of musical theater. It is highly readable. It can be read straight through for its historical narrative information or dipped into for sheer pleasure, or for researching a favorite show, singer, or director. It is packed with narrative and critical information and analysis.—**Charles Neuringer**

P
378.   Hischak, Thomas S. **Off-Broadway Musicals since 1919: From Greenwich Village Follies to** *The Toxic Avenger.* Lanham, Md., Scarecrow, 2011. 469p. index. $75.00. ISBN 13: 978-0-8108-7771-9; 978-0-8108-7772-6 (e-book).

Previous to 1919, the theatrical activity of Broadway was exclusively dramatic as promulgated by such enterprises as The Provincetown Players, The Neighborhood Playhouse, The Washington Square Players, and other less-well-known venues. This volume chronicles the history of Off-Broadway musical theater's debut in 1919 with the opening performance of the *Greenwich Village Follies* and following its course to 2009 with *The Toxic Avenger*. This history of Off-Broadway musicals deals with 381 selected productions from the most famous (*The Fantasticks* and *Little Shop of Horrors*) to the most obscure but historically important enterprises that illustrate some innovative musical or dramatic aspect.

The text opens with an alphabetic list of Off-Broadway musicals starting with *A . . . My Name is Alice* and ending with *Zombies from Beyond*. There follows a chronological year-by-year listing of Off-Broadway musicals. This is followed by an opening general historical essay and is in turn followed by a chronological decade-by-decade list of the Off-Broadway musicals. Each entry consists of information about opening dates, performance venue, number of performances, creative personnel, and cast, and is followed by a description of the show and its historical importance.

This volume concludes with an alphabetic guide to recordings of the musicals, a bibliography, and a name and production index. These are preceded by a postscript in which the author bemoans the future of Off-Broadway theater because its very success is destroying it through roadway transfers as well as actors being recruited by cinema and television as a consequence of their off-Broadway recognition.

The present volume is exhaustive but the writing is excellent thus making it difficult to put down. It is a fun read for both scholars and fans and, not least important, it is a nostalgia trip.—**Charles Neuringer**

P
379.   Naden, Corinne J. **The Golden Age of American Musical Theatre: 1943-1965.** Lanham, Md., Scarecrow, 2011. 266p. index. $39.95. ISBN 13: 978-0-8108-7733-7.

The author, Corinne J. Naden, has written over 100 nonfiction books primarily for a juvenile audience. This volume, which unfortunately contains no illustrations, cover the part of American musical theater history the author calls "the Golden Age." It begins with March 31, 1943, the opening night of *Oklahoma* and ends with the premier of *On a Clear Day You Can See Forever* on October 17, 1965. This period of 23 years saw the twilight productions by such composers as Porter, Arlen, and Berlin; the mature woks of Jerry Herman, Frank Lesser, Lerner and Lowe, Kander and Ebb, and Block and Harnick; and the emergence of new talents like Stephen Sondheim and Cy Coleman. After a 23-page history of the Broadway musical theater (which ends in 1965), there is a list of the 183 musicals discussed in the text arranged chronologically by opening night. The body of the book consists of factual material on each of these shows arranged alphabetically by title. The amount of material given varies in length and depth depending on the importance of the show and the length of its run. For most of the shows (over three-fourth of the titles) the material is extensive and involves length of run, production credits, complete original casts lists (with roles played), a list of the show's songs, a brief synopsis, awards won, and an occasional gossipy comment. For shows considered "flops" and other shows with short runs, the material is truncated and consists chiefly of bare bones production credits without song or cast lists. The chapter, "The Golden Stars of Broadway," consists of about 200 brief (average eight lines) biographies of Broadway luminaries organized under actors, directors, composers and lyricists, and choreographers. This is followed by a list and brief history of each of the current Broadway theaters and a rundown of the most important awards and prizes associated with Broadway theater. The book ends with a useful alphabetically arranged listing of all the songs mentioned in the text followed by the show in which each originated, plus a brief general bibliography and an index of personal show names.

Although this volume contains a lot of good basic material, it faces stiff competition. The most comprehensive and widely used book on the subject is still Stanley and Kay Green's *Broadway Musicals: Show by Show* (Applause Books, 2008), which covers the subject from the beginning to the present day and contains hundreds of attractive illustrations. Perhaps the most scholarly remains Gerald Bordman's *American Musical Theater: A Chronicle* (Oxford University Press, 2010), and the most lavishly illustrated, Ken Bloom's coffee-table opus *Broadway Musicals: The 101 Greatest Shows of All Time* (Black Dog, 2004). The Naden volume, however, supplies solid, basic, and some esoteric statistical information in a well-organized, accessible format that will make it of value in medium to large theater collections.—**John T. Gillespie**

Dictionaries and Encyclopedias

C, P

380.   Fisher, James. **Historical Dictionary of Contemporary American Theater: 1930-2010.** Lanham, Md., Scarecrow, 2011. 2v. (Historical Dictionary of Literature and the Arts). $175.00/set. ISBN 13: 978-0-8108-5532-8; 978-0-8108-7950-8 (e-book).

This reference work is the third volume (and as yet only number published) in a projected set of three dictionaries dealing with the American theater from 1800 to 2010. This third volume covers the years from 1930 to 2010.

There are over 1,700 entries dealing with plays, playwrights, actors, directors, producers, designers, technical specialists, critics, agents, Broadway, Off and Off-Off Broadway, regional theaters, acting companies, publications, genres, archives, and more. Only entries referring to the legitimate theater are included here. Musical comedy, film, radio, and television are excluded from this work. The alphabetically arranged selections are restricted to those that the author feels are important and significant in some way to the history of the American theater.

The reference work opens with a fact-laden, year-by-year historical chronology. This is followed by an essay interpreting in detail the facts given in the proceeding chronology. Following this essay is the heart of this reference work, which starts on page 19 with an entry on "George Abbot" and ends on page 894 with "Catherine Zuber." A very extensive twenty-section bibliography follows the entries. These bibliographic citations are organized around such topics as "Historical and Critical Works," "Acting and Actors," and "Playwrights." No name or subject indexes are included.

A great deal of information can be found in this work. But the reader must realize that such information is limited to the author's opinions of what is important or significant. This is to be expected when there is essentially only one contributor. The lack of name or subject indexes (or any other kind of index such as a play index) limits the accessibility of information. The author does provide an extensive cross-referencing system.

This is a well-written book and is easy and fun to read. It is a good starting point for researchers as well as lovers of the theater. One looks forward to seeing and reading the two as yet unpublished volumes.—**Charles Neuringer**

28 Philosophy and Religion

Philosophy

C

381. Sandywell, Barry. **Dictionary of Visual Discourse: A Dialectical Lexicon of Terms.** Burlington, Vt., Ashgate Publishing, 2011. 702p. $225.00. ISBN 13: 978-1-4094-0188-9.

With the increased emphasis on visual understanding today it becomes critical to have a work that discusses the interrelatedness of image and text for completeness of the topic. The work in review is a step along the path in that discussion and understanding.

With three lengthy prefatory essays on historicism, methodology, and thematic orientation setting the context for the ensuing dictionary of terms on visual discourse, the dictionary itself is arranged in a standard alphabetic arrangement with multiple cross-references to allow the user to chart a path most appropriate to themselves in navigating the work. As the author states, the cross-references allow for hypertext in a traditional linear, static organization of a conventional dictionary. In the front matter is a list of lexiconical terms used in the dictionary portion of the work; an unusual, but useful feature for quick look-up of the material covered in the work. Over 900 entries are listed. The entries are concepts or ideas, many of which may be initially stated in one word, such as *void*, while many others require a more extensive statement, such as reflexivity as the irony of unintended consequences or languages as vehicle of representations. Most entries are from a half page to a page in length with a few of paragraph length with a brief bibliography included at the end of the discussion. A much more extensive bibliography for further exploration and consumption of the material covered in the volume follows the dictionary portion of the work.

This work will appeal most readily to those working in the visual, textual, and philosophical areas of knowledge and exploration. It will be of special interest to faculty and those pursing graduate studies in those disciplines. Although presented in a traditional dictionary format, the user will find that mere consultation for definition of a term leads to an extensive reading of the work that may imply some other location than the ready-reference section of the library.—**Gregory Curtis**

Religion

General Works

P

382. Brockman, Norbert C. **Encyclopedia of Sacred Places.** 2d ed. Santa Barbara, Calif., ABC-CLIO, 2011. 2v. illus. index. $173.00/set. ISBN 13: 978-1-59884-654-6; 978-1-59884-655-3 (e-book).

These two volumes, revised and updated, provide the reader with approximately 400 entries, both religious and secular, of places around the globe considered to be sacred. These are places where the seeker encounters the holy and, as the author comments, "experiences a call to move beyond the self." The sacred places described in these two volumes are categorized by nine general headings: places sanctified by events in the life of a prophet, saint, or deity; sites of miracles and healing; places of apparitions or visions; locales dedicated to special religious rituals; tombs of saints; shrines of a miraculous statue, icon, or relic; the ancestral or mythical abodes of the gods; places that manifest the energies or mystical powers of nature; and places marked by evil that have been a turning point for a religious community. The reader will be pleased that the author has included additional references at the end of each entry, further reference works for research, and an adequate glossary of technical terminology. Also of benefit to the reader are maps covering the continents of the world and the locations of the sites referenced in the two volumes.

Written with clarity and precision, replete with a significant number of pictures, and cross-referencing, the author completes these volumes with two worthwhile appendixes—a list of sacred sites by religious tradition (entries listed by country), and entries on the UNESCO World Heritage list. Any library, including public school, college (private or public), or public library, will want to have these volumes included among its collection. They provide the interested reader and the student with a foundation for going beyond the obvious and digging deeper into a site or subject of interest.—**Joseph P. Hester**

C, P

383.   Chryssides, George D. **Historical Dictionary of New Religious Movements.** 2d ed. Lanham, Md., Scarecrow, 2011. 415p. (Historical Dictionaries of Religions, Philosophies, and Movements). $80.00. ISBN 13: 978-0-8108-6194-7; 978-0-8108-7967-6 (e-book).

The 2d edition of this resource (first published in 2001), updates and adds new religious movements that have occurred during the past 10 years, updates older entries with new information that has come forward, and provides an introduction in which the author addresses the phenomena of new religions. New religious movements are often misnamed "cults" and present an enormous array of worldwide organizations. To bring together in one volume such a varied group of religious data is difficult and nearly impossible to make complete. New religious movements may be conservative, radical, or heretical within traditions, or present a totally new religious reality. More than 600 groups are defined and bibliographies provided. The entries address key figures, ideas, themes, and places. The question of when is a movement "new" underlies the presentation. This volume is helpful for quick reference questions and the bibliography will come in handy to some. The chronological pages are useful for contextualizing. This is one of the few Historical Dictionaries that contains an index; a very useful feature. General students of culture and religion will find this useful and scholars may find quick references for unfamiliar religious traditions.—**Linda L. Lam-Easton**

C, S

384.   **World Religions: Belief, Culture, and Controversy. http://www.abc-clio.com/Previews/index. aspx.** [Website]. Santa Barbara, Calif., ABC-CLIO, 2011. Price negotiated by site. Date reviewed: 2012.

This electronic resource from ABC-CLIO is designed specifically with teachers and students in mind and can be purchased at the middle and high school level, or at the more advanced academic level. It is a new addition to ABC-CLIO's suite of online databases, which focus on history, military, pop culture, and social studies. The design of these databases has recently been revamped to provide an even more student-friendly design, allowing user to research assigned topics, search for resources to support a topic, or prepare for a class discussion or debate. This Website focuses on world religions, a timely topic considering the study of religions within the various cultures is a key element to understanding their politics, history, and social make up. More than 50 religious overviews are covered here, including Christianity, Islam, Buddhism, agnosticism, and more. Its many interactive features allow for statistical comparisons between countries. New content, which is continually be added, will keep students abreast of how religion is affecting current events across all regions. The essays on each topic are thorough and will be easy for students to understand, and the photographs and maps are clear.

Searching this site is straightforward. Along with the option to search by keyword or perform an advanced search, users can also click on a specific religion to browse its content. The middle and high school version has a strong focus on resources that will enhance student research, and the essays are written to engage students in critical thinking and forming reasoned arguments. The academic version has content provided from top scholars, and includes essays that serve as companions to lectures. The articles promote scholarly debate and will engage more advanced users in critical thinking.

The *World Religions* Website is a remarkable tool that will give students a new appreciation for the role religion has in shaping history, politics, and society as a whole. They will be able to see how various religions interconnect as well as where there are distinct differences between them. The use of clearly written essays, topics that promote debate and critical thinking, and an abundance of photographs will appeal to students from the middle grades up. This site should be considered by all types of libraries and libraries are encouraged to take advantage of the publisher's free trial offer to see if this site will be worthwhile in their library.—**Benet Steven Exton**

Bible Studies

Handbooks and Yearbooks

C, P

385.   **Concordia's Complete Bible Handbook for Students.** Edward A. Engelbrecht, ed. St. Louis, Mo., Concordia, 2011. 449p. illus. $23.99pa. ISBN 13: 978-0-7586-2968-5.

This book is a one-stop introduction and ready-reference to the Bible that is intended for use by high school and undergraduate age students. The book begins with an introduction that addresses such questions as: Who wrote the Bible?; How is the Bible organized?; How do you use the various translations?; How reliable is the information in the Bible?; and What is the best approach to reading the Bible? The bulk of the guide provides surveys of the 66 books of the Bible; these are organized by sections, such as The Book of Moses, The Books of the Prophets, The Time Between the Testaments, The Gospels and Acts, and The General Epistles and Revelation. The work is supplemented with charts, illustrations, maps, outlines, and timelines. There are numerous diagrams and genealogy charts included, which will prove very useful for those new to the Bible. This book is ideal for personal study of the Bible as well as a group study. Public and undergraduate libraries would find it to be the most useful as it will answer basic questions about the Bible and is simple to use for general research.—**Alice Crosetto**

P

386.   **The Eerdmans Companion to the Bible.** Gordon D. Fee and Robert L. Hubbard Jr., eds. Grand Rapids, Mich., William B. Eerdmans, 2011. 834p. illus. $40.00. ISBN 13: 978-0-8028-3823-0.

The publisher's stated purpose for this work is to "serve as a guide to the Word." Ideally, the reader would approach the study of Scripture "with the Bible in one hand and the Companion in the other." Likewise, one of the contributors to *The Eerdmans Companion to the Bible* informs the reader that "we come [to Scripture] not so much to retrieve facts or to gain information, but to be formed." To that end, general editors Gordon D. Fee (Regent College) and Robert L. Hubbard Jr. (North Park Theological Seminary) have sought to provide the reader the results of biblical scholarship that is recent, "responsible," and light on the theological jargon so that "modern readers [will] benefit." Perusing the list of 65 contributors, one cannot help notice that only two are affiliated with schools in the Northeast.

The main body of the *Companion* is preceded by a series of essays addressing topics that include biblical inspiration and authority as well as the transmission and translation of the sacred text. This is followed by more than 650 pages of straightforward commentary in Bible book order from Genesis to Revelation. The commentary, which reads more like synopsis, is in easy-on-the-eyes, two-column format. Headings with chapter and verse cross-references nicely break up the text into sense paragraphs. All of the commentary is by Connie Gundry Tappy, a freelance author and editor. Thematic articles of one to six pages in length, each signed by one of the contributor-subject specialists and positioned at key sections within the commentary, help provide context to that particular section. The Book of Psalms, for example, elicits articles on "Music and Musical Instruments" and "The Psalms in Worship."

Lists of works for further reading are provided at the end of each article. The articles stand out as their pages are in a soft gray. In fact, the whole work, heavily illustrated with black-and-white photographs, drawings, charts, and maps, is in nuts-and-bolts gray scale. The *Companion* ends with a glossary of terms, "a Nations and People" section, a gazetteer of places, index of subjects, and finally with an index of scripture and other ancient sources.

Similar guides or companions to the Bible abound, of which, *The Cambridge Companion to the Bible* (see ARBA 98, entry 1377), *The Illustrated Guide to the Bible* (see ARBA 96, entry 1459), and *The Oxford Companion to the Bible* (see ARBA 93, entry 1545) are only a few. Readers of *The Eerdmans Companion to the Bible*, especially those in public libraries and Bible colleges, will find the thematic articles that have been provided by the contributors of particular interest for the light they shed on the ancient text.—**Anthony F. Verdesca Jr.**

Buddhism

C

387. Li-tian, Fang. **China's Buddhist Culture.** Farmington Hills, Mich., Gale/Cengage Learning Asia, 2010. 160p. index. $150.00. ISBN 13: 978-9-814-28142-3.

This handbook is designed to aid the research o f undergraduates interested in Chinese religions and philosophies. It looks closely at the historical evolution of Chinese Buddhism and the ancient books, records, and doctrines it is based on. Famous historic and culture sites related to Buddhism are covered as well. Another key aspect of this religion that the author focuses on is its influence on Chinese politics, ethics, philosophy, literature, art, and customs. The author succinctly summarizes how Buddhism has influenced all aspects of Chinese culture. How Buddhism relates to Confucianism and Taoism is also discussed in depth. The author is a leading scholar of Buddhism in mainland China and does a good job of covering each of the intended topics. This will be a valuable resource in university libraries with extensive religion collections.—**Shannon Graff Hysell**

Christianity

C, P

388. Abbott, Margery Post, Mary Ellen Chijioke, Pink Dandelion, and John William Oliver Jr. **Historical Dictionary of the Friends (Quakers).** 2d ed. Lanham, Md., Scarecrow, 2012. 574p. (Historical Dictionaries of Religions, Philosophies, and Movements). $99.00. ISBN 13: 978-0-8108-6857-1.

This expanded 2d edition is an excellent starting point for anyone interested in the Religious Society of Friends, or Quakers. The four editors are all or have been Quakers, and all have been deeply involved in the life of the group in Great Britain, the United States, and Africa. For a religious body that today numbers less than 340,000 worldwide, Quakers have exerted extraordinary influence and are known the world over for their humanitarian work. Plain dress and peaceful behavior notwithstanding, seventeenth-century Quakers were seen as radical heretics, owing largely to the doctrine of the inward Light, the presence of Christ in all people, young and old, women and men. Such a notion struck at the heart of Calvinistic predestination and pointed toward a society in which all people were equal. For such views four Quakers were hanged on Boston Common in 1659. As time progressed the Quakers suffered internal dissension over matters of theology and church governance. Numerous schisms resulted, eventually bringing considerable diversity. While most contemporary Quakers believe in the saving grace of Jesus, some as readily see the Light in all religions, or even in people of no religious affiliation. Some Quakers still gather in silent worship, others in weekly services resembling those of mainline Protestants.

This, volume in the Historical Dictionaries of Religions, Philosophies, and Movements series, follows a prescribed format. An informative chronology beginning in 1624, the birth date of founder George Fox, and ending in 2012, with the sixth world gathering of Friends to be held in Kenya. A clearly written introductory essay tracing the origins, development, and beliefs of the movement precedes the dictionary, which comprises almost three-quarters of the work. Aiming at a general audience, the editors focus on persons, places, events, associations, and economic, cultural, and religious activities. One finds entries ranging from a line or two to two pages or more on topics from abolition, Susan B. Anthony, heaven and hell, and Shakers to sexuality, temperance, war tax resistance, and women. An exhaustive index affords easy access to this wealth of material, while an extensive bibliography leads serious students to additional sources. High school and university libraries should consider this volume for their reference collections.—**John W. Storey**

C, P

389.   Gassmann, Günther, with Duane H. Larson and Mark W. Oldenburg. **Historical Dictionary of Lutheranism.** 2d ed. Lanham, Md., Scarecrow, 2011. 530p. (Historical Dictionaries of Religions, Philosophies, and Movements). $90.00. ISBN 13: 978-0-8108-7232-5; 978-0-8108-7482-4 (e-book).

A concise introduction to the history of a large Protestant denomination, this volume includes a updated chronology, hundreds of signed entries, a handy appendix listing Lutheran church membership by continent and country in 2009, and a substantial bibliography. Within individual entries, the many cross-references, conveniently printed in bold typeface, will help readers negotiate a very useful book identifying important church events, leaders, institutions, and issues since 1517. Gassmann (retired after a distinguished career with the Lutheran World Federation and the World Council of Churches and now a visiting professor at the Lutheran Theological Seminary in Gettysburg, Pennsylvania) composed about two-thirds of the entries, while his able co-authors, Larson (former President of Wartburg Theological Seminary in Dubuque, Iowa) and Oldenburg (dean and professor at the Lutheran Theological Seminary in Gettysburg, Pennsylvania) produced the remaining articles. The 2d edition includes an updated chronology, updates and corrections for most of the original entries, several new entries, and an updated bibliography and list of Lutheran Churches.

Theological libraries that own Julius Bodensieck's *The Encyclopedia of the Lutheran Church* (out of print) and Paul D. Peterson's *Luther and Lutheranism: A Bibliography Selected from the ATLA Religion Database* (out of print) should acquire both this new dictionary and Donald L. Huber's *World Lutheranism: A Selected Bibliography for English Readers* (see ARBA 2001, entry 1294). The dictionary's broad scope and clear style make it a fine addition for academic or public library religion collections as well.—**Julienne L. Wood**

C, P

390.   Picken, Stuart D. B. **Historical Dictionary of Calvinism.** Lanham, Md., Scarecrow, 2012. 261p. (Historical Dictionaries of Religions, Philosophies, and Movements). $80.00. ISBN 13: 978-0-8108-7224-0; 978-0-8108-7471-8 (e-book).

Like all introductory dictionaries on aspects of intellectual history, Picken's volume compresses a great deal of information about Calvinism into a handy space and is necessarily selective in its choice of topics. But for general readers, students, and those new to Calvinism, this book is a good start. A chronology of relevant historical events spans the years 65 to 2011, and the readable introductory essay (which might have included boldface cross-references) summarizes Calvin's life and his influence upon subsequent eras, though without explaining the essentials of Calvin's theology; for these, one must consult the rather brief entry on "Five Points of Calvinism." Helpful citations to Calvin's Institutes are given for many concepts (e.g., Ascension, Christology) but not for all (e.g., Atonement, Eschatology). Entries link Calvin to theologians both ancient (e.g., Oecolampadius, Beza, Luther) and modern (e.g.,

Tillich, Barth, Niebuhr) and to more denominational figures (e.g., B. B. Warfield, Cornelius Van Til), though the emphasis can be uneven. For example, there are three paragraphs on Woodrow Wilson but three sentences for Dietrich Bonhoeffer. Scholars will most appreciate the very well-organized 43-page concluding bibliography, an excellent springboard for further study.—**Christopher Baker**

Hinduism

C, P

391. Long, Jeffery D. **Historical Dictionary of Hinduism.** new ed. Lanham, Md., Scarecrow, 2012. 365p. (Historical Dictionaries of Religions, Philosophies, and Movements). $75.00. ISBN 13: 978-0-8108-6764-2; 978-0-8108-7960-7 (e-book).

Originating in India over 4,000 years ago, Hinduism is practiced today by over 900,000,000 people and is the world's third largest religion. Due to the widespread diaspora of Indians across the globe, Hinduism is becoming part of the fabric of society in regions of the world far beyond its homeland. According to the editor's foreword, this title is a completely new edition of the work originally published by Scarecrow in 1997, written by Bruce M. Sullivan (see ARBA 98, entry 1392).

An opening reader's note explains the diacritical marks used in transliterating words from Sanskrit and other Indic languages (which typically have about 50 letters) into English, as well as their pronunciation. A brief list of acronyms and abbreviations is included, as is an eight-page historical chronology. A 22-page introductory essay traces the history of Hinduism from its origins in the Indus Valley Civilization of antiquity to its interactions with the West and other developments in modern times, and discusses some of the reasons for its continuing vitality today.

The topics covered by the dictionary's main body of entries include religious and philosophical concepts, key historical figures and movements, deities, important scriptures, and significant places. In addition to Hinduism, entries on related faiths such as Jainism and Sikhism are included. There are typically about four entries per page, although some entries are as long as two and a half pages, such that on Mohandas K. Gandhi. Entries may include cross-references (in bold) and *see also* references. Biographical entries include the subject's dates of birth and death. The volume is rather sparsely illustrated with black-and-white photographs, mainly of works of art depicting deities and interior shots of temples illustrating altars and pujas (rituals). A bibliographic essay and an up-to-date selective bibliography of primary sources in Sanskrit and other Indic languages, translated primary sources, modern secondary works in English, and Internet sources completes the volume. This title is recommended for purchase by academic as well as medium and large public libraries.—**Kenneth M. Frankel**

Islam

C, S

392. Stokes, Jamie. **The Muslim World.** New York, Facts on File, 2011. 379p. index. (Global Issues). $45.00. ISBN 13: 978-0-8160-8086-1.

The Muslim World is part of Facts on File's Global Issues series and is divided into three parts. The first part outlines the issues pertaining to the topic. The second reproduces excerpts of primary documents. The last provides statistical information, thumbnail biographies of relevant people, contact information of relevant organizations, and an extensive bibliography. A chronology of events, extensive glossary, and index complete the book.

Part 1 is composed of three chapters. Chapter 1 provides background information pertaining to the Muslim World (difficulties of defining it, some of the issues it faces, and a brief history). Chapter 2 focuses on the United States, specifically on Muslims living in the United States and U.S. interests in the Middle East. The primary focus is on recent areas of conflict. Chapter 3 is titled "Global Perspectives" and apart from a section addressing the Taliban, it looks at United Arab Emirates, Indonesia, and Algeria.

Part 2 is composed of two chapters. The first reproduces documents that pertain to the United States (either relating to Muslims living in the United States or to U.S. policies). The second focuses on international documents, but the primary focus is restricted to the countries highlighted in chapter 2 and the Taliban. Documents that were written during the time of the Prophet Mohamed are not reproduced. After Umar's Covenant (637), the next chronologically is Balfour declaration (1917) with no mention of documents from pre-modern Muslim Empires.

The first chapter in part 3 provides guidelines for writing a paper on the Muslim World (these guidelines would be most useful to high school students). The remaining chapters provide reference material for additional research. The most valuable part of this work is an extensive list of reference material. However, the text's scope is narrower than the reference materials suggest.—**Muhammed Hassanali**

Judaism

P

393.   **The Eerdmans Dictionary of Early Judaism.** John J. Collins and Daniel C. Harlow, eds. Grand Rapids, Mich., William B. Eerdmans, 2010. 1360p. illus. $95.00. ISBN 13: 978-0-8028-2549-0.

This dictionary emphasizes Second Temple Judaism, from the time of Alexander the Great (332 B.C.E.) to the Bar Kokhba Revolt (132-135 C.E.). It collects 13 major essays, 520 alphabetic entries, and numerous illustrations and maps. After an Alphabetical List of Entries (pp. xix-xxiii) and a Topical List of Entries (pp. xxiv-xxix) are a list of abbreviations, and a brief chronology from 525 B.C.E. to 200 C.E. The essays (pp. 1-290) cover scholarship of early Judaism, Jewish history from Alexander to Hadrian, the diaspora, Hebrew Bible, Dead Sea Scrolls, and early Christianity.

Sources in the entries include historical research, the Old and New Testaments, Apocryphal literature, Dead Sea Scrolls, and historians such as Josephus. The Qumran scrolls are listed in the topical list by the cave number (11Q13), and as dictionary entries by the title of the scroll (Melchizedek Scroll). Entries describe people of the era (e.g., Alexander the Great, Cyrus the Great), groups (e.g., Essenes, Pharisees, Roman emperors), writings important at the time (e.g., Ezra, Book of; Revelation, Book of; the gospels), places (e.g., Jerusalem, Rome, Galilee), and certain rites (e.g., Sabbath, Sacrifices and Offerings). There are entries for biblical figures that are outside the timeline: Abraham, Enoch, Moses, are treated in the way that their stories are interpreted in the literature and culture of Second Temple Judaism. Activities (Creation, pp. 496-500) are approached from the viewpoints of Genesis, Apocrypha, Pseudepigrapha, Philo of Alexandria, Josephus, the New Testament, and Rabbinic literature. Since they were concurrent with early Judaism, several Christian writings and personages are treated, including Jesus of Nazareth (pp. 803-808). Several entries include extensive bibliographies.

The volume employs a solid syndetic structure that allows users to easily find the entries. For example, if searching for "Booths, Festival of" or "Tabernacles, Feast of" users are directed to "Festivals and Holy Days" (pp. 636-645). One downside is that essays and entries do not reference each other. The entry for Antiochus IV (pp. 338-339) presents several details, but the essay "Jewish History from Alexander to Hadrian" also presents information on the Roman monarch (pp. 32-34). The dictionary proves useful to a wide cross-section of users, from those seeking basic information in the entries, to the highly detailed essays, with specific Qumran documents cited. Some entries display highly detailed lists as well, particularly in relation to the Qumran sources. Hebrew and Greek words are Romanized for easy usage as well.—**Ralph Hartsock**

Part IV
SCIENCE
AND
TECHNOLOGY

29 Science and Technology in General

Catalogs and Collections

C

394.   **AccessScience. http://www.accessscience.com/.** [Website]. Price negotiated by site. Date reviewed: 2011.

This is the McGraw-Hill Encyclopedia of Science and Technology on the Web. It provides full access to articles, dictionary terms, and hundreds of research updates in all areas of science and technology. Applied Science and Technology Abstracts (ASTA)—1983 to the present; abstracts 1994 to the present. Applied Science and Technology Abstracts covers core English-language scientific and technical publications. Topics include engineering, acoustics, chemistry, computers, metallurgy, physics, plastics, telecommunications, transportations, and waste management. Periodical coverage includes trade and industrial publication, journals issued by professional and technical societies, and specialized subject periodicals, as well as special issues such as buyers' guides, directories, and conference proceedings.—**James E. Bobick**

C

395.   **HSTM: History of Science, Technology, and Medicine.** [Website]. Dublin, Ohio, OCLC. Price negotiated by site. Date reviewed: 2011.

This resource contains references to journal articles, chapters, and reviews within the fields of general science, technology, and medicine. It covers the influence of these fields on society and culture from prehistory to the present. Citations reflect the contents of nearly 9,500 journals. Covering a vast array of topics, from agricultural sciences to anthropology, medical sciences to military technology, the site can be searched by key word or browsed by subject. The site links to a number of other scholarly databases, including ABI/INFORM, Electronic Collections Online, and Wilson Select Plus. It will be useful to a wide range of science historians.—**James E. Bobick**

S

396.   **Science Online. http://www.infobase.com/.** [Website]. New York, Facts on File. Price negotiated by site. Date reviewed: 2012.

S

397.   **Today's Science. http://www.infobase.com/.** [Website]. New York, Facts on File. Price negotiated by site. Date reviewed: 2012.

Facts on File's *Science Online* has been around for several years and has received numerous awards based on its usefulness in the educational setting. The content is organized by subject area and has been written and organized according to national and state science education standards for middle and high school students. Users can search thousands of entries on science and technology subjects. There are some 8,300 diagrams, illustrations, and images that liven up the text. Additionally, users will have access to biographies of leaders in science, definitions of scientific terms, a timeline of scientific history (which can be searched by specific topic or time period), and experiments and activities. The site features more than 500 videos and animations that will further engage young learners. The database can be searched with a basic search or by using Boolean search capabilities and results can be printed, e-mailed, or saved.

Science Online complements Facts on File's other science database, *Today's Science*, which focuses more on current topics and new discoveries in science. It provides nearly 20 years worth of information on the developments in biology, chemistry, environmental science, space sciences, physics, and technology. New information is added on a weekly basis to keep the database current. The database is designed for middle and high school students and the articles are written to support classroom curriculum according to the National Science Education Standards. Along with news articles there are encyclopedic articles on specific topics, biographical entries on notable scientists, a pop-up glossary, links to related entries, and a "Need a Research Topic?" feature that provides suggestions for their own scientific research. Designed with classroom use in mind, there are suggested activities, assignments, and research tools for teachers and media specialists.

Both of these sites are accessible and easy to use and students are likely to find research on these sites fun and even interesting. They are solid science sources for school media centers that present scientific topics in an engaging way.—**Shannon Graff Hysell**

Handbooks and Yearbooks

C

398.   Day, Robert A., and Nancy Sakaduski. **Scientific English: A Guide for Scientists and Other Professionals.** 3d ed. Santa Barbara, Calif., Greenwood Press/ABC-CLIO, 2011. 225p. index. $55.00. ISBN 13: 978-0-31339-173-6.

Scientific English: A Guide for Scientists and Other Professionals is intended to "provide some simple guidelines to help you improve your knowledge of English and your ability to communicate scientific information in English" (preface). Twenty themed chapters and three appendixes offer information in the areas of writing style, name words and action words, redundancies and jargon, phrases and clauses, voice, person and tense, punctuation, and problem words and expressions. This revised edition updates sections and examples written in the 1995 edition, and includes new sections on self-editing and electronic media.

Chapters are presented in narrative form, with the occasional cartoon added for a bit of humor. Each chapter has several subheadings, headlining the topic being addressed. There are ample illustrative examples of correct language and style within each chapter. Famous quotations are also included as examples. Chapters average 3-10 pages in length and cover the topics succinctly yet completely. Appendixes include information on proper punctuation use, problem words and expressions, and words and expressions to avoid. There is a short glossary of grammar terms, a notes section, and an index.

There is great improvement in layout and format in the new edition of *Scientific English* when compared to the 2d edition. Overall, this is a handy resource for scientists and researchers who write. Consider adding this book to the general collection rather than the reference collection.—**Caroline L. Gilson**

P, S

399.   Gates, Phil. **Nature Got There First: Inventions Inspired by Nature.** Boston, Kingfisher/Houghton Mifflin, 2010. 64p. illus. index. $16.95. ISBN 13: 978-0-7534-6410-6.

Young and older readers will be encouraged to look closely and think in different ways as they peruse information about inventions inspired by both natural and physical science. Tree frogs have a kind of antifreeze in their blood which allows them to survive freezing winters; this is similar to the antifreeze used in engines. Velcro fasteners were inspired by hooked seed heads of burrs clinging to the clothes of a Swiss engineer. Pincers and tweezers, fungus and compost, magnetism and gravity, light and electricity, jet propulsion and buoyancy are among chapters useful for curricular support. The work includes a glossary and index. Interest in mathematics and science combine well for both research and browsing.—**Ann Bryan Nelson**

P, S

400.   **The Handy Science Answer Book.** 4th ed. Compiled by the Carnegie Library of Pittsburgh. Canton, Mich., Visible Ink Press, 2011. 679p. illus. index. 421.95pa. ISBN 13: 978-1-57859-321-7.

The useful *Handy Science Answer Book* contains 13 excellent chapters: General Science, Mathematics, and Technology; Physics and Chemistry; Astronomy and Space; Earth; Climate and Weather; Minerals, Metals, and Other Materials; Energy; Environment; Biology; Plant World; Animal World; Human Body; and Health and Medicine. A topic from the General Science, Mathematics, and Technology is computers. A subject in Physics and Chemistry is electricity and magnetism. A section from Astronomy and Space chapter is universe. An area covered in Earth chapter is air. Information in the chapter Climate and Weather includes wind. The Minerals, Metals, and Other Materials chapter reveals data on manmade products among other areas of interest. The chapter Energy covers specifics on nuclear energy. The chapter Environment discloses particulars on recycling and conservation. Biology describes cells and other topics. Plant diversity is one of the subjects discussed in the chapter Plant World. Animal World explains mammals surrounded by other branches of learning. The chapter Human Body educates on many specialties such as digestion. Health and Medicine chapter enlightens about health care and other fields of study.

An example of the numerous fascinating facts shared in the chapter Health and Medicine reveals that the Romans did not produce as many offspring because of lead in the citizens' water. Any academic, public, and high school library should add the *Handy Science Answer Book* to their library as a superior source on essential science data for their patrons.—**Melinda F. Matthews**

P, S

401.   Parsons, Paul. **Science in 100 Key Breakthroughs.** Richmond Hills, Ont., Firefly Books, 2011. 416p. illus. index. $29.95. ISBN 13: 978-1-55407-808-0.

Authored by the same man who wrote *Science 1001* (see ARBA 2011, entry 1160), this title looks at 100 breakthroughs in scientific history that shaped and defined modern-day Western science. The work covers topics as varied as astronomy and physics to medicine and mathematics. An example of the 100 topics covered includes: Newton's Principle, Chaos theory, relatively, the computer, X-rays, Pi, and the human genome. Each subject is told in an easy-to-understand style and explains how the scientific thought of the time molded the discoveries and oftentimes advanced our ways of thinking. Each breakthrough is accompanied by at least one full-color photograph or illustration. It complements his original volume, *Science 1001*, and will serve as a concise, general work that can be used for browsing or for looking up specific topics in both high school and public libraries.—**Melinda F. Matthews**

Indexes

C

402.   **Applied Science and Technology Abstracts (ASTA).** http://www.hwwilson.com/ast/applieds.cfm. [Website]. Bronx, N.Y., H. W. Wilson. Price negotiated by site. Date reviewed: 2011.

Applied Science and Technology abstracts covers core English-language scientific and technical publications. Topics include engineering, acoustics, chemistry, computers, metallurgy, physics, plastics, telecommunications, transportation, and waste management. Periodical coverage includes trade and industrial publications, journals issued by professional and technical societies, and specialized subject periodicals, as well as special issues such as buyers' guides, directories, and conference proceedings.

The site provides access to more than 220 periodicals as far back as 1997. Also, nearly 800 periodicals have been fully indexed and abstracted, including 400 peer-reviewed journals, going back as far as 1984. The abstracts range in length from 50 to 300 words. Other features of the database include podcasts from well-respected museums, links to full-text articles, .pdf and page images, and the ability to link to your library's OPAC so patrons can easily find the cited materials on your shelves.—**James E. Bobick**

C

403.   **Scitopia. http://scitopia.org/.** [Website]. Free. Date reviewed: 2011.

Scitopia searches more than three and a half million documents, including peer-reviewed journal content and technical conference papers from leading voices in major science and technology disciplines. Through simple and advanced searches users can find bibliographic records in each partner's electronic library; patents from the U.S. Patent and Trademark Office, European Patent Office, and Japan Patent Office; and U.S. government documents on the Department of Energy Information Bridge site.—**James E. Bobick**

30 Agricultural Sciences

General Works

C

404.   **Encyclopedia of Agricultural, Food, and Biological Engineering.** 2d ed. Dennis R. Heldman and Carmen I. Moraru, eds. Boca Raton, Fla., CRC Press, 2011. 2v. index. (Dekker Agropedia Collection). $636.00/set. ISBN 13: 978-1-4398-111-5.

This two-volume set is an expansion of the 1st edition (see ARBA 2004, entry 1256). The scope remains largely the same, describing the progression from raw agricultural material to finished product. The new edition has doubled in size, with approximately 425 short (3-5 pages on average) entries. Previous entries have been replaced, expanded, and, in many cases, split (e.g., "Heat Transfer" has been divided into seven entries). The entries vary somewhat in tone—this edition seems directed more toward a technical audience than the 2003 edition, but there is still material for the less technically oriented reader, and each entry's abstract and introduction serve as a brief readable introduction to the topic. Entries also contain bibliographies plus diagrams, charts, and occasional photographs. Each volume contains alphabetic and subject tables of contents, an index, and a list of contributors. While marketed as an encyclopedia, this resource functions practically as a handbook for its rather broad field, providing a great deal of formulas and similar tools. However, the binding showed significant signs of wear and failure; it is unlikely that this resource would survive the regular use expected of a handbook. With this caveat, it would be a useful addition to any agriculture or food science library.—**Peter Larsen**

C

405.   **Encyclopedia of Animal Science.** 2d ed. Duane E. Ullrey, Charlotte Kirk Baer, and Wilson G. Pond, eds. Boca Raton, Fla., CRC Press, 2011. 2v. illus. index. $472.00/set. ISBN 13: 978-1-4398-5098-5.

This two-volume, 2d edition of the *Encyclopedia of Animal Science* indicates that by the year 2050 the world population will reach 10 million and animal origin products will provide approximately one-sixth of the human food energy and one-third of the human food protein. The demand is accelerating with a growth of population and is influenced particularly by developing countries. Animal products play a major role in preventing malnutrition in the world. In this encyclopedia there are over 300 entries covering the broad field of animal science. This 9-x-11-inch book contains 1,129 pages. Major subjects within the volumes include bioavailability, feedstuff, eggs, adaptation, hormones, nutrients, omega, poultry, slaughter, and ultrasound. There are numerous subdivisions under each of these major categories. The editors and the contributors are well qualified in the subject matter. The binding is above average, paper quality is average, and the font size is slightly small but since users will be reading a small section at a time it is adequate. As with the 1st edition (see ARBA 2005, entry 1333), this updated version will become a key reference for policy-makers, government bodies, private and public research professionals, agricultural producers, students, and the general public. There is a succinct overview that will provide adequate familiarity with the key terms and current knowledge of the subject.—**Herbert W. Ockerman**

Food Sciences and Technology

Catalogs and Collections

C, P

406.   **Nutrition and Food Sciences Database. http://www.cabi.org/nutrition/.** [Website]. Center for Agriculture and Biosciences International. Price negotiated by site. Date reviewed: 2011.

This is a specialist database covering human nutrition, food science, and food technology. No other database can provide such a comprehensive view of the food chain or of the interactions between diet and health. This database contains more than 880,000 records dating back to 1973, with over 50,000 added annually. It annually selects records from over 5,000 serials, as well as 400-500 nonserial publications, covering literature from 125 countries. It also covers books, conference proceedings, bulletins, reports, and published theses.—**James E. Bobick**

Chronology

C, P, S

407.   **American Food by the Decades.** Sherri Liberman, ed. Santa Barbara, Calif., Greenwood Press/ABC-CLIO, 2011. 250p. illus. index. $85.00. ISBN 13: 978-0-313-37698-6; 978-0-313-37699-3 (e-book).

This book is a decade-by-decade analysis of American food taste and innovations. It covers the history from 1900 to the 1990s. It evaluates the influence of commercial, ethnic, and cultural forces in the American diet. It is followed by a list of references. It suggests that the meat, potatoes, cake, and pies of the early 1900s have changed due to refrigeration, improved food production, railways which provide easier access to a wide variety of food stuff, commercial manufacturing and packaging, women's liberation, frozen food, microwave ovens, fast food, more immigration and ethnic foods available, and World War II with food rationing. The book indicates changes due to *The Jungle*, by Upton Sinclair, which brought about food inspection reforms. Other influences include home economics classes in school, calorie restrictions, obesity problems, women's magazines, television and publications including chefs recommendations for a wider variety of food, refined sugar, orange juice, home refrigerators, convenience foods, packaged foods, TV dinners, and a rise in the consumption of sugar including candy bars, soda, and ice cream. The Great Depression also altered our food eating habits along with stainless steel and chrome appliances, and federally funded school lunch programs. During the Second World War, victory gardens were established and 40 percent of vegetables were home grown. Chicken separation into parts and the Delaney Amendment changed our diets as well. "Silent Springs" condemned DDT, when fat became a problem; this encouraged production of leaner animals. Food stamps have also changed the way we eat. Currently low salt is being pushed and people are eating out more in restaurants. This book is very interesting reading and well written. It should be in libraries that focus on food and history.—**Herbert W. Ockerman**

Dictionaries and Encyclopedias

P

408.   **Encyclopedia of Organic, Sustainable, & Local Food.** Leslie A. Duram, ed. Lincoln, Nebr., University of Nebraska Press, 2010. 462p. illus. index. $34.95pa. ISBN 13: 978-0-8032-3625-7.

This encyclopedia covers the topics of organic sustainability and local food for production, with more than 140 entries written by international respected scholars, government experts, and activists. It discusses health issues, organic big business in the United States, economic terms, and organic food standards and labels and organizations involved in the long-term environmental impact and economic viability of organic farming. The book has an introduction, chronology, list of important dates, a list of entries, list of figures, and the 1990 Farm Bill title XXI, as well as other farm bills that influence this area. A major portion of the book is in encyclopedia format, alphabetically listing various terms along with definitions of these terms, and a general discussion of how each term occurred and the influence it has had on the agricultural sector. It has four appendixes: recommendations on organic farming; organic food production act; U.S. organic farming in the 1990s; and recent growth patterns in organic food markets. This is followed by a selected bibliography, information on the editor and contributors, and an index. The font is small but is probably adequate for reading small sections at one time. It should be in all general libraries that have an interest in organic, sustainable, and local food farming problems and successes.—**Herbert W. Ockerman**

C, P, S
409.   **Food: In Context.** Farmington Hills, Mich., Gale/Cengage Learning, 2011. 2v. illus. maps. index. $270.00/set. ISBN 13: 978-1-4144-8652-9.

This two-volume encyclopedia, one of the In Context series by Gale, was written with high school students in mind and is cross-disciplinary. It is a great place for students to begin research about various food science topics. Approximately 250 alphabetically arranged articles cover subjects such as food and nutrition, world health issues, agriculture, environmental concerns, and political decision-making in food policy, to name just a few. There are 47 primary documents included, such as articles from the Food and Agriculture Organizations of the United Nations. The articles, written by experts in their fields, allow students to come to their own conclusions about a variety of social, economic, political, and food and agricultural issues that scientists and other world leaders face every day. Since the series is designed with students in mind the information provided crosses many disciplines, including chemistry and biology, earth sciences, social sciences, history, and government. The more than 300 full-color photographs, glossary, and chronology will enhance learning. Students who wish to supplement their research may also consult *Food Cultures of the World Encyclopedia* (see entry 410) and the *Encyclopedia of Food and Culture* (see ARBA 2003, entry 1307). This new, easy-to-read source, written especially for the high school population, updates the older sources and provides excellent illustrations, timelines, a glossary, bibliographies at the end of each entry, and an easy-to-use index. This set is recommended for high school libraries, public libraries, and community college libraries.—**Diane J. Turner**

C, S
410.   **Food Cultures of the World Encyclopedia.** Ken Albala, ed. Santa Barbara, Calif., Greenwood Press/ABC-CLIO, 2011. 4v. illus. index. $380.00/set. ISBN 13: 978-0-31337-626-9; 978-0-31337-627-6 (e-book).

Food is an integral part of every culture. Daily life, celebrations, and economies all involve food. This four-volume encyclopedia, edited by a professor of history, looks at the foods of all the countries and peoples of the world. The articles are by contributors who are academics and food professionals. The volumes each cover a region of the world: Africa and the Middle East, the Americas, Asia and Oceania, and Europe. Within each volume, the entries are alphabetical in each region. Each entry includes an overview of the country and its culture, major foodstuffs, cooking techniques, typical meals, eating out, special occasions, diet and health, and a few recipes. A food culture snapshot offers a portrait of a family and its meals. All entries include references for further reading. Black-and-white illustrations augment the text. In addition to articles on countries, the encyclopedia covers peoples such as the Roma Gypsies, the Maori of New Zealand, and the Saami of northern Europe. It also has an article about food in outer space.

This encyclopedia is a useful resource for students and those interested in world cuisine. It is more focused on the food traditions of individual countries than *The Encyclopedia of Food and Culture* from

Charles Scribner's Sons/Gale (see ARBA 2003, entry 1307), which includes more information about culinary techniques and general food culture. Libraries lacking the Scribner set will want to add *Food Cultures of the World Encyclopedia.*—**Barbara M. Bibel**

P

411.   Kroner, Zina. **Vitamins and Minerals.** Santa Barbara, Calif., Greenwood Press/ABC-CLIO, 2011. 383p. illus. index. $85.00. ISBN 13: 978-0-31338-224-6; 978-0-31338-225-3 (e-book).

Dr. Kroner provides people who take nutritional supplements a reference about self-medication with vitamins and minerals. *Vitamins and Minerals* is an informative, evidence-based source book and guide to 39 supplements. The author writes in a very authoritative yet understandable way. She breaks the supplements down and explains the details of how they work on a molecular level that the reader can understand.

This reference is an overview of the most commonly used, as well as some not so common, supplements, dispelling misinformation and providing facts from an experienced, qualified, unbiased, certified physician's point of view.

Chapters are designed to help readers make informed decisions about use of under-regulated, over-the-counter "nutraceuticals." Descriptions include a brief overview, the hype, safety, deficiency, food sources, mechanism of action, how it works, primary uses, common doses, potential side effects (toxicity), and fact versus fiction. There is also a bibliography at the end of each chapter; the book provides over 1,000 medical references. It reveals little-known facts about these common supplements. Additionally, there is an introduction explaining the purpose of this book, a table of contents, and a detailed index. A glossary of medical terms would have been helpful to understand the medical terms.

Vitamins and Minerals is recommended as a timely, well-documented book that separates the facts from the hype. It is appropriate as a handy reference book for both physicians as well as any health conscious person's library.—**Nadine Salmons**

C, S

412.   Smith, Andrew F. **Fast Food and Junk Food: An Encyclopedia of What We Love to Eat.** Santa Barbara, Calif., Greenwood Press/ABC-CLIO, 2012. 2v. illus. index. $189.00/set. ISBN 13: 978-0-313-39393-8.

It is no doubt that fast food and junk food have become a part of America's daily lives and culture. Despite warnings from the health care industry, insurance industry, and even the politicians, we continue to be big consumers of these products. The goal of the book is to tell the stories behind many of America's favorite fast foods and junk foods and explain how these foods have come to be a commercial and social hit in the past century. It also delves into the health-related and environmental issues that these foods pose in our society. The work includes more than 700 A-Z entries on all aspects of fast food and junk food, including specific commercial chains, specific foods, targeted age groups, and people in the industry and people fighting the industry. Entries are written in a conversational style and are typically one to three pages in length and include *see also* references and further reading lists. The author stays as objective as possible and concedes that while many Americans are overweight the problem lies in excess consumption of food in general, not necessarily fast food products. A secondary focus of the volume is to explain how many fast food chains and junk food products are becoming international hits and changing the diets and health needs on an international scope.

This set is remarkably similar to the author's 2006 title, the *Encyclopedia of Junk Food and Fast Food* (see ARBA 2008, entry 1122), and although the author states this is a 2d edition to that title in the preface, the publisher does not indicate that it is a 2d edition anywhere on the book's cover or title page. Compared to the 1st edition, this set provides 270 new entries (many of which focus on other countries), and provides updated and expanded entries of those previously published. For public and academic libraries needing this type of information, this is a good source of information.—**Herbert W. Ockerman**

C, P, S

413.   Williams, Elizabeth M., and Stephanie Jane Carter. **The A-Z Encyclopedia of Food Controversies and the Law.** Santa Barbara, Calif., ABC-CLIO, 2011. 2v. index. $165.00/set. ISBN 13: 978-0-313-36448-8.

This 2-volume, 648-page encyclopedia evaluates the influence of law, regulations, guidelines, and labels on food. Volume 1 starts with a table of contents followed by a list of entries that subdivides food and food processes into categories. This is followed by a topical list of entries that are subdivided into topics, laws, and a variety of subjects that influence food law and regulation. Next is a preface, introduction, and chronological arrangement of situations related to food and nutrition, regulations with laws, and rules. A major portion of this volume is an alphabetic listing covering food, food agencies, food organizations, labeling, marketing, problems, regulations, and law. Volume 2 continues the alphabetic listing followed by appendixes (court cases, laws, regulations, and regulatory reviews), international agreements, selected bibliographies, an index, and information about the authors.

This is a comprehensive encyclopedia of topics that have a major influence on how food and law are intertwined. The encyclopedia should be of interest to individuals who are interested in the food industry. It would be very helpful to students that are interested in the interaction of food components and food laws. This encyclopedia set should be in all general libraries.—**Herbert W. Ockerman**

Handbooks and Yearbooks

S

414.   **The Science of Nutrition Series.** New York, Crabtree, 2011. 6v. illus. index. $29.27/vol.; $9.95pa./vol.

A different person authors each volume in this set of six books, yet each volume follows a similar format. The works each include a chapter on food for fuel, the topic of the book, where the topic is found, on the label, what the item does, digestion, and food allergies and special diets. Filled with colorful photographs and illustrations that include age-appropriate and diverse models, the authors use proper terms for body parts and situations, defining these in a glossary at the end of the book. Whether wanting to know more about fats, proteins, minerals, vitamins, water and fiber, or carbohydrates, these books will provide brief bits, tips on being healthy, experiments to try, and knowledge suitable to start researching at the upper-elementary and middle school levels. Labeled with a guided reading level T, this series is appropriate for health, science, and personal care classes, as well as for students who might need a bit more help with a difficult-to-understand topic related to nutrition.—**Sara Marcus**

P, S

415.   Webb, Lois Sinaiko, and Lindsay Grace Roten. **Holidays of the World Cookbook for Students.** updated ed. Santa Barbara, Calif., Greenwood Press/ABC-CLIO, 2011. 442p. index. $95.00; $32.95pa. ISBN 13: 978-0-31338-393-9; 978-0-313-39790-5pa; 978-0-31338-394-6 (e-book).

This is an absolutely fun updated volume not only for students but for anyone who likes to cook. The book was written specifically for students and covers 152 countries in the world, both small and large. The book provides information on holidays from countries around the globe and presents select recipes from each celebration. Countries are arranged alphabetically within each region: Africa, Asia and the South Pacific, the Caribbean, Europe, Latin America, the Middle East, and North America. In all, 440 recipes are provided and include everything from main entrees to side dishes, desserts, and snacks. Along with each entry is a thumbnail map of the country; brief descriptions of its history, geography, and climate; typical foods served during the holidays; and eating habits. Both secular and religious holidays are discussed as well as independence days and holidays unique to that particular country. Each recipe provides easy-to-follow instructions, cooking equipment needed, and how many people it will serve.

The work concludes with a glossary of cooking and ingredient terms, a bibliography, and an index. The publisher states that over 40 percent of the content has been updated since the last edition was published (1995). This set is highly recommended for all medium-sized and larger public libraries as well as middle and high school libraries. It is useful to both students and adults. Bon appetite!—**Nadine Salmons**

Horticulture

Dictionaries and Encyclopedias

P

416.   Armitage, Allan M. **Armitage's Garden Perennials.** 2d ed. Portland, Oreg., Timber Press, 2011. 347p. illus. index. $49.95. ISBN 13: 978-1-60469-038-5.

This gardening classic was originally published in 2000. The updated 2d edition expands the well-chosen plant selections, adding 300 new perennial choices. Well-known horticulturist Allan Armitage precisely describes his highly discriminating choices of more than 1,300 outstanding perennials with color photographs taken by Armitage himself. The entry for each plant includes scientific and common names and hardiness zone information, as well as ideas on growth and cultivation. Armitage also includes his frank opinions about the garden worthiness of the most popular perennials, and readers will have no doubt about which plants he admires and which do not meet his standards. Readers will find old favorites like sunflowers and clematis along with new introductions like geranium phaeum "Margaret Wilson." New fancy forms of the ever popular Echinacea genus are hitting trial gardens everywhere, like the Big Sky series. This gorgeous resource will find a home in the library of every gardener who wants current, authoritative information as well as public and academic libraries with gardening enthusiasts.—**Susan C. Awe**

P

417.   Armitage, Allan M. **Armitage's Vines and Climbers: A Gardener's Guide to the Best Vertical Plants.** Portland, Oreg., Timber Press, 2010. 212p. illus. index. $29.95pa. ISBN 13: 978-1-60469-039-2.

Horticulturist Allan Armitage, renowned professor of horticulture at the University of Georgia, profiles the huge number of climbing plants available to gardeners for ornamental purpose beautiful and fragrant masses of flowers or just lush greenery. After the introduction, sections include A-to-Z Vines, Lists of Vines with Specific Characteristics and Uses, and Useful Conversions. An index of botanical names and one for common names complete the work. Armitage profiles well-known varieties like clematis, morning glories, and honeysuckle, giving best sites and conditions for growing strong specimens. Unusual choices like Cissus discolor, Dutchman's pipe, Chilean jasmine, Rangoon creeper, and maypop are also covered. He includes woody and herbaceous plants and annual as well as perennials. He names invasive, difficult-to-control species no matter how popular and encourages gardeners to incorporate annual specimens along with their highly prized perennials. Over 115 plants in 70 different genera have been selected.

A profile includes the general description, plant's hardiness, plant family, best method of propagation, method of climbing and etymology of botanical and common names. Readers will also find lists of climbers with specific attributes such as extra hardiness, those with clear fragrance elements, compact size, conspicuous fruit usually for attracting birds, those often used for conservatory culture, and evergreen foliage. Find more information about plants Armitage has tested with good results in Athens, Georgia at his Website (http://www.allanarmitage.net/). Well organized and written with a wry sense of humor, *Armitage's Vines and Climbers* will become a classic.—**Susan C. Awe**

P

418. Bryant, Geoff, and Tony Rodd. **Annuals and Perennials: A Gardener's Encyclopedia.** Richmond Hills, Ont., Firefly Books, 2011. 304p. illus. index. $19.95pa. ISBN 13: 978-1-55407-837-0.

This sturdy but compact handbook will help gardeners select outstanding flowers for every spot. More than 300 plant entries, arranged alphabetically by genus name, includes a detailed description of origins, cultivation needs, flowering season, propagation techniques, frost hardiness, and diseases as well as spread and height estimates, subspecies, hybrids, and cultivars. A chart in the beginning shows where to find the information in the entries. The more than 500 terrific color photographs add interest and help in visualizing what the plant will look like in your garden. More coverage of temperate plants than tropical or alpine is provided since more flower and gardening enthusiasts live in temperate zones. The World Hardiness Zones is an unusual addition, and the entries provide the hardiness for each plant. Also near the front is a cultivation table quickly providing height and spread, frost tolerant or now, planting season, and more. Author Rodd is based in Australia and Bryant in New Zealand, and both have extensive experience writing and identifying plants. Sturdy enough to take to the nursery, use this wonderful guide to help beautify your yard and gardens.—**Susan C. Awe**

P

419. Tucker, Arthur O., and Thomas Debaggio. **The Encyclopedia of Herbs: A Comprehensive Reference to Herbs of Flavor and Fragrance.** Portland, Oreg., Timber Press, 2009. 604p. illus. index. $39.95. ISBN 13: 978-0-88192-994-2.

Timber Press has created a beautiful book profiling 500 species of herbs. Within each profile users will find information on how to grow, identify, preserve, and harvest each of the featured herbs. The authors, both winners of The Gertrude B. Foster Award for Excellence in Herbal Literature, are well qualified to write this volume. They have included information on each plant's botanical name, its height, hardiness, light requirements, soil type, water amount needed, and whether it is a perennial or an annual. All of this provides practical advice for those both new to growing herbs as well as those who are experienced herb gardeners but are looking for new varieties to try. Many entries also include information on the history of the plant, its culinary and medical uses, and craft uses. Some 145 line drawings are also provided. This work is written simply enough for the novice but will also be of interest to experienced gardeners. It will be a useful addition to most public libraries. [R: BL, 2 Mar 10]—**Nadine Salmons**

Handbooks and Yearbooks

P

420. Bowe, Alice. **High-Impact, Low-Carbon Gardening: 1001 ways to Garden Sustainably.** Portland, Oreg., Timber Press, 2011. 263p. illus. index. $24.95pa. ISBN 13: 978-0-88192-998-0.

A green approach to backyard ecology, Bowe's manual compiles worthy suggestions for earth stewardship. From Devon walls to loosening clay with gypsum, the text suggests pragmatic methods of accommodating nature. One sidebar enumerates 22 weeds and the types of soil that nourish them. Lists of useful material clarify standard terms—coir, peat moss, porphyry, compost tea, bimodal trees—and propose horticultural specifics (e.g., xeriscaping, meadow planting, viable landscaping, bee-friendly actions, coppicing). There are useful photographs of such heritage plants as cranesbill, goldenrod, and sweet peas. Troubleshooting comments make substitutions, as with oak-leaf hydrangea instead of high-maintenance camellia, coffee grounds rather than poisons to avert slugs, and willow baskets in place of expensive raised beds made from railroad ties and lumber. An unusual text at a low price, Bowe's book belongs in home and public libraries and as reference for gardening, scouting, and school science projects. This gardening reference is highly recommended.—**Mary Ellen Snodgrass**

P

421.   Cohen, Stephanie, and Jennifer Benner. **The Nonstop Garden: A Step-by-Step Guide to Smart Plant Choices and Four-Season Designs.** Portland, Oreg., Timber Press, 2010. 248p. illus. index. $19.95pa. ISBN 13: 978-0-88192-951-5.

A compact guide to seasonal plant groupings, Cohen and Benner's handbook suggests innovative changes to the humdrum yard. Photographs from established gardens propose eye-catching details to unify the landscape; for example, metal statuary, seasoned wooden gates, raised plank walks, and Japanese twig fencing are all included. Perusals of the garden in winter stress the beauty in pyracantha berries, echinacea seed pods, stone paths, and frozen clumps of grasses. A concluding index of plants by type—bulbs, edibles, shrubs, trees, and vines—notes the seasons in which they best perform. A two-page catalog of invasive plants includes the states in which they thrive. The chief weakness occurs in chapter 2, in which the authors discuss plant texture and height without naming the illustrated greenery and flowers. A worthy addition to the home and public library, this work is recommended.—**Mary Ellen Snodgrass**

P

422.   Deardorff, David, and Kathryn Wadsworth. **What's Wrong with My Vegetable Garden?** Portland, Oreg., Timber Press, 2011. 249p. illus. index. $34.95pa. ISBN 13: 978-1-60469-283-9.

P

423.   Gillman, Jeff, and Meleah Maynard. **Decoding Gardening Advice: The Science Behind the 100 Most Common Recommendations.** Portland, Oreg., Timber Press, 2012. 224p. index. $16.95pa. ISBN 13: 978-1-60469-220-4.

Co-authored by two writers who often speak publicly on gardening, plant problems, and ecology, *What's Wrong with My Vegetable Garden?* is written in an easy-to-read style that can be used for a quick look-up or read all the way through. After an introduction titled "Prepare for Success" in which the authors address providing the right temperature, water, light, and soil for optimum results, the book is arranged alphabetically by vegetable name. Nearly 50 vegetables are covered in this book with each entry providing information on its growing season, a thorough description, ideal temperature and soil, light and water needs, garden uses and planting techniques, and a section on common problems and how to solve them. Color photographs are abundant throughout the volume. After the main entries there is a section that provides organic solutions to plant problems according to plant family; this section also provides photographs. Appendixes include a guide to choosing the right cultivar, conversion charts, recommended reading lists, a list of resources, and an index.

Decoding Gardening Advice is a guide designed for anyone who's looking for the logic and science behind common (and not-so-common) gardening advice. It will appeal to those gardening in less-than-ideal climates by providing valuable advice for them and the reasoning behind it. The book is organized into topical chapters (e.g., Soil, Water, Trees and Shrubs, Lawn Care), and then broken down into specific dilemmas pinpointing advice that is "good," "debatable," and "wrong." Many common questions are addressed here, including the best way to prune trees, correctly fertilizing, using organic versus nonorganic mulches, and the best way to treat lawn spots left behind by dogs, to name just a few. This is a useful and oftentimes humorous book that will appeal to a wide range of gardeners.

These books are an ideal read for gardener's looking to grow the healthiest, most problem-free plants and vegetables. They will be useful in most public library gardening collections.—**Diane M. Calabrese**

P

424.   **How to Grow Food: Step-by-Step Techniques for Growing All Kinds of Fruits, Vegetables, Herbs, Salads and More.** By Richard Gianfresco. Richmond Hills, Ont., Firefly Books, 2011. 256p. illus. index. $29.95. ISBN 13: 978-1-55407-806-6.

P

425. **Incredible Edibles: 43 Fun Things to Grow in the City.** By Sonia Day. Richmond Hills, Ont., Firefly Books, 2011. 128p. illus. index. $14.95pa. ISBN 13: 978-1-55407-624-6.

How to Grow Food is a practical guide to growing your own vegetables, fruits, and herbs provides step-by-step instructions for cultivating more than 125 crops, from traditional choices to the more unusual. The author includes techniques that can be applied to any size garden in a variety of locations; he also includes instructions for gardening in window boxes. Included are leafy crops, roots and tubers, fruit crops, grains, edible flower crops, tree fruits, peppers, cane fruits, nuts, and herbs. He provides in-depth instructions on choosing the best site, designing and planting the garden, maximizing space, harvesting and storing, dealing with weeds and pests, and pruning plants. Sidebars provide helpful lists of do's and don'ts, pant ratings describing value and maintenance, and the author's personal picks for any garden. Filled with rich illustrations and photographs, this book will appeal to a wide range of gardeners, making this a useful book for all types of public libraries.

This work is written along the same lines as *Incredible Edibles* but focuses on vegetables, fruits, and herbs that take limited space to grow, making them ideal for city dwellers. Day's focus is on providing clear, concise advice for those who do not have the time or patience to go through more complex gardening books to find those foods that can be grown in containers or window boxes. The work gives clear, step-by-step instructions that are supplemented with numerous color photographs and charts. Although not as detailed or all-inclusive as Gianfresco's title, this book will fill a niche will larger urban libraries.—**Shannon Graff Hysell**

P

426. Ogden, Lauren Springer, and Scott Ogden. **Waterwise Plants for Sustainable Gardens: 200 Drought-Tolerant Choices for All Climates.** Portland, Oreg., Timber Press, 2011. 247p. illus. index. $24.95pa. ISBN 13: 978-1-60469-169-6.

Striking a balance between drought-resistant and water-loving plants is a challenge that many gardeners must meet. In the mid-Atlantic, for instance, a year-to-year swing from 15 inches below average annual rainfall to 15 inches above is not extraordinary. In the West and Southwest, however, dry conditions are more constant and water-use restrictions are becoming the norm. Identifying plants that can tolerate low amounts of rainfall and then, building gardens and landscapes around them ensures that substantial vegetation will survive the harshest conditions. For such core plantings, this book provides an excellent start. The authors suggest trees, perennials, and annuals, as well as subcategories defined by form, such as ground covers. Some suggestions will meet all expectations of novice gardeners. Indian blanket (*Gaillardia aristata*) actually stands through both drought and exceedingly wet conditions and flowers profusely from spring well into fall. Only very hot days suppress flowering. But the oriental poppy (*Paper orientale*) is ephemeral, a mid-spring bloomer in warmer latitudes that completes its flowering phase in two weeks or less. What should a gardener new to waterwise plants do? Use this guide in conjunction with keen observation of successful neighboring gardens. After deciding which plants are a match to personal aesthetic sense, look for matches between the plants that are actually doing well locally and plants the volume showcases. The index to common and scientific names will also help those working from a recommendation of a fellow gardener.—**Diane M. Calabrese**

P

427. Wilson, Andrew. **Contemporary Color in the Landscape: Top Designers, Inspiring Ideas, New Combinations.** Portland, Oreg., Timber Press, 2011. 280p. illus. index. $34.95. ISBN 13: 978-0-88192-996-6.

A visual feast of geometric shapes and flora, Wilson's work coordinates art and architecture with stunning gardens. The photographs connect both powerful and mellow settings with hue and texture, such as the cantilevered overlook at a rose bed of the Savill Garden, a brick walkway in the white garden at Sissinghurst, and a timber deck in Chaumont, France, juxtaposed by banana trees and bird of paradise. Text offers practical advice on growing wine-red cosmos and hollyhock and the purplish globes of echinops. Advice on seasonal plantings ensures a cyclic palette of color and foliage, from red hot pokers and crocosmia to cornflowers, daisies, daylilies, and poppies. Sensitive camera angles pick up the tone-on-tone of swordleafed astelia and a stand of birch saplings. The bibliography precedes a meticulous index by place, designer, and formal and popular names for plants. This work is highly recommended for public libraries.—**Mary Ellen Snodgrass**

P

428.   Wingate, Marty. **Landscaping for Privacy: Innovative Ways to Turn Your Outdoor Space into a Peaceful Retreat.** Portland, Oreg., Timber Press, 2012. 155p. illus. index. $19.95pa. ISBN 13: 978-1-60469-123-8.

P

429.   Young, Beth O'Donnell. **The Nature Scaping Workbook: A Step-by-Step Guide for Bringing Nature to Your Backyard.** Portland, Oreg., Timber Press, 2011. 225p. illus. index. $24.95pa. ISBN 13: 978-1-60469-118-4.

The author of *The Nature Scaping Workbook*, a professional landscaper, encourages readers to landscape their gardens and lawns in a style that accommodates their property's natural habitat. In doing so she makes the case that it will need less weeding, pruning, watering, and fertilizing and will also attract bees, birds, and butterflies. The book is arranged into eight easy-to-read chapters that cover such topics as determining your natural landscape, conserving water, matching plants to place, choosing sustainable materials, developing a landscaping plan on paper, the nuts and bolts of landscaping, and caring for your new garden and lawn. What makes this book unique are the worksheets the author has included at the end of each chapter that help the reader determine exactly how to plan their design. These include a backyard biohabitats chart that helps one select plants native to their area; a worksheet to decide what one will need to include to encourage natural wildlife; and a worksheet to find the best materials to use in your area. The work concludes with conversion tables, a list of suggested reading, and an index.

The author of *Landscaping for Privacy*, a writer and speaker about gardens, provides useful tips on how to make your yard a refuge from the rest of the world, specifically the noise of neighbors and traffic. She provides examples on how to strategically place plants to buffer noise or create barriers and screens with the use of fences and hedges. There is a list of plants provided that are recommended to give an aura of seclusion, including several that require very little maintenance. The work concludes with conversion tables and plant hardiness zones, a list of resources, a list of recommended further reading, and an index. The full-color photographs will provide plenty of visual inspiration for do-it-yourself landscapers.

Filled with full-color photographs, detailed landscaping plans, and sidebars with helpful information, these books will provide plenty of inspiration for gardeners in all types of regions. They are recommended for public libraries.—**Mary Ellen Snodgrass**

31 Biological Sciences

Biology

Dictionaries and Encyclopedias

C, P

430. Cotner, Sehoya, and Randy Moore. **Arguing for Evolution: An Encyclopedia for Understanding Science.** Santa Barbara, Calif., Greenwood Press/ABC-CLIO, 2011. 318p. illus. index. $85.00. ISBN 13: 978-0-313-35947-7; 978-0-313-35948-4 (e-book).

We can always use a new handbook for defending evolution in the public sphere, especially one that is current, thorough, and accessible. This new volume fills the need with precision and creativity. It is designed as a resource for efficiently sorting out arguments about evolution and creationism. It will be most useful not as a reference itself, but to point users to primary sources. Its subtitle shows another value for this book: understanding more about evolution is learning more about science in general.

This book begins with a "Quick A-Z Guide to the Evidence," which is an abridged index to the major elements of evolutionary science. The first chapter summarizes evolutionary theory with a strong philosophical framework. The following chapters present critical fields and questions in evolution, including the age of the Earth; fossils; biogeography; anatomic, behavioral, molecular, and genetic evidence; and human evolution. The long appendix 1 is a reprint of two chapters from "On the Origin of Species" (an odd addition which will not be used often), and the following appendixes cover the geological time scale and the hominin fossil record. A full glossary, index, and bibliography end the book.

Each chapter begins with a "predictions" box outlining what would be expected if evolution were true for that particular topic. This is an effective educational tool for students, who will see the hypothetico-deductive model of science in action. It could even win over an anti-evolutionist or two if they are willing to truly test the evidence. The writing style used by the authors is clear and unencumbered, so scientific jargon will be no excuse for not understanding the arguments.

This book is recommended for all libraries, especially those with natural history collections. It will be useful for high school students through professionals.—**Mark A. Wilson**

C, P

431. **Encyclopedia of Biological Invasions.** Daniel Simberloff and Marcel Rejmanek, eds. Berkeley, Calif., University of California Press, 2011. 765p. illus. index. $95.00. ISBN 13: 978-0-520-26421-2.

Mass transportation has resulted in an unparalleled spread of undesirable species. These nonnative species outcompete their indigenous counterparts, threatening the survival of local species, and often causing major environmental damages. Simberloff and Rejmanek's work addresses the patterns and processes of invasion, the underlying theories, and various species accounts. This over 700-page source is organized into 153 topics. Entries are written for general readers and composed by 197 leading scientists.

The encyclopedia is arranged alphabetically, with a complete listing of entries in the table of contents. Additional access is through a topical subject arrangement and complete index. Although individual species are mentioned, they tend to be discussed briefly as part of broader groups (e.g., reptiles and amphibians, fishes, plant pathogens). Very few receive their own entry. Entries average 4 to 5 pages, with some going as high as 10. The structure of each entry varies, and this variability can be frustrating when moving from topic to topic, but expected considering the scope and numerous authors. A further reading list of 5 to 10 sources is provided at the end of each entry for more detailed or lengthy discussions. Many colored figures, maps, and images appear throughout, although text dominates. A glossary helps clarify concepts unfamiliar to general readers and a list is provided on the 100 worst invasive species. This encyclopedia is unique in its scope and comprehensiveness. Other similar works are older (*Invasive Alien Species: A New Synthesis* [Island Press, 2005]), cover less material, or are more focused (*Invasive Species Management: A Handbook of Principles and Techniques* [Oxford University Press, 2009]). This book will appeal to those wanting a general introduction to the broad principles and issues surrounding invasive species. Those simply interested in species accounts will need additional sources.—**Kevin McDonough**

P, S

432.   **Grzimek's Animal Life Encyclopedia: Evolution.** Farmington Hills, Mich., Gale/Cengage Learning, 2011. 1v. illus. maps. index. $205.00. ISBN 13: 978-1-4144-8669-7.

For more than 30 years *Grzimek's Animal Life Encyclopedia* has been widely accepted as the authority and the most comprehensive reference for information on the animal kingdom. This volume on evolution is the latest addition to a set that currently has 17 volumes, including a cumulative index. Gale has teamed with the American Zoo and Aquarium Association to complete a total revision of this revered resource. The set is being expanded from 13 to 17 volumes including a cumulative index. An abundance of full-color photographs, illustrations, and maps enhance the appeal and usefulness of this resource. Anatomical drawings are detailed and clearly labeled. The book includes 36 entries that have been written by specialists in the field and peer-reviewed by an editorial board. This work includes in-depth articles on Adaptation and Evolutionary Change, Biodiversity Conservation, Genes and Development, Origins of the Universe, and Scientific Methods and Human Knowledge.

While this is a detailed and scholarly resource, the information is not overly technical. This volume and this set are highly recommended for high school, academic, and public libraries; however, the organization of the information in a consistent format and under bold headings makes these volumes useful to even younger students seeking basic information.—**Elaine Ezell**

C, P

433.   Maczulak, Anne. **Encyclopedia of Microbiology.** New York, Facts on File, 2011. 858p. illus. index. (Facts on File Science Library). $95.00. ISBN 13: 978-0-8160-7364-1; 978-1-4381-3406-2 (e-book).

Facts on File's *Encyclopedia of Microbiology* is a single volume source of 850 pages that provides a general introduction to fungi, algae, viruses, bacteria, and protozoa. Written for the educated layperson or lower-level undergraduate student, the *Encyclopedia* consists of over 200 entries connected through two main themes: the interrelationship of microorganisms and their diversity. Most of the entries are at least two to three pages in length, although some are significantly longer. The emphasis is on microbes and less on people. Some entries will mention scientists that have played an important role in a topic, but only Louis Pasteur and Robert Koch receive their own entries, with the latter discussed under Koch's Postulates. Also included throughout the *Encyclopedia* are 13 essays ranging from 1-2 pages in length addressing topical areas that the author notes "prompt active discussions amongst scientists." Over one-half are written by the *Encyclopedia*'s author with the rest by respected scientists in industry and academia. Not particularly image rich, the *Encyclopedia* includes approximately 130 black-and-white photographs, with additional tables, graphs, and line illustrations. An eight-page color insert shows close-ups of various microbes in the lab or their natural environment. Seven appendixes are included: chronology of events, glossary, further resources, proposed hierarchy of biota, classification of bacteria and archaea, viruses of animals and plants, and major human diseases caused by microorganisms. Unfortunately, most of these are too brief or oversimplified to be very useful. The 25-page index is reasonably complete, with the page numbers for main entries listed in bold. Overall, the author has done a good job explaining microbiology topics for the layperson. As microbiology is a science, though, there is some language and concepts that will be difficult for the nonspecialist to fully understand. This work is recommended for public, community college, and undergraduate libraries.—**Kevin McDonough**

Handbooks and Yearbooks

S

434.   **Lifecycles Series.** Boston, Kingfisher/Houghton Mifflin, 2011. 2v. illus. index. $12.99/vol.

The covers for these books will attract readers with their large, color photographs. The series covers the life cycles and food chains in each ecosystem for various animals and plants. Each book includes an introduction with a world map to the ecosystem and is divided into three different food chains. Animals and plants discussed each have a two-page spread with the life cycle and a "Did you know?" section. Small pictures in the form of tabs help the reader follow which food chain they are reading about. A large food web map is included. The layout, colors, and photography are well organized and very eye-catching. These books would be useful for browsing, as well as teaching and researching ecosystems and life cycles.—**Renee Byers Gentry**

Anatomy

P, S

435.   **Human Body from A to Z.** Tarrytown, N.Y., Marshall Cavendish, 2012. 480p. illus. index. $79.95. ISBN 13: 978-0-7614-7946-8; 978-0-7614-9976-3 (e-book).

The *Human Body from A to Z* is a hardbound volume full of information geared toward teenagers about the human body, how it works, and how physical ailments affect it. It includes 168 articles presented in alphabetic order. The articles vary in complexity of topic from simple items such as birthmarks to more meaty features such as the digestive system and the circulatory system. Regardless of the topic the prose is well written and graphic illustrations accompany every topic, making each more interesting and understandable.

Some topics include a question and answer panel, where common questions are asked and answered. These could be highly valuable to a young reader, as they are specifically geared toward a teen audience. Other features of the volume include a *see also* graphic for each topic, which leads the reader to other related topics and a detailed index. Other useful features include 600 illustrations, side bars filled with helpful information on the topic at hand, and lists for further research.

Human Body A to Z is not a highly technical medical encyclopedia, but it is not striving to be. It presents health topics in plain language with colorful graphics, which make it ideal for its target audience of young people. As such, this reviewer highly recommends it for any library that caters to teens and pre-teens.—**Alicia Brillon**

Botany

General Works

Dictionaries and Encyclopedias

C, P

436.   Fayaz, Ahmed. **Encyclopedia of Tropical Plants: Identification and Cultivation of over 3,000 Tropical Plants.** Richmond Hills, Ont., Firefly Books, 2011. 720p. illus. index. $75.00. ISBN 13: 978-1-55407-489-1.

The pictures in this most recent guide to tropical plants are jaw dropping. Just as anyone can be overwhelmed with the beauty of tropical forest or garden, the reader is overwhelmed with the gorgeous pictures in this book. In order to include descriptions of over 3,000 tropical plants and selected subtropical plants with a photograph of almost every one, each of the 720 pages has at least 4 to 8 outstanding pictures.

Besides the wonderful pictures, what makes this book especially useful and timely is the arrangement of the plants in the natural order they evolved (phylogenetic order) with the careful description of each species on the same page as the picture. (Specifically, plants are arranged by the 2009 Angiosperm Phylogeny Group III.) Previously published books with pictures are arranged alphabetically by family or genus with the description apart from the picture.

The immense diversity of tropical plants is what drives much of the fascination with these plants that cover the majority of the world's continents. The largest family of plants, orchids, which have become the symbol of tropical plants, will grab the interest of many readers. But the book also includes non-flowering plants (e.g., mosses, ferns, trees).

The description of each plant is what a serious plant scientist expects, yet it is also useful for the layperson. It includes full scientific data, distribution, ecology, ethnobotany, phenology, and cultivation. The glossary and indexes for both common and scientific names are extensive and thorough. This work is highly recommended for public and academic libraries. [R: Choice, Jan 12, p. 850]—**Georgia Briscoe**

C, P

437.   Moerman, Daniel E. **Native American Medicinal Plants: An Ethnobotanical Dictionary.** Portland, Oreg., Timber Press, 2009. 799p. index. $29.95pa. ISBN 13: 978-0-88192-987-4.

This work, focusing on the traditional medicinal use of plants by Native American groups, is an abridged version of the author's *Native American Ethnobotany* (Timber Press, 1998), a larger volume that also included plants used for nonmedicinal purposes, such as for food or shelter. This volume covers the uses of more than 3,000 plants by 218 Native American tribal groups. It was compiled by analyzing and indexing over 170 different ethnobotanical publications including both journal articles and monographs. The work opens with a brief essay on plant use by Native Americans, along with lists of drug usage categories (e.g., analgesic, expectorant) and the Native American groups included. The following "Catalog of Plants" lists the plant species alphabetically by their scientific names. Each entry also includes the popular name, followed by an alphabetic listing of the groups that use it, the medicinal purpose(s) they use it for, and a cross-reference to the bibliography of sources. The length of the entries can vary considerably based upon the number of groups using a plant as well the number of purposes the species is used for. Entries for some species include a black-and-white botanical line drawing. An index of tribes lists each Native American group followed by the categories of drug usage and the species they use for them. An index of plant uses lists the drug use categories, followed by the species and which tribal group uses them. An index of common plant names provides the nonspecialist with the scientific name for each species. This volume is recommended for academic libraries serving institutions that offer programs in ethnobotany, Native American studies, or pharmaceutical sciences.—**Kenneth M. Frankel**

Handbooks and Yearbooks

P

438.   Turner, Nancy J., and Patrick von Aderkas. **The North American Guide to Common Poisonous Plants and Mushrooms.** Portland, Oreg., Timber Press, 2009. 375p. illus. index. $29.95. ISBN 13: 978-0-88192-929-4.

This new revision of a 1991 guide to toxic plants and fungi is intended especially for the amateur and intermediate botanist. With a chapter each on poisonous mushrooms, poisonous plants in the wild, poisonous cultivated plants, and poisonous houseplants, it has ready-reference and more detailed information on more than 100 plants: a physical description, occurrence in North America, toxicity, and a small color photograph. Both common and scientific names (family, genus, and species) are provided; in the case of mushrooms, the entries are alphabetized by genus because of the many variations in common names. Plants are alphabetized by common name. An introductory chapter is an overview of poisoning, its effects, and treatment. Appendixes offer lists of edible plants that have poisonous parts or are poisonous when consumed raw, those that are skin/eye irritants, those that can poison honey or milk, and medicinal plants. Throughout, the authors, both professional botanists, provide cautionary information to avoid poisoning and recommendations for seeking professional help in the case of an actual poisoning. A glossary, a lengthy reference list, and an index by plant names round out the book. This work is highly recommended for most public libraries.—**Lori D. Kranz**

Flowering Plants

P

439.   **Flowering Plants: A Pictorial Guide to the World's Flora.** Leon Gray, ed. Richmond Hills, Ont., Firefly Books, 2011. 288p. illus. index. $24.95pa. ISBN 13: 978-1-55407-767-0.

This introductory guide to some of the more colorful and familiar angiosperms (flowering plants) describes 86 dicotyledon and 20 monocotyledon families from around the globe. Not intended to be comprehensive, this selection is drawn from the definitive *Flowering Plant Families of the World*, a 2007 reference book by the same editor and authors (see ARBA 2008, entry 1157). Arranged alphabetically by scientific family name, each entry, ranging from two to seven pages long, includes common name(s), a general description, physical description, distribution, and the plants' economic uses. The numerous full-color and two-color drawings for each were rendered by botanical artists, are both attractive and detailed, and have identifying captions. At the end of the book, the reader will find an up-to-date APGIII classification list (based on the new DNA-sequencing data), a list of resources, a glossary, and a common- and scientific-name index.—**Lori D. Kranz**

Fungi

C, P

440.   Roberts, Peter, and Shelley Evans. **The Book of Fungi: A Life-Size Guide to Six Hundred Species from Around the World.** Chicago, University of Chicago Press, 2011. 655p. illus. maps. index. $55.00. ISBN 13: 978-0-226-72117-0.

An attractive photographic guide to common fungi from around the world, this volume illustrates common or interesting mushrooms, truffles, lichens, and other fungi. The authors provide a nice introduction to the fungal kingdom, discussing the taxonomy, biology, ecology, use, conservation, and collection of mushrooms. The bulk of the book consists of individual species accounts of 600 important, famous, or typical species. There is a visual guide to the major groups of fungi, followed by individual species accounts. Each species is illustrated with a life-sized photograph of the fruiting body as well as a line drawing. Many accounts also include either an enlarged or shrunken photograph illustrating features of the fruiting body. The accounts also include a range map, description, similar species, and information on edibility of the mushroom. As well as the usual agarics, boletes, bracket fungi, and puffballs that most people think of as mushrooms, *The Book of Fungi* covers truffles, lichens, stinkhorns, and jelly fungi, but not slime molds. Appendixes list resources for further study and provide a brief overview of fungal classification as well as the usual glossary.

The book is designed as an introduction to the range of fungal species, not as an identification guide. Many mushroom species are widely distributed and may look very different in various parts of their range, so users should be very careful about using this guide to identify mushrooms. As a visual introduction to the range of mushroom types, however, this guide is a valuable addition to public and academic libraries.—**Diane Schmidt**

Trees and Shrubs

P

441.   Bryant, Geoff, and Tony Rodd. **Trees and Shrubs: A Gardener's Encyclopedia.** Richmond Hills, Ont., Firefly Books, 2011. 416p. illus. index. $19.95pa. ISBN 13: 978-1-55407-836-3.

This handy encyclopedic guide provides information on 1,500 species or cultivars of trees and shrubs suitable for cultivation around the world, although the emphasis is on temperate regions. Species covered in the encyclopedia are arranged in alphabetic order by genus name. Each genus is described with the number of species worldwide, original range, horticultural value, and general cultivation information. Selected species within each genus are illustrated with color photographs and described with recommended cultivars and the Plant Hardiness Zones listed. A table provides an easy overview of each species' characteristics such as height, spread, and horticultural information. The authors include both common plants such as oaks and roses and rarer, more unusual plants like the recently discovered Wollemi Pine or African proteas. The authors are from New Zealand and Australia, so their coverage of alternatives from Down Under is more extensive than most similar guides. While the encyclopedia is aimed at gardeners, its worldwide focus makes it a good option for academic and public libraries in need of a handy reference to common or interesting trees and shrubs.—**Diane Schmidt**

P

442.   Dirr, Michael A. **Dirr's Encyclopedia of Trees & Shrubs.** Portland, Oreg., Timber Press, 2011. 951p. illus. index. $79.95. ISBN 13: 978-0-88192-901-0.

So much beauty, yet so little time and space to make all the trees and shrubs that capture our imagination part of our landscape. This dream-maker of an encyclopedia helps us narrow our choices, even as we are swayed by more possibilities. Spellbound by the many gorgeous species of cedar (*Cedrus*), we realize all of them require more growing room that we can provide. As for that statuesque Spanish fir (*Abies pinsapo*), we do not want to supplant or overshadow the vegetable garden. A paperbark maple (*Acer griseum*) is something we ought to try because it will lend texture and color to winter, once it slowly takes root. Anyone planning to add trees and shrubs to their established or new landscape ought to consult this book first. There are a few omissions of tempters, such as cashew (*Anacardium occidentale*). But the luscious and weighty volume is a genuine surfeit of riches. The conversational nugget that accompanies the superb photograph of each tree or shrub includes essential information about size, suitable zones, threats, hardiness, and sources. The separate indexes to scientific and common names are complemented by lists of good selections for everything from salty soil to urban setting. Gardeners who love their snow fountains (*Prunus xyedoensis*) will be surprised to read that it lacks grace. Finally, we could not agree more with his advocating for gardening as the way to find solace during the most difficult times.—**Diane M. Calabrese**

Natural History

Dictionaries and Encyclopedias

C, S

443.   Woodward, Susan L., and Joyce A. Quinn. **Encyclopedia of Invasive Species: From Africanized Honey Bees to Zebra Mussels.** Santa Barbara, Calif., Greenwood Press/ABC-CLIO, 2011. 2v. illus. maps. index. $189.00/set. ISBN 13: 978-0-313-38220-8.

These volumes are either depressing with their detailed accounts of the damage done by invasive species in the United States, or they are a tribute to the extraordinary adaptations and tenacity of life. The authors have produced one of the few comprehensive and user-friendly accounts of the dramatic ecological changes wrought by organism migrations in historic times.

Defining an "invasive species" is one of the first tasks the authors tackled. Many terms, such as "alien", "non-native" and "non-indigenous," have fuzzy meanings and sometimes pejorative implications. Even defining the "native" flora and fauna of the United States is difficult because Native Americans also caused significant ecological changes, both on purpose and inadvertently. The working definition of invasive species used in these volumes is essentially those species introduced that are causing significant disruption to native communities.

There are two volumes, one for animals (also including microorganisms and fungi) and one for plants. Each entry begins with the scientific name and classification of the organism, and then its native range and distribution in the United States. This is followed by a thorough description, a comparison to similar species (much like a field guide) and a history of its introduction. The final portion is an assessment of the impact of the species by examining its diet, life history, and ecological effect on the surrounding physical and biological environment. Most entries also have a section discussing management options and history. The prose is supported by range maps and photographs.

The diversity and penetration of invasive species in the United States is astonishing. Some animals (like the European starling) have invaded every state; others have small distribution but frightening profiles (like the Nile monitor lizard in Florida). [R: LJ, Jan 12, p. 136]—**Mark A. Wilson**

Handbooks and Yearbooks

C, P

444.   Pilkey, Orrin H., William J. Neal, Joseph T. Kelley, and J. Andrew G. Cooper. **The World's Beaches: A Global Guide to the Science of the Shoreline.** Berkeley, Calif., University of California Press, 2011. 283p. illus. index. $29.95pa. ISBN 13: 978-0-520-26872-2.

Beaches, those beautiful places where sediment accumulates on the shore of a body of water, fascinate everyone. They are the overlapping edges of two very different environments and so offer unique challenges to the life that lives there, and they are often the first places to change in response to pollution, human activities, and global sea level fluctuations. This book is a comprehensive view of the world's beaches from a scientific perspective, but it is written for anyone with an interest in these shorelines. The prose is especially well crafted, and every page is drenched in color with spectacular photographs.

This book has three parts: the global character of beaches, "how to read a beach," and the many threats to the world's beaches. The first part explains how beaches develop, from the varied materials found as sediments to the current, tide, and wind processes that shape them. The photographs illustrating each feature are again world-class, and they truly cover the global diversity of beaches. The second part is a detailed description and analysis of nearly every feature you can find on a natural beach, down to the tiny lines made in the sand as sea foam is blown across it. This section will be especially useful to geologists and their students. The third part is where these scientists reveal their passion for beaches by describing the numerous threats to their natural integrity. This book is recent enough to mourn the damage from the BP Deepwater Horizon oil spill in the Gulf of Mexico.

The writing, coverage, accuracy, and illustrations of this book make it a real value. All libraries are encouraged to place it on their shelves.—**Mark A. Wilson**

Zoology

General Works

Dictionaries and Encyclopedias

P, S
445.   **North American Wildlife.** Tarrytown, N.Y., Marshall Cavendish, 2011. 240p. illus. maps. index. $69.95. ISBN 13: 978-0-7614-7938-3.

In this title geared toward middle and high school students, 75 articles excerpted from the publisher's *International Wildlife Encyclopedia* (3d ed.; see ARBA 2002, entry 1413) represent the entire spectrum of wildlife found on the continent and in its oceans. Flashy favorites, such as the brown bear, bison, and bald eagle are included, but numerous less-appreciated species like the garter snake, opossum, and robin also get their due. Each article is accompanied by a "fact file" box—listing information such as size, life span, habitat , diet, and endangered status—that is color-coded to reflect whether the animal is a mammal, amphibian, bird, fish, reptile, or invertebrate. Small maps illustrate the range of each species, while two to three large, full-color photographs per article allow readers to see the animals from different angles, engaged in different activities, or at different life stages.

The text is well researched and detailed without being overwhelming for students. It is evident that much thought and care went into highlighting the uniqueness of each animal, rather than simply listing similar dry facts throughout the book. The article on millipedes, for instance, discusses whether they are more harmful or beneficial to crops and continues with coverage of the poisonous species, while the one on polar bears largely focuses on conservation efforts. *North American Wildlife* is recommended for middle school, high school, and public libraries, particularly those that do not already own the *International Wildlife Encyclopedia* set.—**Maren Williams**

C, P, S
446.   Piper, Ross. **Pests: A Guide to the World's Most Maligned, Yet Misunderstood Creatures.** Santa Barbara, Calif., Greenwood Press/ABC-CLIO, 2011. 282p. illus. index. $55.00. ISBN 13: 978-0-313-38426-4; 978-0-313-38427-1 (e-book).

Author Piper's book deals with animal species having lifestyles that adversely affect humans, their crops, pets, livestock, and health. Piper is a Ph.D. zoologist who has authored a number of books on animals. The narrative is organized into eight units, each subdivided by subtopics. Unit titles include the introduction, arachnids, crustaceans, insects, mollusks, nematodes, platyhelminthes, and vertebrates. The introduction discusses the author's intentions and follows with subtopics on insecticides, acaricides, antihelminthics, rodenticides, and the futures of pesticides. Subtopics of all other chapters focus on animal groupings or individual species. The animal topics themselves vary considerably but typically provide an overview of the particular pest and then discussions on the biology, types of damage or health problems caused by the pest, and control measures. Most animal topics include a black-and-white photograph representing the group. Many include tables of pertinent information on such things as included species, species distribution, host species (if parasitic), and diseases (if relevant), and all close with one or more literature sources included as suggested readings. A glossary, brief selected bibliography, and index complete the volume. The book has 305 pages and 60 percent of the pagination is devoted to arthropods and, mostly, to insects. It is obviously intended for the general public. The narrative is accurate, current, well written, and easily comprehensible for readers with little or no scientific background. It is informative rather than entertaining. This work is recommended for general purchase by municipal, high school, and college libraries.—**Edmund D. Keiser Jr.**

Handbooks and Yearbooks

C, P
447.   Hunter, Luke. **Carnivores of the World.** Illustrated by Priscilla Barrett. Princeton, N.J., Princeton University Press, 2012. 240p. illus. maps. index. $75.00; $29.95pa. ISBN 13: 978-0-691-15227-1; 978-0-691-15228-8pa.

The remarkable diversity of the world's carnivores is well illustrated in this guide to all 245 species. We often think of exotic wildlife such as lions, cheetahs, or bears when thinking of carnivores; however, this book focuses on the smaller varieties as well, including weasels, mongooses, and red pandas. Written by Lake Hunter, President of Panthera, a global wildcat conservation group, and illustrated with rich color plates by Priscilla Barrett, a talented artist, the book is a top-notch team effort. For each species account there is text and a distribution map, along with an illustration or photograph. Terse but sufficient text describes key identification features, distribution and habitat, feeding ecology, behavior, reproduction, threats, and conservation status. The author also provides a concise overview of taxonomy, conservation, and the distinct families within the order Carnivora. The publisher maintains a Web page for the title that keeps range maps accurate for status and distribution (http://www.panthera.org/carnivoreguide). This title could easily be used as a standalone reference for specialists and academics in the fields of biology and conservation. General audiences and students will also enjoy it for its beautiful illustrations and accessible species accounts.—**Charles Leck**

Birds

Atlases

C, P, S
448.   Unwin, Mike. **The Atlas of Birds: Diversity, Behavior, and Conservation.** Princeton, N.J., Princeton University Press, 2011. 144p. illus. maps. index. $22.95pa. ISBN 13: 978-0-691-14949-3.

The Atlas of Birds is a profusely illustrated guide to the world's birds, designed to further our understanding of birds in terms of geography. Narrative chapters discuss such topics as biology, taxonomy, ecology, and more. Several chapters deal with the relationship between birds and men, with a strong emphasis on the conservation and protection of birds. Each chapter is illustrated by bird photographs, outline maps, and graphs and diagrams, most of them in color. A Bird Table provides statistical information for each country of the world: bird species, endemic bird species, threatened bird species, human population, agricultural land, fisheries, carbon dioxide emissions, and more. A list of sources, a bird index, and a general index are included. Unwin is a natural history writer and illustrator whose publications include the *RSPB Guide to Birdwatching* (A & C Black, 2008). Much of the statistical information is provided by Bird Life International.

This is a very attractive book with a great deal of information presented in a readable format that is appropriate for both the educated lay person and the secondary school student. It contains the most up-to-date information available in book form. The nearest equivalent is probably *State of the World's Birds* (Bird Life International, 2004). There is a slight British emphasis to the text, which is unobtrusive except for a few vernacular names (e.g., Little Auk instead of Dovekie). One error was discovered in the Bird Table; it states that there are 1,821 species of birds in the Comoros, which is highly unlikely. The price is reasonable. Public, academic, and secondary school libraries will find it useful, either for reference or circulation.—**Jonathan F. Husband**

Handbooks and Yearbooks

P

449.   **The American Bird Conservancy Guide to Bird Conservation.** By Daniel J. Lebbin, Michael J. Parr, and George H. Fenwick. Chicago, University of Chicago Press, 2010. 446p. illus. maps. index. $45.00. ISBN 13: 978-0-226-64727-2.

The American Bird Conservancy is a broad-based environmental group that has published influential guides for bird preservation in the Americas, particularly for North America (including Hawaii). Here the authors (both scientists and ornithologists) have produced a remarkable overview of our birds, their habitat requirements, environmental threats, and potential solutions. It is a timely and inspiring reference. The two major sections of the guide include a watchlist chapter that reviews over 200 endangered birds by individual species accounts, and a habitat overview that illustrates important birdscapes and their biodiversity (e.g., Platte River Basin, Everglades, Big Bend National Park). Other chapters elaborate on threats such as pollution and feral cats, and present strategies and actions for citizen conservation. There is also a review of international bird conservation efforts in Central and South America. Throughout, the volume is beautifully illustrated with an abundance of high-quality photographs, paintings, and maps. Birders and biologists concerned with avian survival will be thankful for this useful resource.—**Charles Leck**

P

450.   **National Geographic Backyard Guide to the Birds of North America.** By Jonathan Alderfer and Paul Hess. Washington, D.C., National Geographic Society, 2011. 254p. illus. maps. index. $18.95pa. ISBN 13: 978-1-4262-0720-4.

This is a small but fact-filled guide to enjoying birds in one's own backyard. An estimated 62 million Americans feed and watch yard birds through the seasons and can appreciate the hints contained here. Information on the most common species (150 birds) includes identification clues (with great illustrations and photographs), range maps, foods, and nesting needs. Introductory basics show and review many types of bird feeders, seeds and other foods, and bird houses. Plantings for bird-friendly yards are summarized regionally. There are listings of Websites devoted to "citizen science" projects wherein one can contribute our own backyard data to nationwide studies. With this easy guide novices young and old will get a fast start in the pastime of observing nature at home.—**Charles Leck**

P

451.   Thompson, Bill, III. **Identifying and Feeding Birds.** New York, Houghton Mifflin, 2010. 246p. maps. index. $14.95pa. ISBN 13: 978-0-618-90444-0.

In this work the author shares an abundance of bird feeding ideas he has tested in more than 40 years of catering to feathered friends. The light-hearted style of the text introduces the beginner to everything needed to enjoy a remarkable backyard hobby. Topics include many suggestions on avian attractions, from shelter, nest boxes, and food plants (e.g., berries, nectar, seeds) to various styles of feeders (e.g., commercial, homemade). The importance of food diversity is discussed in detail (e.g., many seed types, suet, fruits, bird treats), with instructions for offering unusual items such as mealworms. As long-time editor of *Bird Watcher's Digest*, Thompson amassed a splendid overview of bird feeding questions and answers that are shared here, including common mistakes and squirrel problems. A large chapter presents 125 "common backyard bird species," each with a large photograph, range map, identification notes, habitat preferences, and suggestions for backyard attraction. With this book better bird feeding is easy.—**Charles Leck**

Fishes

C, P

452. Kells, Val, and Kent Carpenter. **A Field Guide to Coastal Fishes from Maine to Texas.** Berkeley, Calif., University of California Press, 2011. 447p. illus. index. $25.00pa. ISBN 13: 978-0-8018-9838-9.

This very fine field guide to Atlantic coast fishes commences with a brief introduction discussing diversity and classification, aquatic adaptations, fish identification (with useful figures illustrating terminology), and conservation. Next is a list, with brief characterizations, of fish families arranged under orders. The main section offers brief descriptions and color paintings on opposite pages of 937 species of brackish and marine fish found between the intertidal and 660 feet (200 m.). Rare species are largely omitted, although 72 additional species are available online. The book ends with a brief list of print and online resources, with a full bibliography online. Author and date of original description of each species is given, which is unusual in field guides but a nice touch. Each description includes terse notes on range, habitat, and biology as well as physical characteristics.

The most comparable book is *A Field Guide to Atlantic Coast Fishes of North America*, by C. Richard Robins and G. Carleton Ray (Houghton Mifflin, 1986), which offers similar coverage. The present book has the decided advantage of having all color illustrations that are adjacent to the descriptions. The Robins/Ray book has partly black-and-white illustrations that are segregated from the descriptions. The *National Audubon Society Field Guide to Fishes*, by Carter Rowell Gilbert and James D. Williams (see ARBA 2003, entry 1387), includes both freshwater and marine (both coasts) fishes and includes only about 700 common species. This is an essential purchase for any library near the Atlantic coast and for academic libraries anywhere.—**Frederic F. Burchsted**

Marine Animals

P

453. Allen, Sarah G., Joe Mortenson, and Sophie Webb. **Field Guide to Marine Mammals of the Pacific Coast: Baja, California, Oregon, Washington, British Columbia.** Berkeley, Calif., University of California Press, 2011. 569p. illus. maps. index. $24.95pa. ISBN 13: 978-0-520-26545-5.

There are few places on Earth with more marine mammals than the Pacific Coast of North America. These nutrient-rich cool waters have produced complex ecosystems with an astonishing diversity of mammals at the top, from massive baleen whales to playful sea otters. This field guide provides up-to-date scientific information on these animals, as well as the tools to identify them in their natural environments. This book contains much more than the usual guidebook when it comes to details about the species it covers.

This field guide begins with a pictorial overview of the marine mammal's communities by habitat, and then brief discussions of their biology, evolutionary history, and tragic encounters with humans in the last two centuries. The bulk of the book is the guide to the 45 marine mammal species in this region. The illustrations are key to identifications, so the authors have included several views of the animals in various orientations. The descriptions are clear, although the occasional use of the term "unmistakable" may be a little optimistic. The photographs of seals, sea lions, and otters are especially good. The discussions for each species include many details of physiology, growth and development, ecological relationships, migration patterns, and geographical ranges. The end pages of this guide include a glossary, references for further reading, and a thorough index. This guide book is highly recommended for all libraries with natural history collections. Those on the Pacific Coast will want to order multiple copies.—**Mark A. Wilson**

Reptiles and Amphibians

C, P

454.   Beolens, Bo, Michael Watkins, and Michael Grayson. **The Eponym Dictionary of Reptiles.** Baltimore, Md., Johns Hopkins University Press, 2011. 296p. $100.00. ISBN 13: 978-1-4214-0135-5.

This dictionary provides concise information on the 2,330 persons who have had reptiles named after them. Individuals honored by taxonomic names (e.g., *Oxybelis wilsoni* is named for Dr. Larry David Wilson) and persons honored by being in common names (e.g., Williams' Canyon Lizard is named for Dr. Kenneth L. Williams), are included in the listing. The authors undertook a huge task in developing a resource book on 4,130 reptiles named for individuals. Their objective was complicated by reptile names that only sound like human names and those who were named for fictional, mythical, and biblical names. Names relegated to extinct species are not included if the extinctions occurred before recent times. Scientific and common names that are dubious or obviously incorrect are not included.

A preface and introduction begin the narrative. These are followed by the accounts of alphabetically listed individuals for which reptiles have been named. Each listing includes the name of the person honored followed by a chronologically ordered list of the animals which bear a person's name. The names of reptiles associated with a person in error are also noted. Each taxon entry includes the scientific and vernacular names, the describer(s), and the date of the initial description. Alternative English names and scientific synonyms are also included. This information is followed by a brief biographical sketch of each biographee. Additional information is provided as necessary. The book closes with a bibliography. There are no illustrations.

This is an interesting, informative, and easy-to-read book. While it will satisfy occasional reader curiosities and perform a valuable role for certain specialists, it will have a limited audience due to the nature of the subject matter. It is also over-priced at $100. It is recommended for purchase by municipal and college libraries when specifically requested by potential readers.—**Edmund D. Keiser Jr.**

C, P

455.   Ernst, Carl H., and Evelyn M. Ernst. **Venomous Reptiles of the United States, Canada, and Northern Mexico. Volume 1.** Baltimore, Md., Johns Hopkins University Press, 2011. 352p. illus. maps. index. $75.00. ISBN 13: 978-0-8018-9875-4.

C, P

456.   Ernst, Carl H., and Evelyn M. Ernst. **Venomous Reptiles of the United States, Canada, and Northern Mexico. Volume 2.** Baltimore, Md., Johns Hopkins University Press, 2012. 391p. illus. index. $75.00. ISBN 13: 978-0-8018-9876-1.

These fascinating books cover all the venomous lizards and snakes. Volume 2 exclusively covers rattlesnakes of the genus *Crotalus*. They aim to include complete natural history information for each species and a full, and rather technical, treatment of venoms, bringing these subjects up to date with coverage of the extensive literature (each volume has a 90-page bibliography) since C. H. Ernst's *Venomous Reptiles of North America* (see ARBA 93, entry 1576). The authors consistently point out gaps in available knowledge.

Volume 1 covers much of the same subject matter as Campbell and Lamar's *The Venomous Reptiles of the Western Hemisphere* (see ARBA 2005, entry 1399). Campbell and Lamar also cover the rich Central and South American fauna. In Campbell and Lamar's book most natural history and venom information is presented in the generic level descriptions, with species entries reserved for names, physical description, distribution, and habitat. Being limited to the northern region allows the Ernsts room for a much more thorough treatment of the natural history than Lamar and Campbell. Volume 2, on *Crotalus*, provides information on this species venom delivery system, how rattles function, what rattlesnakes eat, and what eats rattlesnakes. For each there is a photograph, map of geographic location, and explanations of the limits to their distribution. These volumes are an essential purchase for academic and large public libraries, and a very worthwhile acquisition for smaller libraries, especially in the southern and western United States.—**Frederic F. Burchsted**

C, P, S

457.   Mattison, Chris. **Frogs and Toads of the World.** Princeton, N.J., Princeton University Press, 2011. 192p. illus. index. $29.95. ISBN 13: 978-0-691-14968-4.

Chris Mattison, author of numerous books on amphibians and reptiles and an accomplished photographer, has produced another quality volume on anurans of the world. The narrative is organized into an introduction and 10 chapters. The introduction defines the taxon and provides an overview of variation within the 5,858 species of frogs and toads currently recognized by scientists.

Chapter 1 deals with evolutionary history, diversity, and classification and includes a two-page table on families, genera, species, and family ranges. Chapter 2 specifies frog sizes, shapes, and coloration, often detailed by anatomical parts, sexual dimorphism, color changes, and use in identification. Chapter 3 involves respiration, water balance, thermoregulation, and other interactions with the physical environment. Chapter 4 concerns frog enemies and defense mechanisms and responses, while chapter 5 covers food and feeding of larvae and adults. Chapter 6 provides details on reproduction and early development. Chapter 7 details aspects of aquatic, terrestrial, and aerial egg deposition and life cycles in general, and chapter 8 generalizes habitats and distribution. Chapter 9 describes relationships of frogs and humans. The final chapter presents details on the frog families of the world. A section on further information and an index conclude the book.

All sections of this book are lavishly illustrated with some of the finest color photographs of frogs yet to appear in the literature. This book is easy to read and comprehend, highly informative, accurate, and as up to date as possible in an era dominated by changes due to new molecular insights. This work is highly recommended for purchase by municipal, high school, and college libraries.—**Edmund D. Keiser Jr.**

32 Engineering

General Works

C

458.   **EI Compendex. http://www.ei.org/compendex.** [Website]. San Diego, Calif., Elsevier Science. Price negotiated by site. Date reviewed: 2011.

Compendex, also knows as the Engineering Index, is the most comprehensive bibliographic database of scientific and technical engineering research available, covering all engineering disciplines, including chemical, civil, mining, mechanical, and electrical. It includes millions of bibliographic citations and abstracts from thousands of engineering journals and conference proceedings. When combined with the engineering index Backfile (1884-1969), Compendex covers well over 120 years of core engineering literature. It currently holds 12 million records across 190 engineering disciplines and provides users access to 1,031 journals. It is a standard resource in most academic science and engineering library.— **James E. Bobick**

Biomedical Engineering

C, P

459.   **Plunkett's Biotech & Genetics Industry Almanac.** 2012 ed. Jack W. Plunkett, ed. Houston, Tex., Plunkett Research, 2011. 550p. index. $299.00pa. (includes online editions). ISBN 13: 978-1-60879-649-6; 978-1-60879-911-4 (e-book).

Plunkett's Biotech & Genetics Industry Almanac is the 10th edition and an update from the 2011 almanac. The editors continue to provide the first step for researchers in the biotech and genetics industry. Not written for in-depth analysis of the industry, the monograph instead provides students and researchers with self-contained segments readers can access without going through the entire book. Structured into four chapters dealing mainly with the industry in America, the sections give snapshots of different components of the industry. The first chapter contains several sections of varying length dealing with current trends. These trends include the interest in ethanol as a fuel alternative and hot topics such as stem cell research and rising drug prices. The almanac also provides key statistical information on funding and company rankings. One of the most useful parts of the text was the company profiles for the biotech 400. The companies listed, predominately based in the United States, have significant presence in the industry and openly accessible financial information. The typical entry includes company name, Web address, NAIC code, company ranking, types of business, brands, basic financial data, and contact information. Other useful aspects of the book include a short glossary; an index of subsidiaries, brand names, and affiliations; and an index of companies noted for promoting women and minorities.

The language is relatively jargon-free. The paper binding will not stand up to heavy use but the pages are thick with large clear type. With the purchase of the print edition users will also be given access to the online edition. Overall, this directory will complement the collections of large public and academic libraries.—**Melissa M. Johnson**

Civil Engineering

P, S

460. Barratt, Claire, and Ian Whitelaw. **The Spotter's Guide to Urban Engineering: Infrastructure and Technology in the Modern Landscape.** Richmond Hills, Ont., Firefly Books, 2011. 224p. illus. index. $24.95pa. ISBN 13: 978-1-55407-708-3.

We all rely on modern civil engineering everyday. This book is an introduction to the technology that provides modern life convenience. For those that are curious as to how suspension bridges work, how we get clean drinking water, or the intricacies of the telephone system, this book peels away the layers and provides user a closer look at the technology that enables us to enjoy these modern-day conveniences. The book is arranged into six main areas of infrastructure: raw materials (e.g., mining, concrete plants); water (e.g., dams, water treatment plants); power (e.g., electricity grids, oil and gas distribution); transportation (e.g., sidewalks, aviation); communication (e.g., television, telephone), and waste (e.g., sewers, recycling). For each of the nearly 100 engineering processes featured in this book there is information on what it is, where it can be found, its physical dimensions, architectural notes, and history. Color photographs, detailed diagrams and charts, and sidebars with interesting facts provide additional information and are essential in a book such as this where much of the information can be better understood in visual format. The work concludes with a glossary, a list of references, and an index. With information too general for academic libraries, this work is best suited for high school libraries and public libraries to satisfy the curious customer.—**Shannon Graff Hysell**

Electrical Engineering

C

461. **IEEE Xplore. http://ieeexplore.ieee.org/Xplore/guesthome.jsp?reload=true.** [Website]. Price negotiated by site. Date reviewed: 2011.

This site provides full-text access to IEEE transactions, journals, and conference proceedings and IEE journals from 1988 to the present, as well as all current IEEE standards. This database provides users with a single source leading to almost one-third of the world's current electrical engineering and computer science literature, with unparalleled access to IEEE and IEE publications.—**James E. Bobick**

C

462. **The Industrial Electronics Handbook: Fundamentals of Industrial Electronics.** 2d ed. Bogdan M. Wilamowski and J. David Irwin, eds. Boca Raton, Fla., CRC Press, 2011. 5v. illus. index. $299.95/set. ISBN 13: 978-1-4398-0289-2.

This resource covers all aspects of electrical engineering in an industrial setting in five volumes: "Fundamentals of Industrial Electronics," "Power Electronics and Motor Drives," "Control and Mechatronics," "Industrial Communications Systems," and "Intelligent Systems." The first volume contains basic scientific and design principles, while the later volumes focus on their individual areas. Each volume is subdivided by broad topic and then further by chapter. Chapters range from 4-20 pages, and may either be a single essay or broken into smaller subchapters depending on the complexity of the topic. As necessary, the chapters are illustrated with well-executed photographs, charts, drawings, graphs, and diagrams, along with the necessary equations and other supporting materials. Most chapters have a further reading list at the end as well. Much of the material is derived from articles in the *IEEE Transactions on Industrial Electronics*, but the *Handbook* is not a reprint of articles. Each volume contains a brief introduction to the topic, explaining the organization of the volume, and a volume-specific index. There is no master index for the set, which, given the inevitable overlap between topics, is a small but unfortunate oversight. As is usual for handbooks, this would be a solid addition to any library with the relevant specialty.—**Peter Larsen**

33 Health Sciences

General Works

Bibliography

P

463. **ALA Guide to Medical & Health Sciences Reference.** Chicago, American Library Association, 2011. 742p. index. $75.00pa. ISBN 13: 978-0-8389-1023-8.

The ALA Guide to Reference series will be familiar to librarians who have used *Guide to Reference Books* in the past. The *ALA Guide to Medical & Health Science Reference* offers brief annotations on over 1,500 research, clinical, and consumer health-related print and electronic reference sources. Resources are grouped first by broad subsection (including Medicine, Bioethics, Consumer Health, Dentistry, Nursing, Nutrition, Public Health, and Toxicology), and then by subcategory. Types of sources covered range from bibliographies, dictionaries, directories, encyclopedias, guides, and handbooks as well as Internet-based sources (free and for-fee) and digital image collections. Publication/access information is listed for each source, accompanied by a brief description or a table of contents for each resource. No prices are given.

Individual entries are numbered, and have publication information and LC and Dewey call number designations. Information describing sources is brief and often taken directly from the source introduction or website. Cross-references to other entries in the guide are provided within source summaries. The online edition of this source is not included in this review. An index lists sources in A-Z order, with references to the main entry number.

The strength of the *ALA Guide to Medical & Health Science Reference* is the variety of sources covered; as a bibliography for introductory or retrospective collection building, this is good source to consult. Older publication dates for some sources included are a concern, especially for medical collections where currency is a factor. Most appropriate for medical libraries and universities that support a medical studies program.—**Caroline L. Gilson**

Dictionaries and Encyclopedias

C, P

464. **Encyclopedia of Family Health.** Martha Craft-Rosenberg and Shelley Rae Pehler, eds. Thousand Oaks, Calif., Sage, 2011. 2v. index. $350.00/set; e-book available. ISBN 13: 978-1-4129-6918-5.

Family health encompasses a variety of disciplines, including health and nursing, social and behavioral sciences, and public policy. This resource, available both in print and e-book formats, discusses a variety of issues and policies as they related to family health, such as how the changes in family life affect the health of family members, the affects on families due to rising costs of insurance, and how health care providers can best intervene when working with families. The two-volume work consists of 350 articles written from a variety of fields, with the majority being from the health sciences, psychology, and behavioral sciences. The entries are arranged under 11 themes, with Families Experiencing Transitions (63), Families and the Health Care System (52), and Family Interventions (49) containing the most entries and Family Health Assessment (12) and Education of Health Care Providers (7) containing the fewest. Each of the entries is signed by its author and provides *see also* references, a list of related articles, and a list of further reading suggestions. The writing is clear and jargon-free but will be best understood by undergraduate students and graduate students familiar with this field of study. The cross-references used throughout the text are very useful and straightforward; for example, while researching under "Caregiving: Infants" users will discover relevant entries on Babysitting and the Family, Maternal Lactation, and Sudden Infant Death Syndrome, along with many others.

As with most Sage reference titles, this two-volume encyclopedia provides a wealth of information on a hot topic for both health professionals and public policy makers. Cross-references throughout and the thorough index at the end of volume 2 make this useful as a reference tool, though researchers may find themselves browsing the entries as well. This work would be a worthwhile addition to any public or university library.—**Shannon Graff Hysell**

P, S

465.   **Family Health from A to Z.** Tarrytown, N.Y., Marshall Cavendish, 2012. 480p. illus. index. $59.95. ISBN 13: 978-0-7614-7945-1; 978-0-7614-7945-1 (e-book).

The editors of this "family" encyclopedia indicate that their work is intended for the younger reader, and caution that no treatment should be initiated unless the patient has been advised by or consulted with a licensed medical practitioner. The text then proceeds to identify multiple medical topics in no logical order other than an alphabetic listing reflecting common illnesses and health-related issues such as Abrasions and Cuts, Adolescence, Child Development, Exercise, Infection and Infectious Diseases, Lacerations, Sore Throat, Stroke, Vitamin A, and Zest. However, users can scan a one-page contents at the beginning of the volume to find if there is a heading on Chicken Pox or Lice or Occupational Hazards. In reality, the editors have established five health categories and provided a color key code to the Questions and Answers found in each article: blue is the human body, tan is diseases and other disorders, magenta refers to treatments and cures, deep pink is prevention and diagnosis of disease, and green is human behavior. However, there is no index of what goes under each of the categories.

Entries may be as short as a page or as long as seven or eight pages. Topics vary widely with respect to breadth and/or depth of information; for example, Cancer has six pages with sections on symptoms, diagnosis, types, treatments, and general questions and answers. Hygiene has five pages covering an assortment of related areas such as pets, learning abut hygiene, travel, washing, common precautions, and, as in all articles, selected questions and answers. An article on Warts fills three pages (mostly illustrations) and speaks to causes, appearance, and treatment, but one-quarter of a page is devoted to "magic" cures. It should also be noted that several articles do suggest treatment despite the disclaimer noted above; for example, Abrasions and Cuts, Dislocations, Mumps, and almost every article has some information about treatments or "dos and don'ts." Moreover, the last pages of the work are titled First Aid Handbook (pp. 428-455). Illustrated articles in this handbook begin with Artificial Respiration and include, for example, Burns, Fractures, Sprains and Strains through Wounds. Therefore, as the introduction states, "the information provided here is valuable to users of any age." Clearly this work offers suggestions to adults and younger users in first aid.

The volume is attractively designed with an eye to layout. Multicolored boxes show different types of information and "photographs, charts, graphs, and artworks with clear descriptive captions" (p. 4) adorn every article. Following the first aid handbook is a second A-Z listing titled medical glossary, which provides very brief definitions of terms such as abdomen, enteritis, and yellow fever. The final pages include a brief bibliography, a list of Internet resources and hotlines along with a useful index; for example, celiac disease sends you to a page in an article on allergies.

Similar titles and coverage are found in every bookstore and may continue to be there although widespread Internet connectivity makes such volumes almost obsolete. Rather than struggle to figure out whether one can locate relevant info in Bites and Stings in this volume or find detailed information on multiple types of bee versus wasp bites online may already be a moot point. Whether to treat at home or chat with a specialist after posting a clear picture of the bite site and reaction will be an easy choice for those on the right side of the digital divide. In the meantime, this update to the public library's children's collection may still be useful if introductory, but only available when the library is open—unless this title is acquired as an e-book. The work cannot be recommended for first aid or real substance, but might be useful when looking at prevention or an overview of a health topic.—**Laurel Grotzinger**

Directories

P

466.   **The Complete Directory for People with Chronic Illness 2011/2012.** 10th ed. Millerton, N.Y., Grey House Publishing, 2011. 866p. index. $165.00pa.; $300.00 (online database; single user); $400.00 (print and online editions). ISBN 13: 978-1-59237-741-1.

The 10th edition of this reference contains almost 11,000 updated and new listings for patients, caregivers, researchers, and healthcare professionals. As stated in the introduction, these resources are crucial for people with chronic illness "as they transition from diagnosis to home, home to work, and work to community life." After the table of contents, readers will find a section of steps to follow after diagnosis that provides valuable information about whom to contact, where to find support, and more. Of particular interest are pictures and commentary of actual patients who illustrate and restate the benefits of following the steps outlined in the book.

In this directory there are 89 chronic conditions that are listed alphabetically by name. Each chapter describes the condition in lay terms, and following the descriptions are resources including agencies, information resources in all formats, and personnel who could provide more contacts for support and treatment. There are indexes by entry name as well as geographic location.

In addition to this print volume, the *Directory* is available online for a subscription price. Users can quickly find the information they need through keyword or advanced searches. Libraries in need of access for multiple users can contact Grey House Publishing for pricing information. This volume is recommended for public, medical, and university science libraries.—**Laura J. Bender**

P

467.   **Encyclopedia of Medical Organizations and Agencies: A Subject Guide to Organizations, Foundations, Federal and State Governmental Agencies . . ..** 22d ed. Farmington Hills, Mich., Gale/Cengage Learning, 2010. 3v. index. $584.00/set. ISBN 13: 978-1-4144-4668-4. ISSN 0743-4510.

This volume is a directory of various health and medical entities. The bulk of the *Encyclopedia* is the "List of Medical Organizations and Agencies," subdivided by subject areas such as aging, biomedical engineering, environmental health, genetics, health care industry, and nutrition. Each category lists federal government agencies, foundations and other funding organizations, national and international organizations, research centers, and state and regional organizations. The entries provide a brief description and contact information. In addition, there is a helpful subject cross-index and an alphabetic name and keyword index. This reference contains much of the information in the *Medical and Health Information Directory*, which is also from the Gale Group (26th ed.; see ARBA 2012, entry 1247), but, containing 21,500 entries as opposed to the 28,000 entries in *Medical and Health Information Directory*, is about half the price. In addition, the descriptions are more helpful. This reference is an adequate resource for most public, academic, and health libraries. For a wider array of organizations, but without many of the useful descriptions, consult the *Medical and Health Information Directory*.—**Elaine Lasda Bergman**

C, P

468.   Wischnitzer, Saul, and Edith Wischnitzer. **The Top 100 Health-Care Careers: Your Complete Guidebook to Training and Jobs in Allied Health, Nursing, Medicine, and More.** 3d ed. St. Paul, Minn., JIST Works, 2011. 488p. index. $25.95pa. ISBN 13: 978-1-59357-809-1.

The 3d edition of *The Top 100 Health-Care Careers* offers career information, educational requirements, and training for the latest job options in the health care industry, including practitioners, associated health-care workers, technicians and technologists, therapists, health care administrators, and affiliated health care workers. It also includes topical information such as time management, leadership, professional standards, and information on communication with patients.

This book is divided into four sections: part 1 helps the reader decide if a health-related career is right for them; part 2 discusses what it's like to work in the health care field; part 3 covers the job search process; and part 4 describes 100 positions in the health care field and includes educational requirements and training programs. Chapters are presented in narrative form, with brief paragraphs, bulleted lists, and informational charts. There are also checklists and charts (workbook style) for self-assessment. Additional content includes salary ranges for various positions and résumé and job application information. Each of the 100 careers profiled offers a brief narrative that describes the career, and provides information on educational requirements, prerequisites, and licensure or certification information. Specific colleges and universities that offer educational programs are then listed. The appendixes include a listing of health care education admission tests, professional organizations, and additional job search resources. A general topic index is also included.

Overall, this source offers solid information on planning for a health-related career, with training and educational information. It is most appropriate for medical libraries, community colleges, and public libraries where medical career information would be useful.—**Caroline L. Gilson**

Handbooks and Yearbooks

P, S

469.   Callahan, Joan R. **50 Health Scares That Fizzled.** Santa Barbara, Calif., Greenwood Press/ABC-CLIO, 2011. 361p. index. $85.00. ISBN 13: 978-0-313-38538-4; 978-0-31338-539-1 (e-book).

In the book *50 Health Scares that Fizzled*, Callahan, an epidemiologist for the Naval Health Research Center, co-mingles scientific information with hyped up media health scare hysterias and medical misconceptions. The reader learns about current and past health scares and health threats while being entertained by quirky anecdotes and Internet lore. The introduction explains how a health scare starts and how it keep going and sometimes builds up to a frenzy, and then how a health scare ends or "fizzles out." What is compelling is that the author not only explains how the health scares end, she has also left the reader with questions that have arisen on the subjects leading to thoughts about further research.

The entries begin with a summary of the topic, history of when the fear or scare began, and the science behind the issue and history on how the public reacted to it. For example the Fear of Red Dye entry focuses on the history of red M&Ms. Because of the red dye no.2 health scare, red M&Ms were not made from 1976-1987. The author explains that Red dye no. 40 is used today and some scientists are still not sure if it is any safer. The red dye story ends with more questions than answers. The entries all end with a comprehensive list of references and recommended readings that come from medical journals, newspapers, and popular periodicals. The blending of epidemiology, folklore and quirky human behavior, mass media hysteria, and psychology makes this a highly readable enlightening book that would be useful for both graduate and undergraduate students studying topics in public health. *50 Health Scares that Fizzled* intensifies curiosity to do further research in the public health fields on these controversial topics.—**Amy B. Parsons**

P

470.   Hohler, Sharon E. **Caregiver's Guide: Care for Yourself While You Care for Your Loved One.** Jefferson, N.C., McFarland, 2012. 272p. index. (McFarland Health Topics). $35.00pa. ISBN 13: 978-0-7864-4962-0.

This well-written guide is a timely and valuable resource. It is meant to be a comprehensive resource for those who find themselves in the position of caring for a loved one, either unexpectedly or gradually over a period of time. The contents of the guide are comprehensive. It begins with a table of contents that lists the book's 15 chapters. The first 10 chapters address topics that will aid the caregiver, while the last 5 chapters address specific diseases often encountered in this situation (e.g., cancer, Alzheimer's Disease, diabetes). Topics discussed in depth include the stages of caregiving, children involved in caregiving, how to deal with stress, practical decisions, grieving, and strategies for healthy aging. Specific details and resources for those caring for loved ones with cancer, diabetes, heart disease, Alzheimer's Disease, and arthritis round out the volume. The text is easy to read and understand and provides plenty of resources that those in the caregiving role can turn to for help.

This text is likely to be useful to individuals caring for loved ones or those who know that they will be in the future due to a loved one's progressing disease. The emphasis on maintaining one's own physical and mental health is key, as well as the sound advice on doctor's visits, avoiding mistakes with medicines, and safety around the home.—**Shannon Graff Hysell**

C, P, S

471.   Koch, Tom. **Disease Maps: Epidemics on the Ground.** Chicago, University of Chicago Press, 2011. 330p. illus. maps. index. $45.00. ISBN 13: 978-0-226-44935-7.

Tom Koch's premise that demographics shine a light on the mysteries of pestilence introduces a mathematical and geographical matrix for understanding disease. A standard method of graphing public health statistics, disease maps have become crucial to the tracking of pathogens via immigration, trade, and travel. From cholera, consumption, and typhoid fever to AIDS and West Nile Fever, mapping helps readers picture the grip of sickness on the human community. Koch's maps and charts illustrate the need for cooperation between the medical profession and government. Through engaging discussion of history and insets from classic maps, the text models the advance of mapping as a means of picturing the vectors and effects of invisible microbes, such as the Black Death and yellow fever. Informative notes and 16 pages of bibliography attest to Koch's command of medical history and scholarship. This work is highly recommended for high school, college, and university shelves and for the offices of city planners and public health officials.—**Mary Ellen Snodgrass**

P

472.   Kronenfeld, Jennie Jacobs. **Medicare.** Santa Barbara, Calif., Greenwood Press/ABC-CLIO, 2011. 199p. illus. index. (Health & Medical Issues Today). $35.00. ISBN 13: 978-0-313-36405-1.

Medicare consists of three parts: an overview section, a section on issues and controversies, and a references and resources section. By far the most valuable part of the work is the issues and controversies section. Each of the chapters discuss a controversial issue in Medicare, such as drug coverage, HMOs and Managed Care options, long-term care coverage, Medicare and the demographic-based funding crisis, and health care reform. The author presents a balanced view and does a good job highlighting ethical dilemmas in the current world of Medicare and government sponsored health care programs.

The introductory material is informational and can serve as background reading material for students just delving into a topic. The "Annotated Primary Source Documents" in the references and resources section takes up quite a bit of space, with extensive annotations. This volume will be useful for those looking for a good overview of the topic of Medicare that touches on controversies within the program.—**Danielle Marie Carlock**

Medicine

General Works

Catalogs and Collections

C, P

473.   **MEDLINE. http://www.nlm.nih.gov/.** [Website]. Date reviewed: 2012.

MEDLINE (Medical Literature Analysis and Retrieval System Online), is a product of the U.S. National Library of Medicine (NLM), which describes it as their "premier bibliographic database" containing "approximately 13 million references to journal articles" in the life sciences, with a focus on biomedicine. Date coverage is generally from 1966 to the present, although some older material is also available. *MEDLINE* is a journal citation database (many citations offer links to full text, but the database itself does not contain full-text), and international in scope: it selectively covers approximately 5,200 journals from all over the world, in 37 languages. The NLM enhances records from non-English language journals by supplying translated article titles; English translations of abstracts are dependent on the article authors. The database is updated daily, from Tuesday through Saturday, with the addition of between 2,000–4,000 new citations each day. This phenomenal effort is the result of a distribution of labor among the NLM, its international partners, and collaborating institutions.

A key distinguishing feature of *MEDLINE* is its carefully crafted thesaurus, known as "MeSH," for Medical Subject Headings. This highly developed, hierarchical system of subject headings is also the work of the National Library of Medicine, which has a whole branch devoted to continuous maintenance, revision, and updating of the MeSH vocabulary. The impression one gets is that this is a dynamic system, continually growing and changing in response to developments in scientific and medical research and practice. Statistics about MeSH are impressive: it contains 24,767 subject headings, augmented with 97,000 *see* references, and more than 172,000 other entry points.

Overall, the results make clear that *MEDLINE* is very much a professional tool. Medical librarians can go through weeks of training learning all of its functions and what they mean. For general consumer health queries, however, there are better choices: subscription databases such as *Health Reference Center* (Gale-Cengage Learning), or free government Websites such as *MedlinePlus.gov* (also a product of the National Library of Medicine).—**Suzanne S. Bell**

Dictionaries and Encyclopedias

C, P

474.   **The Gale Encyclopedia of Children's Health.** 2d ed. Farmington Hills, Mich., Gale/Cengage Learning, 2011. 4v. illus. index. $748.00/set. ISBN 13: 978-1-4144-8641-3.

The 2d edition of *The Gale Encyclopedia of Children's Health* is a four-volume reference source that covers 793 pediatric wellness issues, including specific diseases and medical conditions as well as behavioral and developmental issues. More than 200 new entries have been added to this new edition. Examples of specific topics covered include allergies, birthmarks, dyslexia, orthodontics, personality development, puberty, tantrums, and vitamins. The target audience for this source would include parents, students, and general readers interested in children's health issues.

Each volume begins with a comprehensive table of contents and an alphabetic list of all entries. At the end of the fourth volume there is a glossary, followed by a growth charts appendix, a common childhood medications appendix, and complete topic index to all volumes. Main entries are arranged alphabetically and have been written by medical experts. Entries fall into one of four broad categories: Diseases and Disorders, Development, Immunizations/Drugs, and Procedures. Entry lengths vary from

500 to 4,000 words. Some entries have accompanying color images, including photographs, charts, or tables. Within each entry the information presented is broken down into categories such as definition, description, causes and symptoms, treatment, prognosis, and parental concerns. Bolded terms within entries indicate they have their own main entry listing. Specific key vocabulary terms are defined within individual entries. Brief bibliographies and cross-references to related topics follow most entries. All entries are signed.

The 2d edition of *The Gale Encyclopedia of Children's Health* offers students, parents, and teachers a general introduction to children's health and wellness topics. This set is appropriate for school and public libraries.—**Caroline L. Gilson**

C, P, S

475.   **The Gale Encyclopedia of Medicine.** 4th ed. Farmington Hills, Mich., Gale/Cengage Learning, 2011. 6v. illus. index. $919.00/set. ISBN 13: 978-1-4144-8646-8.

Health information is vital. With physicians having less time to explain diseases and treatment options, patients often head to the library to learn more. The 4th edition of *The Gale Encyclopedia of Medicine* is an excellent resource for these questions. It provides more information than single-volume medical encyclopedias in language that is more accessible than that of a medical textbook. The signed articles are by experienced medical writers, including physicians, nurses, pharmacists, and other health practitioners.

This new edition contains more than 1,700 articles, ranging in length from 500 to 4,000 words. About one-quarter of the entries have been updated. The encyclopedia also has approximately 650 color illustrations, charts, and tables as well as sidebars containing biographical and historical information. Shaded boxes define key terms used in the text.

The entries are arranged alphabetically. They include information about diseases and conditions, diagnostic tests, therapies, and drugs. There are entries for alternative as well as conventional treatments, but the articles on alternative therapies are less detailed than those in *The Gale Encyclopedia of Alternative Medicine* (23 ed.; see ARBA 2009, entry 1255). All articles have resource lists of books, articles, and Websites for further research. A master list of organizations and a general index are in the last volume. This work is available as an e-book with a price determined by account type and population served. *The Gale Encyclopedia of Medicine* remains an outstanding resource for public, school, and consumer health libraries.—**Barbara M. Bibel**

C, P

476.   **Salem Health: Infectious Diseases & Conditions.** Hackensack, N.J., Salem Press, 2011. 3v. illus. index. $395.00/set. ISBN 13: 978-1-58765-776-4.

This 3-volume encyclopedia contains 610 entries related to infectious diseases. Topics include pathogens and pathogenicity, transmission, the immune system, vaccines, prevention, epidemiology, drug resistance, and general terminology one encounters when discussing infectious diseases. The work also addresses the social concerns of infectious diseases among social groups, such as the elderly, children, lower-income families, and more. All are written by medical practitioners such as doctors, nurses, and pharmacists. A common entry will include alternate terms for the entry topic, and brief paragraphs that provide essential information at a glance. For example, the entries on procedures include: a definition; why it is performed; patient preparation; what to expect before, during, and after the procedure; risks; and results. Each entry includes references for further information and other resources. The writing styles of the various contributors are somewhat inconsistent—some use quite a bit of medical jargon whereas others are easily understandable by the layperson. Nonetheless, the work is very thorough and informative and would be of use to those recently diagnosed with cancer, their loved ones, or students in health sciences programs.

Purchase of the print edition comes with free online access. The online version currently contains the content of *Salem Health: Cancer, Psychology & Mental Health* (see ARBA 2011, entry 699),

Genetics & Inherited Diseases (see ARBA 2011, entry 1275), *Infectious Diseases & Conditions*, and *Magill's Medical Guide* (4th ed.; see ARBA 2008, entry1233). In the coming years several new titles will be added to this resource, including *Addictions & Substance Abuse* and *Nutrition & Eating Disorders*. Searching is simple. Users can type in a topic or keyword and choose to search any or all of the resources selected. Results can be shown in full-text, abstract, title, or key topic. This title is recommended for public and academic libraries.—**Elaine Lasda Bergman**

Handbooks and Yearbooks

C, P
477.   **Diet and Nutrition Sourcebook.** 4th ed. Laura Larsen, ed. Detroit, Omnigraphics, 2011. 656p. index. (Health Reference Series). $85.00. ISBN 13: 978-0-7808-1152-2.

This is the 4th edition of the *Diet and Nutrition Sourcebook* by Omnigraphics. The main parts of the book include part 1 "Guidelines for Healthy Food Consumption"; part 2 "The Elements of Good Nutrition"; part 3 "Nutrition Through the Life Span"; part 4 "Lifestyle and Nutrition"; part 5 "Nutrition-Related Health Concerns"; part 6 "Nutrition and Weight Control"; part 7 "Nutrition for People with Other Medical Concerns"; and part 8 "Additional Help and Information." The book contains information on the new MyPlate food guidance system; the new dietary guidelines; how to eat healthy away from home; nutritional needs of the elderly; school and senior adult programs on nutrition; and specific diets for illnesses such as diabetes, heart disease, lactose intolerance, food allergies, celiac disease, eating disorders, and cancer. While all of this information is reprinted from elsewhere, the book nicely pulls it together in one place. It is a bit pricy for smaller consumer health collections but not for larger library collections. One drawback is that it is only presented in black and white with minimal diagrams, charts, or tables. For a library wanting something more visual for patrons it will not be a good choice. This book is a good buy for larger public libraries and medical or academic libraries that have consumer health collections.—**Leslie M. Behm**

S
478.   **Diet Information for Teens: Health Tips About Nutrition Fundamentals and Eating Plans.** 3d ed. Zachary Klimecki and Karen Bellenir, eds. Detroit, Omnigraphics, 2011. 427p. index. (Teen Health Series). $62.00. ISBN 13: 978-0-7808-1156-0.

This new edition of *Diet Information for Teens* debuts the new look of the Teen Health Reference series. The series books are a bit larger than previous volumes and the covers include photographs and a more modern look. The organization of information within the volume remains much the same as other volumes. It is a very quick and pleasant read, using a lot of white space, bullet lists, and sidebars to grab readers' interest. The writing is informal and speaks directly to the reader; it uses technical terms, while going to great length in explaining them. It does not talk down to the reader. The material is authoritative. It comes from documents put out by most of the federal agencies dealing with health and nutrition and also includes information from professional societies. There is an M.D. on the editorial board as well.

The book has 58 chapters in 7 parts. They are: "Nutrition Fundamentals," which deals with the food groups and reading food labels; "Vitamins and Minerals," which explains all of the essential vitamins and minerals and the use of supplements; "Other Elements Inside Food," which covers sodium, sugars, fats, and additives; "Smart Eating Plans," which goes into healthy shopping, ordering healthy while eating out, and nutrition for athletes and vegetarians; "Eating and Weight-Related Concerns," which discusses a healthy BMI, body image, and choosing a weight loss program; "Eating and Disease," which provides information on health problems associated with obesity, poor oral health, diabetes, and more; and "If You Need More Information," which wraps it up with cooking tips, resources for dietary information, and resources for physical fitness. One of the great pleasures in using this book is finding a professionally prepared index. It makes all the difference in the world in getting to specific information. In fact, even though this is a handbook, the index makes it a solid reference tool.

It is nice to see that this updated volume focuses more on healthy eating and the benefits of good nutrition than on weight loss and dieting. Teaching young adults to live a healthy lifestyle without dieting will be more beneficial to them in the long run. Even though it was written for teenagers, it really is a book for anyone concerned about diet and nutrition. The very good writing makes it accessible to anyone with a middle school level of reading.—**Lillian R. Mesner**

P

479.   **Medical Tests Sourcebook.** 4th ed. Joyce Brennfleck Shannon, ed. Detroit, Omnigraphics, 2011. 649p. index. (Health Reference Series). $85.00. ISBN 13: 978-0-7808-1151-5.

This book is written for the medical consumer as part of the Health Reference Series. This is an extensive series that pulls together recent articles from authoritative sources, usually national health organizations. The book divides medical tests into several general categories: screening and preventive care tests (e.g., for newborns, preventive care); laboratory tests (e.g., blood tests, bone marrow tests); imaging tests (e.g., x-rays, MRIs, sonography); cathertierization, endoscopic, and electrical tests and assessments (e.g., EKGs, stress testing); screening and assessment for specific conditions (e.g., allergies, cancer, diabetes); and home and self-ordered tests (e.g., cholesterol home use test, ovulation and pregnancy tests, HIV home test). Each section is further divided into types of tests within the category and specific tests. Most sections include background information about the history and development of the test, a description, and preparation for the test if important. Most chapters include references for further reading and information and the addresses and telephone numbers for any groups that deal with the medical problem. An additional chapter provides a glossary of medical terms, online health screening tools, a special directory for breast and cervical cancer early detection programs, and resources for more information. An extensive topical index aids the reader.

As a whole, the volume is fairly user-friendly despite its tendency to fall into medical terminology without explanation or glossary entries. Most individual test entries explain what the test shows and how the test is done. Very little information is provided to aid the patient in interpreting test results. Many sections dealing with specific tests include a bibliographic reference for the information at the beginning of the section, but this information is provided on an inconsistent basis. Taken as a whole, this volume can be a valuable reference guide and will serve as a first-stop resource when one is beginning their personal research into this topic. [R: LJ, Jan 12, p. 134-136]—**Shannon Graff Hysell**

P

480.   **The Merck Manual of Diagnosis and Therapy.** 19th ed. Robert S. Porter, ed. West Point, Pa., Merck, 2011. 2990p. index. $79.95. ISBN 13: 978-0-911910-19-3.

Questions about sickness, health, and medicine are commonplace in many reference departments. Fortunately, the quality and amount of consumer health information has increased over the past few years. Although reference librarians should not attempt to provide medical advice, a number of handbooks assist the user in understanding health-related issues. Merck Research Laboratories publishes *The Merck Manual of Diagnosis and Therapy*, a widely used medical handbook that provides essential information on diagnosing and treating medical disorders, with 22 major sections by body system and medical specialty. *The Merck Manual of Medical Information* (2d home ed.; see ARBA 2004, entry 1437) is a comprehensive consumer health version of the previous title, offering straightforward discussions of diseases and other health problems. It describes symptoms and suggests possible treatments. Both titles are also available online.—**Caroline L. Gilson**

C, P

481.   Thompson, Lana. **Plastic Surgery.** Santa Barbara, Calif., Greenwood Press/ABC-CLIO, 2012. 200p. illus. index. (Health & Medical Issues Today). $58.00. ISBN 13: 978-0-313-37568-2; 978-0-313-37569-9 (e-book).

In this volume of Greenwood Press's Health & Medical Issues Today series, Thompson tackles the medical and social issues in both necessary and elected plastic surgery. Examining it all from all angles, the author presents a fair and well-balanced overview of extraordinarily diverse subject matter.

Adhering to the standard arrangement of this series, section 1 of *Plastic Surgery* explains the history, applications, and challenges of the surgeries in a very readable way. Other highlights include discussions of breast reconstruction, altering of ethnic traits, Botox, plastic surgery on Down Syndrome patients, and repairing cleft palates and cleft lips. Several primary documents are included: Cases of Deformity from Burns, Successfully Treated by Plastic Operations, Thomas mutter, 1843; Safety of Silicone Breast Implants (1999); and Position Statement on Cosmetic Surgery for Children with Down Syndrome (2011). Supplementary materials include a chronology, glossary, and list for further reading.

This slim volume aimed particularly at the layperson or novice researcher proves to be an excellent starting point for navigating the vast literature on this topic and related subtopics. While resources on plastic surgery abound, what sets this one apart is its clear and very accessible language. *Plastic Surgery* is appropriate and highly recommended for public libraries and undergraduate academic collections.—**Leanne M. VandeCreek**

Alternative Medicine

C, P
482.   Morrow, John Andrew. **Encyclopedia of Islamic Herbal Medicine.** Jefferson, N.C., McFarland, 2011. 225p. index. $55.00pa. ISBN 13: 978-0-7864-4707-7.

Since the 1970s, the traditional medical systems of China (acupuncture) and India (Ayurveda) have gradually and steadily grown in popularity with U.S. consumers seeking complementary and alternative treatments for health issues. These systems have a number of philosophical bases and treatment modalities in common, including tailoring treatments to the unique constitution of the patient, employment of pulse and tongue diagnosis, and the use of massage, herbal medicine, and diet as interventions. A similar traditional medical system, generally known as Unani Tibb, is widespread throughout the Muslim world, ranging from Morocco to India, but has not yet achieved the same level of prominence as its Chinese and Indian counterparts in the West, and remains little known here. Unani Tibb's historical roots lie in the medicine of the ancient Greek and medieval Arab physicians, such as Hippocrates, Galen, and Avicenna. This work focuses exclusively on one aspect of Unani Tibb, Prophetic phytology, which is herbal medicine based on the prescriptions of the prophet Muhammad, as discussed in the Qur'an, the Hadith, and the writings of the Twelve Imams of Shi'ism.

The introductory section covers the historical development and current status of this system of herbal medicine. The main body of the encyclopedia consists of entries on the individual herbs, which are typically from one to three pages in length, and arranged alphabetically by their English names. The medicinal uses of over 100 different plants are described, including many well known to Americans as foods and spices, including basil, celery, cloves, dates, and ginger. Each entry includes the English and Arabic name of the plant, the Latin botanical name, and additional common names in a variety of languages; a safety rating; the Prophetic prescription (scriptural quotations on traditional usage); issues in identification, especially regarding translation of the scriptures; properties and uses; and scientific studies discussing the efficacy of the herb for various medical issues. Each entry includes notes, which encompass both Arabic publications and Western scholarly journals. Illustrations of the plants are not included. A general note on the transliteration of Arabic terms is included, along with a glossary of technical terms, and a bibliography. The index, which includes main entries in italics, would allow the user to access a list of those herbs prescribed for specific conditions.

Due to the paucity of resources on this subject in English, this title is a welcome addition to the body of reference works on complementary and alternative medicine, and is recommended for purchase by academic libraries, the libraries of schools of alternative medicine, and public libraries in areas with significant Muslim populations. The amount of research and scholarship that the author put into compiling this information over the course of 10 years is quite impressive, and this reviewer would welcome an additional volume by him covering the broader scope of Unani Tibb medicine in the future.—**Kenneth M. Frankel**

Specific Diseases and Conditions

AIDS

C, P, S

483.   Bell, Sigall K., Courtney L. McMickens, and Kevin J. Selby. **AIDS.** Santa Barbara, Calif., Greenwood Press/ABC-CLIO, 2011. 151p. index. (Biographies of Disease). $45.00. ISBN 13: 978-0-313-37682-5.

This small book is packed with information on AIDS. It opens with a timeline of the disease and its history. The following chapters cover what it is, how it affects the immune system, global epidemiology, transmission, how it affects the body, diagnosis and treatment, sociology, lessons learned and the future direction for medical science, and articles by people living with AIDS. The book includes a glossary, bibliography, and extensive index. The book is very readable and recommended for public and health care libraries. It is a good purchase for the cost.—**Betsy J. Kraus**

Arthritis

P

484.   Taylor, Guy, and C. Michael Stein. **The Encyclopedia of Arthritis.** 2d ed. New York, Facts on File, 2011. 420p. index. (Facts on file Library of Health and Living). $75.00. ISBN 13: 978-0-8160-7767-0; 978-1-4381-3305-8 (e-book).

Written by two practicing rheumatologists, *The Encyclopedia of Arthritis* is an updated edition of a comprehensive source of information for arthritis sufferers, researchers, or anyone interested in musculoskeletal disorders. The main body of the work contains more than 250 alphabetic entries covering body parts, types of arthritis, medical specialties, and conditions. New to this edition is a section dealing with risk factors and preventative measures for specific types of arthritis. Here, the authors have tried to present evidence-based information on treatments; however, since this information is not available for all treatments it is noted in the text when there is an exception. Entries on conditions cover causes, symptoms, diagnosis, treatment, and outcome. Cross-references lead the user to terms in the main section as well as to entries in the appendixes. The detailed appendixes contain information on drugs used to treat arthritis and related conditions, on common lab and diagnostic tests, and on useful arthritis-related Websites. The work concludes with a glossary, bibliography, and an index. The concise and authoritative information is useful to laypersons and scholars alike.—**Denise A. Garofalo**

Autism

C, P, S

485.   **Autism and Pervasive Developmental Disorders Sourcebook.** 2d ed. Joyce Brennfleck Shannon, ed. Detroit, Omnigraphics, 2011. 603p. index. (Health Reference Series). $85.00. ISBN 13: 978-0-7808-1146-1.

The 2d edition of the *Autism and Pervasive Developmental Disorders Sourcebook* contains updated information for general readers about a poorly understood condition afflicting a growing number of children. From Autistic Disorder, Asperger Syndrome, Autism Spectrum Disorders, and more, there are sections dealing with causes, conditions, assessment, treatments and intervention, and education. A section on transitioning to adulthood contains useful information on housing, employment, and transition models. A glossary of terms and acronyms and a directory of additional resources are both practical and beneficial. The title also has a helpful index. Of interest to parents, students, educators, and anyone with an interest on the subject of autism and developmental disorders.—**Denise A. Garofalo**

Cancer

C, P, S

486.   **Cancer Sourcebook.** 6th ed. Karen Bellenir, ed. Detroit, Omnigraphics, 2011. 1090p. index. (Health Reference Series). $85.00. ISBN 13: 978-0-7808-1145-4.

The 4th and 5th editions of this title have previously been reviewed in *American Reference Books Annual* and both reviewers found this title to be reliable and useful as also noted in the *Midwest Book Review*, which states that "the *Cancer Sourcebook* provides consumers with a wealth of information on the major forms and stages of cancer, from blood cell, skin and bone cancers to the latest treatments, identifying and reducing cancer risks, and strategies for coping with diagnosis and treatment."

The 6th edition includes a detailed table of contents that identifies 78 chapters divided into 6 key sections. The five parts are: Cancer Risk Factors and Cancer Prevention; Common Types of Cancer (the bulk of the book); Cancer-Related Tests and Treatments; Recurrent and Advanced Cancer; Cancer Research; and Additional Help and Information. This last section has a glossary of cancer terms, a directory of cancer-related organizations, information on how to find resources within your own community, and tips on avoiding online cancer fraud. There is also an extensive index.

Since the book is designed for the layperson, the preface briefly describes how to use this cancer source; emphasizes other cancer-related titles in the reference series (some of which focus on major types of cancer such as breast cancer and pediatric cancer); outlines the content in the six parts of the text; notes selected Websites for further information; and states that the "material in this book has been collected from a wide range of government agencies, nonprofit organizations, and periodicals." Users of the book will generally find references to the sources of the information; however, there is no general bibliography of sources and the content varies in sophistication and coverage depending on the source used.

Omnigraphics' Health Reference series consists of dozens of volumes related to multiple aspects of consumer health issues. The series' titles are listed on the front and back cover papers of the *Cancer Sourcebook*. The final pages of the *Cancer Sourcebook* are an annotated listing with reviewers' comments on the various titles in the Health Reference series. Clearly, this publisher offers a wide array of general health-related reference tools for the general public.

The *Cancer Sourcebook* has served as a useful and inexpensive resource in public and hospital libraries since this single volume offers readable, organized, across-the-board, and reasonably current information; it also serves a similar purpose in undergraduate academic libraries. However, the Internet now offers several excellent alternatives, including direct access to association and government sources. When looking for specific types of cancer (e.g., mantle cell lymphoma, referenced in this sourcebook in a single sentence), one general volume can never provide the detail that is now found through any Internet search engine. And, of course, anyone specializing in one of the health sciences will want to use more sophisticated and specialized scholarly resources for research.—**Laurel Grotzinger**

Diabetes

C, P, S

487.   Petit, William A., Jr., and Christine Adamec. **The Encyclopedia of Diabetes.** 2d ed. New York, Facts on File, 2011. 436p. index. (Facts on File Library of Health and Living). $75.00. ISBN 13: 978-0-8160-7948-3; 978-1-4381-3622-6 (e-book).

A comprehensive treatment of the prevalent disease of diabetes can be found in the 2d edition of *The Encyclopedia of Diabetes*. A history of this metabolic syndrome and its treatment from 1500 B.C.E. to today is followed by alphabetic entries for articles explaining about the causes of diabetes, medications, lifestyle adaptations, and more. Eleven appendixes cover sources for additional information, such as organizations, periodicals, research centers, and Websites, as well as provide key issues and statistical data about the disease. Further sources are provided in the bibliography. A thorough index rounds out the title. This title will be of interest to students, lay persons, and anyone interested in learning more about diabetes.—**Denise A. Garofalo**

Heart Disease

C, P

488. Randall, Otelio S., Nathan M. Segerson, and Deborah S. Romaine. **The Encyclopedia of the Heart and Heart Disease.** 2d ed. New York, Facts on File, 2011. 392p. index. (Facts on File Library of Health and Living). $75.00. ISBN 13: 978-0-8160-7751-9; 978-1-4381-3355-3 (e-book).

This encyclopedia is a useful resource that focuses on the human heart and heart disease. The authors have crafted a well-written text that is likely to be informative and interesting for individuals that are interested the heart, cardiovascular disease (heart disease), and overall wellness.

This hardback text spans more than 370 pages. The contents begin with a foreword, preface, and introduction. The body of the text includes entries arranged alphabetically. There are three appendixes: organizations and resources; common abbreviations and symbols; and diagrams. Following the appendixes there is a selected bibliography and further reading section followed by an index.

The text is well written and well researched. Information specific to heart conditions, medications, complications, and general heart wellness is presented in a user-friendly and easy-to-read format. Cross-references are clearly indicated and easy to locate within the text. The appendix including associations and resources provides information on heart health information, professional organizations, Website-based resources, clinical research study information, and workplace and disability resources. The appendix containing common abbreviations and symbols ranges from the symbol for "alpha" to the abbreviation for the Women's Health Initiative (WHI). The final appendix includes several black-and-white diagrams relating to the heart. Examples include the anterior view of anatomy showing major arteries and veins, anterior and posterior views of the heart, a section showing blood flow through the atria and ventricles, a section showing impulse-conduction system, circulation in pulmonary veins and left heart, and an anterior view showing arteries and veins. Following the appendixes are the selected bibliography and further reading sections that includes listings of books and journals. The index has numerous entries that are easily located.

The authors have successfully combined their expertise and knowledge of the heart, heart disease, and factors relating to heart disease to create a well-written and comprehensive text. Individuals that are interested in the heart, heart disease, or overall wellness are likely to find this text informative.—**Paul M. Murphy III**

Sexually Transmitted Diseases

P, S

489. **Sexual Health Information for Teens: Health Tips About Sexual Development, Reproduction, Contraception, and Sexually Transmitted Infections.** 3d ed. Elizabeth Magill, ed. Detroit, Omnigraphics, 2011. 429p. index. (Teen Health Series). $62.00. ISBN 13: 978-0-7808-1155-3.

Part of the Omnigraphics Teen Health Series, this 3d edition presents information related to the emotional, physical, and biological development of both males and females that occurs during puberty. It also strives to address some of the issues and questions that may arise. The work is intended as a reference set for teens in middle and high school who may be seeking factual information on puberty, sex, pregnancy, or STDs. The text is easy to read and understand for young readers, with satisfactory definitions within the text to explain new terms. Small fact boxes are interspersed throughout the text. There are important chapters included on protecting your sexual health that includes chapters on risky behaviors, abuse and rape, sexual predators, and virginity as a choice. The language and brevity may be helpful for young readers; however, the list of agencies to contact for further information appears to be more intended for adults than for adolescents seeking information relevant to their needs. Although teens may be more apt to search for this type of information on this Internet, the purchase of a book such as this may still be a good idea of high school and public libraries due to the fact that the information provided here is from reputable sources and up to date. This cannot be said for much of the information that kids may find on the Internet on this topic.—**Shannon Graff Hysell**

Sleep Disorders

P
490.   Brodsky, Phyllis L., and Allen Brodsky. **Living with Insomnia: A Guide to Causes, Effects and Management, with Personal Accounts.** Jefferson, N.C., McFarland, 2011. 194p. index. (McFarland Health Topics). $35.00pa. ISBN 13: 978-0-7864-5971-1.

This well-written guide is a timely and valuable resource. It is likely to be useful to individuals, including healthcare providers, who are involved or interested in learning more about topics related to insomnia. The contents of the guide are comprehensive. It begins with a table of contents that lists the book's 11 chapters. Topics discussed in depth include an overview of what insomnia is, how normal sleep is defined, how sleep patterns vary throughout the life span, sleep disorders and underlying pathologies, parasomnias (e.g., sleepwalking, narcolepsy, nightmares), the consequences of insomnia, and how to manage it. This text also includes a questionnaire to determine if you have insomnia and to what degree, a selected bibliography, and an index. The text is easy to read and understand and provides plenty of first-person accounts to help users determine how common their symptoms are and the extent of their sleeping problems.

This text is likely to be useful to individuals diagnosed with insomnia or their relatives. It is also a resource that a variety of healthcare providers may find helpful, especially if they are involved in providing care to patients who suffer from insomnia.—**Shannon Graff Hysell**

Nursing

C
491.   **CINAHL: The Cumulative Index to Nursing and Allied Health Literature. http://www. ebscohost.com/cinahl/.** [Website]. Ipswich, Mass., EBSCO. Price negotiated by site. Date reviewed: 2011.

This database is the most comprehensive resource for nursing and allied health literature. CINAHL subject headings follow the structure of the Medical Subject Headings, or MeSH, used by the National Library of Medicine. There are currently over 12,000 subject heading used in this database, which efficiently and effectively retrieves information for literature citations and text. It covers the literature in the fields of nursing, allied health, and related fields from 1981 to the present.—**James E. Bobick**

Pharmacy and Pharmaceutical Sciences

Handbooks and Yearbooks

P
492.   Graedon, Joe, and Terry Graedon. **The People's Pharmacy Home Remedies: Q&As for Your Common Ailments.** Washington, D.C., National Geographic Society, 2011. 263p. index. $16.95pa. ISBN 13: 978-1-4262-0711-2.

This volume is a handy guide to remedies you can literally pick off your shelf, from your refrigerator, or your garden. It is presented by a pharmacologist and a medical anthropologist with more than 30 years of expertise. It is written in an accessible question-and-answer format in alphabetic order by the 62 most common ailments and their natural remedies.

The effectiveness of some of these remedies can be explained by science, and others remain a mystery. The authors explain, when possible, why they work. They are careful to warn that home remedies should not substitute for medical attention. Additionally, the Graedons give us, in sidebars, 24 beneficial foods "from garlic to coconut . . . to chocolate with their corresponding up-to-date research report on just what, how and why these food contribute to your daily diet." There are three basic diets that have proven health benefits: the DASH (low salt) diet, the Mediterranean diet, and a low-carbohydrate diet. In addition to recipes for remedies throughout the book there are nine pages of simple healthy recipes using common ingredients created by the authors and leading health experts. Websites are given where more information can be found on a topic. A helpful index is available when you want to use a remedy for more than one health problem.

This work is a down-to-earth, two-part, natural remedy book primarily based on science is for the everyday person. It reads like a novel and would be recommended to have in one's home for simple solutions to common health problems.—**Nadine Salmons**

C, P
493.   **PDR for Nonprescription Drugs, Dietary Supplements, and Herbs 2012.** 33d ed. Montvale, N.J., Thomson Healthcare, 2012. 576p. index. $59.95. ISBN 13: 978-1-56363-797-1.

The 33d edition of *PDR for Nonprescription Drugs, Dietary Supplements, and Herbs* provides entries and information on hundreds of over-the-counter medications, supplements, and herbal remedies. Entries are presented according to therapeutic categories, and both by scientific name and common name. The guide provides complete descriptions of the most common OTC drugs, with additional information on ingredients, indications, interactions with other drugs, and recommended dosages for symptomatic relief. Also included are a listing of devices, diagnostics, and nondrug products; and two full sections on dietary supplements and herbs (fully cross-referenced and alphabetically organized for ease of use).

Indexing herbs by both botanical name and common name is appreciated for the academic as well as general public audiences. Language within can get technical, so a cautionary note to public libraries considering this source: have a chemistry or medical dictionary handy. *PDR for Nonprescription Drugs, Dietary Supplements, and Herbs* is becoming a standard reference sources in the medicinal field. This new edition is recommended to college and university libraries supporting medical and botanical collections and to public libraries supporting advanced alternative medicine information.—**Caroline L. Gilson**

34 Technology

General Works

Directories

C, P
494. **Plunkett's Games, Apps, & Social Media Industry Almanac 2012.** Jack W. Plunkett, ed. Houston, Tex., Plunkett Research, 2012. 500p. index. $299.99pa. (includes online edition). ISBN 13: 978-1-60879-643-4; 978-1-60879-905-3 (e-book).

Plunkett Research is a well-known publisher of industry directories and almanacs. This particular title covers fast-growing industry of games, apps, and social media. This new edition focuses on the role the internet and mobile devices play in business collaboration and online retailing. Games, both online and offline, continue to be very popular and a high-dollar industry as well. This work is designed for the general reader and business owner to compare the top 300 American game, app, and social media companies. An overview of the industry trends is provided and graphs and tables are provided for easy interpretation of the information.

The top gaming and social media companies included here are the largest and most successful companies from all areas of the industry. The alphabetic listing of these top companies provides the industry group, types of business, brands, divisions, subsidiaries, plans for growth, current news, contact information for the officers, annual financials, salaries and benefits, and provides an assessment of the company's hiring and advancement of minorities and women. Within the volume users will find industry analysis and market research. Topics include: social media privacy concerns, 3-D games and new opportunities, the latest trends in mobile table entertainment devices, and virtual worlds opening up new revenue sources. Indexes to the industry, sales, brand names, and the subsidiaries are provided. The information in this book is also available online through the publisher. This work is a fine addition of Plunkett Research's growing list of industry guides and will be useful in academic and public library's business collections.—**Kay M. Stebbins**

Handbooks and Yearbooks

C
495. **Technology and Young Children: Bridging the Communication-Generation Gap.** Sally Blake, Denise Winsor, and Lee Allen, eds. Hershey, Pa., Information Science Reference, 2012. 299p. index. $175.00; $265.00 (e-book); $350.00 (print and e-book edition). ISBN 13: 978-1-61350-059-0; 978-1-61350-060-6 (e-book).

This volume brings together 12 chapters by 24 scholars and practitioners in the area of early childhood and pre-school education and technology. Organized into four sections, the work begins with five chapters on understanding the digital communication generation gap—the values, beliefs, social cultural systems that influence teaching practice. The second section, consisting of one chapter, focuses on bridging the gap between technology-based educational methods and child development. The third section presents five chapters addressing the bridging of the gap between pedagogy and technology; while the final chapter addresses in a single chapter the bridging of the gap between policy and practice in science, math, second language, and special needs education. A detailed table of contents and extensive index enables quick location of desired materials, while the chapters themselves are easily read by novices and provide substance of use to the seasoned practitioner and researcher. Each chapter begins with objectives and ends with a section of questions and activities, making this book good not only as a reference source but also as a text for an education course or professional development. The materials and research are mostly United States-focused, so one cannot use this for an international view.—**Sara Marcus**

Games

C

496.   **Computer Games as Educational and Management Tools: Uses and Approaches.** Maria Manuela Cruz-Cunha, Vitor Hugo Costa Carvalho, and Paula Cristina Almeida Tavare, eds. Hershey, Pa., Information Science Reference, 2011. 337p. index. $180.00; $255.00 (e-book): $360.00 (print and e-book editions). ISBN 13: 978-1-60960-569-8; 978-1-60960-570-4 (e-book).

Edited by three professors at the Polytechnic Institute of Cavado and Ave in Portugal, this volume brings together 17 chapters authored by 44 international scholars and researchers. Presented without organization into categories, these chapters address the technology, industry, and human and social aspects of using computer games in education. Providing both a theoretical and practical view of the topic, the contributors present new developments and applications, issues, challenges, opportunities, and trends in the use of computer games in education and management, providing ideas and research-based support for integration in their own work. The detailed table of contents, compiled list of references, and index make this useful as a resource to turn to again and again, while the use of images throughout the chapters make the work approachable to all. This is a useful addition to any academic collection where the use of games is being considered.—**Sara Marcus**

Internet

Dictionaries and Encyclopedias

P, S

497.   Dingwell, Heath. **The Truth About the Internet and Online Predators.** New York, Facts on File, 2011. 134p. index. $35.00. ISBN 13: 978-0-8160-7648-2; 978-1-4381-3628-8 (e-book).

The Truth About the Internet and Online Predators provides information on topics related to this very serious subject, such as identity theft, cyberbullying, and the real danger of sexual predators. As part of The Truth About series it is specifically written for young adults seeking information on this timely issue with an intended purpose to inform for support. This resource may also be used by those who interact with adolescents, such as teachers, parents, or counselors, as a resource to refer young adults to read when they are seeking information.

About 30 specific topics related to the Internet and online predators are presented in alphabetic format. The topic is broadly introduced at the beginning of the A-Z list, discussing both the good and the bad that Internet access has brought to individuals' lives. Each topic covered includes a basic definition followed by relevant facts and statistics. An emphasis has been placed on presenting research-based data and facts in order to overcome misconceptions. Each topic also includes a section of questions and answers interspersed with sections titled "Teens Speak" where teens discuss their real-life experience with the subject. A selected list of additional resources to consult concludes each entry. Illustrations consist of black-and-white tables and charts. The list of Hotlines and Help sites provides an excellent compilation of resources to consult by those who may be seeking answers on their own. *The Truth About the Internet and Online Predators* provides good coverage of this topic for the intended audience, in an easy-to-read and easy-to-comprehend format that should appeal to young adults.—**Susan E. Thomas**

Directories

C, P

498. Aloi, Michael J., Marjorie Fusco, and Susan E. Ketcham. **Digital Collections Worldwide: An Annotated Directory.** New York, Neal-Schuman, 2011. 345p. index. $250.00pa. ISBN 13: 978-1-55570-701-9.

In *Digital Collections Worldwide*, the authors attempt to provide access to "authoritative, useful, and permanent worldwide digital collections" while reducing the frustration involved in locating quality image collections through Web pathfinders or search engines. Over 1,400 sites are included in this book, originating from educational institutions, government bodies, museums, libraries, archives, or scholars' personal Websites. Corporate sites were also listed, but only those that were not created to promote products. Although the primary audience is researchers, the authors' claim anyone will find this collection useful. One of the limitations of this source is the organization. The authors chose to group resources geographically by continent, and then subdivided into countries or states. Maybe researchers can appreciate this structure, but for most people subject access is preferable. There is an index with subject access, but an overall subject arrangement would allow for greater discovery. Another potential limitation is the ephemeral nature of Website addresses. In the preface and back cover, the authors mention a companion Website that will eliminate the problem of broken links and make newer collections accessible. Without the companion site, entering some of the Web addresses will be difficult as they can be fairly long with back slashes, question marks, equal signs, and underscores. That said, the entries themselves are well described, including the scope of the images present, the identity and intent of the creator, and the best means for exploring a site. The authors' selections seem good, along with the quality of the images in the collections. Whether a book like this will be sought out by users needing digital images is the key question to consider before purchasing.—**Kevin McDonough**

C, P, S

499. **Complete Planet: A Deep Web Directory. http://www.completeplanet.com/.** [Website]. Free. Date reviewed: 2011.

According to the creators of this database, "there are hundreds of thousands of databases that contain Deep Web Content. CompletePlanet is the front door to these Deep Web databases on the Web and to the thousands of regular search engines." They consider it a first step in trying to find highly topical information. By tracing through CompletePlanet's subject structure or searching Deep Websites, you can go to various topic areas, such as energy or agriculture or food or medicine, and find rich content sites not accessible using conventional search engines." CompletePlanet is one of the Websites that the literature describes as a good starting point for entrance into the Invisible Web (Websites that cannot be accessed by search engines such as Google or Yahoo).—**William O. Scheeren**

Handbooks and Yearbooks

C, S

500.   **Social Networking.** Kenneth Partridge, ed. Bronx, N.Y., H. W. Wilson, 2011. 216p. index. (The Reference Shelf, v.83, no.1). $50.00pa. ISBN 13: 978-0-8242-1110-3.

Social Networking is the newest volume in H. W. Wilson's The Reference Shelf series. As in other volumes in this series, the content includes reprints, excerpts, and reproductions of articles, books, addresses, and studies pertaining to the topic at hand. In this case the book focuses on social networking itself, such as its history, the benefits and detriments to social media, and questions posed by David Fincher's film, *The Social Network*.

The book is organized into six sections of similarly themed content, including a historical look at social media, the business aspect of social media, the intersection of social media with politics and activism, social media and education, the dangers of social media, and the way in which social media integrates and affects lives. The editor does an excellent job of combining materials from a wide variety of sources, including Websites (e.g., MacLife.com, TechCrunch.com), newspapers (e.g., *The San Francisco Chronicle*, *The New York Times*), popular journals/magazines (e.g., *Women's Health*, *The Economist*), and others. Many of these pieces can be found on one's own, but the benefit of this publication is having an editor who has filtered through the thousands of relevant articles to identify those of most importance to providing a foundation for research on social networking and social media.

Although the editor has done an admirable job of pulling together these resources, and appears to have done so with an eye for longevity, such a rapidly evolving topic will always raise some questions of timeliness. As of now, though, the content is current and provides a sound resource for research on the topic.—**Tyler Manolovitz**

Telecommunications

Directories

C, P

501.   **Plunkett's Telecommunications Industry Almanac.** 2012 ed. Jack W. Plunkett, ed. Houston, Tex., Plunkett Research, 2011. 604p. index. $299.99 (includes online edition). ISBN 13: 978-1-60879-648-9; 978-1-60879-910-7 (e-book).

This guide is a comprehensive overview, from a business and investment perspective, of the companies participating in the worldwide telecommunications industry. Overall an excellent guide to the industry, it has two main components. About the first quarter of the book is a discursive guide to industry trends—discussing market trends, historical and projected for the next five years, by category of service. It discusses worldwide variation in the technologies used, the potential market, and the degree and character of government involvement. The role of new technologies and products and select lists of companies that might be attractive investment opportunities are also covered. Overall, this coverage is careful, complete, and accurate. This section provides a good, balanced look at the range of telecommunications technologies in use, the firms that provide them, and the markets they serve.

The second section, provided in both print and online edition, is a database of the "Telecom 500," a listing of 500 companies chosen specifically for their prominence in telecommunications and related support industries. Each gets (in the print version) a one-page listing, including company contact information, a narrative description of the company's lines of business, revenues and profits for the past five years, and a few more details. Company selection seems good. The company descriptions are generally informative, but the financial detail is a bit sparse.—**Ray Olszewski**

35 Physical Sciences and Mathematics

Physical Sciences

Earth and Planetary Sciences

Astronomy

Atlases

C

502.   **The Cambridge Photographic Star Atlas.** By Axel Mellinger and Ronald Stoyan. New York, Cambridge University Press, 2010. 176p. illus. maps. index. $40.00. ISBN 13: 978-1-10701-346-9.

The authors of this book have used the latest methods in digital photography and image processing to share with readers photographic images of the whole sky. To do this they use large-scale photography and corresponding charts. The work is arranged into double-page spreads that show a section of the sky with a chart depicting and naming the double stars, open clusters, planetary nebulae, globular clusters, and galaxies. In all there are 82 charts identifying over 1,500 objects and 2,500 stars. The volume concludes with a object index. This work is a genuine feast for the eyes for those studied in astronomy. It is appropriate for academic collections supporting programs in astronomy and astrophysics.—**Margaret F. Dominy**

Handbooks and Yearbooks

S

503.   Aguilar, David A. **13 Planets: The Latest View of the Solar System.** Washington, D.C., National Geographic Society, 2011. 64p. illus. index. $16.95. ISBN 13: 978-1-4263-0770-6.

Black cosmic space contrasting with colorful planets on the cover will attract readers of all ages. Ceres, the 5th planet, was reclassified in 2006, as was Pluto, as one of the dwarf planets. Eris, a dwarf planet, now accepted by astronomers completes the thirteen planets. Awe-inspiring views of planets and ice striations are artistically exceptional, as the publisher's reputation promises. Many classrooms and school libraries desperately need this quality update of the solar system at this affordable price. Websites for further exploration, Earth weight chart with weight on other planets, and a Planet Chart are included. This work will be useful in middle and high school libraries.—**Ann Bryan Nelson**

P, S

504.   Gott, J. Richard, and Robert J. Vanderbei. **Sizing Up the Universe: The Cosmos in Perspective.** Washington, D.C., National Geographic Society, 2011. 247p. illus. index. $35.00. ISBN 13: 978-1-4262-0651-1.

Beautiful color photographs of terrestrial and celestial objects highlight this engaging book dealing with developing a better comprehension about the size of the planets, stars, solar systems, and more in the universe as well as imparting interesting astronomical information. A fold-out, full-color Gott-Juric Map of the Universe represents planets, satellites, stars, and galaxies in relation to their distance from Earth. Diagrams, photographs, and drawings are provided to help explain various concepts, such as how Earth is measured, what happens during an eclipse, the relative size of a sunspot, lakes and volcanoes, and more. Students, amateur astronomers, and anyone interested in our universe will find this title useful.—**Denise A. Garofalo**

C, P

505.   Moore, Patrick, and Robin Rees. **Patrick Moore's Data Book of Astronomy.** New York, Cambridge University Press, 2011. 576p. illus. index. $55.00. ISBN 13: 978-0-521-89935-2.

If one were to count the people who have most influenced popular astronomy, Patrick Moore will come in at or near the top. For over five decades he has published astronomy articles and books for the ravenous public in such a way that promoted astronomical science around the world. This latest endeavor compiles in one place factual astronomical information. Beginning with the Solar System, in general, then the Sun, Moon, planets, he then takes us outward to the galaxies and the universe. Additional chapters with constellation charts, a star catalogue, telescopes and observatories, a history of astronomy, and short biographies of astronomers complete the rest of this tome. Written in a voice respectful of the reader, this book is both informative and instructive. It is more than just recitation of dry facts, and the author shows restraint on the sensational. It is bursting with tables, charts, and illustrations. A glossary and substantial index finish the book.

Although the principal purpose of this work would be to efficiently retrieve numbers and factual information, it is also quite a delight just to browse and peruse. Both professional and arm-chair astronomers will benefit from the up-to-date, well-organized, and thoroughly presented data offered in this work. This resource is appropriate for academic and public library collections.—**Margaret F. Dominy**

Climatology and Meteorology

S

506.   **Confronting Global Warming Series.** Farmington Hills, Mich., Greenhaven Press/Gale/Cengage Learning, 2011. illus. index. $37.10/vol.

This relatively new series from Greenhaven Press, Confronting Global Warming, discusses the full range of current challenges that the Earth faces due to global warming. The publisher admits that there are still some in the scientific community that argue that global warming is a myth; however, the fact is that global warming is a widely accepted theory among scientists and policy makers and needs to be addressed. The series addresses the problem from a variety of angles, including the scientific and geological, the political, problems related to health concerns, and environmental. Each book addresses its key issue from a variety of perspectives and provides the pros and cons of the various solutions to each problem. Titles recently added to the series include: *The Role of Industry*; *The Role of the Individual*; *Farming and Food Supply*; *Population, Resources, and Conflict*; and *Nature and Wildlife*> Each book offers a background on the subject; 8-12 chapters that discuss key issues; sidebars with statistics, firsthand accounts, and primary source documents; charts, maps, and graphs; full-color photographs; a glossary and bibliography; organizations to consult for further information; and an index. The books could feasibly be used individually, but are much more effective and informative as a series. This series is most appropriate for high school age students with the critical thinking skills to understand the more complex language in the pro/con essays.

In general, these books are excellent sources for high school readers to enhance their knowledge of global warming and use their critical thinking skills to weigh the pros and cons behind the debates. They could easily be used as jumping off points for research projects and debate topics. This is a continuing series that looks to expand about five volumes per year, which could make it an expensive series in the long run for a school library collection. Libraries needing this type of information on global warming may need to pick and choose titles based on their library's needs.—**Shannon Graff Hysell**

C, P, S

507.   **Encyclopedia of Climate & Weather.** 2d ed. Stephen H. Schneider and Michael D. Mastrandrea, eds. New York, Oxford University Press, 2011. 1344p. illus. index. $450.00. ISBN 13: 978-0-19-976532-4.

While it may be true that "Everyone talks about the weather, but nobody does anything about it," we have certainly had a lot to talk about over the past 15 years since the 1st edition of this title was published in 1996 (see ARBA 97, entry 1396). Every month we are faced with more deadly after affects of weather, including hurricanes, tornadoes, flooding caused by rain, blizzards, and extreme drought conditions. This makes this update of a well-received reference on the weather and climatology all the more timely.

This new edition has been updated with new articles on such topics as global warming, extreme weather, the Intergovernmental Panel on Climate Change, tradable permits, and the Kyoto Protocol. Overall, it includes some 330 entries that include scientific concepts used in climatology, processes that produce weather, classification of climates, and the history of atmospheric sciences. The editors have used more than 300 maps, photographs, and charts to illustrate the various concepts and topics throughout the text. Each entry is typically several pages in length, has subtopics within that help organize the text, has a bibliography, and is signed by the contributor. The audience for this resource remains high school students, undergraduate students, and the general reader, making this a worthwhile addition for high school, university, and public libraries. [R: Choice, Jan 12, p. 850]—**Shannon Graff Hysell**

C, S

508.   Favor, Lesli J. **Natural Disasters.** New York, Facts on File, 2011. 414p. index. (Global Issues). $45.00. ISBN 13: 978-0-8160-8260-5.

Natural Disasters, part of the Facts on File Global Issues series (billed by the publishers as "a first-stop resource for hot button issues"), is divided as are other works in the series, into three parts: a problem statement, selected primary documentary sources, and "useful research tools." The problem statement section attempts to define the issues covered in the volume, provide a background to natural disasters in the United States, and describe a number of global disaster issues (earthquakes/tsunami, famine, volcanic eruptions, and flood/drought). This section contains a number of teaching moments, such as when the text talks in the water resource management in China section about Yu the great, there is mention of the "Greek legends of the Trojan Horse, and the 12 labors of Hercules," thereby creating opportunities for further investigation on the part of the student. Typical of the primary document section is an NOAA publication entitled "Heat Wave: A Major Summer Killer." This document, which is undated, was pulled of the NOAA Website in 2009, and outlines the "Excessive Heat Products" issued by the agency; the effects of heat on the body; the national Heat Health Warning System (HHWS); and a series of cautions and safety tips for dealing with excessive heat. Other typical documents include: Pliny's description of the eruption of Vesuvius; the St. Louis blizzard of 1982; the 1900 Galveston Hurricane; eyewitness account of the 1833 eruption of Krakatoa; food problems in China in 1922; and "China's Actions for Disaster Prevention and Reduction 2010." The "useful research tools" section includes hints to the student on how to conduct basic research: getting started, selecting a topic, evaluating information sources, online library catalogs, printed periodical indexes, online periodical indexes, how to develop a thesis statement, and more. This final section concludes with a basic statistical compendium, a bibliography, "Key players: A-Z," a chronology, a glossary, and an index.

In one handy volume this work picks a topic, provides the student with issues to solve, supplies a selection of primary source readings, and gives suggestions for further inquiry. While the cover of the volume is attractive, there are no illustrations interspersed within the large blocks of text that make up the bulk of the work. Some pages contain a variety of bolded, un-bolded, italic, non-italic, highlighted, un-highlighted, blocked and un-blocked texts along with variations in type size that make reading somewhat confusing to the reader. These variations, which undoubtedly mean something, only serve as a poor substitute for good layout. Nevertheless, this work is a good treatment of the topic for students grade 9 and up.—**Ralph Lee Scott**

Ecology

S
509.   **The Living Earth Series.** Chicago, Encyclopaedia Britannica, 2011. 8v. illus. maps. index. $51.70/vol.

This series focuses on eight different ecological units and issues. Most books explore a region's biotic and abiotic systems; the scientific content is technical. Explanations of climate, physical environments, and biodiversity are explained with great detail. Annotated color photographs or diagrams highlight environmental conditions and symbiotic relationships. A useful feature is that notable ecosystems, regions, or explorers are highlighted in each book. Two books in the series discuss climate and climate change, and conservation and ecology. The science of the ecological threats, the history, and discussions from eminent people and their efforts to battle them are included. This series can be used to supplement classroom materials or for further research. Each volume includes a bibliography, glossary, and index. This set is recommended for high school libraries.—**Christine Brandt**

Oceanography

C
510.   Hinrichsen, Don. **The Atlas of Coasts and Oceans: Ecosystems, Threatened Resources, Marine Conservation.** Chicago, University of Chicago Press, 2011. 128p. illus. maps. index. $22.00pa. ISBN 13: 978-0-226-34226-9.

The main title of this slim volume, in which most maps do not take up more than half a page, is a bit overly ambitious. As is noted in the foreword, it is not intended as a comprehensive oceanographic atlas, but rather as "an attempt to map human impacts upon [oceans and coastlines]." At this it succeeds well enough, providing maps, graphs, and textual explanations for issues as varied as pollution, overfishing, energy production (from winds, tides, and waves as well as oil and natural gas), climate change, and piracy. The final section of the six found in the book concentrates on efforts to wisely and conscientiously manage the oceans through national and international management plans, as well as marine protected areas. There is also a glossary of key terms, a list of online and print sources, and a country-by-country table of oceanographic data such as length of coastline, tons of seafood caught and farmed per year, and number of endangered fish species.

Unfortunately, many of the maps are simply too small to show much detail below the country level. Likewise, relatively small but heavily used bodies of water such as the Gulf of Mexico and the North Sea are often nearly obscured by cartographic symbols, making it difficult to draw any useful meaning from those maps. The *Atlas* would certainly be a useful supplement to other oceanographic atlases in large universities.—**Maren Williams**

Paleontology

C, S

511.   **Dinosaurs.** John J. Meier, ed. Bronx, N.Y., H. W. Wilson, 2011. 221p. illus. index. (The Reference Shelf, v.83, no.2). $55.00pa. ISBN 13: 978-0-8242-1107-3.

This book is a compendium of popular dinosaur articles over the past few years. It is part of the publisher's Reference Shelf collection. The idea is to present to general readers "the basic facts as well as the latest scholarship" on these extinct beasts. It includes five sections with five to six articles in each on dinosaur biology, dinosaur collecting, the bird-dinosaur relationship, dinosaur extinction, and new discoveries. Most but not all of the authors are science writers (there are some scientists), and the articles come from sources as diverse as *Scientific American* and *Wired Magazine*.

With all these talented writers, this book is readable and useful in many ways, especially as a history of recent ideas about dinosaurs and their demise. There are two significant problems, however. Most articles do not have their original illustrations, leaving out a critical part of their mission (an example would be the *National Geographic* piece on "extreme dinosaurs" by John Updike shorn of all images). The second problem is more conceptual: popular science writers make errors that would be caught in scientific peer review (an example is the very first photograph showing a dinosaur skeleton said in the caption to be "some seven or eight million years old"—it is actually 70 or 80 million years old). On some contentious scientific issues there is an illusion of consensus (on preserved dinosaur soft tissues, for example) and on others a history of debate that repeats wrong ideas in a popular format without the requisite data (outdated extinction theories come to mind). The informed reader will understand the context, the careful reader will pick it up; the casual reader may dip in and extract a large helping of misinformation.—**Mark A. Wilson**

Volcanology

C, P

512.   Siebert, Lee, Tom Simkin, and Paul Kimberly. **Volcanoes of the World.** 3d ed. Berkeley, Calif., University of California Press, 2010. 551p. illus. maps. $50.00. ISBN 13: 978-0-520-26877-7.

Volcanic eruptions are probably the most complex, beautiful, and terrifying natural events we can witness. They have brought misery to countless numbers of people, even to the point of destroying civilizations, and they also shape our landscapes, change our climates, and rejuvenate our soils. Understanding volcanoes and their associated hazards is critical for our future. This massive volume is a richly detailed database to further that geological knowledge to help mitigate future disasters. This is not a book for casual volcano watchers—it is the professional source for basic information on thousands of volcanoes and their eruptions.

This is the 3d edition of this famed volume. It begins with an explanation of the volcano and eruption data it presents, carefully assessing the relevance and accuracy of each measure and analyzing historical and geographical trends. The bulk of the book contains a directory of volcanoes organized by regions and a universal numbering system. The data for each volcano contain location, elevation, nearby populations, eruption dates, rock types, eruptive characteristics, and other technical details. All the terms and abbreviations are defined inside the front cover of the book and at the head of the chapter, and there are maps throughout, including a global map inside the back cover. The directory is followed by a chronology of eruptions (over 100 pages in small type) and then sections on large-volume Holocene eruptions and related fatalities and evacuations. New to this volume is an extensive (and preliminary) list of Pleistocene volcanoes. Hundreds of references are also included. A gazetteer makes finding particular volcanoes easy in the databases. There are even some color plates of spectacular volcanoes and eruptions.

Libraries will not find a more detailed and complete source for data on volcanoes than this volume. It is highly recommended for all libraries with science and natural history collections.—**Mark A. Wilson**

Mathematics

C, P, S

513.   Greenwald, Sarah J., and Jill E. Thomley. **Encyclopedia of Mathematics & Society.** Hackensack, N.J., Salem Press, 2012. 3v. illus. index. $595.00/set. ISBN 13: 978-1-58765-844-0.

The *Encyclopedia of Mathematics & Society* is a fascinating approach to the role mathematics plays in our everyday life. For the most part students plod through the constant stream of problem sets, theorems, and equations just to satisfy some requirement to then put aside once the course is over. Most do not see the mathematics behind everything. This reference work quickly, and most convincingly, enlightens everyone who approaches it. Who would guess the mathematics behind chemotherapy, deforestation, movies, or water quality? Topics include Mathematics Around the World, Mathematics Culture and Identity, and Medicine and Health, just to name a few. The signed articles range from about 500 to about 3,000 words. Nearly 200 contributors, most writing from colleges and universities, provided almost 560 articles over 3 volumes, writing for the audience they know best, college students and the motivated reader. The articles are further augmented by cross-references to related articles, further readings, and a sprinkling of illustrations, plots, and graphs. The first volume lists the articles (by title) and then offers a list of topics, making it convenient to see the articles as they fall within topics. At the end of the third volume, there is an extensive index, tying together this formidable work. This reference work is highly recommended for academic, public, and possibly high school collections. There is a complementary Website available to purchasers of the encyclopedia.—**Margaret F. Dominy**

C, S

514.   **MathWorld. http://mathworld.wolfram.com/.** [Website]. Champaign, Ill., Wolfram Research. Free. Date reviewed: 2011.

This is the Web's most extensive mathematics resource. MathWorld continues to be the most popular and most visited mathematics site on the Internet and its mathematical content continues to steadily grow and expand. It includes definitions of more than 300 mathematical terms, citations to book and journal articles (with hyperlinks), downloadable Mathematica notebooks, interactive entries that help teach complex topics such as three-dimensional geometry, and more. MathWorld is provided as a free service to the world's mathematics and Internet communities as part of a commitment to education and educational outreach by Wolfram research, makers of Mathematica.—**James E. Bobick**

36 Resource Sciences

Energy

Directories

C, P

515. **Plunkett's Green Technology Industry Almanac 2012.** Jack W. Plunkett, ed. Houston, Tex., Plunkett Research, 2012. 450p. index. $299.99pa. (includes online edition). ISBN 13: 978-1-60879-672-4; 978-1-60879-934-3 (e-book).

Plunkett's Green Technology Industry Almanac is a new addition to Plunkett Research's vast offering of industry almanacs and seems like a worthwhile industry survey to pursue since green technology is the wave of the future. Not written for in-depth analysis of the industry, the monograph instead provides students and researchers with self-contained segments readers can access without going through the entire book. While energy conservation is the key focus, the book also focuses on related topics in the area of recycling, water technology, building materials, heating and air conditioning, transportation, and manufacturing processes. Features of this volume include an industry trend analysis, statistical tables, profiles and directory information of leading companies, contact information for executives, a glossary, and a listing of industry associations and professional societies. Within this volume users will find statistics and information on such topics as corporate giants (e.g., Wal-Mart, General Electric) investments in green technology, new transportation technologies that cut emissions, and China's role as an emerging player in green technology. The typical entry includes company name, Web address, NAIC code, company ranking, types of business, brands, basic financial data, and contact information. Other useful aspects of the book include an index of subsidiaries, brand names, and affiliations, and an index of companies noted for promoting women and minorities.

The language is relatively jargon-free. The paper binding will not stand up to heavy use but the pages are thick with large clear type. Overall, this directory will complement the collections of large public and academic libraries.—**William C. Struning**

Handbooks and Yearbooks

P, S

516. **A Student Guide to Energy.** By John F. Mongillo. Santa Barbara, Calif., Greenwood Press/ABC-CLIO, 2011. 5v. illus. index. $255.00/set. ISBN 13: 978-0-313-37720-4; 978-0-313-37721-1 (e-book).

This five-volume set is introductory on renewable and non-renewable energy sources. The information covers many subjects in addition to scientific concepts. A history of United State's energy use and other countries' renewable energy facilities are discussed. The primary purpose of *A Student Guide to Energy* is to describe the need to use renewable energies today because of the growing human population and political and financial constraints on limited supply of fossil fuels.

Volume 1 covers the oil (the associated chapter is titled "Petroleum"), natural gas, coal, and nuclear energy fossil fuels. Topics include different geographic locations, method how to obtain, environmental issues, and future use. Many chapters in the five volumes include an interview with an individual with expertise in a specific subject. For instance, Charles Ferguson of the Council on Foreign Relations describes his academic study, career, and suggestions for employment in the nuclear industry. Volume 2 is on solar energy and hydrogen fuel cells. The process on how semiconductors inside solar cells produce energy is explained. This energy type most promising for reducing fossil fuel use but one limiting factor is that it is not continuously available during nighttime. Volume 3 covers wind energy, oceanic energy, and hydropower. Wind power is one of lowest cost renewable energies but may not be feasible to many developing countries due to high startup cost. A "Video" section (this section is in all volumes) includes a Website to watch CBS News video showing how underwater turbines create electricity from hydropower. Volume 4 is on geothermal and biomass energy. Biomass includes municipal waste material and used for automobile fuel and heating buildings. Volume 5 describes energy efficiency, conservation, and sustainability. The Leadership in Energy and Environmental Design (LEED) certification program includes measurable benchmarks for building "design, construction, and operations" to prevent environmental degradation.

The excellent illustrations and flow charts can help the reader visually see how processes occur. For instance, the direction of groundwater flow through open and closed loop geothermal heating systems shows how these two types are different. A rectangular box titled "Feature" is on many pages and has interesting examples on energy topics applied in the real word. One example is a high school using a wind turbine for electrical lighting and in science class studies. A separate section is on careers in the energy industry and includes Websites for government agencies, nonprofit organizations, and job opportunity listings.

The word "green" is used in many contexts, including green school, "Green Faith in Action Project," green vehicle, and "Green biz." The different meanings for this word should be in introductory section for clarification purposes. Many chapters end with suggested activities to do but often include just checking a Website. More physical activities requiring easily accessible items can also help students better understand concepts. There is a brief description given for each of the 11 schools that obtained LEED certification. If a school has a Website describing their certification, this information should be included for an additional reading option. This publication would be a good addition to a public library's reference collection and beneficial to individuals researching renewable energy technologies and employment.—**Mike Parchinski**

Environmental Science

Dictionaries and Encyclopedias

C, S

517.   Brosnan, Kathleen A. **Encyclopedia of American Environmental History.** New York, Facts on File, 2011. 4v. illus. maps. index. (Facts on File Library of American History). $350.00/set. ISBN 13: 978-0-8160-6793-0.

The *Encyclopedia of American Environmental History* is a four-volume set that covers the United States' overuse of natural resources from pre-colonial to the present time. The emphasis is on environmental degradation worldwide. The purpose of this reference resource is to show how the physical environment shapes American history. More than 750 articles covering a wide spectrum of topics and a chronology strongly support this objective.

Volume 1 starts with eight essays defining characteristics of environmental history. The rest of this volume and other three volumes contain articles, charts, and overview maps. Each main entry is shown in boldface letters and additional main entries associated with the one read are capitalized words. This feature helps the individual find more easily other useful topics to read. For instance, the main entry on Climate Change includes entries pertaining to specific individuals, geographic locations, government regulations, and national parks. The geographic maps provide good additional material to clarify statements. One example is the Ratification of the Kyoto Protocol map showing a global view of countries that did and did not endorse an international agreement to reduce greenhouse gas emissions. The clear, nontechnical wording helps in comprehending diverse topics.

The index section has acronyms shown without the associated full term. The main entry "water, drinking" has the main entry "CVP" listed underneath and refers to Central Valley Project. This information can be found by looking in the alphabetic listing for the space where "CVP" would be listed. An individual new to reading this publication or not familiar with acronyms may not find this information as easily. An environmental impact statement is a document with comprehensive information about the purpose and activities of a planned project. The potential negative effects on the surrounding environment are also identified. This subject is an entry but should be a main entry because of its close associations with many other main entries discussed.

This encyclopedia set provides a wealth of information in a beneficial format that interconnects human society with the physical environment; it will serve as an excellent addition to any academic and public library reference collection. The audience is high school, undergraduate, and graduate students as well as individuals interested in the broad subject environmental history.—**Mike Parchinski**

C, P, S

518. **Encyclopedia of Environmental Issues.** Craig W. Allin, ed. Hackensack, N.J., Salem Press, 2011. 4v. illus. index. $495.00/set. ISBN 13: 978-1-58765-735-1.

A daunting topic is covered very well in this set of four encyclopedia volumes. Environmental issues is a broad category of nearly overwhelming diversity, from antibiotics to zoos. There are over 250 expert authors and 772 articles here in about 1,400 pages, and the editor kept the writing even and focused on human interactions with nature and other aspects of environment broadly conceived. The material is up to date and scientifically sound for an introduction to often very complex topics.

Each article begins with a category, a brief definition, and a statement of significance to the environment. Many have black-and-white photographs, charts, tables, and inset boxes. The index is essential for navigation. Who would have thought, for example, that to read about Trofim Lysenko you would have to find the article "Soviet Plan for the Transformation of Nature"? The appendixes are extensive and very useful. They include a list and brief descriptions of environmental organizations (with Web page addresses), brief biographies of environmentalists (and anti-environmentalists), major federal environmental laws, directories of national parks, an environmental timeline, a glossary, and a bibliography.

This encyclopedia set comes with free online access to the electronic version of the text, along with additional material from the publisher. This makes searching through the complex organization of the volumes very easy. *The Encyclopedia of Environmental Issues* is recommended for any library with science and social science holdings.—**Mark A. Wilson**

C, P, S

519. Gates, Alexander E., and Robert P. Blauvelt. **Encyclopedia of Pollution.** New York, Facts on File, 2011. 2v. illus. maps. index. (Facts on File Science Library). $170.00/set. ISBN 13: 978-0-8160-7002-2; 978-1-4381-3491-8 (e-book).

This encyclopedia has over 300 entries which are up-to-date, educational, and enlightening. Numerous biographies of pioneers of pollution study plus early activists, such as Rachel Carson and John Muir, add to this two-volume set. Covering a variety of pollution topics from 9/11 to Katrina to colony collapse to the Rocky Mountain Arsenal, this source will be of value to the general public as well as undergraduates looking for interesting research paper topics. Pollution research is an ever-expanding field, and this reference details how our lives have been and are drastically affected and informs the reader about the multitude of challenges and issues we all face. The appendixes have a wealth of information, including Superfund sites, the top 25 oil spills in the world, and EPA Drinking Water Standards. Expanding on the reference source *Pollution A to Z* (see ARBA 2004, entry 1550), this set contains a detailed glossary, indexes, a timeline, tables, and cross-references that will enhance research. Almost 300 color photographs and illustrations add to this informative and clear-cut encyclopedia. This set will be an excellent addition for all academic libraries and public libraries. [R: Choice, Jan 12, p. 851]—**Diane J. Turner**

Handbooks and Yearbooks

C, S
520. **The Environmental Debate: A Documentary History, with Timeline, Glossary and Appendixes.** 2d ed. Peninah Neimark and Peter Rhoades Mott, eds. Millerton, N.Y., Grey House Publishing, 2011. 460p. index. $165.00. ISBN 13: 978-1-59237-676-6; 978-1-59237-677-3 (e-book).

The 2d edition of this informative source provides an updated timeline; new information covering 2000-2010; and names, addresses, and Websites of many environmentally significant organizations. The main part of this reference is comprised of 168 primary documents expressing wide ranging attitudes from environmentalists (e.g., John Muir, Theodore Roosevelt), naturalists, philosophers, artists and poets, lawyers, and other groups concerned with the use of natural resources and the environment. Government reports as well as legislation from federal, state, and local governments and court cases are also presented. Each of the eight sections is introduced with short essays to provide context. This is an excellent resource for high school or college students researching or working on or working with controversial issues. Reading about how environmental thought has changed over the years, students can select viewpoints on a variety of issues from fracking to overpopulation to environmental impacts on human diets. The easy-to-read print and informative introduction, as well as the glossary, a further reading section for more in-depth research, and a well-designed index will make this a valuable source for high school, college, and university libraries.—**Diane J. Turner**

37 Transportation

General Works

C

521. **A Dictionary of Transport Analysis.** Kenneth Button, Henry Vega, and Peter Nijkamp, eds. Northhampton, Mass., Edward Elgar, 2010. 515p. index. $245.00. ISBN 13: 978-1-84376-375-8.

A Dictionary of Transport Analysis provides detailed definitions to terminology used in transportation policy and administration. These terms can often be confusing to those new to the industry or those crossing between various industries as terms often vary between industries. The terms concentrate on the social science aspects of transportation and some terms may be familiar to those outside of the industry but when seen in the context of this title will take on a whole new meaning. Each term is defined in several paragraphs and often time bullet lists are used to make the definitions even more clear. Many entries conclude with a list for further reading and all are signed by the contributor. This will be a useful addition to academic and research libraries that serve students studying transportation at the advanced level.—**Shannon Graff Hysell**

C, P

522. **Plunkett's Automobile Industry Almanac.** 2012 ed. Jack W. Plunkett, ed. Houston, Tex., Plunkett Research, 2011. 562p. index. $299.99pa. (includes online edition). ISBN 13: 978-1-60879-651-9; 978-1-60879-651-9.

Plunkett's Automobile Industry Almanac provides an overview of the automobile industry and the key players. It is intended to be a general guide and offers many easy-to-use charts and tables.

The opening chapters describe the state of the industry and the major trends and technologies affecting the industry; provide statistics from trade associations and government sources; and offer the industry contacts such as government agencies, associations, publications, job-hunting resources, and various information sources related to the industry. It includes information on recent car ad truck industry mergers and globalization efforts, information regarding automobile loans and insurance, and the affects of e-commerce in the automobile industry and the fact that most people now shop online before even stepping foot in a dealership. Chapter 4 is the core of this publication, and includes ranking charts and leading companies' profiles. The companies were selected from all U.S. and many foreign automobile and related industry segments: manufacturers; dealerships; financial services; and many others, including makers of trucks and specialty vehicles. Alphabetic and geographic indexes are provided for chapter 4. Each company profile includes the following: company name; ranks; business activities; types of business; brands/divisions/affiliations; names and positions of top officers; address; telephone and fax numbers; Website address; key financials; salaries/benefits; number of apparent women officers; growth plans; and office locations. There are two additional indexes at the end of the publications: index of firms noted as hot spots for advancement for women/minorities, and index by subsidiaries, brand names, and selected affiliations. The glossary at the beginning the publication covers basic industry terminology.

This almanac seems especially useful for market research and job hunting. The inclusion criteria of chapter 4 are not clear and the information provided is not in depth, but the volume provides a good overview of the automobile industry. This work is recommended for business reference collections.—**Mihoko Hosoi**

Author/ Title Index

Reference is to entry number.

A-Z ency of food controversies & the law, 413
Aalen, F. H. A., 42
Abbott, Margery Post, 388
Abshire, Jean E., 136
AccessScience [Website], 394
Adamec, Christine, 487
Adamec, Ludwig W., 37
African American almanac, 11th ed, 107
African American experience [Website], 109
Aguilar, David A., 503
AIDS, 483
ALA bk of lib grant money, 8th ed, 168
ALA gd to economics & business ref, 45
ALA gd to medical & health scis, 463
Alaska, 33
Albala, Ken, 409
Alcohol & alcohol problems sci database [Website], 243
Alderfer, Jonathan, 450
AllBusiness [Website], 46
Allen, Lee, 495
Allen, Sarah G., 453
Allin, Craig W., 518
Almanac of …
    American educ 2011, 84
    American pol, 2012, 201
    famous people, 10th ed, 9
Aloi, Michael J., 498
AMA hndbk of business docs, 83
AMA hndbk of financial risk mgmt, 61
American Bird Conservancy gd to bird conservation, 449
American buyers, 250
American centuries, 131
American food by the decades, 407
American hist [Website], 130
American Indian hist online [Website], 114
American marketplace, 10th ed, 251
American musical theatre, 4th ed, 377
American novel, 327
American presidency, 196
American presidency online [Website], 197
American women's hist online [Website], 261
Americans & their homes, 3d ed, 252
America's college museums hndbk & dir, 2d ed, 23
America's top-rated cities 2011, 18th ed, 256
Ammer, Christine, 300
Anatomy of muscle building, 226

Ancient & medieval hist online [Website], 142
Ancient Egypt & the Near East, 139
Anderson, Margo J., 248
Anderson, Richard Paul, 345
Animated film ency, 2d ed, 373
Annuals & perennials, 418
Antarctica, 2d ed, 44
Anthem dict of literary terms & theory, 307
Anti-immigration in the U.S., 132
Applegate, Edd, 276
Applied sci & tech abstracts (ASTA) [Website], 402
Archer, J. Clark, 32
Archinform index of persons [Website], 293
Arguing for evolution, 430
Armitage, Allan M., 416, 417
Armitage's garden perennials, 2d ed, 416
Armitage's vines & climbers, 417
Arnold, Kathleen R., 132
AssociationExecs.com [Website], 17
Associations yellow bk, Winter 2011 ed, 15
At issue series, 29
Atkins, Stephen E., 207
Atlas of …
    birds, 448
    coasts & oceans, 510
    global inequalities, 253
    sports, 219
    the great plains, 32
    the Irish rural landscape, 2d ed, 42
    the transatlantic slave trade, 129
Auger, Peter, 307
Autism & pervasive developmental disorders sourcebk, 2d ed, 485

Baby boomer ency, 249
Baer, Charlotte Kirk, 405
Baker, Elizabeth A., 86
Baldino, Thomas J., 200
Baltic, Sarah E., 84
Banerjee, Tridib, 258
Bankston, Carl L., III, 108
Barnes, Amber, 236
Barone, Michael, 201
Barratt, Claire, 460
Barrett, Priscilla, 447
Bartlett's familiar quotations, 17th ed, 25
Baseball now! 2d ed, 224

Basher basics series, 30
Basic business lib, 5th ed, 162
Battles that changed hist, 181
Baugh, Gail, 287
Bearport digital lib [Website], 89
Beary, Brian, 190
Bell, Sigall K., 483
Bellenir, Karen, 478, 486
Benner, Jennifer, 421
Beolens, Bo, 454
BEOnline [Website], 47
Berger, Clare, 271
Bernadowski, Carianne, 92
Beshara, Tony, 74
Biographical ency of scientists & inventors in
    American film & TV since 1930, 364
Black America, 110
Blake, Sally, 495
Blauvelt, Robert P., 519
Blevins, Dave, 220
Blume, Kenneth J., 64
Bodart, Joni Richards, 319
Bodden, Valerie, 272
Book of ...
    fungi, 440
    the states 2011, v.43, 18
    U.S. govt jobs, 11th ed, 77
Booker, M. Keith, 367, 368
Books that teach kids to write, 94
Bordman, Gerald, 377
Bortolotti, Dan, 224
Bowe, Alice, 420
Bray, Ilona, 161
Breuning, Marijke, 193
Bridges to understanding, 310
Britannica bk of the yr 2011, 20
Britannica gd to the world's most influential people,
    10
Britannica online [Website], 11
Brockman, Norbert C., 382
Brodsky, Allen, 490
Brodsky, Phyllis L., 490
Brooks, F. Erik, 95
Brosnan, Kathleen A., 517
Bryant, Geoff, 418, 441
Buranbaeva, Oksana, 41
Burch, John R., Jr., 212
Burgess, Susan, 237
Business decision [Website], 81
Business plans hndbk, vols.21-22, 79
Business source premier [Website], 48
Business stats of the US 2011, 16th ed, 55
Button, Kenneth, 521

Callahan, Joan R., 469
Cambridge photographic star atlas, 502
Cancer sourcebk, 6th ed, 486
Canfield Reisman, Rosemary M., 338, 339
Canon of violin lit, 346
Carangelo, Lori, 120
Caregiver's gd, 470
Carnivores of the world, 447
Carpenter, Kent, 452
Carrigan, Esther, 163
Carstensen, Angela, 315
Carter, Stephanie Jane, 413
Carvalho, Vitor Hugo Costa, 496
CaseBase: case studies in global business, 70
Catalog of fed domestic assistance [Website], 238
Catherwood, Christopher, 144
Cavalier, Stephen, 357
Cawthon, Elisabeth A., 151
Celebrating women in American hist, 263
Celebrity in the 21st century, 361
Chamber orchestra & ensemble repertoire, 349
Chapman, Bert, 191
Chijioke, Mary Ellen, 388
Children's core collection, 20th ed, 163
China's Buddhist culture, 387
Chryssides, George D., 383
Ciment, James, 154
CINAHL: the cumulative index to nursing & allied
    health lit [Website], 491
Cite right, 2d ed, 274
Cities & building database [Website], 294
Cities in American pol hist, 257
Citro, Constance F., 248
City crime rankings, 18th ed, 155
Civil War era & Reconstruction, 134
Civil War naval ency, 185
Classical tradition, 268
Cohen, Stephanie, 421
Collaborative grantseeking, 240
College financing info for teens, 2d ed, 101
Collins, John J., 393
Collins, John W., III, 85
Comic bk collections for libs, 359
Companion to urban design, 258
Comparative gd to American suburbs 2011/12, 6th
    ed, 259
Complete bk of patchwork, quilting & appliqué, 285
Complete bk of soccer, 2d ed, 231
Complete costume dict, 286
Complete dir for people with chronic illness
    2011/12, 10th ed, 466
Complete dir for people with disabilities 2012, 20th
    ed, 235

Complete planet [Website], 499
Computer games as educl & mgmt tools, 496
Comrie, Bernard, 296
Concordia's complete Bible hndbk for students, 385
Condé, H. Victor, 159
Conflict & conquest in the Islamic world, 178
Confronting global warming series, 506
Congress investigates, 202
Contemporary color in the landscape, 427
Contemporary world fiction, 305
Cook, Sarah, 192
Cooper, J. Andrew G., 444
Copyright law for librarians & educators, 3d ed, 169
Core collection for YAs, 2d ed, 167
Cotner, Sehoya, 430
Countries at the crossroads 2010, 192
Cousins, A. D., 332
CQ global researcher [Website], 189
Crabtree connections series, 21
Craft-Rosenberg, Martha, 464
Crash course in the world of genealogy, 170
Crews, Kenneth D., 171
Crime writers, 323
Crisp, Richard J., 217
Critical companion to J. R. R. Tolkien, 334
Critical companion to Maya Angelou, 329
Crow, Ben, 253
Crutchfield, James A., 133
Cruz-Cunha, Maria Manuela, 496
Cuhaj, George, 279
Culture & customs of Hungary, 41
Cunion, William, 198
Curriculum resource center [Website], 90

Daily life in colonial Latin America, 138
Daily life in the Ottoman Empire, 140
Daily life of women during the civil rights era, 266
Daily life through American hist in primary docs, 135
Daily life through hist [Website], 143
Dali, Keren, 305
Damp, Dennis V., 77
Dandelion, Pink, 388
Danilov, Victor J., 23
Danver, Steven L., 146, 212
Database of award-winning children's lit (DAWCL) [Website], 311
Day, Robert A., 270, 398
Day, Sonia, 425
Deardorff, David, 422
Debaggio, Thomas, 419
Decoding gardening advice, 423

DemographicsNow, lib ed [Website], 247
Developmental editing, 273
Diamond, Marie Josephine, 309
Dictionary of ...
    literary characters, 322
    transport analysis, 521
    visual discourse, 381
Diet & nutrition sourcebk, 4th ed, 477
Diet info for teens, 3d ed, 478
Digital collections worldwide, 498
Dilevko, Juris, 305
Dilworth, Richardson, 257
DiMare, Philip C., 370
Dingwell, Heath, 215, 497
Dinosaurs, 511
Direction of trade stats [Website], 67
Dirr, Michael A., 442
Dirr's ency of trees & shrubs, 442
Discovery educ streaming plus [Website], 91
Disease maps, 471
Ditmore, Melissa Hope, 242
Dixon, Pam, 160
Dizard, Jake, 192
Documentary filmmakers hndbk, 374
Dodds, Mark, 221
Doskow, Emily, 150
Dowding, Keith, 27
Dowell, David R., 169
Drew, Bernard A., 325
Dreyer, David R., 209
Drug info for teens, 3d ed, 246
Drugs of abuse, 244
Duerr, Sasha, 283
Dunmore, Tom, 232
Duram, Leslie A., 408

Eckhardt, Ned, 374
Education state rankings 2011-12, 93
Eerdmans companion to the Bible, 386
Eerdmans dict of early Judaism, 393
EI compendex [Website], 458
Eltis, David, 129
Encyclopedia of ...
    African American music, 341
    African American popular culture, 111
    agricultural, food, & biological engineering, 2d ed, 404
    American business, rev ed, 53
    American environmental hist, 517
    animal sci, 2d ed, 405
    arthritis, 2d ed, 484
    Asian American folklore & folklife, 352
    biological invasions, 431

Encyclopedia of ... (*Cont.*)
   climate & weather, 2d ed, 507
   consumer culture, 59
   contemporary social issues, 26
   diabetes, 2d ed, 487
   disaster relief, 210
   drug policy, 147
   emerging industries, 6th ed, 65
   environmental issues, 518
   family health, 464
   geography terms, themes, & concepts, 126
   herbs, 419
   human rights in the US, 2d ed, 159
   invasive species, 443
   Islamic herbal medicine, 482
   math & society, 513
   medical orgs & agencies, 22d ed, 467
   microbiology, 433
   natl anthems, 2d ed, 343
   Native American hist, 115
   N American Indian wars 1607-1890, 116
   organic, sustainable, & local food, 408
   pollution, 519
   power, 27
   religion & film, 369
   right-wing extremism in modern American hist, 207
   sacred places, 2d ed, 382
   school crime & violence, 152
   small business, 4th, 52
   S Africa, 36
   sports mgmt & mktg, 221
   TV shows, 1925-2010, 2d ed, 372
   TV theme songs, 371
   the heart & heart disease, 2d ed, 488
   the U. S. Census, 2d ed, 248
   the U.S. govt & the environment, 211
   the Vietnam War, 2d ed, 179
   themes in lit, 308
   tropical plants, 436
   vampires & werewolves, 2d ed, 354
   war crimes & genocide, rev ed, 144
   water pol & policy in the US, 212
   women in today's world, 262
   world writers, 309
Engelbrecht, Edward A., 385
Environmental debate, 2d ed, 520
Eponym dict of reptiles, 454
Ernst, Carl H., 455, 456
Ernst, Evelyn M., 455, 456
Essential world atlas, 6th ed, 124
Ethiopia, 35
Ethnic groups of Africa & the Middle East, 106
Europe: a pol profile, 206

Evans, Robert C., 327
Evans, Shelley, 440
Eye on art series, 292

Factmonster.com [Website], 2
Facts on File dict of clichés, 3d ed, 300
Fagan, Bryan D., 359
Fagan, Jody Condit, 359
Family health from a to Z, 465
Family in lit for young readers, 312
Famous trials in hist, 151
Fashion designer's textile dir, 287
Fast food & junk food, 412
Favor, Lesli J., 508
Fayaz, Ahmed, 436
Federal reserve stats & histl data [Website], 60
FedStats [Website], 254
Fee, Gordon D., 386
Fenwick, George H., 449
Field gd to coastal fishes from Maine to Tex., 452
Field gd to marine mammals of the Pacific coast, 453
50 health scares that fizzled, 469
Fighting elites, 183
Film & TV music, 340
Financial aid for African Americans, 2002-14, 98
Financial aid for Hispanic Americans, 2012-14, 99
Finding the answers to legal questions, 173
Finley, Laura L., 152
Firefly's step-by-step ency of needlecraft, 284
First research industry profiles [Website], 63
Fisher, James, 380
Flowering plants, 439
Folklore, 2d ed, 353
Folsom, W. Davis, 53
Food: in context, 410
Food cultures of the world ency, 409
Forte, Eric, 168
Foundation grants to individuals, 20th ed, 239
Fowler, Susan G., 234
Frasier, David K., 362
Fredriksen, John C., 176, 183, 186
Free, Rhona C., 56
Frogs & toads of the world, 457
Fusco, Marjorie, 498

Gagné, Nicole V., 347
Gale business insights: global [Website], 49
Gale ency of children's health, 2d ed, 474
Gale ency of medicine, 4th ed, 475
Gaquin, Deirdre A., 84
Garbutt, Glenda, 305
Gassmann, Günther, 389

Gastel, Barbara, 270
Gates, Alexander E., 519
Gates, Phil, 399
Geis, Gilbert, 156
Gellman, Robert, 160
Gender & women's leadership, 264
Geopolitics, 191
Gianfresco, Richard, 424
Gillespie, John T., 312
Gillman, Jeff, 423
Gitlin, Martin, 249
Gods & goddesses of Greece & Rome, 356
Golden age of American musical theatre, 379
Gott, J. Richard, 504
Governing America, 198
Graedon, Joe, 492
Graedon, Terry, 492
Grafton, Anthony, 268
Graham, Allison, 269
Graphic novels & comic bks, 360
Graphic novels for young readers, 313
Graphic novels in your school lib, 171
Grasso, John, 225, 233
Gray, Leon, 439
Grayson, Michael, 454
Great lives from hist: African Americans, 108
Great lives from hist: Jewish Americans, 118
Greek poets, 338
Greenwald, Sarah J., 513
Greenwood dict of educ, 2d ed, 85
Grey House performing arts dir 2011/12, 7th ed,
     363
Griffith, Jerry, 240
Grove ency of American art, 288
Grover, Robert J., 234
Grover, Sharon, 278
Grzimek's animal life ency: evolution, 432
Guide to fed terms & acronyms, 1
Guide to private special educ 2011/12, 103
Guiley, Rosemary Ellen, 354
Gun digest, 2012, 281

Halliday, Fred, 180
Hampton, John J., 61
Handbook of ...
     intl rivalries 1494-2010, 209
     natural plant dyes, 283
     U.S. labor stats 2011, 14th ed, 75
Handy personal finance answer bk, 62
Handy presidents answer bk, 2d ed, 203
Handy sci answer bk, 4th ed, 400
Hang, Xing, 343
Hanks, Reuel R., 126

Hannegan, Lizette D., 278
Harlow, Daniel C., 393
Hawdon, James E., 147
Haynes, Elizabeth, 323
Hays, Peter L., 187
Haywood, John, 141
Heijmans, Jeroen, 227
Heldman, Dennis R., 404
Helping those experiencing loss, 234
Herald, Nathan, 313
Hess, Paul, 450
Higa, Mori Lou, 163
High-impact, low-carbon gardening, 420
Hillstrom, Kevin, 76, 213
Hines, James R., 230
Hinrichsen, Don, 510
Hischak, Thomas S., 378
Historical dict of ...
     Afghanistan, 4th ed, 37
     American cinema, 367
     Angola, 2d ed, 34
     Australian Aborigines, 112
     basketball, 225
     Byzantium, 2d ed, 137
     Calvinism, 390
     children's lit, 318
     contemporary American theater, 380
     cycling, 227
     English music ca. 1400-1958, 342
     figure skating, 230
     golf, 229
     Hinduism, new ed, 391
     Lutheranism, 2d ed, 389
     modern & contemporary classical music, 347
     neoclassical art & architecture, 290
     new religious movements, 2d ed, 383
     postwar Japan, 39
     rococo art, 289
     romantic art & architecture, 291
     sci fiction cinema, 368
     soccer, 232
     tennis, 233
     the Chinese communist party, 205
     the Friends (Quakers), 2d ed, 388
     the U.S. maritime industry, 64
Historical fiction for teens, 316
Historical thesaurus of the Oxford English
     Dictionary, 301
Historically black colleges & universities, 95
History of American presidential elections, 4th ed, 195
History of Singapore, 136
Hohler, Sharon E., 470
Holidays of the world cookbk for students, updated
     ed, 415

Hombs, Mary Ellen, 241

Honig, Megan, 320

Hoover, William D., 39

Hornsby, Alton, Jr., 110

Horvitz, Leslie Alan, 144

How to grow food, 424

How to write & pub a scientific paper, 7th ed, 270

HSTM: history of sci, tech, & medicine [Website], 395

Hubbard, Robert L., Jr., 386

Hudson, David L., Jr., 203

Human body from A to Z, 435

Hunt, Chris, 231

Hunter, Luke, 447

Hyatt, Wesley, 365

I am hip-hop, 351

IBISWorld [Website], 68

Icons of African American lit, 328

Identifying & feeding birds, 451

IEEE Xplore [Website], 461

Ihrie, Maureen, 336

Incredible edibles, 425

India today, 38

Industrial electronics hndbk, 2d ed, 462

Information please almanac online [Website], 3

International literary market place 2012, 174

International trade stats [Website], 69

Irwin, J. David, 462

Ishiyama, John T., 193

Israel, Fred L., 195

Issues [Website], 28

Jacobs, Sean, 36

James, W. Martin, 34

Jefferson, Ann, 138

Jensen, Vickie, 153

Jerris, Randon, 229

Johnson, Krista, 36

Johnson, Murray, 112

Journalism in the US, 276

Junior worldmark ency of world cultures, 2d ed, 105

Kalaitzidis, Akis, 208

Kaminsky, Arnold P., 38

Kan, Kat, 360

Karp, Jesse, 167

Kelley, Joseph T., 444

Kells, Val, 452

Kepler, Ann, 172

Kernodle, Tammy L., 341

Ketcham, Susan E., 498

Kia, Mehrdad, 140

Kimberly, Paul, 512

Kingfisher geography ency, 2d ed, 127

Kinnear, Karen L., 265

Kleiman, Mark A. R., 147

Klimecki, Zachary, 478

Koch, Tom, 471

Kreider, Kyle L., 200

Kress, Rush, 167

Kronenfeld, Jennie Jacobs, 472

Kroner, Zina, 411

Kummings, Donald, 331

Kupperman, Karen Ordahl, 131

Lampson, Marc, 165

Landmark Supreme Court cases, 2d ed, 148

Landscaping for privacy, 428

Lansford, Tom, 177

Larousse concise dict: English-German/German-English, 303

Larousse unabridged dict: French-English/English-French, 302

Larsen, Laura, 477

Last name meanings dict [Website], 123

Latino American experience [Website], 119

Lavin, Stephen J., 32

Lebbin, Daniel J., 449

Lee, Jerry, 282

Lee, Jonathan H. X., 352

Legal answer bk for families, 150

Legal rights & responsibilities of teachers, 87

Legends of American Indian resistance, 117

Leiter, Richard A., 148

LeMaster, J. R., 330, 331

Lems, Kristin, 295

Leslie, Larry Z., 361

Levy, Joel, 216

Lewandowski, Elizabeth J., 286

Li-tian, Fang, 387

Liberman, Sherri, 407

Life stories, 337

Lifecycles series, 434

Lindstrom, Matthew, 211

Lipson, Charles, 274

Listening to learn, 278

Literary market place 2012, 175

Literary research & Canadian lit, 335

Living Earth series, 509

Living with insomnia, 490

Lodha, Suresh K., 253

Lokken, Paul, 138

Long, Jeffery D., 391
Long, Roger D., 38
Loukaitou-Sideris, Anastasia, 258

Maczulak, Anne, 433
Magill, Elizabeth, 101, 246, 489
Magill's cinema annual 2012, 375
Make mine a mystery II, 324
Mallette, Leo, 271
Mallon, Bill, 227, 229
Mancall, Peter C., 115
Marill, Alvin H., 366
Marley, David F., 157
Marshall Cavendish digital [Website], 12
Marter, Joan, 288
Mastrandrea, Michael D., 507
MathWorld [Website], 514
Mattison, Chris, 457
Maxile, Horace J., Jr., 341
Maynard, Meleah, 423
Mazur, Eric Michael, 369
McCaffrey, Paul, 260
McClinton-Temple, Jennifer, 308
McCormick, Charlie T., 353
McCutcheon, Chuck, 201
McGuire, Charles Edward, 342
McMickens, Courtney L., 483
McVicker, Mary F., 348
Medical Lib Assn's master gd to authoritative info
    resources in the health scis, 164
Medical tests sourcebk, 4th ed, 479
Medicare, 472
MEDLINE [Website], 473
Medoff, Rafael, 118
Meier, John J., 511
Mellinger, Axel, 502
Melton, J. Gordon, 358
Merck manual of diagnosis & therapy, 19th ed, 480
Mersky, Roy M., 148
Meyer, Dirk, 349
Middle East, 43
Middle East almanac, 176
Mikaberidze, Alexander, 178
Milam, Jennifer D., 289
Militarization of space, 188
Milkias, Paulos, 35
Miller, Leah D., 295
Miller, Randall M., 135
Miner, Jeremy T., 240
Miner, Lynn E., 240
MLA intl bibliog [Website], 8
Mladineo, Vanja, 41
Modern homelessness, 241

Modern piracy, 157
Moerman, Daniel E., 437
Money for graduate students in the physical & earth
    scis, 2010-12, 100
Mongillo, John F., 516
Monteith, Sharon, 269
Moon, Danelle, 266
Moore, Patrick, 505
Moore, Randy, 430
Moraru, Carmen I., 404
Morgan, Kathleen O'Leary, 93, 155, 255
Morgan, Scott, 93, 155, 255
Morgano, Kelly, 92
Morris, Vanessa Irvin, 321
Morrow, John Andrew, 482
Mortenson, Joe, 453
Most, Glenn W., 268
Mott, Peter Rhoades, 520
Movies in American hist, 370
Movies made for TV 2005-09, 366
Music production, 344
Muslim world, 392

Nadeau, Kathleen M., 352
Naden, Corinne J., 379
Nardolillo, Jo, 346
Naske, Claus M., 33
National Geographic atlas of the world, 9th ed, 125
National Geographic backyard gd to the birds of N
    America, 450
National Geographic kids almanac 2012, 4
National trade & professional assns dir 2011, 16
Native American medicinal plants, 437
Natural disasters, 508
Nature got there first, 399
Nature scaping workbk, 429
Neal, William J., 444
Neimark, Peninah, 520
Nelson, Paul, 173
New atlas of world hist, 141
New ency of southern culture: media, v.18, 269
New literacies, 86
New York Times on gay & lesbian issues, 237
Newbery & Caldecott Awards, 2011 ed, 314
Niebuhr, Gary Warren, 324
Nijkamp, Peter, 521
9/11 & the wars in Afghanistan & Iraq, 177
Nonfiction, 272
Nonstop garden, 421
North American coins & prices CD, 2012 ed, 280
North American gd to common poisonous plants &
    mushrooms, 438
North American wildlife, 445

Norton, Scott, 273
Nutrition & food scis database [Website], 406

O'Brien, Nancy Patricia, 85
O'Connor, Karen, 264
O'Connor, Maureen, 337
Off-Broadway musicals since 1919, 378
Ogden, Lauren Springer, 426
Ogden, Scott, 426
Oliver, John William, Jr., 388
Olson, Danel, 326
100 most popular contemporary mystery authors, 325
Online privacy, 160
Oppenheim, Michael R., 168
Oropesa, Salvador A., 336
Osborne, Allan G., Jr., 87
O'Sullivan, Emer, 318
Outstanding bks for the college bound, 315
Oyster, Carol K., 262

Page, Joseph S., 228
Page, Yolanda Williams, 328
Palmer, Allison Lee, 290, 291
Parr, Michael J., 449
Parsons, Paul, 401
Partridge, Kenneth, 500
Patrick Moore's data bk of astronomy, 505
Pavonetti, Linda M., 310
PDR for nonprescription drugs, dietary
    supplements, & herbs 2012, 33d ed, 493
Pearlmutter, Jane, 173
PebbleGo biogs [Website], 88
Pehler, Shelley Rae, 464
Penuel, K. Bradley, 210
People's pharmacy home remedies, 492
Pests, 446
Peterson, Herman A., 113
Peterson's 4-yr colleges 2011, 96
Peterson's graduate & professional programs 2012,
    46th ed, 97
Petit, William A., Jr., 487
Phillips, Joseph, 80
Philpott, Don, 1
Phobiapedia, 216
Pianist's craft, 345
Picken, Stuart D. B., 390
Pilkey, Orrin H., 444
Piper, Ross, 446
Plank, Steven E., 342
Plastic surgery, 481
Plunkett, Jack W., 54, 66, 459, 494, 501, 515, 522

Plunkett's almanac of Asian companies 2012, 72
Plunkett's almanac of middle market companies
    2012, 54
Plunkett's automobile industry almanac, 2012 ed,
    522
Plunkett's biotech & genetics industry almanac,
    2012 ed, 459
Plunkett's games, apps, & social media industry
    almanac 2012, 494
Plunkett's green tech industry almanac 2012, 515
Plunkett's insurance industry almanac 2012 ed, 66
Plunkett's telecommunications industry almanac,
    2012 ed, 501
Pond, Wilson G., 405
Pool, Jeannie Gayle, 376
Popular controversies in world hist, 146
Porter, Robert S., 480
Prefaces to Shakespeare, 333
Price, Emmett G., III, 341
Pro football championships before the Super Bowl,
    228
Project mgmt for small business, 80
ProQuest entrepreneurship [Website], 50
Prostitution & sex work, 242
PsycINFO [Website], 214
Purdy, Elizabeth Rholetter, 263

Quinn, Joyce A., 443
Quirk, Paul J., 198

Rabey, Melissa, 316
Ramsay, Craig, 226
Randall, Otelio S., 488
Rausch, Andrew J., 351
Read on . . . Audiobks, 165
Readers' advisory gd to street lit, 321
Rees, Robin, 505
Reid, Rob, 317
Reid's read-alouds 2, 317
Reiss, Steven A., 223
Rejmanek, Marcel, 431
Religious celebrations, 358
Research gd to film & TV music in the US, 376
Reznowski, Gabriella Natasha, 335
Richardson, David, 129
Rielly, Edward J., 117
Roberts, Peter, 440
Robertson, Ann E., 188
Robinson, Mark A., 371
Rodd, Tony, 418, 441
Rodriguez, Junius P., 145
Rolls, Mitchell, 112

Romaine, Deborah S., 488
Rosser, John H., 137
Roten, Lindsay Grace, 415
Routledge ency of …
    Mark Twain, 330
    social & cultural anthropology, 2d ed, 104
    Walt Whitman, repr ed, 331
Rubin, Barry, 43
Russian poets, 339
Russo, Charles J., 87
Ruud, Jay, 334

Saccardi, Marianne, 94
Sakaduski, Nancy, 398
Salem health: infectious diseases & conditions, 476
Salvo, Joseph J., 248
Sandywell, Barry, 381
Saricks, Joyce g., 166
Schlachter, Gail Ann, 98, 99, 100
Schlesinger, Arthur M., Jr., 195
Schneider, Stephen H., 507
Science behind sports series, 222
Science in 100 key breakthroughs, 401
Science of nutrition series, 414
Science online [Website], 396
Scientific English, 3d ed, 398
Scitopia [Website], 403
Segerson, Nathan M., 488
Selby, Kevin J., 483
Senior high core collection, 18th ed, 166
Separatist movements, 190
Settis, Salvatore, 268
Settlement of America, 133
Seward, Linda, 285
Sexual health info for teens, 3d ed, 489
Shakespeare, 332
Shally-Jensen, Michael, 26
Shannon, Joyce Brennfleck, 479, 485
Shelley, Fred M., 32
Sherk, Warren M., 340
Shidler, Dan, 281
Shocked & awed: a dict of the war on terror, 180
Shoup, John A., 106
Show business homicides, 362
Siebert, Lee, 512
Simberloff, Daniel, 431
Simkin, Tom, 512
Sizing up the universe, 504
Skaine, Rosemarie, 184
Slavery in the modern world, 145
Sloan, Jane, 262
Sloan, Kathryn A., 267
Slomp, Hans, 206

Slotnick, Herman E., 33
Small business resource center [Website], 51
Small public lib mgmt, 172
Smith, Andrew F., 412
Smith, Jessie Carney, 111
Snodgrass, Mary Ellen, 134
Social networking, 500
Social psychology, 217
Sollars, Michael D., 322
Soro, Tenena M., 295
Southerton, Dale, 59
Space & security, 187
Sports Hall of Fame ency, 220
Sports in America, 223
Spotter's gd to urban engineering, 460
Standard catalog of firearms, 2012, 282
Standard catalog of world coins 1601-1700, 5th ed, 279
Stange, Mary Zeiss, 262
Starks, Glenn L., 95
State rankings 2011, 255
Statesman's yrbk 2011, 147th, 31
Statler, Matt, 210
Steiger, Brad, 355
Stein, C. Michael, 484
Stewart, John, 44
Stewart, Marcia, 150
Stokes, Jamie, 392
Stout, Matthew, 42
Stoyan, Ronald, 502
Streich, Gregory W., 208
Streissguth, Tom, 215
Stress-related disorders sourcebk, 3d ed, 218
Student gd to energy, 516
Substance abuse, addiction, & treatment, 245
Sullivan, Lawrence R., 205
Supreme Court & the environment, 158
Survey of American industry & careers, 73
Sutton, Amy L., 218
Swayne, Linda E., 221

Tanner, Tony, 333
Tavare, Paula Cristina Almeida, 496
Taylor, Guy, 484
Teaching histl fiction with ready-made lit circles for
    secondary readers, 92
Teaching reading to English lang learners, 295
Technology & young children, 495
Television's top 100, 365
Terrace, Vincent, 372
TheStreet Ratings' ultimate guided tour of stock
    investing, Spring 2011, 58
They suck, they bite, they eat, they kill, 319
13 planets, 503

Thomley, Jill E., 513
Thompson, Bill, III, 451
Thompson, Lana, 481
Thompson, Laurie L., 163
Thompson, William R., 209
Thursby, Jaqueline S., 329
Time almanac 2011, 5
TinkerPlots [Website], 102
Tobia, Rajia, 163
Today's sci [Website], 397
Tomlinson, Alan, 219
Top 100: the fastest growing careers for the 21st
    century, 5th ed, 78
Top 100 health-care careers, 3d ed, 468
Top stories 2010, 22
Trail of tears, 113
Trees & shrubs, 441
Troy, Gil, 195
Truth about family life, 2d ed, 236
Truth about stress mgmt, 215
Truth about the Internet & online predators, 497
Tucci, Paul A., 62
Tucker, Arthur O., 419
Tucker, Spencer C., 116, 179, 181, 182, 185
Tucker, Virginia, 165
Turner, Nancy J., 438
21st century economics, 56
21st-century gothic, 326
21st century novels, 306
21st century pol sci, 193

Ullrey, Duane E., 405
Ulrich's per dir 2011, 49th ed, 24
Ultimate playlist, 350
Ultimate search bk, 2011 ed, 120
Unbeatable resumes, 74
United States Marine Corps, 186
United States presidents [Website], 194
Unwin, Mike, 448
Urban grit, 320
U.S. election campaigns, 200
U.S. foreign policy, 208
U.S. health policy & pol, 213
U.S. immigration made easy, 15th ed, 161
U.S. infrastructure, 260
U.S. justice system, 149
USA.gov [Website], 19
USGenWeb [Website], 121
Utter, Glenn H., 204

Van Riper, A. Bowdoin, 364
Vanderbei, Robert J., 504

Vega, Henry, 521
Venomous reptiles of the US, Canada, & N Mexico,
    v.1, 455
Venomous reptiles of the US, Canada, & N Mexico,
    v.2, 456
Venture deal [Website], 57
Vitamins & minerals, 411
Volcanoes of the world, 3d ed, 512
von Aderkas, Patrick, 438

Wadsworth, Kathryn, 422
Walker, Christopher, 192
Washington info dir 2011-12, 199
Waterwise plants for sustainable gardens, 426
Watkins, Julia A., 236
Watkins, Michael, 454
Wauson, Jennifer, 83
Webb, Graham, 373
Webb, Lois Sinaiko, 415
Webb, Robert, 350
Webb, Sophie, 453
Weber, R. David, 98, 99, 100
Website mktg plan [Website], 82
Webster's dict & thesaurus for students, 2d ed, 297
Webster's dict for students: special ency ed, 4th ed,
    298
Webster's everyday Spanish-English dict, 304
Webster's rhyming dict, 299
Welch, Rollie James, 170
Werewolf bk, 2d ed, 355
What's wrong with my vegetable garden?, 422
Whelan, Kevin, 42
White-collar & corporate crime, 156
White, Kim Kennedy, 353
Whitelaw, Ian, 460
Wilamowski, Bogdan M., 462
Williams, Elizabeth M., 413
Wilson, Andrew, 427
Wilson, James D., 330
Wilson, Kevin, 83
Wilson, Steven Harmon, 149
Wingate, Marty, 428
Winsor, Denise, 495
Wischnitzer, Edith, 468
Wischnitzer, Saul, 468
Wolf, Michael Allan, 158
Women composers of classical music, 348
Women criminals, 153
Women in combat, 184
Women in developing countries, 265
Women's roles in Latin America & the Caribbean,
    267
Woodward, Susan L., 443

Workers unite, 76
World almanac for kids online [Website], 7
World almanac online [Website], 6
World & its peoples: Sub-Saharan Africa,
        Australasia, & the Pacific, 40
World Bk advanced [Website], 14
World Bk ency 2012, 13
World economic factbk 2012, 19th ed, 71
World Heritage Sites, 3d ed, 128
World hist of animation, 357
World lit in Spanish, 336
World news digest [Website], 277
World religions [Website], 384
World terrorism, 154

World War II at sea, 182
WorldGenWeb [Website], 122
World's beaches, 444
World's major langs, 2d ed, 296
Wright, H. Stephen, 376
Writer's ref center [Website], 275
Writing for conferences, 271

Young, Beth O'Donnell, 429
Youth & pol participation, 204

Zager, Michael, 344

Subject Index

Reference is to entry number.

ABORIGINAL AUSTRALIANS
Historical dict of Australian Aborigines, 112

ACTORS. *See also* **CELEBRITIES; MOTION PICTURES**
Biographical ency of scientists & inventors in American film & TV since 1930, 364
Show business homicides, 362

ADVERTISING. *See* **MARKETING**

AESTHETICS
Dictionary of visual discourse, 381

AFGHANISTAN
Historical dict of Afghanistan, 4th ed, 37

AFRICA
World & its peoples: Sub-Saharan Africa, Australasia, & the Pacific, 40

AFRICAN AMERICAN AUTHORS
Critical companion to Maya Angelou, 329
Icons of African American lit, 328

AFRICAN AMERICAN HISTORY
African American experience [Website], 109

AFRICAN AMERICAN MUSIC
Encyclopedia of African American music, 341

AFRICAN AMERICANS
African American almanac, 11th ed, 107
Black America, 110
Encyclopedia of African American popular culture, 111
Great lives from hist: African Americans, 108

AFRICAN AMERICANS - EDUCATION
Historically black colleges & universities, 95

AFRICANS
Ethnic groups of Africa & the Middle East, 106

AGRICULTURE
Encyclopedia of agricultural, food, & biological engineering, 2d ed, 404

AIDS (DISEASE)
AIDS, 483

ALASKA
Alaska, 33

ALCOHOLISM
Alcohol & alcohol problems sci database [Website], 243

ALMANACS
Factmonster.com [Website], 2
Information please almanac online [Website], 3
National Geographic kids almanac 2012, 4
Time almanac 2011, 5
World almanac for kids online [Website], 7
World almanac online [Website], 6

ALTERNATIVE MEDICINE
Encyclopedia of Islamic herbal medicine, 482
People's pharmacy home remedies, 492

AMERICAN LITERATURE. *See also* **AUTHORS, AMERICAN**
American novel, 327
Icons of African American lit, 328

AMPHIBIANS
Frogs & toads of the world, 457

ANATOMY
Human body from A to Z, 435

ANCIENT HISTORY
Ancient & medieval hist online [Website], 142
Ancient Egypt & the Near East, 139

ANGOLA
Historical dict of Angola, 2d ed, 34

ANIMAL INDUSTRY. *See also* **AGRICULTURE**
Encyclopedia of animal sci, 2d ed, 405

ANIMALS
Carnivores of the world, 447
North American wildlife, 445
Pests, 446

ANIMATION
Animated film ency, 2d ed, 373
World hist of animation, 357

ANTACTICA
Antarctica, 2d ed, 44

ANTHROPOLOGY
Routledge ency of social & cultural anthropology,
    2d ed, 104

APPLICATION SOFTWARE
Plunkett's games, apps, & social media industry
    almanac 2012, 494

ARCHITECTURE
Archinform index of persons [Website], 293
Cities & building database [Website], 294
Historical dict of neoclassical art & architecture,
    290

ART
Eye on art series, 292
Grove ency of American art, 288

ART HISTORY
Historical dict of neoclassical art & architecture,
    290
Historical dict of rococo art, 289
Historical dict of romantic art & architecture, 291

ARTHRITIS
Encyclopedia of arthritis, 2d ed, 484

ASIA, BUSINESS
Plunkett's almanac of Asian companies 2012, 72

ASIAN AMERICANS
Encyclopedia of Asian American folklore &
    folklife, 352

ASSOCIATIONS
AssociationExecs.com [Website], 17
Associations yellow bk, Winter 2011 ed, 15
National trade & professional assns dir 2011, 16

ASTRONAUTICS
Space & security, 187

ASTRONOMY
Cambridge photographic star atlas, 502
Patrick Moore's data bk of astronomy, 505
Sizing up the universe, 504
13 planets, 503

ATHLETES. *See also* **SPORTS**
Sports Hall of Fame ency, 220

ATLASES
Essential world atlas, 6th ed, 124
National Geographic atlas of the world, 9th ed, 125

AUDIOBOOKS
Listening to learn, 278
Read on . . . audiobks, 165

AUSTRALASIA
World & its peoples: Sub-Saharan Africa,
    Australasia, & the Pacific, 40

AUTHORS
100 most popular contemporary mystery authors,
    325
21st century novels, 306

AUTHORS, AMERICAN
Critical companion to Maya Angelou, 329
Routledge ency of Mark Twain, 330
Routledge ency of Walt Whitman, repr ed, 331

AUTHORS, ENGLISH
Critical companion to J. R. R. Tolkien, 334
Prefaces to Shakespeare, 333
Shakespeare, 332

AUTHORSHIP
Books that teach kids to write, 94
Cite right, 2d ed, 274
Developmental editing, 273
How to write & pub a scientific paper, 7th ed, 270
Nonfiction, 272
Scientific English, 3d ed, 398
Writer's ref center [Website], 275
Writing for conferences, 271

AUTISM
Autism & pervasive developmental disorders
    sourcebk, 2d ed, 485

AUTOBIOGRAPHY
Life stories, 337

AUTOMOBILE INDUSTRY
Plunkett's automobile industry almanac, 2012 ed,
    522

AWARDS
Database of award-winning children's lit (DAWCL)
    [Website], 311
Newbery & Caldecott Awards, 2011 ed, 314

BABY BOOM GENERATION
Baby boomer ency, 249

BANKS & BANKING. *See also* **FINANCE**
Federal reserve stats & histl data [Website], 60

BASEBALL
Baseball now! 2d ed, 224

BASKETBALL
Historical dict of basketball, 225

BEACHES
World's beaches, 444

BIBLE - HANDBOOKS & YEARBOOKS
Concordia's complete Bible hndbk for students, 385
Eerdmans companion to the Bible, 386

BIBLIOGRAPHY
MLA intl bibliog [Website], 8

BIOGRAPHY
Almanac of famous people, 10th ed, 9
Britannica gd to the world's most influential people, 10
PebbleGo biogs [Website], 88

BIOLOGICAL SCIENCES
Encyclopedia of biological invasions, 431
Encyclopedia of microbiology, 433
Lifecycles series, 434

BIOMEDICAL ENGINEERING
Encyclopedia of agricultural, food, & biological engineering, 2d ed, 404
Plunkett's biotech & genetics industry almanac, 2012 ed, 459

BIRDS
American Bird Conservancy gd to bird conservation, 449
Atlas of birds, 448
Identifying & feeding birds, 451
National Geographic backyard gd to the birds of N America, 450

BODYBUILDING
Anatomy of muscle building, 226

BOOK INDUSTRIES & TRADE
International literary market place 2012, 174
Literary market place 2012, 175

BOTANY. *See also* **GARDENING; PLANTS**
Encyclopedia of tropical plants, 436
Flowering plants, 439
Native American medicinal plants, 437

BUDDHISM
China's Buddhist culture, 387

BUSINESS - BIBLIOGRAPHY
ALA gd to economics & business ref, 45
Basic business lib, 5th ed, 162

BUSINESS - CATALOGS & COLLECTIONS
AllBusiness [Website], 46
BEOnline [Website], 47
Business source premier [Website], 48
First research industry profiles [Website], 63
Gale business insights: global [Website], 49
ProQuest entrepreneurship [Website], 50
Small business resource center [Website], 51

BUSINESS - DICTIONARIES & ENCYCLOPEDIAS
Encyclopedia of American business, rev ed, 53
Encyclopedia of emerging industries, 6th ed, 65
Encyclopedia of small business, 4th, 52

BUSINESS - DIRECTORIES
Plunkett's almanac of middle market companies 2012, 54

BUSINESS - HANDBOOKS & YEARBOOKS
AMA hndbk of business docs, 83
Business stats of the US 2011, 16th ed, 55

BUSINESS LIBRARIES
ALA gd to economics & business ref, 45
Basic business lib, 5th ed, 162

BUSINESS MANAGEMENT
Business plans hndbk, vols.21-22, 79
Project mgmt for small business, 80

BUSINESS STATISTICS
Business stats of the US 2011, 16th ed, 55
FedStats [Website], 254

BYZANTINE EMPIRE
Historical dict of Byzantium, 2d ed, 137

CALDECOTT AWARD
Newbery & Caldecott Awards, 2011 ed, 314

CALVINISM
Historical dict of Calvinism, 390

CANADIAN LITERATURE
Literary research & Canadian lit, 335

CANCER
Cancer sourcebk, 6th ed, 486

CAREERS
Book of U.S. govt jobs, 11th ed, 77
Survey of American industry & careers, 73
Top 100: the fastest growing careers for the 21st
       century, 5th ed, 78
Top 100 health-care careers, 3d ed, 468
Unbeatable resumes, 74

CAREGIVERS
Caregiver's gd, 470

CARIBBEAN
Women's roles in Latin America & the Caribbean,
       267

CARNIVORES
Carnivores of the world, 447

CARTOONS
Animated film ency, 2d ed, 373
World hist of animation, 357

CELEBRITIES
Almanac of famous people, 10th ed, 9
Celebrity in the 21st century, 361
Show business homicides, 362

CHAMBER ORCHESTRA MUSIC
Chamber orchestra & ensemble repertoire, 349

CHILDREN'S LIBRARY SERVICES
Graphic novels in your school lib, 167
Reid's read-alouds 2, 317

CHILDREN'S LITERATURE
Books that teach kids to write, 94
Bridges to understanding, 310
Children's core collection, 20th ed, 163
Database of award-winning children's lit (DAWCL)
       [Website], 311
Family in lit for young readers, 312
Historical dict of children's lit, 318
Newbery & Caldecott Awards, 2011 ed, 314
Reid's read-alouds 2, 317

CHILDREN'S REFERENCE
Basher basics series, 30
Britannica gd to the world's most influential people,
       10

Factmonster.com [Website], 2
National Geographic kids almanac 2012, 4
Phobiapedia, 216
World almanac for kids online [Website], 7

CHINA - POLITICS & GOVERNMENT
Historical dict of the Chinese communist party, 205

CHINA - RELIGIONS
China's Buddhist culture, 387

CHRISTIANITY
Historical dict of Calvinism, 390
Historical dict of Lutheranism, 2d ed, 389
Historical dict of the Friends (Quakers), 2d ed, 388

CITIES & TOWNS
America's top-rated cities 2011, 18th ed, 256
Cities in American pol hist, 257
Companion to urban design, 258
Comparative gd to American suburbs 2011/12, 6th
       ed, 259
U.S. infrastructure, 260

CIVIL ENGINEERING
Spotter's gd to urban engineering, 460

CIVIL RIGHTS
Daily life of women during the civil rights era, 266

CIVILIZATION - ANCIENT
Ancient & medieval hist online [Website], 142
Ancient Egypt & the Near East, 139

CLASSICAL MUSIC
Historical dict of modern & contemporary classical
       music, 347
Women composers of classical music, 348

CLIMATOLOGY
Confronting global warming series, 506
Encyclopedia of climate & weather, 2d ed, 507
Natural disasters, 508

COASTS
World's beaches, 444

COINS & PAPER MONEY
North American coins & prices CD, 2012 ed, 280
Standard catalog of world coins 1601-1700, 5th ed,
       279

COLLECTIBLES
Gun digest, 2012, 281
North American coins & prices CD, 2012 ed, 280

Standard catalog of firearms, 2012, 282
Standard catalog of world coins 1601-1700, 5th ed,
    279

COLLECTION DEVELOPMENT
Children's core collection, 20th ed, 163
Core collection for YAs, 2d ed, 167
Senior high core collection, 18th ed, 166

COMIC BOOKS. *See also* **GRAPHIC
NOVELS**
Comic bk collections for libs, 359
Graphic novels & comic bks, 360
World hist of animation, 357

COMMUNICATION
New ency of southern culture: media, v.18, 269

COMMUNISM
Historical dict of the Chinese communist party, 205

COMPOSERS (MUSIC)
Women composers of classical music, 348

CONSERVATISM
Encyclopedia of right-wing extremism in modern
    American hist, 207

CONSUMER SPENDING
American marketplace, 10th ed, 251
Encyclopedia of consumer culture, 59

COPYRIGHT LAW
Copyright law for librarians & educators, 3d ed,
    169

COSTUMES
Complete costume dict, 286

CRAFTS
Complete bk of patchwork, quilting & appliqué,
    285
Firefly's step-by-step ency of needlecraft, 284

CRIME
City crime rankings, 18th ed, 155
Encyclopedia of school crime & violence, 152
Modern piracy, 157
Show business homicides, 362
White-collar & corporate crime, 156
Women criminals, 153

CRIMINAL JUSTICE
Famous trials in hist, 151

CULTS
Historical dict of new religious movements, 2d ed,
    383

CULTURES
Culture & customs of Hungary, 41
Junior worldmark ency of world cultures, 2d ed,
    105

CYCLING
Historical dict of cycling, 227

DEATH
Helping those experiencing loss, 234

DEMOGRAPHICS
American buyers, 250
American marketplace, 10th ed, 251
Americans & their homes, 3d ed, 252
Business decision [Website], 81
DemographicsNow, lib ed [Website], 247
Encyclopedia of the U. S. Census, 2d ed, 248

DETECTIVE & MYSTERY STORIES
Crime writers, 323
Make mine a mystery II, 324
100 most popular contemporary mystery authors, 325

DIABETES
Encyclopedia of diabetes, 2d ed, 487

DIGITAL LIBRARIES
Bearport digital lib [Website], 89
Digital collections worldwide, 498

DINOSAURS
Dinosaurs, 511

DIRECTORIES
AssociationExecs.com [Website], 17
Associations yellow bk, Winter 2011 ed, 15
National trade & professional assns dir 2011, 16

DISASTER RELIEF
Encyclopedia of disaster relief, 210

DRAMA
Shakespeare, 332

DRUG ABUSE
Alcohol & alcohol problems sci database [Website], 243
Drug info for teens, 3d ed, 246
Drugs of abuse, 244
Encyclopedia of drug policy, 147
Substance abuse, addiction, & treatment, 245

DRUG CONTROL
Encyclopedia of drug policy, 147

DRUGS
PDR for nonprescription drugs, dietary
      supplements, & herbs 2012, 33d ed, 493

DYES & DYING
Handbook of natural plant dyes, 283

EARTH SCIENCE
Living Earth series, 509

ECOLOGY
Living Earth series, 509

ECONOMICS
ALA gd to economics & business ref, 45
Encyclopedia of consumer culture, 59
21st century economics, 56

**EDUCATION - DICTIONARIES &
ENCYCLOPEDIAS**
Greenwood dict of educ, 2d ed, 85

EDUCATION - ALMANACS
Almanac of American educ 2011, 84

EDUCATION - DIRECTORIES
Guide to private special educ 2011/12, 103
Peterson's 4-yr colleges 2011, 96
Peterson's graduate & professional programs 2012,
      46th ed, 97

EDUCATION, ELEMENTARY
Bearport digital lib [Website], 89
Books that teach kids to write, 94
Curriculum resource center [Website], 90
Discovery educ streaming plus [Website], 91
PebbleGo biogs [Website], 88

**EDUCATION - HANDBOOKS &
YEARBOOKS**
Education state rankings 2011-12, 93
Legal rights & responsibilities of teachers, 87

EDUCATION, HIGHER
Historically black colleges & universities, 95
Peterson's 4-yr colleges 2011, 96
Peterson's graduate & professional programs 2012,
      46th ed, 97

EDUCATION, SECONDARY
Books that teach kids to write, 94
Curriculum resource center [Website], 90

Discovery educ streaming plus [Website], 91
Teaching histl fiction with ready-made lit circles for
      secondary readers, 92

EDUCATIONAL GAMES
Computer games as educl & mgmt tools, 496

EDUCATIONAL TECHNOLOGY
Discovery educ streaming plus [Website], 91
New literacies, 86
Technology & young children, 495
TinkerPlots [Website], 102

EGYPT
Ancient Egypt & the Near East, 139

ELECTIONS
American presidency, 196
American presidency online [Website], 197
History of American presidential elections, 4th ed,
      195
U.S. election campaigns, 200

ELECTRICAL ENGINEERING
IEEE Xplore [Website], 461
Industrial electronics hndbk, 2d ed, 462

ELECTRONIC BOOKS
Bearport digital lib [Website], 89
Digital collections worldwide, 498

EMIGRATION & IMMIGRATION
Anti-immigration in the U.S., 132
U.S. immigration made easy, 15th ed, 161

ENCYCLOPEDIAS & DICTIONARIES
Britannica online [Website], 11
Marshall Cavendish digital [Website], 12
World Bk advanced [Website], 14
World Bk ency 2012, 13

ENERGY
Plunkett's green tech industry almanac 2012, 515
Student gd to energy, 516

ENGINEERING
EI compendex [Website], 458
IEEE Xplore [Website], 461
Spotter's gd to urban engineering, 460

ENGLISH LANGUAGE - DICTIONARIES
Webster's dict & thesaurus for students, 2d ed, 297
Webster's dict for students: special ency ed, 4th ed,
      298

ENGLISH LANGUAGE - DICTIONARIES - FRENCH
Larousse unabridged dict: French-English/English-French, 302

ENGLISH LANGUAGE - DICTIONARIES - GERMAN
Larousse concise dict: English-German/German-English, 303

ENGLISH LANGUAGE - DICTIONARIES - RHYMING
Webster's rhyming dict, 299

ENGLISH LANGUAGE - DICTIONARIES - SPANISH
Webster's everyday Spanish-English dict, 304

ENGLISH LANGUAGE - DICTIONARIES - SYNONYMS & ANTONYMS
Historical thesaurus of the Oxford English Dictionary, 301
Webster's dict & thesaurus for students, 2d ed, 297

ENGLISH LANGUAGE - TERMS & PHRASES
Facts on File dict of clichés, 3d ed, 300

ENTREPRENEURSHIP
AllBusiness [Website], 46
ProQuest entrepreneurship [Website], 50

ENVIRONMENTAL HISTORY
Encyclopedia of American environmental hist, 517
Encyclopedia of the U.S. govt & the environment, 211
Environmental debate, 2d ed, 520

ENVIRONMENTAL LAW
Supreme Court & the environment, 158

ENVIRONMENTAL SCIENCE
Encyclopedia of environmental issues, 518
Encyclopedia of pollution, 519

EPIDEMICS
Disease maps, 471

ETHIOPIA
Ethiopia, 35

ETHNIC STUDIES
Ethnic groups of Africa & the Middle East, 106
Junior worldmark ency of world cultures, 2d ed, 105

EUROPE, HISTORY
Historical dict of Byzantium, 2d ed, 137

EUROPE, POLITICS
Europe: a pol profile, 206

EVOLUTION
Arguing for evolution, 430
Grzimek's animal life ency: evolution, 432

FAMILIES IN LITERATURE
Family in lit for young readers, 312

FAMILY
Legal answer bk for families, 150
Truth about family life, 2d ed, 236

FASHION
Complete costume dict, 286
Fashion designer's textile dir, 287

FEDERAL GOVERNMENT
Guide to fed terms & acronyms, 1

FEMALE OFFENDERS
Women criminals, 153

FESTIVALS
Religious celebrations, 358

FICTION
American novel, 327
Contemporary world fiction, 305
Crime writers, 323
Dictionary of literary characters, 322
Historical fiction for teens, 316
Make mine a mystery II, 324
100 most popular contemporary mystery authors, 325
Readers' advisory gd to street lit, 321
21st-century gothic, 326
21st century novels, 306
Urban grit, 320

FIGURE SKATING
Historical dict of figure skating, 230

FINANCE
AMA hndbk of financial risk mgmt, 61
Federal reserve stats & histl data [Website], 60
Handy personal finance answer bk, 62
TheStreet Ratings' ultimate guided tour of stock investing, Spring 2011, 58
Venture deal [Website], 57

FINANCIAL AID & SCHOLARSHIPS
College financing info for teens, 2d ed, 101
Financial aid for African Americans, 2002-14, 98
Financial aid for Hispanic Americans, 2012-14, 99
Money for graduate students in the physical & earth
    scis, 2010-12, 100

FIREARMS
Gun digest, 2012, 281
Standard catalog of firearms, 2012, 282

FISHES
Field gd to coastal fishes from Maine to Tex., 452

FITNESS
Anatomy of muscle building, 226

FLOWERS
Annuals & perennials, 418
Armitage's garden perennials, 2d ed, 416
Flowering plants, 439

FOLKLORE
Encyclopedia of Asian American folklore &
    folklife, 352
Folklore, 2d ed, 353
Werewolf bk, 2d ed, 355

FOOD HABITS
American food by the decades, 407
Fast food & junk food, 412
Food cultures of the world ency, 409
Holidays of the world cookbk for students, updated
    ed, 415

FOOD INDUSTRY
A-Z ency of food controversies & the law, 413

FOOD SCIENCE
Encyclopedia of agricultural, food, & biological
    engineering, 2d ed, 404
Encyclopedia of organic, sustainable, & local food,
    408
Food: in context, 410
Nutrition & food scis database [Website], 406
Science of nutrition series, 414

FOOTBALL
Pro football championships before the Super Bowl,
    228

FRENCH LANGUAGE DICTIONARIES
Larousse unabridged dict: French-English/English-
    French, 302

FROGS
Frogs & toads of the world, 457

FRUITS
How to grow food, 424
Incredible edibles, 425

FUNDRAISING. *See also* **GRANTS-IN-AID**
ALA bk of lib grant money, 8th ed, 172

FUNGI
Book of fungi, 440
North American gd to common poisonous plants &
    mushrooms, 438

GAMES
Computer games as educl & mgmt tools, 496
Plunkett's games, apps, & social media industry
    almanac 2012, 494

GARDENING
Annuals & perennials, 418
Armitage's garden perennials, 2d ed, 416
Armitage's vines & climbers, 417
Contemporary color in the landscape, 427
Decoding gardening advice, 423
Encyclopedia of herbs, 419
High-impact, low-carbon gardening, 420
How to grow food, 424
Incredible edibles, 425
Landscaping for privacy, 428
Nature scaping workbk, 429
Nonstop garden, 421
Trees & shrubs, 441
Waterwise plants for sustainable gardens, 426
What's wrong with my vegetable garden? 422

GAYS
New York Times on gay & lesbian issues, 237

GENEALOGY
Crash course in the world of genealogy, 170
Ultimate search bk, 2011 ed, 120
USGenWeb [Website], 121
WorldGenWeb [Website], 122

GENETICS
Plunkett's biotech & genetics industry almanac,
    2012 ed, 459

GENOCIDE
Encyclopedia of war crimes & genocide, rev ed,
    144

GEOGRAPHY
Encyclopedia of geography terms, themes, &
     concepts, 126
Kingfisher geography ency, 2d ed, 127

GEOPOLITICS
Geopolitics, 191

GERMAN LANGUAGE DICTIONARIES
Larousse concise dict: English-German/German-
     English, 303

GLOBAL WARMING
Confronting global warming series, 506

GOLF
Historical dict of golf, 229

GOTHIC LITERATURE
21st-century gothic, 326

GOVERNMENT INFORMATION
USA.gov [Website], 19

GRANTS-IN-AID. *See also* **FINANCIAL AID &
SCHOLARSHIPS**
ALA bk of lib grant money, 8th ed, 168
Catalog of fed domestic assistance [Website], 238
Collaborative grantseeking, 240
Foundation grants to individuals, 20th ed, 239

GRAPHIC NOVELS
Comic bk collections for libs, 359
Graphic novels & comic bks, 360
Graphic novels for young readers, 313
Graphic novels in your school lib, 171

GREAT PLAINS
Atlas of the great plains, 32

GREECE
Gods & goddesses of Greece & Rome, 356

GREEK LITERATURE
Greek poets, 338

GREEN TECHNOLOGY. *See also*
ENVIRONMENTAL SCIENCE
Plunkett's green tech industry almanac 2012, 515

GRIEF
Helping those experiencing loss, 234

GUNS
Gun digest, 2012, 281

Standard catalog of firearms, 2012, 282

HANDBOOKS, VADE MECUMS, ETC.
Britannica bk of the yr 2011, 20
Crabtree connections series, 21
Top stories 2010, 22

HEALTH CARE - BIBLIOGRAPHY
ALA gd to medical & health scis, 463
Medical Lib Assn's master gd to authoritative info
     resources in the health scis, 163

HEALTH CARE CAREERS
Top 100 health-care careers, 3d ed, 468

**HEALTH CARE- DICTIONARIES &
ENCYCLOPEDIAS.** *See also* **MEDICINE –
DICTIONARIES & ENCYCLOPEDIAS**
Encyclopedia of family health, 464
Family health from a to Z, 465
Gale ency of children's health, 2d ed, 474
Gale ency of medicine, 4th ed, 475
Salem health: infectious diseases & conditions, 476

HEALTH CARE - DIRECTORIES
Complete dir for people with chronic illness
     2011/12, 10th ed, 466
Encyclopedia of medical orgs & agencies, 22d ed,
     467

**HEALTH CARE - HANDBOOKS &
YEARBOOKS**
Caregiver's gd, 470
50 health scares that fizzled, 469

HEALTH CARE POLICY
U.S. health policy & pol, 213

HEALTH INSURANCE
Medicare, 472

HEALTH SCIENCES LIBRARIES
ALA gd to medical & health scis, 463
Medical Lib Assn's master gd to authoritative info
     resources in the health scis, 163

HERBS
Encyclopedia of herbs, 419
People's pharmacy home remedies, 492

HINDUISM
Historical dict of Hinduism, new ed, 391

HISTORY - AMERICAN
American centuries, 131

American hist [Website], 130
Anti-immigration in the U.S., 132
Atlas of the transatlantic slave trade, 129
Celebrating women in American hist, 263
Daily life through American hist in primary docs, 135
Settlement of America, 133

HISTORY - ANCIENT
Ancient & medieval hist online [Website], 142
Ancient Egypt & the Near East, 139

HISTORY - WORLD
Daily life through hist [Website], 143
New atlas of world hist, 141
Popular controversies in world hist, 146
World news digest [Website], 277

HOLIDAYS
Religious celebrations, 358

HOMELESSNESS
Modern homelessness, 241

HORROR FICTION
They suck, they bite, they eat, they kill, 319
21st-century gothic, 326

HUMAN ANATOMY
Human body from A to Z, 435

HUMAN RIGHTS
Encyclopedia of human rights in the US, 2d ed, 159

HUMANITIES
Classical tradition, 268

HUNGARY
Culture & customs of Hungary, 41

IDEOLOGIES
Encyclopedia of right-wing extremism in modern
        American hist, 207

INDIA
India today, 38

INDIANS OF NORTH AMERICA
American Indian hist online [Website], 114
Encyclopedia of Native American hist, 115
Encyclopedia of N American Indian wars 1607-
        1890, 116
Legends of American Indian resistance, 117
Native American medicinal plants, 437
Trail of tears, 113

INDUSTRY
Encyclopedia of emerging industries, 6th ed, 65
First research industry profiles [Website], 63
Historical dict of the U.S. maritime industry, 64
Plunkett's almanac of middle market companies
        2012, 54
Plunkett's automobile industry almanac, 2012 ed,
        522
Plunkett's games, apps, & social media industry
        almanac 2012, 494
Plunkett's insurance industry almanac 2012 ed, 66
Plunkett's telecommunications industry almanac,
        2012 ed, 501

INFORMATION LITERACY
New literacies, 86

INSECTS
Pests, 446

INSOMNIA
Living with insomnia, 490

INSTRUMENTS
Canon of violin lit, 346

INSURANCE
Plunkett's insurance industry almanac 2012 ed, 66

INTERNATIONAL BUSINESS. *See also*
INTERNATIONAL TRADE
CaseBase: case studies in global business, 70
Gale business insights: global [Website], 49
IBISWorld [Website], 68
World economic factbk 2012, 19th ed, 71

INTERNATIONAL RELATIONS
CQ global researcher [Website], 189
Handbook of intl rivalries 1494-2010, 209
U.S. foreign policy, 208

INTERNATIONAL TRADE
Direction of trade stats [Website], 67
IBISWorld [Website], 68
International trade stats [Website], 69
Plunkett's almanac of Asian companies 2012, 72

INTERNET
Truth about the Internet & online predators, 497

INTERNET - DIRECTORIES
Complete planet [Website], 499
Digital collections worldwide, 498

INTERNET IN EDUCATION
Technology & young children, 495

INTERNET - LAWS & LEGISLATION
Online privacy, 160

INTRODUCED ORGANISMS
Encyclopedia of invasive species, 443

INVENTORS & INVENTIONS
Nature got there first, 399

INVESTMENTS
TheStreet Ratings' ultimate guided tour of stock
    investing, Spring 2011, 58
Venture deal [Website], 57

IRELAND
Atlas of the Irish rural landscape, 2d ed, 42

ISLAM
Encyclopedia of Islamic herbal medicine, 482
Muslim world, 392

ISLAMIC EMPIRE
Conflict & conquest in the Islamic world, 178

JAPAN
Historical dict of postwar Japan, 39

JEWS
Great lives from hist: Jewish Americans, 118

JOBS. *See* **CAREERS**

JOURNALISM
Journalism in the US, 276

JUDAISM
Eerdmans dict of early Judaism, 393

LABOR
Handbook of U.S. labor stats 2011, 14th ed, 75
Survey of American industry & careers, 73
Workers unite, 76

LANDSCAPING
Contemporary color in the landscape, 427
Landscaping for privacy, 428
Nature scaping workbk, 429

LANGUAGE & LINGUISTICS
Historical thesaurus of the Oxford English
    Dictionary, 301
Teaching reading to English lang learners, 295
World's major langs, 2d ed, 296

LATIN AMERICA
Daily life in colonial Latin America, 138
Women's roles in Latin America & the Caribbean,
    267

LATIN AMERICAN LITERATURE
World lit in Spanish, 336

LATIN AMERICANS
Latino American experience [Website], 119

**LAW - DICTIONARIES &
ENCYCLOPEDIAS**
A-Z ency of food controversies & the law, 413
Encyclopedia of drug policy, 147
Famous trials in hist, 151

LAW - HANDBOOKS
Legal answer bk for families, 150

LAW, UNITED STATES
Landmark Supreme Court cases, 2d ed, 148
Supreme Court & the environment, 158
U.S. immigration made easy, 15th ed, 161
U.S. justice system, 149

LEADERSHIP
Gender & women's leadership, 264

LEGAL RESEARCH
Finding the answers to legal questions, 173

LESBIAN STUDIES
New York Times on gay & lesbian issues, 237

LIBRARY MANAGEMENT
Small public lib mgmt, 172

LITERACY
New literacies, 86

LITERARY AWARDS
Database of award-winning children's lit (DAWCL)
    [Website], 311
Newbery & Caldecott Awards, 2011 ed, 314

LITERATURE - BIBLIOGRAPHY
Contemporary world fiction, 305

LITERATURE - BIO-BIBLIOGRAPHY
American novel, 327

LITERATURE - CRITICISM
21st century novels, 306

LITERATURE - DICTIONARIES & ENCYCLOPEDIAS
Anthem dict of literary terms & theory, 307
Dictionary of literary characters, 322
Encyclopedia of themes in lit, 308
Encyclopedia of world writers, 309

MAMMALS. *See also* **ANIMALS**
North American wildlife, 445

MARINE ANIMALS
Field gd to marine mammals of the Pacific coast, 453

MARINE BIOLOGY
Atlas of coasts & oceans, 510

MARITIME INDUSTRY
Historical dict of the U.S. maritime industry, 64

MARKETING
American buyers, 250
Business decision [Website], 81
Website mktg plan [Website], 82

MASS MEDIA
New ency of southern culture: media, v.18, 269

MATHEMATICS
Encyclopedia of math & society, 513
MathWorld [Website], 514

MEDICAL TESTS
Medical tests sourcebk, 4th ed, 479

MEDICARE
Medicare, 472

MEDICINAL PLANTS
Native American medicinal plants, 437

MEDICINE - BIBLIOGRAPHY
ALA gd to medical & health scis, 463
HSTM: history of sci, tech, & medicine [Website], 395
Medical Lib Assn's master gd to authoritative info resources in the health scis, 164

MEDICINE - CATALOGS & COLLECTIONS
MEDLINE [Website], 473

MEDICINE - DICTIONARIES & ENCYCLOPEDIAS
Encyclopedia of arthritis, 2d ed, 484
Encyclopedia of diabetes, 2d ed, 487

Encyclopedia of the heart & heart disease, 2d ed, 488
Family health from a to Z, 465
Gale ency of children's health, 2d ed, 474
Gale ency of medicine, 4th ed, 475
Salem health: infectious diseases & conditions, 476

MEDICINE - DIRECTORIES
Complete dir for people with chronic illness 2011/12, 10th ed, 466
Encyclopedia of medical orgs & agencies, 22d ed, 467

MEDICINE - HANDBOOKS & YEARBOOKS
Merck manual of diagnosis & therapy, 19th ed, 480
Plastic surgery, 481

MEDICINE - POPULAR
AIDS, 483
Autism & pervasive developmental disorders sourcebk, 2d ed, 485
Cancer sourcebk, 6th ed, 486
Living with insomnia, 490
Medical tests sourcebk, 4th ed, 479
Sexual health info for teens, 3d ed, 489

MENTAL HEALTH. *See also* **PSYCHOLOGY**
Phobiapedia, 216
Stress-related disorders sourcebk, 3d ed, 218
Truth about stress mgmt, 215

MICROBIOLOGY
Encyclopedia of microbiology, 433

MIDDLE EAST
Ethnic groups of Africa & the Middle East, 106
Middle East, 43

MIDDLE EAST, HISTORY
Ancient Egypt & the Near East, 139
Middle East almanac, 176

MILITARY HISTORY
Battles that changed hist, 181
Civil War naval ency, 185
Encyclopedia of N American Indian wars 1607-1890, 116
Middle East almanac, 176
9/11 & the wars in Afghanistan & Iraq, 177
United States Marine Corps, 186
World War II at sea, 182

MILITARY STUDIES
Fighting elites, 183
Militarization of space, 188

Shocked & awed: a dict of the war on terror, 180
Women in combat, 184

MINERALS
Vitamins & minerals, 411

MOTION PICTURE MUSIC
Film & TV music, 340

MOTION PICTURE PRODUCTION
Documentary filmmakers hndbk, 374

MOTION PICTURES
Animated film ency, 2d ed, 373
Biographical ency of scientists & inventors in
    American film & TV since 1930, 364
Encyclopedia of religion & film, 369
Historical dict of American cinema, 367
Historical dict of sci fiction cinema, 368
Magill's cinema annual 2012, 375
Movies in American hist, 370
Research gd to film & TV music in the US, 376

MULTICULTURAL LITERATURE
Bridges to understanding, 310

MUSEUMS
America's college museums hndbk & dir, 2d ed, 23

MUSIC - CATALOGS & COLLECTIONS
Chamber orchestra & ensemble repertoire, 349

**MUSIC - DICTIONARIES &
ENCYCLOPEDIAS**
Encyclopedia of African American music, 341
Historical dict of English music ca. 1400-1958, 342
Historical dict of modern & contemporary classical
    music, 347

MUSIC - HANDBOOKS & YEARBOOKS
Encyclopedia of natl anthems, 2d ed, 343
Music production, 344
Research gd to film & TV music in the US, 376

MUSICALS
Golden age of American musical theatre, 379
Off-Broadway musicals since 1919, 378

MUSICIANS. *See also* **COMPOSERS (MUSIC)**
I am hip-hop, 351

MYTHOLOGY
Gods & goddesses of Greece & Rome, 356

NATIONAL SONGS
Encyclopedia of natl anthems, 2d ed, 343

NATURAL DISASTERS
Natural disasters, 508

NATURAL HISTORY
Encyclopedia of invasive species, 443

NATURAL MEDICINE
Encyclopedia of Islamic herbal medicine, 482
People's pharmacy home remedies, 492

NEEDLECRAFT
Complete bk of patchwork, quilting & appliqué,
    285
Firefly's step-by-step ency of needlecraft, 284

NEWBERY AWARD
Newbery & Caldecott Awards, 2011 ed, 314

NEWSPAPERS
World news digest [Website], 277

NONFICTION
Life stories, 337

NURSING
CINAHL: the cumulative index to nursing & allied
    health lit [Website], 491

NUTRITION. *See also* **FOOD HABITS; FOOD
SCIENCE**
Diet & nutrition sourcebk, 4th ed, 477
Diet info for teens, 3d ed, 478
Nutrition & food scis database [Website], 406
Science of nutrition series, 414
Vitamins & minerals, 411

OCEANIA
World & its peoples: Sub-Saharan Africa,
    Australasia, & the Pacific, 40

OCEANOGRAPHY
Atlas of coasts & oceans, 510

OFFICE PRACTICES
AMA hndbk of business docs, 83

ONLINE SOCIAL NETWORKS
Plunkett's games, apps, & social media industry
    almanac 2012, 494
Social networking, 500

OTTOMAN EMPIRE
Daily life in the Ottoman Empire, 140

PALEONTOLOGY
Dinosaurs, 511

PEDIATRIC MEDICINE
Gale ency of children's health, 2d ed, 474

PERFORMING ARTS
Grey House performing arts dir 2011/12, 7th ed,
    363

PERIODICALS
Ulrich's per dir 2011, 49th ed, 24

PERSONAL NAMES
Last name meanings dict [Website], 123

PERSONS WITH DISABILITIES
Complete dir for people with disabilities 2012, 20th
    ed, 235

PHARMACEUTICAL SCIENCES
PDR for nonprescription drugs, dietary
    supplements, & herbs 2012, 33d ed, 493

PHILANTHROPY. *See also* **GRANTS-IN-AID**
Catalog of fed domestic assistance [Website], 238
Foundation grants to individuals, 20th ed, 239

PHOBIAS
Phobiapedia, 216

PIANO MUSIC
Pianist's craft, 345

PIRACY
Modern piracy, 157

PLANTS. *See also* **GARDENING**
Armitage's vines & climbers, 417
Encyclopedia of tropical plants, 436
Flowering plants, 439
Native American medicinal plants, 437
Waterwise plants for sustainable gardens, 426

POETRY
Greek poets, 338
Russian poets, 339

POISONOUS PLANTS
North American gd to common poisonous plants &
    mushrooms, 438

POLITICAL LEADERS. *See* **PRESIDENTS –**
UNITED STATES

POLITICAL PARTICIPATION
Youth & pol participation, 204

POLITICAL SCIENCE
Governing America, 198
21st century pol sci, 193

POLLUTION
Encyclopedia of pollution, 519

POPULAR CULTURE
Celebrity in the 21st century, 361
Encyclopedia of African American popular culture,
    111

POPULAR MUSIC
Ultimate playlist, 350

POVERTY
Atlas of global inequalities, 253
Modern homelessness, 241

POWER
Encyclopedia of power, 27

PRESIDENTS – UNITED STATES
American presidency, 196
American presidency online [Website], 197
Handy presidents answer bk, 2d ed, 203
History of American presidential elections, 4th ed,
    195
United States presidents [Website], 194

PRIVACY - RIGHT OF
Online privacy, 160

PROSTITUTION
Prostitution & sex work, 242

PSYCHOLOGY
Phobiapedia, 216
PsycINFO [Website], 214
Social psychology, 217
Stress-related disorders sourcebk, 3d ed, 218

PUBLIC HEALTH
Disease maps, 471
Encyclopedia of family health, 464
50 health scares that fizzled, 469
Salem health: infectious diseases & conditions, 476

PUBLIC POLICY
Encyclopedia of the U.S. govt & the environment, 211
Encyclopedia of water pol & policy in the US, 212
U.S. health policy & pol, 213

PUBLISHERS & PUBLISHING
International literary market place 2012, 174
Literary market place 2012, 175

QUILTING
Complete bk of patchwork, quilting & appliqué, 285

QUOTATION BOOKS
Bartlett's familiar quotations, 17th ed, 25

RADICALISM
Encyclopedia of right-wing extremism in modern American hist, 207

RAP MUSIC
I am hip-hop, 351

READERS' ADVISORY
Children's core collection, 20th ed, 163
Graphic novels for young readers, 313
Historical fiction for teens, 316
Life stories, 337
Make mine a mystery II, 324
Read on . . . audiobks, 165
Readers' advisory gd to street lit, 321
Senior high core collection, 18th ed, 166
Urban grit, 320

READING. *See also* **LITERACY**
Teaching histl fiction with ready-made lit circles for secondary readers, 92
Teaching reading to English lang learners, 295

REFERENCE SERVICES
Finding the answers to legal questions, 165

RELIGION
Historical dict of new religious movements, 2d ed, 383
World religions [Website], 384

RELIGION - CHRISTIANITY
Historical dict of Calvinism, 390
Historical dict of Lutheranism, 2d ed, 389
Historical dict of the Friends (Quakers), 2d ed, 388

RELIGION - DICTIONARIES & ENCYCLOPEDIAS
Religious celebrations, 358

REPTILES
Eponym dict of reptiles, 454
Venomous reptiles of the US, Canada, & N Mexico, v.1, 455
Venomous reptiles of the US, Canada, & N Mexico, v.2, 456

ROMAN HISTORY
Gods & goddesses of Greece & Rome, 356

SACRED SPACE
Encyclopedia of sacred places, 2d ed, 382

SCHOLARLY WEBSITES
Digital collections worldwide, 498

SCHOOL LIBRARIES
Graphic novels in your school lib, 171

SCHOOL VIOLENCE
Encyclopedia of school crime & violence, 152

SCIENCE
AccessScience [Website], 394
Applied sci & tech abstracts (ASTA) [Website], 402
Handy sci answer bk, 4th ed, 400
HSTM: history of sci, tech, & medicine [Website], 395
Nature got there first, 399
Science in 100 key breakthroughs, 401
Science online [Website], 396
Scitopia [Website], 403
Today's sci [Website], 397

SCIENCE FICTION
Historical dict of sci fiction cinema, 368

SCIENTIFIC WRITING
How to write & pub a scientific paper, 7th ed, 270
Scientific English, 3d ed, 398

SEPTEMBER 11 TERRORIST ATTACKS, 2011
9/11 & the wars in Afghanistan & Iraq, 177

SEX STUDIES
Prostitution & sex work, 242

SEXUALLY TRANSMITTED DISEASES
Sexual health info for teens, 3d ed, 489

SHAKESPEARE, WILLIAM
Prefaces to Shakespeare, 333
Shakespeare, 332

SINGAPORE
History of Singapore, 136

SLAVERY
Atlas of the transatlantic slave trade, 129
Slavery in the modern world, 145

SMALL LIBRARIES
Small public lib mgmt, 172

SNAKES
Venomous reptiles of the US, Canada, & N Mexico,
    v.1, 455
Venomous reptiles of the US, Canada, & N Mexico,
    v.2, 456

SOCCER
Complete bk of soccer, 2d ed, 231
Historical dict of soccer, 232

SOCIAL ISSUES
At issue series, 29
Encyclopedia of contemporary social issues, 26
Issues [Website], 28

SOCIAL MEDIA
Plunkett's games, apps, & social media industry
    almanac 2012, 494
Social networking, 500

SOCIAL NETWORKS. *See* **ONLINE SOCIAL
NETWORKS**

SOCIAL SCIENCES
Statesman's yrbk 2011, 147th, 31

SOUTH AFRICA
Encyclopedia of S Africa, 36

SPACE SCIENCES
Cambridge photographic star atlas, 502
Patrick Moore's data bk of astronomy, 505
Sizing up the universe, 504
13 planets, 503

SPACE WARFARE
Militarization of space, 188

SPANISH LANGUAGE DICTIONARIES
Webster's everyday Spanish-English dict, 304

SPANISH LITERATURE
World lit in Spanish, 336

SPECIAL COLLECTIONS (LIBRARIES)
Basic business lib, 5th ed, 162
Comic bk collections for libs, 359
Crash course in the world of genealogy, 170
Medical Lib Assn's master gd to authoritative info
    resources in the health scis, 164

SPECIAL EDUCATION
Guide to private special educ 2011/12, 103

SPECIAL FORCES (MILITARY STUDIES)
Fighting elites, 183

SPORTS
Atlas of sports, 219
Baseball now! 2d ed, 224
Historical dict of basketball, 225
Historical dict of cycling, 227
Historical dict of figure skating, 230
Pro football championships before the Super Bowl, 228
Science behind sports series, 222
Sports Hall of Fame ency, 220
Sports in America, 223

SPORTS INDUSTRY
Encyclopedia of sports mgmt & mktg, 221

STATISTICS
Atlas of global inequalities, 253
Education state rankings 2011-12, 93
FedStats [Website], 254
Handbook of U.S. labor stats 2011, 14th ed, 75
State rankings 2011, 255
TinkerPlots [Website], 102

STRESS
Stress-related disorders sourcebk, 3d ed, 218
Truth about stress mgmt, 215

STYLE GUIDES. *See also* **WRITING**
Cite right, 2d ed, 274
Developmental editing, 273
Nonfiction, 272
Writer's ref center [Website], 275

SUBSTANCE ABUSE
Alcohol & alcohol problems sci database [Website],
    243
Drug info for teens, 3d ed, 246
Drugs of abuse, 244
Encyclopedia of drug policy, 147
Substance abuse, addiction, & treatment, 245

TEACHING
Legal rights & responsibilities of teachers, 87

TECHNOLOGY
AccessScience [Website], 394
Applied sci & tech abstracts (ASTA) [Website], 402
HSTM: history of sci, tech, & medicine [Website], 395
Scitopia [Website], 403

TEENAGERS
College financing info for teens, 2d ed, 101

TEENAGERS - HEALTH & HYGIENE
Diet info for teens, 3d ed, 478
Drug info for teens, 3d ed, 246
Sexual health info for teens, 3d ed, 489

TELECOMMUNICATIONS
Plunkett's telecommunications industry almanac, 2012 ed, 501

TELEVISION BROADCASTING
Encyclopedia of TV shows, 1925-2010, 2d ed, 372
Encyclopedia of TV theme songs, 371
Movies made for TV 2005-09, 366
Research gd to film & TV music in the US, 376
Television's top 100, 365

TELEVISION MUSIC
Film & TV music, 340

TENNIS
Historical dict of tennis, 233

TERRORISM
9/11 & the wars in Afghanistan & Iraq, 177
World terrorism, 154

TEXTILES
Fashion designer's textile dir, 287

THEATER
American musical theatre, 4th ed, 377
Golden age of American musical theatre, 379
Historical dict of contemporary American theater, 380
Off-Broadway musicals since 1919, 378

TOLKIEN, J. R. R.
Critical companion to J. R. R. Tolkien, 334

TRANSPORTATION
Dictionary of transport analysis, 521

TRAVEL
World Heritage Sites, 3d ed, 128

TREES & SHRUBS
Dirr's ency of trees & shrubs, 442
Trees & shrubs, 441

TWAIN, MARK
Routledge ency of Mark Twain, 330

UNITED STATES
Atlas of the great plains, 32
Book of the states 2011, v.43, 18
State rankings 2011, 255

UNITED STATES CENSUS
Encyclopedia of the U.S. Census, 2d ed, 248

UNITED STATES - CIVIL WAR, 1861-1865
Civil War era & Reconstruction, 134
Civil War naval ency, 185

UNITED STATES - CONGRESS
Congress investigates, 202

UNITED STATES - HISTORY
American centuries, 131
American hist [Website], 130
Anti-immigration in the U.S., 132
Atlas of the transatlantic slave trade, 129
Celebrating women in American hist, 263
Daily life through American hist in primary docs, 135
Settlement of America, 133

UNITED STATES MARINE CORPS
United States Marine Corps, 186

UNITED STATES NAVY
Civil War naval ency, 185
World War II at sea, 182

UNITED STATES - POLITICS & GOVERNMENT
Almanac of American pol, 2012, 201
American presidency, 196
American presidency online [Website], 197
Book of the states 2011, v.43, 18
Cities in American pol hist, 257
Governing America, 198
Guide to fed terms & acronyms, 1
Handy presidents answer bk, 2d ed, 203
History of American presidential elections, 4th ed, 195
United States presidents [Website], 194

U.S. election campaigns, 200
Washington info dir 2011-12, 199
Youth & pol participation, 204

UNITED STATES - SOCIAL CONDITIONS
Baby boomer ency, 249
Civil War era & Reconstruction, 134
Encyclopedia of contemporary social issues, 26

UNITED STATES SUPREME COURT
Landmark Supreme Court cases, 2d ed, 148
Supreme Court & the environment, 158

URBAN STUDIES. *See also* **CITIES & TOWNS**
Companion to urban design, 258
U.S. infrastructure, 260

VAMPIRES
Encyclopedia of vampires & werewolves, 2d ed,
354

VEGETABLES
How to grow food, 424
Incredible edibles, 425
What's wrong with my vegetable garden? 422

VIETNAM WAR, 1961-1975
Encyclopedia of the Vietnam War, 2d ed, 179

VIOLIN
Canon of violin lit, 346

VITAMINS
Vitamins & minerals, 411

VOLCANOES
Volcanoes of the world, 3d ed, 512

WAR CRIMES
Encyclopedia of war crimes & genocide, rev ed,
144

WARS
Battles that changed hist, 181
Civil War naval ency, 185
Encyclopedia of N American Indian wars 1607-
1890, 116
Middle East almanac, 176
9/11 & the wars in Afghanistan & Iraq, 177
Shocked & awed: a dict of the war on terror, 180
World War II at sea, 182

WATER RESOURCES DEVELOPMENT
Encyclopedia of water pol & policy in the US, 212

WEAPONS. *See also* **FIREARMS**
Militarization of space, 188Space & security, 187

WEATHER
Confronting global warming series, 506
Encyclopedia of cliate & weather, 2d ed, 507
Natural disasters, 508

WEBSITES
AccessScience [Website], 394
African American experience [Website], 109
AllBusiness [Website], 46
American hist [Website], 130
American Indian hist online [Website], 114
American presidency online [Website], 197
American women's hist online [Website], 261
Ancient & medieval hist online [Website], 142
Applied sci & tech abstracts (ASTA) [Website], 402
Archinform index of persons [Website], 293
AssociationExecs.com [Website], 17
Bearport digital lib [Website], 89
BEOnline [Website], 47
Britannica online [Website], 11
Business decision [Website], 81
Catalog of fed domestic assistance [Website], 238
CINAHL: the cumulative index to nursing & allied
health lit [Website], 491
Cities & building database [Website], 294
Complete planet [Website], 499
CQ global researcher [Website], 189
Curriculum resource center [Website], 90
Daily life through hist [Website], 143
Database of award-winning children's lit (DAWCL)
[Website], 311
DemographicsNow, lib ed [Website], 247
Direction of trade stats [Website], 67
Discovery educ streaming plus [Website], 91
EI compendex [Website], 458
Factmonster.com [Website], 2
Federal reserve stats & histl data [Website], 60
FedStats [Website], 254
First research industry profiles [Website], 63
Gale business insights: global [Website], 49
HSTM: history of sci, tech, & medicine [Website],
395
IBISWorld [Website], 68
IEEE Xplore [Website], 461
Information please almanac online [Website], 3
International trade stats [Website], 69
Issues [Website], 28
Last name meanings dict [Website], 123
Latino American experience [Website], 119
Marshall Cavendish digital [Website], 12
MathWorld [Website], 514

MEDLINE [Website], 473
MLA intl bibliog [Website], 8
Nutrition & food scis database [Website], 406
PebbleGo biogs [Website], 88
ProQuest entrepreneurship [Website], 50
PsycINFO [Website], 214
Science online [Website], 396
Scitopia [Website], 403
Small business resource center [Website], 51
TinkerPlots [Website], 102
Today's sci [Website], 397
USA.gov [Website], 19
USGenWeb [Website], 121
Venture deal [Website], 57
Website mktg plan [Website], 82
World almanac for kids online [Website], 7
World almanac online [Website], 6
World Bk advanced [Website], 14
World news digest [Website], 277
World religions [Website], 384
WorldGenWeb [Website], 122
Writer's ref center [Website], 275

WEREWOLVES
Encyclopedia of vampires & werewolves, 2d ed,
     354
Werewolf bk, 2d ed, 355

WHITE-COLLAR CRIME
White-collar & corporate crime, 156

WHITMAN, WALT
Routledge ency of Walt Whitman, repr ed, 331

WOMEN AUTHORS
Critical companion to Maya Angelou, 329

WOMEN COMPOSERS
Women composers of classical music, 348

WOMEN IN BUSINESS
Gender & women's leadership, 264

WOMEN SOLDIERS
Women in combat, 184

WOMEN'S STUDIES
American women's hist online [Website], 261
Celebrating women in American hist, 263

Daily life of women during the civil rights era, 266
Encyclopedia of women in today's world, 262
Women in developing countries, 265
Women's roles in Latin America & the Caribbean,
     267

WORLD HERITAGE SITES
World Heritage Sites, 3d ed, 128

WORLD HISTORY
Daily life through hist [Website], 143
New atlas of world hist, 141
Popular controversies in world hist, 146
World news digest [Website], 277

WORLD POLITICS
Countries at the crossroads 2010, 192
CQ global researcher [Website], 189
Geopolitics, 191
Separatist movements, 190
Statesman's yrbk 2011, 147th, 31
Top stories 2010, 22

WORLD WAR, 1939-1945
World War II at sea, 182

WRITING
Books that teach kids to write, 94
Cite right, 2d ed, 274
Developmental editing, 273
How to write & pub a scientific paper, 7th ed, 270
Nonfiction, 272
Scientific English, 3d ed, 398
Writer's ref center [Website], 275
Writing for conferences, 271

YOUNG ADULT LIBRARY SERVICES
Core collection for YAs, 2d ed, 167
Outstanding bks for the college bound, 315

YOUNG ADULT LITERATURE
Family in lit for young readers, 312
Historical fiction for teens, 316
Outstanding bks for the college bound, 315
Readers' advisory gd to street lit, 321
Senior high core collection, 18th ed, 166
They suck, they bite, they eat, they kill, 319

COMMUNITY COLLEGE

3 1717 00097 935

Recommended reference books
for small and medium sized
libraries and medica centers